WORKPLACE INDUSTRIAL RELATIONS

and the

GLOBAL CHALLENGE

Edited by
JACQUES BÉLANGER, P.K. EDWARDS, LARRY HAIVEN

Cornell International Industrial and Labor Relations Report Number 25
ILR PRESS *Ithaca, New York*

Library of Congress Cataloging-in-Publication Data

Workplace industrial relations and the global challenge / Jacques
Bélanger, P. K. Edwards, and Larry Haiven, editors.
    p.   cm. — (Cornell international industrial and labor
relations report: no. 25)
    Includes bibliographical references and index.
  ISBN 0-87546-327-4 (alk. paper). — ISBN 0-87546-328-2 (pbk.:
alk. paper)
    1. Comparative industrial relations.   2. Comparative management.
3. Industrial management—Case studies.   4. Industrial sociology—
Case studies.   5. Work environment—Case studies.   I. Bélanger,
Jacques.   II. Edwards, P. K. (Paul K.)   III. Haiven, Larry.
IV. Series: Cornell international industrial and labor relations
reports: no. 25.
HD6971.W856   1994
331—dc20   94-1668

Copies may be ordered through bookstores or directly from

ILR Press
School of Industrial and Labor Relations
Cornell University
Ithaca, NY 14853-3901

Printed on acid-free paper in the United States of America
5   4   3   2   1

Contents

iii

Tables and Figures

Tables

Figures

Preface

In the wake of the restructuring of the world economy and its redivision into distinct trading blocs, comparative industrial relations is once again a subject of great interest. The dialectic of cooperation and conflict between employers and employees (and their trade unions) in different countries is a key to understanding comparative economic performance and to analyzing economic trends. As more and more corporations operate and subcontract internationally, an appreciation of variations in industrial relations systems becomes more crucial. As trade unions attempt to cope with this phenomenon, they too must become international in their strategic thinking.

Scholarly effort has not kept pace with these developments. To be sure, there has been no dearth of edited volumes containing individual reports on selected countries, tied together with very general but untheoretical introductions. These are admittedly useful. Anything that reports on a wide array of countries, especially in times of rapid change, provides much-needed information. The breadth involved, however, makes empirical work all the more frustrating. Considerably rarer and desperately needed are scholarly projects that attempt any one or a combination of three goals: comparisons, employing the same criteria and methodology, of groups of countries; the application and/or construction of a unifying theoretical framework to explain variations and similarities among countries; and studies that focus on the workplace.

This volume attempts to address some of these needs. It began with discussions between faculty and graduate students of the Industrial Relations Research Unit at the University of Warwick. Out of these discussions emerged a recognition that a growing number of lonely researchers around the world were engaged in comparative workplace studies but needed to get together to compare methodologies, problems, and theory, and, not least, to give each other encouragement. The next step was a conference at Laval University in Québec City, Canada, in August 1991 entitled "Workplace Industrial Relations and Industrial Conflict in International Perspective." The call for papers requested reports on original studies from researchers working in the following areas:

Intensive studies. Research that directly compares labor-management relations in specific workplaces in two or more countries and that examines the frontier of control and the nature of the effort bargain.

Extensive studies. Research that is more broadly comparative in one of three senses of the word:

- Studies comparing workplace relations in two or more countries, at the level of an industry, for example. Such studies would contain a strong emphasis on labor regulation at the point of production and include those assessing the impact of the state and the law on workplace relations in these countries.
- Studies comparing patterns of industrial conflict across a large sample of countries that take a broadly political economy approach and attempt to relate observed patterns to the character of shopfloor relations in the countries examined.
- Studies of workplaces in *one* country which engage theoretically with the literature on conflict in the workplace and/or in an international comparative perspective.

The response to the call was gratifying, and all of those participating agreed that the conference was a great success. Not only were all the papers submitted in advance and thoughtfully critiqued by selected experts and the discussion (and there was plenty of time set aside for that) conducted at a very high level, but there seemed to be an intellectual intimacy, a palpable scholarly excitement, in those three warm August days in Québec City as participants from ten countries shared their insights. Such an atmosphere is rare in the staid world of academic conferences. No small amount of thanks for this is due to the charm of the city (a description that transcends cliché), the excellence of the facilities, and the genuine warmth of our hosts from the Industrial Relations Department at Laval.

After the conference came the unenviable task of selecting papers for inclusion in this volume. None of the papers delivered was unworthy of inclusion per se, so the editors had to establish certain criteria. To provide cohesion, we decided to focus on papers that did the following: concentrated on the workplace, as opposed to broad national-level analysis; provided international comparative analysis (i.e., of comparable workplaces in two or more countries); and used ethnographic methodology. Those papers that addressed most of these objectives and whose work fit into an overall framework were chosen.

Next came the task of tracing common themes and asking the authors to rewrite so that the book would be more than a collection of individual essays. The editors decided to further this process by framing the individual contributions by three chapters on theory, methodology, and globalization. Although some chapters may be of more interest to some readers than others, we trust you will find that the whole is more than the sum of its parts.

In addition to those whose work is included herein, we would like to thank all of those who spent their time and energy delivering papers, acting as commentators on those papers, and chairing sessions at the conference: Gilles Laflamme (director of the Laval Industrial Relations Department), Jean-Paul Montminy, Marc Maurice, Jean Boivin, Jeffrey Haydu, Chris Huxley, Jeff Wareham, Bob Russell, Richard Price, Willy Brown, Leon Grunberg, Gilles Breton, Mària Ladò, Alicja Kozdroj, Roy Adams, Tony Giles, Gregor Murray, Walther Müller-Jentsch, and Hans Joachim Sperling. Special thanks go to Céline Saint-Pierre and Stephen Wood, who presented a final session commenting on *all* the papers. In addition to the above, we would like to thank those who attended the conference simply because they were interested in the topics being discussed. Their contribution is no less appreciated.

Funding for the conference and for preparation of the manuscript for this volume came from the Social Sciences and Humanities Research Council of Canada, the Ministry of Labor of the Government of Québec, the College of Commerce at the University of Saskatchewan, the University of Saskatchewan, the Department of Industrial Relations at Laval University, the Faculty of Social Sciences at Laval University, and the Industrial Relations Research Unit at the University of Warwick.

We would like to thank Bob Laurie, who helped produce some of the charts, graphs, and graphics. Martin Dumas, Jean-Noel Grenier, and Francine Jacques helped with the index. We very much appreciate the thoughtful comments on the manuscript made by two anonymous reviewers. To meticulous copy editor Erica Fox: our respect and gratitude are due. Finally, special thanks to Patty Peltekos and Fran Benson of ILR Press, who offered help and encouragement and who listened to our complaints patiently while guiding us toward the final deadlines.

We are not strong believers in dedications, but given the considerable practical obstacles to be overcome and the great amount of time, effort, and intellectual energy required to do comparative workplace studies, we hope this volume will spark the imagination of a new corps of researchers in this very valuable, very rewarding enterprise.

WORKPLACE
INDUSTRIAL RELATIONS
and the
GLOBAL CHALLENGE

Introduction
The Workplace and Labor Regulation in Comparative Perspective

P. K. Edwards, Jacques Bélanger, and Larry Haiven

rimo Levi has said (1988, 80) that "the region of *le boulot,* the job, *il rusco*—of daily work, in other words—is less known than the Antarctic." If that is true, then variations between countries in what we will term "the regulation of labor" are even less well understood. This book sets out to further such understanding. Its heart is a set of original case studies of the workplace in comparative perspective. The goals of these studies are threefold: to add to the limited number of comparative workplace studies; to contribute to a series of debates on comparative issues; and to exemplify a distinctive approach to the workplace, and indeed to the employment relationship more generally. This introduction highlights the analytical approach captured by the term "the regulation of labor," explains the substantive issues tying the case studies together, and outlines the structure of the volume. First, however, it is necessary to comment on the importance of comparative issues in general and the workplace in particular.

Workplace Comparisons

The general importance of comparative study hardly needs justification. As the globalization of production develops, and as national markets are opened up through such developments as the North American Free Trade Agreement and the Single European Market, no country can be immune from external competitive pressure. A key element of competitive advantage is the social organization of production: technology is increasingly freely available, and it is the way in which it is harnessed to workers' skills that is critical (Porter 1990, 14). National systems of labor regulation shape how this harnessing occurs. Such a system can be defined as the rules and expectations governing employment, which develop from the interaction between states, employers, unions, and workers. As Wolfgang Streeck

(1992) in particular has shown, in the case of a country such as Germany, an interlocking set of social institutions can promote a "virtuous circle" of economic growth, low inflation, and low unemployment.

As for the workplace, it is here that all the other aspects of an industrial relations system—its labor laws, collective agreements, and managerial and union policies and philosophies—have their effects on the critical issue of work itself. It is to the workplace that one must look to consider what happens in practice: how the structures of law and agreements combine with workers' and managers' own goals to create a workplace regime that governs how work is actually performed.

This has always been true. But the regulation of the workplace has often laid at the margins of academic interest. In many countries, as Stephen Frenkel (1986) shows, key substantive rules of work were determined through national or industry agreements (most continental European countries), through detailed contracts at the company level (North America), or through state arbitration systems (Australia). Workplace relations were assumed to be determined by national institutions.

This situation began to change in the 1980s, as employers in many countries introduced initiatives to change traditional systems of work organization. Quality circles and teamworking became major issues. As two experienced researchers note in the case of Germany, these developments mean that "the factory level will have to be more actively included in empirical research than at present" (Jacobi and Müller-Jentsch 1990, 182). Some researchers claimed a shift was occurring, away from rules and procedures toward flexibility and employee involvement, or, in the words of Richard E. Walton (1985), from control to commitment. A particularly influential study in this regard is *The Machine That Changed the World* (Womack, Jones, and Roos 1990). This study of the auto industry identifies a form of work organization, labeled lean production, that emerged in Japan and that is presented as the route any company wishing to remain in the global market must follow. Under lean production, the organization of the workplace is made a central issue.

Work of the kind shown in *The Machine That Changed the World* mixes analysis with description and prescription. In particular, as discussed below, it sees workplace change as the pursuit of an unproblematic best practice and does not explore the tensions and conflicts within workplace regimes. Independent critical analysis of workplace behavior in a comparative context is relatively recent. As Robin Cohen has noted (1991, 19), "There is no doubt that all IR [industrial relations] theorists find it difficult to move in a comparative direction beyond Europe, the U.S. and the colonies of Anglo-Saxon settlement and beyond such obviously comparable elements as strike statistics, labour law and the rates of union membership." Some of the limitations of the comparative approach are detailed in chapter 1. The importance of a different direction, exploring the actual workings of national labor relations systems and their implications for competitive advantage, is increasingly emphasized (Kochan and

McKersie 1992; Kochan, Batt, and Dyer 1992); it is notable, however, that the research base of this new agenda remains small. This book contributes to this agenda by focusing on perhaps the most neglected element of all, the workplace.

Regulation of Labor

This volume is inspired by the question of how work gets done. How are workers persuaded to work hard? What is the balance between willing cooperation, routine compliance, generalized discontent, and active protest? How is a sense of order and discipline created and sustained? And how far is the manager-worker relation mediated by collective systems of interest representation? The intellectual tradition from which these questions have emerged (discussed more fully in Edwards 1988 and 1992b) will be reviewed briefly before its analytical themes are isolated and contrasted with other approaches.

Ethnographic Tradition

The basis of the tradition from which this book has developed is detailed ethnographic analysis of the dynamics of the effort bargain. This can be based on participant observation, on interviews and observations of a nonparticipant kind, or on a mixture of both approaches. Though there have been important sociological workplace studies in countries such as France (e.g., Bernoux 1985), the studies of workplace regulation on which this volume builds were done largely in the United States or Great Britain. In America, Stanley B. Mathewson's (1931) is perhaps the best-known early study. Other significant landmarks in the United States include Donald Roy's (1954) series of participant observer studies, conducted at the end of World War II, and Alvin Gouldner's (1954) well-known study of industrial bureaucracy, based on observation and interviews by a team of researchers. In Britain, William Baldamus (1961) produced an important analytical statement focused on the effort bargain. But such studies tended to be isolated inquiries.

The ethnographic approach received its shaping as a systematic method of analysis at the University of Manchester in the 1950s, under the influence of the anthropologist Max Glucksman (see Emmett and Morgan 1982). A series of connected participant observer studies was conducted. Yet even this body of work left no institutional legacy.

Some of the concerns were taken up again in the early 1970s by scholars at the University of Warwick, notably William Brown (1973) and Eric Batstone, Ian Boraston, and Stephen Frenkel (1977 and 1978). The Warwick tradition, in which five of the contributors to this volume (the three editors, plus Stephen Frenkel and Anthony Smith) have their roots, continues to develop detailed workplace inquiry (e.g., Ram 1991 and 1994).

A second impetus to ethnographic inquiry is the influential work of Michael Burawoy. It is no accident that Burawoy was trained in the Manchester school (a tradition that has also influenced one of our contributors, Chung Yuen Kay). Burawoy worked initially in Zambia before applying his ethnographic skills to an American machine shop (Burawoy 1979b). As discussed below, the method of participant observation was combined with an extended argument about what this particular case showed about the American workplace more generally.

In a series of related studies, collected in *The Politics of Production* (1985), Burawoy turned to comparative issues. These included a study in which he contrasted the United States and Britain based on a careful comparison of his own findings with those of one of the leaders of the original Manchester researchers, Tom Lupton (1963), in Britain. Burawoy also developed a framework to explore the differences between capitalist and state socialist factory regimes, drawing on contrasts between the United States and Hungary. Subsequently, Burawoy conducted his own studies in Hungary (Burawoy 1985; Burawoy and Lukacs 1985 and 1989) and elsewhere. A key contribution here was the focus on the links between the workplace and the state, a theme discussed in chapter 1. Burawoy has also led in the production of a set of ethnographic studies (Burawoy et al. 1991), but since these do not focus on the regulation of labor as defined here, we do not discuss this work further.

In view of the importance of the workplace, why have ethnographies been so rare? As well as being time-consuming, the work can be very demanding, calling for the commitment of energy in an environment that is not the researcher's own. The emphasis on quantification and the distrust of case study work in mainstream social science disciplines has also made it difficult to have ethnographic work accepted (Rosen 1991). And for scholars needing to produce research output quickly, becoming involved in lengthy case studies is a high-risk strategy. Projects like this volume aim to overcome resistance to the ethnographic method and, by demonstrating its relevance to major issues, to give collective encouragement to its present and prospective practitioners.

Conflict and the Negotiation of Order

Three issues underlying the ethnographic approach are crucial. The first two are substantive and may be treated together. The third issue, the crucial matter of generalizations based on case studies, requires separate discussion.

There is an emphasis on conflict in ethnographic studies of the workplace. Burawoy asked explicitly how workers are persuaded to cooperate in their own exploitation. Other writers did not spell this out so sharply, but they plainly saw the enterprise as a site in which conflict was an underlying principle shaping day-to-day activity. Conflict, or, to use a more precise term, structured antagonism, lies at the heart of workplace relations because workers are in a subordinate position: their capacity to labor—their labor power—is transformed into effective labor under the authority of management, and the surplus so created is not under their control (Edwards 1986).

Contemporary studies of workplace change, by contrast, often counterpose the rigidity and rules of the past with the flexibility of the future. Underlying this model is a view of the workplace as essentially harmonious. Among the weaknesses of *The Machine That Changed the World* is the very limited attention paid to the costs that lean production imposes on workers. These include pressures to work long hours, a relentless pace of work, and a requirement to conform to the demands of the system (Kamata 1983; Dohse, Jürgens, and Malsch 1985). Studies of Japanese-owned firms in the United States and Britain have noted similar phenomena (Fucini and Fucini 1990; Milkman 1992; Oliver and Wilkinson 1992; Sewell and Wilkinson 1992; Berggren 1993). There are two implications. First, the model of change may need to be qualified: lean production is not a development in the interests of all but a process with costs as well as benefits. Second, the analytical focus on consensus is at best one-sided and at worst seriously misleading.

Perhaps the best-known alternative is the labor process tradition stimulated by the work of Harry Braverman (1974) and developed by Richard Edwards and others (Edwards 1979; Gordon, Edwards, and Reich 1982). The central strength of this approach is its focus on management control: the organization of work involves creation by management of systems of control that subordinate workers. The generation of commitment is seen not as a dissolution of conflict between management and worker but as a particular control strategy.

The problem with this work is that it creates a sharp distinction between managerial control and worker resistance (Nolan and Edwards 1984). It gives no attention to the negotiation of order within the workplace. This is where the second feature of the present approach comes in. As well as conflict, there is also cooperation, for managements need workers' compliance, while workers depend on employers for their jobs and cannot afford to adopt a policy of total resistance (Cressey and MacInnes 1980). The balance between the conflictual and cooperative aspects of work occurs through a negotiation of order. Even in situations where managers are apparently all-powerful, the performance of work depends on the cooperation of workers, and there develops a negotiation of the exact terms of the labor contract. Empirical studies of the eighteenth century British navy (Rodger 1986), nineteenth-century slave plantations (Genovese 1976), and twentieth-century Malaysian peasants (Scott 1985), all situations apparently marked by managerial domination and a worker response of either passivity or rebellion, in fact reveal a complex of customs and understandings that determined how work was to be carried out. There was, in short, an effort bargain—that is, a bargain about the balance between reward and effort. This bargain inscribed the terms of the negotiation between the dominant group (ship's captain, slave owner, or landlord) and the subordinates. There was no simple contrast between cooperation and conflict. Rather, these two principles were intricately intertwined in the operation of the effort bargain.

Burawoy (1979b) explored this bargain by asking not "why do workers resist managerial efforts to make them work hard?" but "why do they work as hard as they do?" As he put it later, when workers found ways to alleviate the boredom of work and to exert some influence over their working lives, they were also "generating consent": they "manufactured not only parts of diesel engines, not only relations of cooperation and domination, but also consent to those activities and relations" (Burawoy 1985, 11). This perspective is in sharp contrast to the managerial control and worker resistance perspective that has characterized much labor process debate.

Much discussion has focused on the workers' side. The logic driving the early Manchester studies, for example, was the need to understand how workers manipulate the effort bargain. Yet the managerial role is also important. A persistent finding from shopfloor studies is that the management of labor follows far fewer clear-cut strategies than is implied either in management textbooks or in certain labor process writing. In the words of one study, there is "chaos on the shopfloor" (Juravich 1985).

The theoretical reason for this chaos has been highlighted by Richard Hyman (1987). "Management" involves the handling of different demands that are inherently contradictory. A contradiction in this sense is a relationship between two principles, both of which are essential to the operation of the enterprise but which are in tension with each other. The contradiction lies in balancing the need to control labor with that of securing workers' cooperation. In addition, there is a contradiction between maintaining harmony within the workplace and ensuring the profitability of the enterprise in the market. These contradictions do not send out direct guides to action. They exert certain pressures and managers then choose which of the conflicting signals to highlight. Antony Ferner (1990), for example, shows that the privatization of enterprises in Britain sent some signals about the need to be competitive and reduce labor costs but others about maintaining public confidence and emphasizing the quality of service. The process was one not of finding a simple "fit" between the organization and the environment as portrayed in management textbooks, but one of negotiating contradictory demands.

This argument underlines the inherent nature of negotiation and bargaining. These processes are not incidental extras or minor qualifications to the relationship between management and workers and unions. They are integral to it. The regulation of labor requires contradictory demands to be actively managed, together with the laws, collective agreements, and customs that are resources in the process.

Issue of Generalizations

Finally, there is the question of the models, explanations, and generalizations that can be offered. Case study work often has to justify itself in the face of the criticism that any one workplace is atypical and that it tends to produce interesting stories but no general lessons. As a blanket criticism, this reaction is simply unwarranted. It is like saying that all surveys merely establish some basic facts but do not address what really happens. The basic rationale for case work is explained in detail by J. Clyde Mitchell (1983, 207), who emphasizes that it involves a different sort of generalization from that employed in quantitative study: not statistical representativeness but analytical connections between social processes. The purpose is to understand why and how different aspects of social life are linked. A well-conducted case study, concludes Mitchell in a powerful peroration, "provides the optimum conditions for the acquisition of those illuminating insights which make formerly opaque connections suddenly pellucid."

Once this basic objective is established, there are five ways in which generalization proceeds (Edwards 1992b). The first is through the discovery of hidden forms of behavior, such as sabotage or pilfering, and of their role in the negotiation of order. This is the most fundamental role of the case study. Gouldner (1954), for example, took the established model of bureaucracy—namely, that there are clear-cut rules everyone acknowledges—and showed that there are in fact different rules, which are the outcome of negotiation. This is now an accepted commonplace in industrial sociology. But it has only become one as the result of investigations like Gouldner's. Moreover, its acceptance remains less than complete. In the field of workplace discipline, for example, personnel texts continue to speak of rules as though they are agreed standards of conduct, thus failing to address issues of power and negotiation (Edwards 1989).

Second, critical cases can be identified: if an alleged phenomenon does not exist in its most likely setting, it is unlikely to occur anywhere. Third, the causal mechanisms linking phenomena can be explored: surveys identify correlations, but to establish causation, it is necessary to understand exactly why the correlation exists. Surveys indicate general tendencies, but in the social world these are not iron laws. Case studies indicate the conditions under which a tendency operates. Equally important, they point to situations that are "exceptions to the rule." Why is a statistical association less than perfect? Case studies indicate the conditions that counteract the general tendency, and thereby enrich understanding of the causal mechanisms involved. This links to the fourth point: case studies can explain variations. Comparative study can reveal why certain forms of effort bargaining occur in one place and not in another. Fifth, and finally, a research program of case studies can advance the understanding of the nature and sources of variation in a given activity. For example, the whole meaning of "output restriction" has been refined and developed as case studies have built on Mathewson's (1931) early observations.

How does all of this relate to the comparative study of systems of labor regulation? Some themes may be identified and then linked back to these modes of generalization. Much comparative work adopts a universalistic approach, identifying common trends throughout the industrialized world. This was true of the early *Industrialism and Industrial Man* (Kerr et al. 1960) tradition as well as the work of James P. Womack, Daniel T. Jones, and Daniel Roos and other commentators such as Robert B. Reich (1991). The main alternative is work that distinguishes by country. This has early examples, notably the Arthur M. Ross and Paul T. Hartman (1960) study of industrial conflict, which identified certain distinct patterns into which individual countries could be located. The tradition has been continued in more recent work identifying corporatist and pluralist models (Korpi and Shalev 1979; Cameron 1984).

Several contributions can be identified in the development of an approach to the regulation of labor. First, any work organization has the problem of transforming labor power into effective labor. But how this is accomplished, case studies show, varies considerably. For example, the effort bargain in the former Soviet system operated on different principles from capitalism, and the significance of behavior such as absenteeism or quitting was also quite different (Sabel and Stark 1982; Arnot 1988; Burawoy 1985). Second, by types of country, how do certain systems really work at the shopfloor level? For example, a great deal has been written about the U.S. system under the "New Deal model" of detailed contracts and rigid job classifications (e.g., Kochan, Katz, and McKersie 1986). But how did the system work in practice on the shopfloor: how was the formal system of rights and responsibilities experienced in practice? Thus, Burawoy (1979b) highlighted the ways in which the seniority system, the structure of collective bargaining, and the grievance system tended to individualize workers' approaches to management.

Third, does a national system really operate as the ideal-typical description says it should? How rigid and inflexible was the New Deal system, for example, and did it not have certain flexibilities within it? Fourth, how much variation is there within a national system: how homogeneous is it? Fifth, do countries that fit into certain "types" really share all the relevant characteristics? How much, for example, do Canada and the United States differ? It is then possible to look at different workplaces to consider variation: how uniform was the system?

In relation to modes of generalization, several themes stand out. The most important point about hidden behavior concerns the ways in which national systems function. Models of these systems tend to treat them as carefully integrated wholes. Much of the case work cited above reveals the uncertainties of the process.

Critical or particularly illustrative cases can help reveal the extent to which national systems are homogeneous and how well countries fit certain "types." As for mechanisms, case studies play a key role in showing how the components of a system are connected. Again taking the North American example, it is widely argued that systems of labor law have tended to constrain certain shopfloor behavior (Brody 1980; Tomlins 1985). Case studies can reveal the processes involved, as well as the connections between labor law and managerial and trade union policies. Stephen Jefferys (1986), for example, shows how North American contract unionism developed more slowly and less completely at Chrysler than in the other auto firms; and, in line with the "exception proving the rule" mode of generalization, he specifies the conditions for this process. Case studies can, moreover, indicate the dynamic role of labor legislation, a point developed below in relation to the present volume.

Comparison can take place within a national system, to explore its internal differences, or between regimes. The differences between these two modes of comparison need to be kept in mind. The approach of the former is likely to emphasize diversity. Thus, Lupton's (1963) classic study examined plants in two industries in Britain and showed that explicit bargaining over the balance of effort and reward was deeply entrenched in one (an engineering firm, "Jay") and absent in the other (a clothing firm, "Wye"). Does this deny Burawoy's use of the former case to characterize the British system? It plainly does, if Burawoy takes Jay to represent everything about Britain. This was not, however, his intention, which was to compare Jay with an American workplace that was similar on some key features (industrial sector, union status, pay system, and so on). Jay represents a specific situation in Britain. One can make the important generalization that in Britain the generic characteristic is the setting of the effort bargain at the point of production (rather than through the detailed, legally enforceable agreement of North America or national or industry-level collective bargaining, as in the rest of Europe), while the specific ways in which this characteristic operates will depend on a range of other factors (Edwards et al. 1992). This point is developed in chapter 1.

Finally, there is the possibility of developing a research program. As noted above, such a program evolved within countries such as Britain and enabled a phenomenon such as "output restriction" to be more carefully delineated. Within the comparative study of labor regulation, such a program has yet to develop. Given the paucity of any workplace studies, let alone comparative ones, this is hardly surprising. The key issue is the way in which the workplace is regulated in different countries, together with the extent of variation within each country and the reasons for and results of different methods of regulation. Some work has been done on this issue in studies that contrast developments in Britain and North America, on which there is an established debate. This debate forms one of the themes of the present volume. We turn now to those themes.

Themes of the Volume

This book makes two kinds of contribution. The first is methodological; two such themes are considered in the first two sections below. The second contribution is substantive. Four such themes tie together the individual chapters. These are outlined in turn.

Emphasis on Explanation in Case Study Work

Several chapters in this book develop the research tradition described above. For example, the need for management to negotiate consent is highlighted by Jacques Bélanger and by Chung Yuen Kay and the uncertainties of managerial "strategy" by Stephen Herzenberg. They also apply the ethnographic method to new issues. Chung, for example, deploys an essentially Burawoyan method to consider the organization of consent. There is no need for her to labor the point. There are, however, some issues about the method that need addressing.

Traditionally, many case studies have adopted a style of "telling it like it is": concentrating on the day-to-day deprivations of labor to paint a picture of life on the shopfloor. The method has been applied in, for example, Britain, France, the United States, and Australia (Beynon 1984; Linhart 1978; Pfeffer 1979; Kriegler 1980). The problem is that explanations are left at best implicit. A recent example is Dorinne K. Kondo's (1990) fascinating inquiry into the world of work in small enterprises in Japan. In the true ethnographic tradition, it explores many hidden processes and thereby qualifies the picture of work in Japan, which is heavily based on large firms. But how much were certain features characteristic of the Japanese national system, of small firms anywhere, or only of small Japanese firms? It is possible for the reader to infer some answers. For example, the emphasis on informality and the personal negotiation of obligations, often based on family ties and interpersonal trust, has been noted in studies of small firms elsewhere (Ram 1991 and 1994). By contrast, a conscious inculcation of a sense of company loyalty may be more common in Japan, so that Kondo's case lies interestingly at the intersection of the Japanese national system and features of small firms. But the relevant connections could be spelled out more fully.

By contrast, the strength of Burawoy's (1979b) work is its emphasis on explanation: workers worked hard because of a bargain over piecework prices that was inscribed in a wider workplace rule of law comprising the seniority system, collective bargaining, and grievance arbitration. The difficulty, though, is to tease out which aspects of the story were specific to this workplace, which to a national regime, which to capitalism as distinct from feudalism or socialism, and which to any form of exploitation. Piecework, for example, is rare in the United States and Canada, while formalized seniority systems are peculiar to the unionized sector of these countries. As for differences between regimes, later work (Burawoy and Lukacs 1985) compared state socialism with capitalism. Yet it did so by contrasting Hungary and the United States, even though each country had important features that were not typical of the modes of production in toto. Finally, some aspects of the negotiation of order embrace any work system, as the discussion of peasants, the navy, and slavery above indicated.

The present book reflects an awareness of this problem. We certainly do not claim to have resolved it, and it is addressed more fully in some chapters than others. But we have endeavored to deal with it more explicitly than is often the case. There are also specific themes within the work of writers such as Burawoy that are taken up within individual chapters. For example, Bélanger explores effort bargaining and shows that the North American system can, under specified circumstances, allow more space for controls on worker effort than Burawoy suggests.

Reliance on Comparative Ethnographic Insight

In terms of approach, three forms of inquiry are represented. First, there is the detailed ethnographic analysis of the workplace using observation and interviews focusing closely on the negotiation of the effort bargain. Two chapters (by Bélanger and by Haiven) are directly comparative. A third (Chung) examines one workplace in one country. Apart from being a particularly rich reconstruction of the negotiation of order, it is included here because it sees this case in comparative light. In the terms introduced above, it presents something of a critical case: it takes a situation in which workers might be expected to be particularly powerless and shows that consent was in fact negotiated.

Second, several of the analyses are somewhat less ethnographically intense but still focus on the negotiation of control (Herzenberg, Shire, Shaiken). The first of these reconstructs the history of shopfloor bargaining in the plants of one firm in two countries. This method does not permit analysis of the micro politics of the negotiation of order; instead, it takes a broader historical view of the changing dynamics of the process, and how these dynamics differed between countries. Shire also conducts a comparative study, looking not at the effort bargain as a whole but at how workplace trade union organizations in two countries responded differently to new managerial initiatives. Its particular strength is its reconstruction of the politics of organizational relations, rather than those around the day-to-day effort bargain. Shaiken's chapter looks at one plant in one country, as Chung does, using it to stand for much broader trends. Nonetheless, a comparison with the model of auto production in the United States and Japan is strongly implicit. The chapter is less able to explore the politics of bargaining or the subtleties of the ways in which workers can respond to managerial initiatives, but it is interesting for its view of the nature of this control and ominous in its argument about the wider implications.

Third, and finally, two chapters (Frenkel, Smith) adopt a more general perspective; the former examines four plants that are owned by one firm but in different countries, and the latter compares twelve sites across four countries. They are included because, apart from their important substantive themes discussed below, they are firmly comparative and focus on the relationship between specific national modes of labor regulation and managerial policy and practice. Thus, although the contributions in this book vary somewhat in the level of generality to which they are tuned, they all rely on some intensity of ethnographic insight, which renders them distinct from most of the comparative literature.

North Atlantic Comparisons

Four substantive themes emerge: comparisons among the Anglo-Saxon countries of the North Atlantic; national systems versus workplace peculiarity; the influence of U.S. capital; and globalization. The first is perhaps the most heavily debated issue in comparative workplace studies—namely, the extent of and reasons for the differing trajectories of workplace relations in Britain and North America. The reason for this attention is that regulation at the level of the workplace has been a more substantial part of the overall regime of labor regulation in these systems than it has elsewhere. In Keith Sisson's (1987) telling phrase, in most other countries it was possible to "neutralize the workplace," that is, to contain the ever-present possibility of conflict over the effort bargain, by developing national and industry-level collective agreements, sometimes buttressed by the force of law. In Britain, the problem was left for the individual employer to resolve. This was also true of North America until the 1930s. The "New Deal system" then brought law into the picture, but the point of production was still the central focus: the law did not shift bargaining to a higher level but helped to define a certain system of workplace governance, what has been called, in another telling phrase, a "workplace rule of law" (Brody 1980).

A picture emerges from a series of studies (Elbaum and Lazonick 1986; Tolliday and Zeitlin 1986 and 1991b; Lazonick 1990; Kochan, Katz, and McKersie 1986; Jacoby 1985 and 1991). The story goes like this: Up to the 1930s, American employers were more able than their British counterparts to root out challenges to their own authority. This reflected the extent to which a legacy of "craft control" survived in Britain. The craft tradition meant that workers were granted the authority to determine key aspects of the work process and in extreme cases to control entry to the trade and issues such as discipline. British employers tolerated this situation because they were too small and fragmented to take on the workers and because of the nature of their product markets. These markets were protected, so that there was little pressure on price, and demanded custommade goods, so that it was possible to continue with traditional manufacturing methods based on craft skills.

Mass markets in the United States, by contrast, called for "Fordist" mass production. American employers established autocracy on the shopfloor. This was challenged by the rebellions of the 1930s. The outcome was state intervention, which, while reinforcing some labor gains, increasingly constrained the independent challenge of workers' shopfloor organizations. The New Deal system inscribed a labor peace in which unions were granted legitimacy but in which a bureaucratic system of rules contained the shopfloor challenge. This system imposed real constraints on management too, however, notably through rigid job classifications. The system began to break down in the 1970s in the face of nonunion and foreign competition.

The unregulated system continued to operate in Britain until the 1970s, although in key sectors such as autos it came under increasing pressure as competition intensified. The arrival of a government of the radical right in 1979 encouraged managements to attack shopfloor trade union organization, although the extent to which this marked a transformation along North American lines was greatly in doubt (Edwards et al. 1992).

This book qualifies this story in several respects. In relation to Britain, the argument does not deal adequately with the many parts of the economy where there was no identifiable craft tradition (Coleman 1988; Glucksmann 1990). As discussed in chapter 2, the British workplaces studied by Haiven and by Bélanger illustrate a deeper dependence by management on an unsystematic approach to labor regulation.

As for North America, Haiven's and Bélanger's chapters, together with Herzenberg's, suggest that the New Deal system was more flexible than is often suggested. As Haiven shows, the system of labor arbitration could indicate norms of good practice to management and thus promote change; and, as Bélanger shows, in some circumstances it could tolerate workers' controls of the pace and timing of work and thus accommodate much more implicit bargaining than the rule-governed image recognizes. Futher, the system of labor arbitration was not always under careful managerial control. Herzenberg describes a case in which management was continually struggling with uncertainty and finding it impossible to develop a carefully planned system. The model of the New Deal system thus needs to be refined.

In relation to both Britain and North America, the chapters demonstrate diversity within national systems. By comparing two Canadian plants with two British counterparts, Haiven points to the tendency in Canada for the system of legal regulation to impose uniformity: weak unions gained from the ability to use arbitration, but strong ones found their ability to flex their bargaining muscles contained. In Britain, by contrast, weak unions were weaker and strong ones more able to deploy their bargaining power. Uniformity is not, however, total, for Bélanger's Canadian case shows that the workers he studied were able to breach constraints. The reason, as his chapter discusses, is the nature of the technology used at the firm (batch production calling for a greater reliance on workers' informal skills than is the case with the mass production or process operations studied by Haiven) and its product market (a nonprice-sensitive product in an oligopolistic market permitting a relaxed shopfloor regime). Herzenberg points to two kinds of diversity. The first is within an industry: most shopfloor studies in North America have focused on auto plants, particularly those belonging to the Big Three. By looking at an auto parts supplier, Herzenberg qualifies the picture of the industry by showing how in this sector the survival of firms was more uncertain, and the shopfloor less rationalized, than in the big firms.

The second kind of diversity exists between the United States and Canada, countries often seen as part of the same pattern of development. The broad divergence of labor relations in the two countries, and hence the extent to which there is one North American case, has been the subject of considerable inquiry for at least ten years (Huxley, Kettler, and Struthers 1986; Chaykowski and Verma 1992).

Although U.S.-based unions traditionally represented more Canadian workers than independent Canadian unions, this ratio was finally transposed (no doubt irreversibly) by the late 1970s. Union density (and the absolute number of trade unionists) and the impact of trade unionism in the United States have been declining for some thirty years, while this has not been the case in Canada. U.S. unions engaged quite openly and extensively in "concession bargaining" in the 1980s, while their Canadian cousins have been much more militant on the whole. Canadian unions have long had a more explicitly social and political orientation than their U.S. counterparts, including organizational support of a social democratic party (the New Democratic party). Thus, it can be said with some confidence that either Canada has overtaken the United States as primary exemplar of the "North American model" of industrial relations or that it represents a distinct variant on that model. The problem is that although considerable work has been done on institutional and legal differences between the two systems, virtually no comparison exists of the workplace in the two countries. This volume makes a modest attempt to rectify that. Herzenberg's contribution explores the themes of differential militancy and shopfloor control and speculates on some of the reasons for the differences.

A wider implication concerns the contrast between the view that the past was rigid and the future will be flexible. There was more flexibility and diversity in the past than sometimes appears. Management has always been the management of uncertainty (Streeck 1987). If the past contained diversity and uncertainty, is this not also likely to be true of the future? This issue of the shift from one mode of regulation to another is taken up in the conclusion.

National Systems or Workplace Peculiarity?

Do these chapters assume that there is a national system that can be studied at the workplace level, or do they wish to undermine the idea of national stereotypes? Recent debate on this point has given extensive attention to Richard M. Locke's (1992) analysis of Italy, which argues that variations within national systems are as important as differences between them. This is an important point, but some commentaries on Locke seem to go further and argue that the idea of any national system must be rejected. Yet variation within systems is hardly a new phenomenon. The question is whether distinct national characteristics can be identified, and how these characteristics shape different kinds of workplaces.

There are certain identifiable features of national systems, such as labor laws, the structure of collective bargaining, and certain generally accepted customs and protocols. These do shape any workplace regime. Consider Bélanger's analysis. This shows that in certain respects workers in a Canadian plant were able to exert control over the pace of work in a way that was different from the picture provided by accounts of the New Deal system. But he does not argue that this case disproves the concept of a "workplace rule of law." On the contrary, he takes pains to show that certain apparently similar workplace practices in Britain and Canada had different implications, because in Britain they developed unchecked to form a system that questioned managerial authority whereas in Canada they remained consistent with such authority.

The shaping of the workplace by national regimes is not, however, total. The national features exert forces that can be counteracted to a degree by other forces, such as technologies and product markets. Bélanger explains in the light of such forces why his workplace had the features he describes. Different workplaces are thus variations on the basic national theme.

The general contribution of these studies thus relates to their mode of explanation. They demonstrate that national systems are neither homogeneous entities nor assemblies of disparate cases. This methodological point also applies to two chapters that are not focused on the North Atlantic. Shire's study compares the introduction of similar workplace initiatives, based on teamworking, in General Motors plants in Austria and what was then West Germany. Her key theme is that these national systems, both of which are sometimes seen as exemplars of a cooperative or corporatist approach to labor management, in fact differed significantly. They did so, moreover, in a direction that some treatments of this approach would not expect.

The Austrian system is widely seen as corporatism in its most developed form: strong and encompassing unions bargain effectively with employers and the state at the national level. Germany, by contrast, tends to be presented as a weaker case: union membership is lower and unions have a much less entrenched role at the national level (Crouch 1993). Shire shows, however, that the German unions were more able to control the impact of teamworking, the key reason being the strength of workplace organizations and their links with national unions, whereas strong corporatism in Austria had resolved most issues at the national level and left the workplace as something of a vacuum. Shire's study is in the tradition of Streeck's (1984b and 1992) analysis of Germany, which emphasizes the strengths of German unions at the workplace level, strengths that are greater than formal measures of membership suggest. As well as addressing the third and fourth themes discussed below, Shire thus develops Herzenberg's comparison between two countries that are at first sight similar and explores the connection between the national and workplace levels of systems of labor regulation.

The latter issue also appears in Smith's analysis of the workplace effects of new technology in three industries across four countries. Smith shows that the links between national and local levels are important in determining how new technologies are implemented: where there is a strong articulation of these links, unions are able to exert more effect than where the links are weaker. Smith's more general contribution is to show that new technology involves what he calls the reregulation of the shopfloor. It is not a matter of determinate impacts but of certain pressures emerging from technical change, which then have to be negotiated within the workplace. There were some similarities within national systems, so that the adversarial bargaining of Canada and Britain reduced union influence relative to the situation in Germany and Italy. But there was also variation within these systems depending on the specifics of each case. Smith thus adds to the understanding of the nature and internal differentiation of systems of labor regulation.

American Capital

The third substantive theme concerns the role of North American firms in different countries. Most of the case studies (Haiven, Herzenberg, Shire, Frenkel, Shaiken, Chung) were conducted in such firms. This issue, however, did not directly inspire the case studies. The theme is an underlying one rather than a direct focus of the case studies. There are nonetheless certain common points.

Several studies confirm that, at least up until the recent past, American multinationals adapted their activities to fit in with national traditions, rather than impose a uniform global system (Copp 1977; for a review, see Enderwick 1985). Haiven's Canadian-owned firm operated in Britain much as similar British-owned firms did; Herzenberg's U.S. firm had to adapt its style to the Canadian context; General Motors, the subject of Shire's study, accepted the workplace arrangements of the two countries examined, Austria and (West) Germany; and Chung's U.S. firm found that it had to develop ways of handling the distinctive shopfloor culture of Singapore. Globalism was, however, not completely absent; it is the fourth theme of the book.

Globalism

Globalism is addressed indirectly in several chapters. Smith and Shire show that national systems had a degree of autonomy in the face of apparent global trends, respectively, the introduction of new technology and team-working.

Chung considers the issue from a different angle. Her focus is women assembly workers in an electronics plant owned by a large American multinational in Singapore, where independent trade unions have been tightly regulated by the state. These conditions might be expected to lead to a particularly extreme form of exploitation. As globalism proceeds, such exploitation would be expected to grow more common. These assumptions may be viewed in the light of Frederic C. Deyo's (1989) important study of four newly industrialized countries (NICs) of Southeast Asia. In contrast to writers who identify only one form of labor subordination, Deyo usefully identifies several, such as the traditional patriarchy of small firms. He firmly places women workers employed by multinationals in a category that he terms hyperproletarian. It is characterized by a high degree of expropriation on all relevant dimensions.

We have already commented on the problem of defining national systems in the absence of field studies. Deyo is limited by the lack of studies within the workplace. His models sound plausible, but they lack detail. One of the few workplace studies compared Korea and the United States and concluded that in many respects American workers were the more individualized and powerless; in Korea, there were family and other sources of cohesion (Cho 1985). As Deyo shows, worker activism has been greater in Korea than in countries such as Singapore, which leaves the question of whether Singapore is a better example of the model of the NIC. Chung's contribution is to show that, although workers certainly were intensely subordinated, there were still ways in which they could assert some autonomy. Chung's study may be set alongside one of the few other detailed ethnographies of such apparently powerless workers, namely, Aiwah Ong's (1987) important study of workers in Japanese-owned plants in Malaya, which develops some similar themes. Ong, however, gives particular weight to workers' preindustrial traditions as a source of a language of resistance. Chung shows that "little resistances" can still be negotiated even when such traditions have lost much of their meaning. Global corporations are certainly powerful, but their control of the labor process always and everywhere depends on the negotiation of order.

The issue of globalism is taken up directly by Shaiken and Frenkel. They both argue that their studies exemplify the possibilities of genuine globalization. In the past, tariff barriers and the difficulties of obtaining information on plants spread across the globe constrained the apparent might of the multinational corporation (MNC). With competition increasingly occurring globally, with technology being in principle available everywhere, and with the growing ease of collecting and transmitting data, these constraints may be weakening.

Shaiken looks at an auto plant in Mexico and argues that it was possible to secure high productivity based on high levels of skill despite low wages. He also draws some bleak conclusions for labor within the United States. Frenkel analyzes the operations of a U.S.-based pharmaceuticals firm with plants in Australia, Britain, Malaysia, and Taiwan. This study is less centrally concerned with the dynamics of the workplace than the other chapters, but it is informed by the problem of labor control. Unlike much of the established literature on multinational companies, which often has a bland and generalized view of control (e.g., Brooke 1984; Doz and Prahalad 1986), Frenkel looks in detail at labor productivity and how it was policed by corporate headquarters. He suggests that, though there were significant national differences of a kind noted in the other chapters, the firm was able to impose a centralized measurement system and that this affected shopfloor practice.

Concluding Remarks

At least as important as the shared substantive themes of the eight case study chapters is the desire to understand the process of labor regulation. Methodologically, the book emphasizes issues such as the operation in practice of systems that are often described only by their formal features; variations within national systems, together with the ways in which the product market and other forces explain these variations; the links between different levels of the systems; and the continuity and uncertainty of the process of determining the effort bargain. Such themes should form part of the developing agenda of workplace studies.

Structure and Content of the Volume

Though wide-ranging, this book does not pretend to be comprehensive. Its content is limited by the nature of the workers, workplaces, and countries considered. All the workplaces were factories, and in most of them the workforces were predominantly male (the exception is Chung's study of female assembly operatives). This focus, in which we are of course far from alone, reflects the fact that the problem of labor management has traditionally been felt to be concentrated in large manufacturing sites in sectors such as the auto industry that are dominated by men. "Neutralizing the workplace" was not a problem in large parts of the service sector, for example. The approach in terms of labor regulation can readily be applied to labor outside manufacturing, and we hope this book encourages such an approach.

There is a substantial literature on women in the workplace, and a growing one on the significance of notions of masculinity in men's workplace experiences. For the purposes of this volume, however, gender can be taken as something of a constant. In Bélanger's study, for example, although masculinity may have been an important element in the experience of workers in each plant he studied, differences in its role were probably not great enough to have explained the observed differences in the workplace regime. This volume chooses to focus on issues other than gender.

The focus is heavily on North America and Europe. Only Chung and Frenkel consider Southeast Asia. There are, of course, good reasons for a specific focus, including the chance to address issues such as American-British differences and similarities in detail. Had studies on other countries been available, it would have been desirable to include them. The aim, however, was not to cover every possible case but to illustrate an approach to the workplace and in the course of doing so to address substantive themes. The collection meets this objective.

The structure of the book is straightforward. Chapter 1 sets the scene by indicating some of the limits in existing approaches to the regulation of labor. As mentioned above, it deals with two topics. The first is the comparative analysis of conflict developed by students of corporatism. Consideration of this tradition points to some weaknesses in the conceptualization of the nature of conflict that ethnographically informed work can correct. Second, it addresses the role of the state in shaping the character of a national system. Since several case studies in this volume discuss aspects of this issue, it is important to place them in context by outlining current debates and suggesting where case studies can take them forward.

Following Chapter 1 are three chapters that provide North Atlantic comparisons. They are followed by two chapters that focus on Europe (Shire) and on Europe and North America (Smith). We then turn to the three cases (Chung, Shaiken, and Frenkel), which examine other parts of the globe and in so doing address the issue of globalization.

The conclusion considers some general implications of the case studies, in particular the relationship between global trends and national systems of regulation, as well as whether national regimes are undergoing a sudden transformation or a more limited and uncertain process of change. The issue of continuity points to the final message of this volume. If regimes are changing fundamentally, studies of the past are of historical interest. To the extent that they are not, lessons from the past retain considerable force.

1

A Comparison of National Regimes of Labor Regulation and the Problem of the Workplace

P. K. Edwards

From the emergence of the proletariat during the nineteenth century to the early twentieth century, employers and reformers worried about the "labor problem." The basis of the problem was the threat to the political system posed by a mass of workers. The response was defined in terms of a set of institutions, operating at the national political level as well as in the workplace, that could be used to bring labor within the fabric of society. The same issue faces any governing class: how are workers to be persuaded to continue to work hard under the authority of others?

Though the language of the labor problem has disappeared, the underlying problem of how workers are integrated into capitalism has continued to fascinate scholars. In the field of comparative inquiry, two main traditions have focused on the problem of containing conflict. This chapter reviews their contributions and indicates the space they leave for the workplace-oriented approach of the rest of this volume.

The first tradition, the political economy approach, sets out to explain variations between countries in the level and, more significantly, the role and meaning of conflict. It is highly pertinent to this volume in view of the general emphasis in the introduction on the importance of conflict and particularly the generation of conflict within the workplace. In practice, however, the political economy approach examines strikes at the level of a whole economy and, though assuming a workplace regime that generates patterns of strikes, it does not address the nature of this regime. It also tends to reduce countries to examples of certain types and thus to play down the dynamics and contradictions of labor regulation.

The second tradition, the historical legacies approach, by contrast, places great weight on these issues. Its exploration of state and employer policies toward the labor problem indicates a set of themes within which the present contributions can be located. The following chapters use state and employer policies to explain workplace labor regimes. In doing so, they do not pluck these explanations out of the air but draw on a well-established tradition of inquiry.

The idea of legacies is also important to the question, raised in the introduction, of whether there are identifiable national systems of labor regulation. It is possible that employers are driven by the conditions facing their industry and thus that any comparison between two countries does not really measure "country effects" at all. Jeffrey Haydu (1988), for example, has applied this point to historical analysis, demonstrating great differences in employers' policies in different American industries. This chapter, by contrast, argues that there are certain national characteristics that limit the degree of variation possible: there *are* national systems of regulation. In focusing on these systems, the historical legacies approach tends, however, to exaggerate the amount of diversity that exists. Each system is treated as an entity, with the system of regulation being explained as the result of historical accident. Such a contingency approach neglects the material basis of the problem of regulating labor. This chapter offers a view grounded in the approach to the labor relation outlined in the introduction. As Burawoy (1979a, 263) puts it, "In exploring changes in the labor process either over time or between places, we are simply trying to approach the limits of variation of the capitalist labor process, that is, its capitalist essence."

The Political Economy of Conflict

The political economy approach has risen to a position of prominence over the past decade or so. It presents itself as an advance on traditional comparative industrial relations, with the latter's familiar problems of its emphasis on collective bargaining, its interest in the regulation of conflict rather than the conditions that promote it, and its pluralist underpinnings (Hyman 1978; Cohen 1991). Political economy thus represents the most developed approach with which an alternative "labor regulation" approach may be contrasted. It also shares substantive interests, for it sees the pattern of conflict in a country as an index of a much wider relationship between labor and the social and political structures of advanced capitalism. In practice, as will be seen, proponents of a political economy approach use strike patterns as their main indicator of conflict, whereas followers of a labor regulation approach try to look at the actual processes of conflict. But the interest in conflict, and the view of it as a key element in a whole pattern of relationships, takes political economy a long way from conventional analyses of strike patterns.

One difficulty is that political economy has become a very widely used term. In some usages it is largely coterminous with what is called here labor regulation. As will be seen, Anthony Giles and Gregor Murray's

(1989) statement has much in common with this view, and Hyman (1989b), though he does not go into great detail about his use of the label, would appear to adopt a very similar style of analysis. For present purposes, political economy is that approach that tries to explain variations in the extent and nature of conflict in terms of the structure of the exchange between employers, unions, and the state; that sees the state as a largely neutral force; and that gives greatest explanatory weight to the powers of unions in the political arena.

Political Perspective on Strikes

Political economy emerged in reaction to two approaches: economics and industrial relations. The former explains strike rates in terms of such conditions as unemployment levels and price inflation. It was argued, however, that such explanations worked only in certain contexts, namely, those in which stable collective bargaining was established. Thus, they worked quite well in the United States in the post-1945 period but broke down in countries such as France and Italy, and indeed failed to function even for the United States in the period before bargaining was well established (Snyder 1975). Orthodox industrial relations as represented by Hugh Clegg (1976) offered an institutional rather than an economic explanation, focusing on the structure of collective bargaining. The low strike rate in Sweden, for example, reflected the level of bargaining (national-level bargaining reduced the number of separate strikes), the nature of contracts (comprehensive agreements reduced the scope for bargaining at the shopfloor level), and so on.

According to Walter Korpi and Michael Shalev (1979), this approach was limited because the institutions of bargaining merely passed on the effects of wider social structures. In countries such as Sweden, industrial relations was overlaid by political exchange (see also Korpi 1983b). The strike ceased to be a major aspect of class conflict. The key reason was that working-class interests were able to establish effective control of the political system. Instead of direct battles between employers and unions over wage levels, political exchange allowed workers' interests, in such matters as unemployment insurance and social welfare, to be pursued through their political party. The economic sphere in general, and the workplace in particular, ceased to be a major site of contestation.

A similar view was developed by Edward Shorter and Charles Tilly (1974) in relation to France. The problem here was not a decay of the strike but a change in its form, with long battles being replaced by short but massive protests. The explanation was again political: unions directed their demands at the state rather than at individual employers, and strikes thus became means to demonstrate symbolically workers' concerns over an issue, rather than weapons of economic attrition.

Both groups of writers used their analyses to consider advanced capitalist countries as a whole. North American strikes, for example, remained long because unions were unable to gain leverage in the political arena. Korpi and Shalev provided detailed descriptions of the extent of social democratic or labor party control of governments, the prediction being that greater control would reduce strike levels. This approach merged with the much wider debate about corporatism, in which numerous writers have measured the political power of labor and also the degree of centralization and unity of labor movements, with the expectation that high scores on these measures would strengthen the ability of unions to maintain political exchange (e.g., Stephens 1979; Schmitter 1979). A related development was the attempt to classify countries according to the extent of their corporatist arrangements. Instead of treating nation states as individual entities, efforts were made to reduce them to examples of certain types.

Problems of Theory and Method

In view of the popularity of the political economy approach, criticism has been surprisingly rare. Three broad difficulties can, however, be identified (Edwards 1983). First, though presented as a break with industrial relations, the approach in fact reproduced a pluralist methodology. The institutionalists saw collective bargaining as a means by which conflicts between capital and labor could be resolved. The political economy writers viewed the state in much the same way: organizations of workers pursued class interests in the industrial and political spheres, and, if they were strong enough, they could establish a system of exchange in the latter. Though Marxist language appears in some accounts, in others (notably Korpi 1983b) it is made plain that the state is seen as a passive, neutral body that merely reflects the balance of forces between capital and labor. As James Fulcher (1987) has argued, what he terms labor movement theorists (who would include Gosta Esping-Andersen [see Esping-Andersen and Korpi 1984] as well as Korpi and John D. Stephens) assume that labor parties can gain effective control of the state.

Why is this a problem? It could be argued that the assumption, though plainly demarcating political economy from any serious Marxist or indeed radical analysis of the capitalist state, is a reasonable approximation that does not damage the explanation: is it not true that working-class interests have been effective in Sweden and have accordingly moderated industrial struggle? One problem arises because the approach directs attention away from the state as an active agent in the management of labor. It sees the state merely as a reflection of other forces and gives no consideration to how state actors can shape the process of labor regulation.

One consequence is an inaccurate reading of key historical periods. The critical exemplar case is Sweden. The country merits some discussion because the political economy interpretation of the historical trajectory has rarely been scrutinized. Thus, much is made of the timing of the decline of strikes. There was allegedly a key turning point in 1934, that is after the electoral victory of the Social Democrats in 1932 but before the famous

Basic Agreement between unions and management of 1938; this is used to argue that politics was the key factor in the decline. Fulcher (1987) shows that 1934 was not in fact a dramatic turning point. The fall in strikes in that year was part of a longer trend, in particular, the decline in the number of large strikes against wage cuts imposed in the depth of the Depression. There is thus no evidence that 1934 was in any way distinctive in terms of the effects of political exchange on strikes.

The Basic Agreement, moreover, reflected not just labor movement power but also, and arguably more importantly, changing strategies by employers and the state concerning the regulation of the workplace. As Peter Jackson and Keith Sisson (1976) show, the state was increasingly concerned about the level of industrial conflict and in essence told the parties to sort out their own affairs or have them sorted out for them. Many other states have been active in shaping national systems of labor regulation, as the American New Deal clearly shows (Harris 1985). Seeing the state as neutral directed attention away from a major actor in the system.

The second problem relates to typologies. They all have anomalies. Britain appeared to be an exception in Shorter and Tilly's account since strikes did not become a political weapon despite the country's fairly high scores on measures of the influence of a labor party in government. Germany was a problem for Korpi and Shalev, since it enjoyed low strike rates without the benefit of corporatist institutions. In accounts that focus on a fairly small number of countries, even one anomaly is a weakness. But the presence of anomalies illustrates a deeper problem. The analysis is mechanical and largely ahistorical, with the assumption being that certain institutions lead to certain outcomes and with the causal mechanisms at work being at best left implicit.

In the case of Britain, it would be reasonably straightforward to construct an account of the continuation of strikes at the workplace level in terms of the fragmentation and weakness of employers, the parallel focus of unions at the shopfloor level (Sisson 1987; Zeitlin 1990), and the limited powers of the state to force through the rationalization of industrial relations or indeed of anything else (Hall 1986). But this would involve a historical reconstruction of the "labor problem" and its regulation that would step beyond the concerns of the political economy approach.

In the case of Germany, David Cameron (1984) offers an account that is more in the spirit of the approach. In brief, unions gained the benefits of low unemployment and low inflation, in return for which they practiced moderate bargaining strategies and rarely struck; this in turn promoted high employment levels and low inflation, so that a virtuous spiral was set in motion. Cameron applies this logic to other countries and demonstrates the relevant correlations between strikes, inflation, unemployment, and economic growth. Since no process of political exchange is necessarily involved, this reasoning does in fact break with the core political economy assumptions. It suggests how an alternative approach might be constructed but does not in fact do this itself. It remains at the level of cross-sectional relationships and does not explore the historical processes permitting virtuous spirals to develop. In short, Cameron's study is a useful starting point but no more than that.

In addition to admitted anomalies, there are difficulties with other countries, even such exemplar cases as Sweden. As Fulcher (1987) argues, labor movement theory posits that workers can secure their goals through political action. It thus has difficulty in explaining the continuation of shopfloor protest, as exemplified by a wave of unofficial strikes at the end of the 1960s. Such protest did not reach the scale of that recorded in many other countries, but it shows that problems of shopfloor order continue even where political exchange is advanced. One illustration is labor turnover. A government inquiry into a shipyard (summarized by Fulcher 1973) found a high rate of turnover, which it explained as the result of shopfloor grievances that had no institutional avenue of expression, so that workers quit. In other words, it is impossible to "neutralize the workplace" entirely by taking capital-labor relations to a higher level.

This leads to the third problem for political economy. Like industrial relations pluralism, it focuses on what happens when organized bodies of unions and employers meet. It does not consider the conditions permitting such mobilization or, crucially, how far the demands that are made in organized bargaining relate to all the interests of workers. It has long been recognized that conflict can be expressed in many ways, including quitting, absenteeism, and sabotage (Kerr 1954). The labor movement view does not address the continuity of relations around the effort bargain. It assumes that unions can simply resolve workers' demands elsewhere, thereby neglecting the ways in which conflict continues to underlie the operation of the workplace. Quitting and absenteeism have long been concerns of Swedish companies. Labor movement theory provides no means to analyze their role on the shopfloor or, more generally, to explore how labor is regulated.

From Political Economy to Mode of Production

An approach that connects the shopfloor to the development of capitalism is suggested in two recent critiques. Giles and Murray (1989) lay out the core features of what they term a political economy view. They include Korpi among its exponents, though perhaps overgenerously, for they emphasize several points that he largely neglects. Burawoy (1990, 783), by contrast, includes Korpi in his list of those who have abandoned the "core tenets of Marxism." For the present purposes, what is or is not Marxism is not the issue. The key point is analytical: labor movement writers adopt an essentially pluralist view that lacks a perspective on the bases of conflict in a capitalist mode of production.

Giles and Murray, by contrast, make four key points. *Conflict* is not just concerned with the distribution of rewards, as it is seen in pluralism, but also revolves around the organization of production. *Trade unions* should be seen not as interest groups but as class-based intermediary organizations. They cannot necessarily, therefore, simply aggregate workers' interests, and they may not be able to handle some shopfloor discontents. The Swedish shipyard would be an example, for the unions were confined to a legally defined bargaining relationship and were unable to address some major shopfloor issues. *The state* is "a set of institutions that reflect and reinforce relations of social power," which contrasts with pluralism's view of the state as passive. Further, patterns of industrial relations need to be related to "the dynamics of international and national social *structures of production and accumulation*," whereas pluralism says little about these dynamics.

These last two points are elaborated in the second critique, that of Roberto Franzosi (1989). Taking Italy as his example, Franzosi detects two problems with a political economy explanation. First, it would be predicted that a strike wave should be a response to political crises, whereas this order of events was often reversed. Second, if strike waves depend on events within individual countries, why do they tend to occur at the same time in most capitalist nations?

Franzosi argues for an integrated approach that would deal with the latter point by exploring forces operating within the mode of production as a whole. The most developed theories at this level of analysis are those identifying long waves of accumulation and relating trends in indexes of conflict to these waves (Screpanti 1987; Silver 1991). Such theories offer some intriguing suggestions (see Edwards 1992a) but need no further comment here. Franzosi also underlines the causative role of conflict: most theories take strikes to be a dependent variable, but the Italian case shows how strikes can significantly affect later developments. He also argues for the need for much more attention to the policies of employers and the state in managing conflict. In short, instead of seeing strikes in particular and conflict in general as the activity of workers and unions and as merely responses to structural conditions, the interrelations of workers, unions, management, and the state must be considered.

Much of this program is not novel. After all, Clegg (1976) had reached a similar view about the importance of employers from a purely conventional analysis. As discussed below, studies of the problem of workplace order have also begun to appear. Franzosi's work remains important, however, in focusing sharply on the weaknesses of political economy. Perhaps the most important implication of his critique is that the approach has ceased to be a progressive research program: once the basic point about political exchange was made, any further development has involved abandoning the core of the approach by exploring the historical dynamics of the labor relation within specific national contexts. A perspective informed by the workplace offers a new route forward.

Conclusion

Political economy claims to address the question of how class conflict
has developed throughout the capitalist nations. Yet its model of conflict is
one-sided, in that it focuses on the demands of labor and neglects the
strategies of employers and the state. It is also one-dimensional, in that it
pays so little attention to the workplace. In accounts of large-scale
phenomena such as class conflict, the workplace tended to be seen as
unimportant, with events here perhaps filling in some details but otherwise
being of little interest. In fact, in any capitalist economy, political
exchange is irrelevant without the production of surplus value within the
workplace. Such exchange can certainly help to "neutralize the workplace,"
but the historical dynamics of this process cannot be reduced to the ideal-
typical and static models of political economy.

The State and Legacies of History

This section turns to two of the issues at the heart of an alternative view,
namely, the roles of the state and employers in the development of
historical traditions within nation states. This is not, of course, to argue
that unions and workers have been unimportant. It is to make two points.
First, the overwhelming emphasis until relatively recently was on unions:
traditional labor history was the history of unions, not of the regulation of
work. At the very least, attention needs to shift toward other key actors
and, even more important, toward how work has been organized and
controlled. Second, it can be argued that employers and the state are the
key influences in explaining variations between countries. As Sanford
Jacoby (1991) argues in the case of the United States, the demands of
unions were not substantially different from those of labor in other
countries. What was critical was the reaction of employers in the context
of the wider social and economic environment. Sweden would be another
example, for early unionism was of the craft character familiar in the
United States or Britain. But the nature of Swedish industry, the organization of employers, and the response of the state led labor relations away
from craft traditions. It is thus important to consider how the state and
employers have been viewed.

Though debate on the state and employers has been wide-ranging, the
center of the analysis has been simple: how can the problem of the
workplace be managed? There is thus a very clear connection between the
"micro politics" of the workplace and the "macro politics" of the state.
Debates on both topics also sharply contrast two different approaches,
namely, a form of contingency theory and a more materially grounded
analysis.

Contingency Theories of the State

In relation to the state, the clearest expositions of contingency theory
are those of Theda Skocpol (1980) and Jonathan Zeitlin (1985). Both

authors were reacting against the determinism and functionalism of certain Marxist theories of the state. These theories tended to assume that the state responded to the "needs" of the capitalist economy and that its interventions were successful in promoting the integration of labor in particular and the continued functioning of capitalism as a whole. It was not difficult to indicate the problems with such a view. But it was not clear what the critics put in its place. Having demonstrated, for example, that key actors within the state do not merely follow some presumed "needs" and instead make important choices, the critics merely suggest that everything is contingent on the balance of political forces at a given time and indeed on accident. They accept that, within any one nation state, traditions of state intervention grow up and that these reflect the institutional structure of the state. Thus, the reluctance of the British state, as compared with Sweden and even the United States, to adopt Keynesianism in the 1930s is explained in terms of the powers of conventional economic theories within the government and civil service (Weir and Skocpol 1985). But any deeper argument about the nature of the state and its dependence on a capitalist economy is ruled out.

As argued elsewhere (Edwards 1986, 144–54), this approach jumps from one extreme to another. The evident failings of certain Marxist theories do not mean that one must reject all efforts to establish the nature of the capitalist state. Capitalist economies may not have "needs" that are automatically recognized by the state, but they do generate pressures and impose constraints on states. The pressures reflect the conditions that are necessary for the economic system to continue to operate. As capitalism develops, these conditions change. Thus, early capitalism could happily operate without much state intervention in the economic infrastructure, but by the late nineteenth century the benefits of a trained workforce and of state-provided education as the means to this end were increasingly voiced. The constraints indicate the limits on the choices open to state actors. Even where capitalism has lost legitimacy, as in the United States in the early 1930s, feasible means of state intervention are defined by what is compatible with a capitalist economy; state planning was not on the agenda.

Different states can adopt different policies as a result of the specific circumstances in which they operate. They are, moreover, not always successful. Contingency theorists often criticize more structuralist accounts for being untestable. Yet a retreat into empirical complexity is hardly an answer. Cases of state failure can be used to establish the conditions for the continued functioning of a capitalist economy. The state in tsarist Russia in 1917 was plainly failing to reproduce the conditions necessary for a capitalist economy, and consideration of the case could well identify which conditions were absent. In short, to speak of conditions and pressures is not to sink into functionalism but to identify forces that constrain but do not determine the behavior of state actors.

A further illustration of the constraints on state intervention comes from the timing of efforts to manage the capital-labor relation. If the state were an autonomous actor, such efforts would occur whenever people within it wished to intervene. That intervention comes only when there is a perceived crisis in the management of labor indicates that it is the relationship between the state and the capitalist economy that is crucial. As Burawoy (1985, 139) puts it, "State politics does not hang from the clouds; it rises from the ground, and when the ground trembles, so does it."

States as Managers of the Labor Relation

As noted in the introduction, Burawoy himself made an important contribution to the discussion of the constraints on state intervention. His starting point was that labor process analysis of the workplace had been underpoliticized, in that few connections had been forged between the shopfloor and power relations in the rest of society. By contrast, discussion of the state was overpoliticized in concentrating on politics in the sense of relations between political parties, the behavior of organized interest groups, and so on, to the neglect of the management of labor.

On the overpoliticization of the state, much debate has turned on the political process at the national level, as though it is cut off from developments in the economic base. For lengthy periods, the regulation of labor may not in fact be an open issue for national politics. But in every major state it has surfaced at least once—during the New Deal in the United States and during World War II in Canada, in the 1930s and 1960s in France, in the early 1900s in Sweden, in the 1890s in Australia—and it is always implicit in the forms of class accommodation reached even when it is not explicitly a topic.

Burawoy argues that the differences in workplace regime that he identified in Britain and the United States—a reliance on informal bargaining at the point of production in the former, compared with detailed, legally enforceable contracts in the latter—stemmed from differences in state regulation. He categorized these differences on two dimensions, as shown in table 1.1. State support for the reproduction of labor power refers to such things as unemployment benefit and welfare systems. State regulation of factory regimes entails direct involvement in the relation between capital and labor, for example, whether any laws require employers to bargain

Table 1.1. Burawoy's Classification of the State Regulation of Labor

Regulation of factory regimes	Support for reproduction of labor power	
	High	Low
High	Sweden	United States
Low	Britain	Japan

Source: Burawoy (1985: 138).

with unions and whether collective agreements are legally enforceable. Britain scores high on the first dimension and low on the second, whereas the reverse is the case for the United States. Burawoy fills in the other two boxes in his diagram with figures for Sweden and Japan.

Burawoy's depiction of the two factory regimes is illuminating, and the general differences in state approach to the workplace between Britain and the United States are incontrovertible. It is difficult, however, to use the model to analyze other countries. For example, Australia's egalitarian society and strongly state-supported bargaining system would place it in the same box as Sweden, and yet such things as its strike pattern and its trade union structure are very different. Burawoy might argue that workplace regimes nonetheless have important similarities. It is true that, in both cases, the use of industrial action is shaped by the legal systems, but the response to the constraints is different. In Australia, strikes reflect two rationales: the use of a brief stoppage to indicate workers' feelings and thus to put pressure on the state's arbitration system; and less organized protests by workers who find that they have no means of bargaining directly over workplace issues such as discipline and health and safety (Waters 1982). Sweden lacks such aggressive tactics (Korpi 1978; Sisson 1987, 28).

In defense of Burawoy, it might be argued that these empirical problems show that he has identified necessary but not sufficient conditions to explain differences in behavior. That is, his dimensions capture certain features of national regimes but not all the key ones. As the political economy school would emphasize, political exchange in Sweden has taken the heat out of workplace grievances, and the form of such exchange is a further dimension that needs to be included. If, however, Burawoy's classification is viewed in this way, then it is not clear why weight is placed on these particular dimensions. They may serve to differentiate Britain and the United States, but their general applicability has not been established.

A further difficulty relates to the explanation of why countries are in specific boxes. Staying with the example of Sweden, Burawoy (1985, 147) explains why national-level bargaining emerged between the LO (the confederation of manual workers unions) and the employers' national federation, the SAF, in terms of late and rapid industrialization, which occurred when labor movements were already influenced by socialism. There are some important elements in the causal story sketched here. As Fulcher (1988 and 1991) has argued, accounts emphasizing industrialization alone are inadequate: what was crucial was the combination of industrial change and political development. By the time Sweden industrialized, a strong socialist ideology had already emerged. The franchise was also very limited, and most of the working class had no vote. Working-class people were thus open to the arguments of socialist organizers, so that party loyalties generated unions and helped to direct aspirations at the political center. Most analysts also emphasize the small number of firms and their export orientation.

The difficulty, warns Fulcher (1988, 271), is that "it is all too easy to take shortcuts and telescope complex historical processes." Care is particularly important in identifying what is being explained and which combination of factors is used to account for it. Is the question the extent of state intervention, the early formation of the SAF, or the specific policy adopted by the SAF? Burawoy's list helps to explain the second issue, although even here specific contingencies have to be addressed. As Sisson (1987, 160) notes, the early formation of the SAF was due less to the concentration of industry than to the difficulties Swedish firms faced in establishing "single-industry organizations at this stage of industrial development." For the other questions, Burawoy's list is even less satisfactory.

Particularly important in the Swedish case is the role of the state. In many ways, the Swedish state did not take a leading role in regulating factory regimes, because of substantial splits within the legislature. As Sisson notes (1987, 157), "Employers were frustrated in their hope that the state would intervene with legislation to deal with the challenge of trade unions." Employers were thus forced to deal with the challenge themselves.

State regulation of workplace regimes was not established in Sweden until confirmation, in 1928, of the legal enforceability of collective agreements. Intervention has in some ways remained limited; for example, the state imposes far fewer rules on the conduct of unions and employers than in the United States or, since 1980, in Britain. Swedish employers cherished their independence from the state, albeit at the price of an accommodation with labor. As for the state, its leaders were conscious of the costs of continuing industrial disruption and felt that there was a need to contain it within acceptable bounds. Thus, though Sweden and the United States both score high on state regulation of the workplace, the origins and nature of this regulation are significantly different. As discussed below, this explanation fits within Burawoy's overall approach, although it also indicates the need for the detailed reconstruction of key historical episodes.

Classificatory boxes can interfere with this approach. Differences between countries, remarks Sisson (1987, 137), "represent variations on a common pattern of development." That is, employers faced the general problem of managing labor, in particular the emergence of organized challenges by unions, and their responses reflected the circumstances in which they found themselves. To place the results in boxes may provide some initial categorizations, but the exercise is at best a starting point.

In directing attention to the state's approach to the labor problem, Burawoy has indicated how these processes might be analyzed. In particular, structural forces exert pressures, but these have to be interpreted at the key turning points when the management of labor enters the political arena. A workplace orientation thus directs attention to the management of labor in ways that tend to be neglected in conventional politically oriented accounts of the state's interventions in the economy. Forms of accommodation carry implications for the future, and decisions at one juncture are shaped by previous choices. National systems of labor regulation have their own dynamics and are not to be reduced to static typologies.

Among the most important illustrations of this point is Alan Fox's (1985) analysis of the role of the British state. Fox characterizes the state's approach to the labor problem as an attempt to manage it through a rule of law. At various key junctures authoritarian solutions were rejected and a form of compromise was engineered. The compromise involved a degree of acceptance of the lower orders within the political system, but there was no clear-cut strategy. Though the state would try to contain certain aspects of trade union behavior, there was no firm commitment to back employers in labor disputes. In contrast to German employers, who could be confident of state support in their key encounters with labor, British employers could never be sure that the state would back them. There was no systematic policy, only the development of understandings as to what was reasonable.

Fox explains this development in terms of the slow evolution of the British political system and the reliance of the ruling class on certain long-established and trusted recipes for responding to the challenge from below. But this is no contingency theory. Fox takes it for granted that there were problems that had to be tackled and that these had a material basis in the capital-labor relation. He does not labor this point but instead focuses on how the problems were interpreted at certain key junctures. These decisions—for example, to adopt a reformist rather than a repressive route during the Reform crisis of 1832 and to avoid authoritarian legislation in the face of the labor challenge of the late nineteenth century—helped to determine the course taken subsequently. The pace and timing of industrialization may have been a background factor, but to explain developments properly calls for a reconstruction of choices and historical dynamics, not a search for static and monocausal explanations.

Legacy of History and Role of Employers

Comparative work on employers' policies has developed in a similar direction (e.g., Jacoby 1985; Sisson 1987; Zeitlin 1990; Gospel 1992). The central question is simple: given that employers make important choices in responding to labor's challenge, how much are these choices freely made, and how much are they dependent on structural conditions?

Contingency theory has again emerged as a significant force, essentially criticizing structural accounts and offering a more voluntaristic model. There are two expressions of it that are relevant here. First, there is the well-known "societal approach" of Marc Maurice, François Sellier, and Jean-Jacques Silvestre (1986). Comparing matched firms in France and Germany, and thus controlling for influences such as technology, these authors found that there were substantial differences in such matters as the structure of the managerial hierarchy, the role of the supervisor, and pay differentials. Other authors (e.g., d'Iribarne 1989) develop a similar approach that goes back at least as far as Michel Crozier's (1963) celebrated identification of the base of a certain approach to organization deep in French culture and society, that organizational structure varies between nations for reasons due to distinct national managerial and cultural traditions. Much of this argument—notably that there are indeed national characteristics—is consistent with the present discussion. It is, however, directed at the overall nature of management and not at the issue of labor regulation as defined here. Nor does it explore the contradictions in the ways in which managements and the state have tried to handle the labor problem. Each nation is presented as a bundle of deeply rooted but essentially unchanging characteristics, and the dynamics of attempts to solve the labor problem do not feature strongly. As Lane (1989, 34–37) explains, the constraints of capitalism are not addressed, and managerial policy is thus ungrounded. Moreover, references to 'actors' notwithstanding, the ways in which managers and workers interact, a key theme in the present volume, are given very little attention. We take up the links between global capitalism and national systems in the conclusion.

A more dynamic approach is provided by Steven Tolliday and Jonathan Zeitlin (1991a and 1991b). They argue that many accounts, the conventional ones associated with Alfred D. Chandler (1977) as well as more radical analyses, tended to assume that "the logic of capitalism itself obliges firms to adopt the form of organization that most efficiently serves their economic interests" (Tolliday and Zeitlin 1991a, 8). Yet analysts have increasingly been forced to recognize that there has been no universal trend toward deskilling and no one best route to competitive success. Nonetheless, this recognition has not changed underlying assumptions, so that even the "most sophisticated" writers are "unwilling to concede a genuine scope for managerial choice" (12). Tolliday and Zeitlin go on to cite substantial evidence that the constraints of the market and technology do not determine managerial behavior. They conclude that outcomes "depend not simply on markets and technology but also on the interaction between the strategic choices of employers, trade unions and the state" (1991b, 324).

Though many of these points are well taken, two problems remain. The first is empirical. Tolliday and Zeitlin offer a magisterial synthesis of the development of employer labor policy in the leading industrial countries. But there remains a nagging question as to why matters developed in the way they did: why were these choices made, and how far, given economic and political traditions and previous patterns of decision, were they genuinely free choices? The relative importance of different factors might be pursued more rigorously through comparisons between two or three countries. Covering an array has the benefit of considering a range of cases, but it tends to weaken an assessment of key causal factors.

Second, there is the same analytical problem as that faced by contingency theories of the state. Many of the specific points made are valid. For example, employers do make mistakes, and there are different ways of managing the labor problem. But what level of critique is this? Does it mean that employers face no common problems and that the demands of product markets and competitive pressure place no constraints on choice? If we consider the policies of unionized American employers since the 1970s, it is clear that the threat of competition from other countries and from nonunion firms within the United States was a major factor leading to change. Firms certainly responded in different ways, but choice needs to be seen not as a factor on a par with other structural conditions but as a means of managing within the limits that these conditions set. The twin needs of producing surplus value in the production process and realizing this value in exchange are the fundamental issues facing any capitalist firm.

Tolliday and Zeitlin (1991a, 13) respond to this argument by questioning how far the market acts as a means of natural selection, allowing only firms that practice efficient policies to survive. Yet the criterion is too strict. There plainly is some room for choice, and markets do not send inefficient firms to the wall immediately. They do exert constraints, however. Tolliday and Zeitlin's own examples make the point. They note that enterprises such as British Leyland (BL), British Steel, and the National Coal Board were able to pursue highly questionable policies that were driven more by internal political logics than by the hand of the market. Yet these firms have experienced massive job losses and, in the case of BL, disappearance as an independent entity. Such losses are the price of making choices that lie for too long outside the bounds of the constraints of the market.

This is not to suggest that there is "one best way" to which all firms must approximate or die. There are different ways of responding to market constraints, for example, a policy of high wages and high skills or one of short-termism and hire and fire. Either may work. But each policy needs to be able to respond to market pressures and to integrate business plans with labor management. The failures of the firms mentioned above stemmed from an inability to develop any particular model of their own and a tendency to try to ape what they saw as "best practice" (Williams, Williams, and Thomas 1983).

Contingency theory thus offers valuable correctives to determinism. But choice (even when sanctified with the adjective "strategic") has to be seen in the light of the material forces shaping firms' environments. We may now consider what specific features of choice have been seen as critical. Most scholarly attention has focused on Britain, for the behavior of employers here is at first sight most difficult to explain. British employers were the first to enter the capitalist era and yet, by the late nineteenth century, they were felt to be acquiescing in shopfloor challenges to their own authority, which their counterparts in Germany or America were able to root out. How could this happen?

There is no doubt that workplace relations in Britain have evolved in distinctive ways. Custom and informal understandings have been crucial. Efforts by the state to regulate the workplace were few and limited, and employers did not develop the sophisticated systems of personnel management that characterized their counterparts in the United States. The result was a reliance on unwritten agreements, creating an environment in which open bargaining could flourish. This bargaining, moreover, covered the organization of work as well as pay systems.

As noted in the introduction, a well-established view explains these developments in terms of a craft legacy that was itself the result of employers' market circumstances. The difficulty is that the account applies only to the minority of industries where craft unions played a role, whereas the weakness of the economy was more deep-seated. The problem was one of employer approaches to labor management, not of craft constraints. It is, for example, well established that until very recently British firms were far less professionalized in handling personnel issues than their American counterparts (Jacoby 1985; Sisson 1989; Thomson 1981). This has been a generic feature of many, if not most, British firms.

Consider the food firm Cadbury's (Smith, Child, and Rowlinson 1990). This company had nothing that could be called, in any exact sense of the term, a craft legacy. Yet by the late 1970s it was facing similar problems to those in the more well-known industries such as autos: loss of market share, technological backwardness, and a sense that control of the shopfloor had slipped away from management (as indexed by problems of productivity and a chaotic wage payment system).

Some elements of the explanation are consistent with William H. Lazonick's (1990) account. Notably, the firm eschewed the Fordist principle of producing a few standard products and instead had a large number of different lines. Yet this factor did not lead to craft controls on the shopfloor. Cadbury's had chosen a form of paternalism to run the shopfloor. By the 1970s this had produced a cozy atmosphere that in itself created few problems but that was increasingly incompatible with the need to rationalize: the shopfloor was not generating problems in the form of strikes or extensive craft controls of production, but reforming it was part of the solution. Two points follow. First, competitive weakness did not necessarily stem from craft traditions. Second, a firm like Cadbury's made choices and was not locked into one style of development. Its production system was consistent with autocracy as well as with paternalism, and its choice of paternalism reflected specific aspects of the management of the firm, and not the inevitable logic of product market forces. Third, paternalism survived only as long as it was consistent with the pursuit of competitive advantage. The firm had no compunction about dismantling its famed traditions of labor management, and in the 1970s it began to impose a more rigid discipline on the shopfloor.

A further revealing illustration is provided by the railroad industries in

Britain and the United States (see Edwards 1991 for more details). Unions became established more slowly in Britain than in America: anything approaching normal collective bargaining was not established until after World War I (Bagwell 1963), whereas written collective agreements and formal grievance procedures developed in America during the last quarter of the nineteenth century (Richardson 1963; Licht 1983). In this case, one would expect craft legacies to restrain the American, not the British, companies. Yet American firms rationalized their networks while British firms failed to do so (Chandler 1977, 133–44; Bagwell 1968, 119, 243). In the 1890s, the average freight train load on Britain's lines with the heaviest loads was 68 tons, versus an average of 484 tons on America's leading line (Aldcroft 1974, 9–14, 38–40).

Failure to rationalize in Britain cannot be explained in terms of craft restraints. What of the size of firms and the fragmentation of markets? The British railroad industry was more oligopolistic than many: in 1914, four companies owned 53 percent of the rail network (Simmons 1978, 240) and they dominated many smaller companies, so that their effective control was greater than this figure suggests. Fragmentation was perhaps more important: unrestrained competition led to a proliferation of lines and made rationalization difficult. But this failure to rationalize was a generic feature of British employers. As Lazonick (1981) himself argues, the British approach was to maximize within constraints, whereas in the United States and other countries these constraints were treated as challenges to be overcome.

Why this should be so in Britain is beyond the scope of the present discussion. The key point is that a failure to rationalize reflects an approach to the management of the enterprise that goes deeper than the limits of a craft legacy. For example, the training of managers was rudimentary, and the companies failed to look outside for new methods: "At the level of management, they came to constitute a closed service" (Simmons 1978, 251). As Howard Gospel (1992, 7) argues of British firms in general, family control of the business and low levels of managerial education and training led to "insufficient organisational capacity . . . to develop and administer strong internal systems of labour management." Some firms partially escaped this national situation, but even they did not do so completely.

Conclusion

Historical accounts of employer and state policies have either identified constraints such as the craft legacy or emphasized the complexities of historical development without placing the numerous factors that they cite into a wider framework. Legacies are certainly important. But perhaps central are the assumptions that emerge among employer and state managers about how to manage the labor problem, and not any external constraint. These assumptions develop a logic of their own, such that the management of labor in, say, Sweden and the United States moved along different paths. But these paths were not built on wholly different principles. They were routes to the common problem of regulating labor.

Conclusion: States, Employers, and the Workplace

This chapter has tried to indicate a set of themes that either locate and justify the approach taken in the rest of the book or that introduce concrete issues pursued in it. Under the former head, the introduction underlined the centrality of conflict within the labor relation. Within traditional industrial relations writings, conflict used to be equated with strikes, leaving the connections between such overt sanctions and the organization of conflict within the production process largely unexplored. Comparative studies followed this approach. The great contribution of political economy was to see strikes as part of a wider relationship between unions, employers, and the state. Its limitation was its typological approach and a lack of evidence on the workplace relations underlying a given strike pattern.

Developments around a mode of production approach have offered a more dynamic view of the labor relation. Yet there is an evident need to complement analysis at a national or industry level with study of the dynamics of conflict within the workplace. As argued in the introduction, with growing employer attention to initiatives within the workplace, it is here that the management of conflict is likely to be particularly significant.

A second theme relates to contingency theory. The theory is correct to question deterministic models of development, but it tends to see the regulation of labor as lacking any logic or material base. The assumption guiding the present collection, by contrast, is that there are identifiable structural forces at work. Managements have to turn labor power into labor, which is an uncertain and contradictory process. Not surprisingly, therefore, the ways in which labor is performed vary both between countries and over time. But this is variation on a theme, and it is constrained by the need to continue to produce a surplus in the production process and to realize it in the market. Variation occurs within limits.

In relation to the state, too, the current fashion is to emphasize its independence and to explain its behavior in terms of its own dynamics. The present argument, by contrast, is that, though states certainly make choices, the choices made, and indeed the fact that states have to take any position at all on workplace issues, are shaped by pressures from the productive sphere. The American state would not have been led to pass the New Deal labor legislation without a "labor problem" that called for attention.

Further, the form of intervention reflected the preexisting nature of class relations. It was taken for granted that collective bargaining between an individual employer and a single union was the natural order and that the state should buttress this system. This reflected the development of employer power within the workplace in the nonunion era, as compared with the development of multiemployer arrangements in a country such as Sweden. The preference for exclusive union jurisdictions reflected long-established workplace practice, whereas in France, with its multiple union traditions, the state would have been unable to impose such an arrangement.

As for concrete issues, the nature of employer and state activity within the workplace features heavily in the following chapters. This chapter has outlined several debates, partly to set the context for the detailed studies and partly to introduce some key arguments. There are three such arguments. First, the state plays a significant role in labor regulation. Reference in later chapters to its impact on workplace regimes is not a chance observation but part of a well-established debate. Second, the state's role varies between countries. The following chapters help to explore the nature of this variation. Third, the state has a generic impact. The literature reviewed in this chapter sees state policies as central to the explanation of historical variation. When following chapters focus on the role of the state and not on other aspects of the environment of a workplace, they have good grounds for doing so. State interventions shape the regulatory regime of a country in clear ways: they impinge directly on the system of labor regulation in the workplace, whereas other external forces do not.

A final concrete issue is variation in the behavior of the employer. There certainly are differences within national systems. For example, sectors such as construction, dominated by small employers and facing specific product market and technological circumstances, differ from mass production. Yet there are approaches to labor that are characteristic of employers within a whole country. Firms in Germany, for example, cannot escape the system of industrywide bargaining. And, as argued above, British rail companies, though free of the constraints that faced their counterparts in many manufacturing sectors, still failed to rationalize the shopfloor; this failure stemmed from their wider lack of interest in rationalizing the production process as a whole. By contrast, American railroads, in their vigorous opposition to industrial unions, were no different from the steel or engineering firms.

Thus, when workplaces in two countries are compared, one can be reasonably confident that real national differences, and not accidental aspects of a particular case, are being explored. This point is important in buttressing arguments about generalization considered in the introduction. The British firms discussed by Bélanger and Haiven were not inhibited by a craft legacy. Their reliance on ad hoc approaches and their lack of coherent labor strategies were part of a wider British approach that has continued even into the 1980s and 1990s (Edwards et al. 1992). Haiven shows that one function of grievance arbitration in Canada was to educate managers in current good practice and thus to promote a systematic, professional style. Even if managers in his British firms had wanted a legally sanctioned grievance procedure, it is doubtful whether they had the organization to handle it effectively. The British firm studied by Bélanger lacked a developed personnel function, and it was driven along by reactions to immediate crises. Its labor policy was one part of its managerial approach.

In addition to all these points, the overall lesson from this chapter is simple. Analyses of variations in labor regulation have advanced our understanding of how labor is regulated and how the workplace may be "neutralized." But what actually happens within the workplace itself? The following chapters take up this question.

2

Job Control under Different Labor Relations Regimes: A Comparison of Canada and Great Britain

Jacques Bélanger

D rawing on fieldwork conducted in Great Britain and Canada, this chapter aims to explore the interaction between specific patterns of labor control and national labor relations regimes. The analysis relates mainly to the way work relations are shaped by the economic and institutional forces outside the enterprise. In examining the connection between "micro" and "macro" levels, it also seeks to achieve a better understanding of the national regimes under study, through an analysis of their effects in particular workplaces.

Research carried out in a car components manufacturing plant in Coventry, England, enabled me to document a particularly pronounced pattern of job control and to explain its basis. The production workers had a great influence on the utilization of their labor power, and especially on job assignments, mobility between workshops, and work intensity. The situation observed subsequently in a large Quebec factory suggested stimulating questions from a comparative perspective. The workers here, in a plant that manufactures subway cars, had as much autonomy in the execution of their tasks and in their relationships with the foremen as did their British counterparts. They were able to reorganize the operations within their work groups, and, given their control of work intensity, they finished their workday a few hours before the end of the shift, a practice that was even more widespread than in the plant in Britain.

This chapter develops in five sections, of which the first seeks to define the problem under study and to show its relevance to recent industrial relations literature. After exposing briefly the theoretical approach and considering some issues of methodology in the second section, the three empirical sections present in turn three levels of analysis, namely, the extent of job control, social regulation in the workplace, and wider influences.

The first level of analysis entails documenting the extent of job control in each of the two factories. At the second level of analysis, the understanding of these patterns of job control calls for an examination of the whole process of workplace regulation, in other words, the "factory regime" (Burawoy 1985, 7–8). Here, it becomes obvious that work practices that are outwardly similar pertain to very different regulation processes and also have very different effects on an organization's efficiency. The third level of analysis deals with the structural and institutional factors that influence and contribute to the similarities and differences between the two factories. Hence, each of these three sections considers progressively wider issues.

In brief, the methodological approach consists of expanding gradually from the workshop toward the forces beyond the bounds of the workplace, to the national institutions and regimes of each country. Thus, advancing from the most microcosmic level, that of production activity, to the macro level, the study shows how rather similar patterns of behavior have very different effects because they are embedded within fundamentally different social structures.

Problem under Study

Practices of job control were studied mainly in Great Britain, especially during the decade following the report of the Donovan Commission (1968). This report linked these practices to pressure exerted by shop stewards and to the informal system of industrial relations. By comparison with this British pattern, it is generally understood that North American production workers have not developed the same degree of shopfloor control, because of the more widespread dissemination of the Fordist labor process and social compromise and because autonomous union activity is constrained by the collective agreement. The latter influence, which relates closely to the argument of this chapter, was emphasized in particular by David Brody, who compared Britain, "where union contracts did not penetrate down to the factory floor," and America, where "the workplace rule of law effectively forestalled the institutionalization of shop-group activity" (1980, 206). Discussion of these two different patterns is developed further in a recent chapter on the historical foundation of different workplace regimes (Brody 1993, 183–88; see also Burawoy 1985).

Although it is widely accepted that different historical paths have been followed on the two sides of the Atlantic, there is now considerable debate on the extent to which the North American collective agreement actually constrains management in the organization of work and production. Within mainstream industrial relations, it is generally held that labor contracts are long and detailed enough to have much impact on management. The classic works of Neil Chamberlain (1948) and of Sumner Slichter, James Healy, and E. Robert Livernash (1960) have become standard references to support this view, although the second study shows in great detail how the union challenge was circumscribed and an important body of procedural and substantive rights enshrined into collective agreements.

More recently, Michael Piore and his colleagues at the Massachusetts Institute of Technology (MIT) have put much emphasis on the importance of union control over work organization in American workplaces. A close study of their publications shows the overwhelming influence of the analysis developed by Piore in *Challenge* in 1982.[1] In a general discussion of what American businesspeople see as their major problems, he emphasized, "These companies—and indeed American management in general—report that their principal concern is with the restraints which unions impose upon the ability to organize production efficiently. They feel unable to design jobs, assign workers, or utilize tools and equipment in a productive way" (1982, 8). The article in *Challenge* became a standard reference, and its line of analysis on work organization was adopted in all major works of the MIT school of industrial relations (for instance, Katz 1984, 209; Kochan and Piore 1984, 178–79; Piore and Sabel 1984; and Kochan, Katz, and McKersie 1986).

Building on this interpretation,[2] Tolliday and Zeitlin challenge the orthodox position and seek to show that

> although this picture of Anglo-American differences has some real purchase on reality, particularly from the vantage point of the late 1960s and early 1970s, recent developments, contemporary and historiographical, on both sides of the Atlantic suggest the contrast between workplace industrial relations in the two countries is overdrawn and misleading in important respects. (1989, 222)

Yet the argument put forward by Tolliday and Zeitlin is not based on a proper comparison of the two models of workplace regulation. Much of the difficulty lies in the fact that their account reproduces a confusion between two different processes of labor regulation—namely, formal collective bargaining and shopfloor control—each model having been built around, and even dominated by, one of these processes. In other words, although each of these two complementary processes can be observed in most unionized workplaces, they do not take the same form and do not have the same importance in the countries under study here.

The North American model rests on a particular form of "workplace contractualism" (Brody 1993), whereas the British model still relies very much on customary and informal regulation, where the uncertainty of production generates much day-to-day bargaining at the most decentralized level. As the two case studies presented here will show, it is important to recognize that job controls, and indeed the whole processes of workplace regulation, have different characters in these countries.

Assumptions about the capacity for collective bargaining to regulate the labor process were so entrenched among industrial relations scholars in

North America that for decades little empirical research was pursued on the complex array of social relations that develop at levels *below* that of the legally binding collective agreement.[3] This view, that the study of workplace relations has been inhibited by the institutionalization of labor relations, is given support by Piore and Charles F. Sabel in *The Second Industrial Divide* (1984). They recall that "in the 1940s, academic observers and authors of handbooks for foremen did define key elements of shop-floor organization. . . . But by the 1960s, these elements were taken for granted, as part of an indisputably successful system of industrial production. From the late 1960s on, the subject of American shop-floor control was treated primarily by foreigners" (1984, 112).[4]

This neglect of the shopfloor as a research problem helps explain why Piore and Sabel's discussion of shopfloor relations is limited mostly to the core issues of the collective agreement, particularly the internal job structure and seniority. They explain how

> the predominant American system of shop-floor control solidified in the mass-production industries in the 1950s. It depends on two central concepts: a job is a precisely defined aggregate of well-specified tasks; and seniority . . . is a criterion in the allocation of jobs. . . . Hence, the struggle for control on the shop floor is a struggle over task classifications and allocative rules; this struggle, in turn, reinforces these two central concepts as structuring elements of American workshop life. (1984, 113)

This false assumption about the possibilities for formal collective bargaining to take over and channel all the pressure emerging from the labor process has led many specialists to believe that the informal bargaining observed in Britain over issues such as staffing levels, production standards, and work intensity, as well as the underlying forms of social pressure on the shopfloor, would be of little importance in North America. To give just one example, the book that is most highly regarded in mainstream industrial relations does not really go into these matters, in spite of its insistence on the "three-tiered framework" and its two chapters dealing with change at the workplace (Kochan, Katz, and McKersie 1986). Hence, the main weakness of this institutionalist approach is that it neglects the extent of conflict and social arrangements occurring below the level of the collective agreement and, accordingly, overestimates the impact of the agreement on the actual working of the production unit. This has led many to exaggerate the constraints imposed by the collective agreement on the efficient management of production.

The rationale of this chapter is different. It holds that a comparison of the different patterns of job control that have developed in Britain and Canada, in close connection with their different models of collective bargaining, may improve our understanding of workplace relations.

Although mainstream industrial relations did not give proper consideration to the study of shopfloor relations in North America, a small number of ethnographic studies have unveiled the complex processes of collective action, bargaining, and social adjustment occurring at the point of production, more or less independently from the collective agreement. In his classic study, Burawoy (1979b) portrays the "game of making out" within the labor process as practically distinct from the collective bargaining arrangements between the union and the management of Allied Corporation. He introduced the concept of "internal state" to characterize the role of union-management institutions in the production of order and consent on the shopfloor.[5]

In his dissertation, based on four years of participant observation of a General Motors plant, Craig A. Zabala (1983) gives a full account of shopfloor bargaining and of the struggle over production standards and related issues. But, unlike Burawoy, he sees mutual support in the union's action through collective bargaining and the more spontaneous pressure generated by United Auto Workers (UAW) members on the shopfloor. His material "shows how sabotage and grieving are intimately bound in the labor process. As in much of the rest of the auto industry, production standards, or job task—output rates, were a chronic issue at Van Nuys" (Zabala 1989, 24). Hence, the idea is not to counterpose these two levels of social regulation, but rather to show how they interact in the process of regulating labor utilization in the workplace.

A Note on Theory and Method

The ethnographic method is meaningful only when it is guided by theory and eventually refers back to it. And it is most important to be explicit about the main theoretical foundations underlying my analysis and interpretation. From the beginning, attention is focused on the labor process, that is, the process of transformation underlying the complex array of social relations studied in this book. It is through the study of the labor process that it is possible to grasp the objective foundations of conflict, which represents the central principle of analysis (Edwards 1986). Thus, the employer and the workers are put in an antagonistic position. They are also in a situation of mutual dependency; market constraints are such that they have to cooperate adequately to produce a surplus and thus reproduce the employment relationship. In this sense, it is not so much conflict that characterizes the employment relationship as, most of all, this obligation, which makes the agents maintain some form of accommodation in spite of their conflictual position. Hence, the idea of social regulation is most important in the field of industrial relations.

The notions of management control and motivation are also crucial, because once the general terms of employment are determined, production norms, and especially those related to the amount and quality of work to be done, remain indeterminate. Moreover, the problem is not simply that of "fixing" production norms in a technical way. More crucial and, sociologically, all the more interesting, this effort bargain will be determined through the power relationship that develops at the workplace, where the employer is in a position of command. Nevertheless, the observation carried out in both firms shows a considerable margin between the "optimal" use of labor power—that is, the maximum possible with a given technical organization—and the amount of work provided in reality.

It follows that the notion of control over labor utilization is central in the field of industrial relations. It is in reference to this notion that we use the term "job control" throughout this study. But job control does not have the same meaning on both sides of the Atlantic, and this has led to confusion in some comparative discussion.

In North America, job control has long been used to characterize various forms of union control over the supply of labor (in the sense of "control over jobs"). Indeed, in his classic work, Selig Perlman explains how the "consciousness of scarcity of opportunity" fostered the development of job control, by which he portrays unions as very much centered upon access to jobs, the protection of access, and what he terms the "rules of occupancy and tenure" (1928, 6–10, 237–79).

In contemporary publications, job control still has more to do with the supply of labor than with the actual use of labor power, which is the meaning of the term in the British literature. But the phrase "job control unionism" is also used in a very broad sense to cover all the rules of a collective agreement that have to do with the internal job structure and the seniority system (Piore 1982, 8–9; Katz 1984, 209; Kochan and Piore 1984, 179). Indeed, in *The Transformation of American Industrial Relations,* job control unionism is seen as one "of the basic principles of the New Deal industrial relations system," and it literally includes all the major principles enshrined in the collective agreement.[6]

It follows that when comparing the extent of job control in North America and Britain, it is most important to be explicit about one's definition. In this book, the term refers specifically to the use of labor power; it refers specifically to the margin of autonomy workers actually have over the way their labor power is utilized by management. In other words, it has to do with the range of discretion workers (and not necessarily their union) have developed over the organization and execution of work, once they have been hired and the general terms of employment have been defined.

It is worth emphasizing that the painstaking fieldwork and analysis that characterize this book would make little sense if the material collected did not have any meaning and relevance outside the gates of the very few factories where observation was conducted. Of course, this brings us into a debate on typicality and generalization, which is indeed a complex issue (Edwards 1992b, 422–25; chap. 1). Considering that this chapter builds on a comparison between two engineering factories that are not only oceans apart in space but also different on several accounts, and that fieldwork was conducted in different research projects, it is worth being more specific about the methodological approach. The intention is to explain that, although, in an ideal world, the comparison would be better controlled, these limits are not so much a problem considering the way we define the object of study and the methodological approach that follows.

Most textbooks on research methods recognize that the ethnographic approach does not rest on the typicality or representativeness of the "case" selected. Indeed, as for all research methods, the value of this approach depends very much on there being a proper definition of the research problem and on the way it is grounded in theory. In our field of study, Burawoy makes a useful point when he emphasizes that all the factories that have become brand names in the literature

> can hardly be regarded as a representative sample. They are not even "typical" of the societies in which they are embedded. Indeed, the very idea of a typical factory is a sociological fiction. It is the artificial construction of those who see one mode of generalization—the extrapolation from sample to population. There is, however, a second mode of generalization, which seeks to illuminate the forces at work in society as a totality rather than to reflect simply on the constancy and variation of isolated factory regimes within a society. This second mode, pursued here, is the extension from the micro context to the totality which shapes it. (1985, 18)

In an important article, Mitchell (1983) discusses the possibilities of generalization from case studies. Building on the distinction between statistical and logical inference, and then between enumerative and analytical induction, he defines the general conditions by which a case study can contribute to more general theoretical debates. One of these conditions is for the writer to give some account of the "particularities of the context" from which the empirical material was extracted. Mitchell concludes by emphasizing how "the extent to which generalization may be made from case studies depends upon the adequacy of the underlying theory and the whole corpus of related knowledge of which the case is analyzed rather than on the particular instance itself" (1983, 203).[7]

It follows that some form of generalization is possible inasmuch as the study rests on a sound theoretical foundation and that proper consideration is given to the historical context and to the whole social structure of which some of the processes were observed. And what may derive from such a methodological approach, which is highly demanding, has to be a form of conceptual generalization, as opposed to empirical generalization. Clearly, the idea is not to suggest that the empirical phenomena discussed in this chapter were generalized in other factories of the same countries or industrial sectors.

In this chapter, and indeed in the book as a whole, the first step of international comparison does not consist of applying the parameters of the national model to the study of concrete behavior, as in the usual "top-down" fashion. Rather, the approach proceeds by observing and documenting concrete patterns of behavior and then seeks to understand these patterns in considering both the rationale of the actors and the social and institutional framework within which they evolve and make arrangements. This means going beyond two serious difficulties that are quite common in the literature. The first, and most usual, is to conceive the relations between the macro and the micro in a rather deterministic way, whereby national regimes are seen as monolithic structures within which agents just have to play their roles. As noted by Tolliday and Zeitlin in a recent comparative work, "National models of labor management should be understood not as homeostatic and self-reproducing systems of action but as complex and contingent historical constructions whose unity and coherence always remain open empirical questions" (1991b, 277).

The second difficulty is that precedence is given to the study of the actors, their strategies, and social arrangements without proper consideration of the specific set of institutions that shape their behavior. In this study, much attention is given to the very different collective bargaining regimes that characterize Britain and Canada, as well as to the many constraints associated with the employment relationship.

In short, this chapter explores the complex connections between similar phenomena observed in two factories and the social entities of which they were part. The approach consists of progressing in an inductive fashion from the level of *concrete behavior*, to the study of the *processes of control* through which comparable normative behaviors develop and have different meanings and effects, and then to the *structural and institutional context* in which these actors evolve and develop their relationships. Each of the following sections corresponds to these three levels of social analysis.

Similar Manifestations of Job Control

The Coventry factory where observation was conducted exhibited many of the characteristic features of the British engineering industry. Established in 1926, its production activities centered gradually on the manufacture of pressed components for the motor industry. After 1955, it was part of a British engineering multinational. Its competitive position had greatly declined by the time fieldwork was conducted in 1979–80. Whereas in the mid-1960s, total employment numbered more than 2,000, by August 1979, it was about 1,250, of whom 830 were blue-collar workers.

The factory illustrated the labor relations crisis diagnosed by the Donovan Commission (1968), especially the incoherence of the wage structure and of the internal dispute procedures. Conflict was particularly manifest in the press shops. For example, company records show that there were ninety-nine wildcat strikes in this part of the plant between January and November 1969; twenty-five lasted less than one hour, twenty-nine lasted between one and four hours, and forty-five extended to more than four hours, (many to more than one shift). Most of the stoppages directly involved only one work group at a time, whereas some mobilized the whole workshop. The greatest proportion of these conflicts had to do with the effort bargain. This pattern of worker resistance led the employer to adopt a more conciliatory approach during the 1970s and to adopt the process of institutional reform recommended by the Donovan Commission.

Particular attention was paid to a homogeneous group of 134 press operators assigned to four workshops. Members of the Transport and General Workers' Union (TGWU), they had secured an important sphere of influence on matters such as work assignment, mobility within the workshop, and allocation of overtime. In fact, even more than influence, they exercised a form of veto on several of these issues (Bélanger and Evans 1988, 162–64). Nevertheless, the effort bargain remained the principal object of tensions in 1980, and this deserves closer study.

The development of job control was closely linked to the technical organization of production, which fostered collective organization. For instance, one shop steward was elected for each type of task (direct production, setting, quality control, and so on) in each workshop and for every shift. This was certainly a major reason for the large number of accredited shop stewards, (fifty during the study), but it also meant that the shopfloor organization was well designed for bargaining over job control issues. Most of the presses were nonautomatic machines, and the work pace thus depended on the operator, who had to repeat the same movements for each cycle, over thousands of times per shift.

The work was organized mainly into line production, such that several presses were linked by a series of conveyor belts. Consequently, the production rhythm of these different presses was determined by the group, and all its members shared the easiest and most trying tasks according to a rotation system they had worked out for themselves. Such technical arrangements greatly promoted social cohesion, and the establishment of production norms became a matter of bargaining. If the tension was less manifest than in the 1960s, the operators had all the means to exert a great deal of pressure on management throughout this continual bargaining process, and their numerous shop stewards were more than confident in their dealings with supervisors.

It is worth giving some idea of the decay of the payment systems. The piecework scheme, introduced with much worker resistance in the late 1960s, was still in operation in 1979. But since 1974, some press shop jobs had been done on the basis of a measured daywork scheme that proved to be a disaster in terms of productivity. By all accounts, the basic standards agreed to were too low from the beginning, and press operators found ways to produce less than the standard on a daily basis.

The various forms of pressure on the effort bargain had led, over time, to the erosion of production norms. But related phenomena also affected productivity. Operators were taking advantage of the anachronistic wage system and of the foremen's weak position to develop a whole range of fiddles, which further affected output. Indeed, in the press shops, fiddling was not limited to a redistribution of time between "good" and "bad" piecework jobs, a practice discussed as "chiseling" by Burawoy (1979b, 58). Operators were also taking advantage of periods booked as downtime to start producing on a piecework job so that they could "get in front" substantially and accumulate time off. This was called "fiddling the clock." Because of the predominance of small batches and the very fragmented nature of the organization of production, the operators might have several occasions to "fiddle the clock" in a single shift. From the data collected, it is possible to estimate that, when adding the three segments of working time (piecework, measured daywork, and downtime), the press operators' average pay corresponded to a performance of about 240 percent (i.e., a ratio of 2.4 times the average piecework standard established on the basis of work study and a fair extent of bargaining). In consequence, any piecework standard with a lower expected yield was not a real incentive and was not worth any intensification of work pace. In fact, work study had so little connection with real production that one should wonder why work study engineers had not given up.

The real problem for the company was that, over time, press operators had developed their controls to the stage where their overriding preoccupation had shifted from "making it pay" to "getting the day in," or managing their working time instead of boosting their piecework earnings. They were able to consolidate high levels of intensity and production over several hours to accumulate a substantial reserve of time off within the duration of the shift. And once they got their day in, they would stop work and retire to their rest area until the end of the shift. The length of these leisure periods varied depending on the availability of work and by individuals and work groups but typically ranged from one to three hours each day.

A subsequent study dealt with work relations in a Quebec factory that employed 950 workers. Located in a rural area, this factory was developed by a local entrepreneur. It remained very small until the mid-1960s, when it went into the fast-growing business of snowmobile manufacturing. In 1972, the family business was sold to the current owner, which has since become a multinational and known as the leader in the manufacture of public transport equipment in North America. Since 1976, most of the factory production has consisted of subway cars. All the stages of fabrication are integrated, including the pressing of components, subassembly, assembly, and the installation of various equipment. It is the principal production center of the subway car division within the company.

Direct observation was carried out in 1987 and focused mainly on two large departments: the assembly line, on which 88 workers assembled the frame, the walls, and the roof of the vehicle over two shifts; and the equipment department, where 176 workers installed various mechanical, electrical, and pneumatic components. Apart from the welders who assembled the frame of the vehicle, these departments employed semiskilled and unskilled labor, just as in the British factory.

At the time of observation, the employees were completing a huge contract to manufacture 825 subway cars for the Metropolitan Transportation Authority of New York. Since fieldwork was carried out toward the completion of this contract, the assembly line and, indeed, the entire production system were fully operational and highly stable. For more than a year, since the output had been set at two vehicles per day, no change had been made in the work organization. Although engineering and technology were quite sophisticated, most of the workers were, nonetheless, using hand tools.

Work was divided, but not really repetitive, throughout the whole shift, since each job was made up of a large number of interconnected operations. Repeating them on a daily basis enabled the employees to memorize all the twists and "angles," which, in turn, enabled them to establish modes of operation and reset the sequence of operations in a more efficient way. Because such a reorganization of the sequence of operations had a great impact on time management, it also involved some arrangements within work groups, especially since two to six employees shared the same work station over a long period of time. Although such a technical organization gave the employees control over the work pace, the fact that the production line moved forward only at the end of each shift also allowed them to get ahead from the beginning of the day and to finish early.

The development of tacit skills was encouraged by management. The company policy was to favor employee involvement in the execution of work, once all the specifications for every given job had been defined by engineers and technicians from the methods department. This autonomy in the execution of work was observed among all categories of workers. For instance, two workers in the equipment department who were classified as unskilled had the task of putting metal panels on the ceiling of each vehicle. It was regarded as a simple task by other workers, consisting mainly of taking the necessary measurements and drilling and screwing on the metal plates with a pneumatic tool. This task was repeated, however, with such deftness and speed by these two employees, who really acted as one person, that they were able to get considerably ahead of the standard time established by the methods department.

Also in the equipment department, a group of six workers was assigned to install electrical equipment inside the vehicle. They had been working together for about eighteen months and had developed quite a remarkable team spirit. At the beginning of the day, four of them worked very methodically in pairs, then everybody completed their individual routine with humor, which helped alleviate the monotony. I spent a day with this group, and five of them finished their work before 1:45 P.M. and then waited for the end of the shift at 4:30 P.M.

Apart from the fact that the workers' autonomy was quite comparable in both plants, in spite of their very different contexts, the phenomenon whereby workers greatly increased the work pace in order to get ahead and then take advantage of a long rest period at the workplace was remarkably similar. The Quebec workers were paid according to a fixed hourly rate. Given the organization of production, it was practically impossible to reduce the volume of work provided, since each employee had to complete a series of specific tasks on a vehicle every day. Indeed, it was imperative that the production line move on twice a day, before the end of each shift. Thus, in this context, just as the British workers did, the Quebec workers turned their attention toward the other side in the equation—the management of time. This preoccupation led them to increase their work intensity enormously during the first half of the shift in order to "get the day in" as early as possible. In fact, the phenomenon of a waiting period at the end of the day was even more diffused and longer than the one observed in Coventry. It is estimated that this period lasted on average two hours and ten minutes per shift on the assembly line and two hours and thirty minutes in the equipment department.

In short, considering the thirty minutes of official breaks, members of the second department were working five hours out of eight, on average. With this in mind, the Quebec plant's workers imposed considerable pressure on themselves and worked very efficiently, using all their resources during a reduced part of their work time. Thus, what was still considered by the engineers and methods department as a "fair day's work" could be produced in a much shorter period, thus leading to a long waiting period before leaving the factory. Indeed, employees were obliged to stay until the end of their shift. Most of them spent their "free" time socializing in small groups in the areas surrounding their work station or within a vehicle in the equipment department.

Different Processes of Labor Regulation

The material presented shows quite a striking similarity between the patterns of job control in these two factories, which are nevertheless located in very different countries and economic and industrial relations environments. In both cases, production workers had a great deal of scope to control the methods of operation and work intensity, and they displayed a marked independence in their relationships with supervisors. These factors, as well as the strong cohesion of the work groups, enabled them to get ahead of their work schedule and spend the last hours of the shift socializing. In both cases, this pattern was standard practice, well known and tolerated by management. A previous article on the Quebec factory tried to explain how this phenomenon helped satisfy the distinct rationalities of both management and labor (Bélanger 1989). This chapter seeks to further that analysis, starting with a comparative approach and locating the manifestations of autonomy in the different processes of social regulation from which they are derived.

Before defining the regulation processes observed in each factory, however, it should be emphasized that several of the workers' practices mentioned above are quite prevalent and have been analyzed by sociologists from several countries. Although not universal (since they require a minimum degree of collective organization), these norms, developed by and imposed on the work groups, are not specific to any particular pattern of control or labor relations regime (Burawoy 1985, 129–33; Edwards 1988, 189–94). For example, output ceilings and the opposite practice of "goldbricking"—that is, working slowly whenever the standard does not allow for a sufficiently interesting bonus—are widespread, as documented by Donald Roy in one of his classic articles (1952).

Since these phenomena have usually been studied in the context of payment-by-results systems, there is a tendency in the literature to link them too closely. In fact, these practices are inherent to the employment relationship. As the quantity to be produced remains undetermined after the initial economic exchange, the wage-effort bargain or, in other words, the question of motivation to produce a surplus, requires an ever fragile arrangement.

The various forms of payment-by-results confront the problem more directly by linking earnings to production; however, they cannot solve this problem and, in many cases, make it more open. By contrast, when the monetary incentive is too weak or the wage is simply constant, workers will focus their attention on the quantity to be produced. In many cases, such pressure can lead to a gradual erosion of production norms.

Finally, when neither the wages nor the quantity to be produced are affected by workers' performance, as was the case at the Quebec plant, workers may shift their attention to time management. Under these circumstances, the practice of increasing the pace to finish early seems quite natural, where the technical organization of production allows it. This phenomenon can be observed in the case of postal carriers and refuse collectors and in various service occupations in which employees can go home on completion of their daily routine ("job-and-finish").

The phenomenon is more complex and more interesting in the case of factory work, however, because it raises the whole question of management control (or lack thereof). Concretely, the behavior discussed in this chapter indicates that wage earners have a substantial period of free time during the working day, inside the factory, in spite of the subordinate relationship. Such a phenomenon contradicts the traditional notion of direct supervision and discipline that led, historically, to the development of factory work.

Thus, it is important to establish, in each case, the link between manifestations of autonomy and the whole process of management control. In the Coventry plant, control over the execution of work was gradually established by the workers and work groups, who had developed their collective organization as a way of adjusting to, and gaining more control within, the labor process (Bélanger and Evans 1988). Originally, this control was developed independently of the unions. From the end of the 1950s onwards, however, the shop stewards gradually imposed themselves as leaders and greatly contributed to the diffusion of job control. Indeed, it is mainly through the continual process of bargaining over production norms, the principal stake of worker resistance, that the shop stewards came to play such an important role during the 1960–80 period.

In keeping with a general trend in the United Kingdom toward workplace reform in the manufacturing sector (Brown 1981; Purcell 1981), from 1971 to 1974, management succeeded in involving the local unions in the elaboration of more efficient bargaining structures and dispute procedures. These reforms led to the adoption of a coherent wage structure and contributed to a decreasing number of work stoppages. The study also showed, however, that management did not regain more control over labor utilization following the process of reform. Indeed, a primary principle of the reforms was to centralize power within management as well as within the shop steward organization, and the effect was to weaken further the power of the foremen and consolidate the entrenched position that workers had established in the labor process (Bélanger 1987).

In the late 1970s, the limitations of a workers' organization that was overly marked by sectionalism as well as the vulnerability of this job control had become all too apparent. The company was in decline and was gradually reducing its workforce. It became obvious that the employees could not count on a collective organization that would elaborate a more comprehensive and progressive strategy, and mobilize them. Indeed, no agent was really in control of the situation. The various programs for change and restructuration proposed by the company did not bear much result, and shopfloor management was neither consistent nor convincing. Workers no longer trusted management.

Over the years, the pressure exerted on production norms and the different tactics that increased the periods of downtime certainly had a negative effect on productivity. Contrary to the other factory studied here, the long period of waiting at the end of the shift was not really compensated by an excessive and continuous pace during the rest of the day. To a certain extent, the workers were conscious of this reality and wished it had been otherwise. Undoubtedly, they would have preferred to produce more under other circumstances. Considering the social structure within which they worked, however, why would they forsake all their control over the labor process? No other mode of rational behavior was available to them. Thus, it was obvious that no significant change would be possible without a major restructuring of work relations, and the company was sold in August 1980.

By comparison, in the Quebec factory, job control was the main component of a pattern of work characterized by workers' cooperation and consent. Although this logic of consent was similar to the one observed by Burawoy (1979b) in a Chicago factory, it had its peculiarities. The work groups made use of all their creative resources and know-how to finish work as early as possible, without affecting the quality of that work. Their relationships with the foremen were also characterized by cooperation, and each party, of course, found this mutually advantageous. In the departments where fieldwork was carried out, each supervisor had, on average, forty workers under his command, and he was not in a position to exercise direct control over their work. Foremen had developed, therefore, an exchange relationship with the wage earners. For example, out of a total of 3,509 instances of absence of three days or less recorded throughout the factory over a period of fourteen months in 1986–87, no less than 58.8 percent were authorized by the supervisor concerned. Whenever they were told in advance, the supervisors used their discretionary power to tolerate brief periods of voluntary absence, inasmuch as it was possible to mitigate the consequences on production with the collaboration of the work group (Bélanger, Bilodeau, and Vinet 1991).

As opposed to the Coventry factory, and although the workers had been unionized since 1972, job control was not the outcome of direct pressure imposed by the workers and their organization. In fact, the local union was not really involved in the determination of production norms. But although shopfloor regulation was distinct from the formal process of collective bargaining, it was not completely independent of it.

It is important to understand the mutual dependence between these two modes of regulation, inasmuch as the cohesion and confidence displayed by the work groups were supported by the institutional power of the local union, which had all the independence and necessary resources to react if management went too far, or carried out unjust dismissals, for instance.

The process of consent at work observed here should not be seen as a simple "management effect." In spite of the company's fierce opposition to unionization in the early 1970s and a long strike in 1975–76, union activity had actually prompted management to adopt a more flexible style. Statements from more senior workers emphasized that the management had been much more authoritarian in the 1960s, before unionization. To summarize, the possibility of resorting to effective means of pressure still existed, although union action had been institutionalized and was heavily concentrated on the collective agreement during these latter years.

Of course, when discussing early finishing, the obvious question is, Why did management tolerate it and not require more work? The answer in this case is that, contrary to the Coventry situation, the general pattern of control contributed to the achievement of a high level of productivity, in spite of the considerable reserve of free time. Indeed, early finishing was an essential component of the social arrangement between management and labor.

Detailed data on worker hours show that productivity remained stable during the whole period from May 1986 to the end of June 1987, in which two vehicles were manufactured every day (Bélanger 1989, 358). Management attached the greatest importance to this regularity in production, since work had to be completed at each work station before the end of the shift, twice a day, to meet the delivery deadline stipulated in this particularly important contract. Given this requirement, the fact of finishing early also brought other definite advantages, such as the possibility of more easily making up for absences or of coping with the consequences of equipment breakdowns, back orders, or other technical problems. This reserve of time also enabled management to carry out preliminary quality control, allowing immediate rectification of any problem. In summary, job control was perfectly compatible with the technical organization of production and belonged to a general system of control.

This case illustrates particularly well Edwards's distinction between detailed control and general control: "Managers can secure a high level of general control without maximizing detailed control" (1986, 6). It also shows how important it is to look beyond any particular form of behavior and consider the pattern of labor control as a whole; this pattern was conducive to the achievement of high and constant production standards. Moreover, the company considered that the employees worked efficiently and at a very high pace during long periods and appreciated that there was much to lose in any attempt to reassess the effort bargain before the end of this huge contract. A social convention had more or less been established between management and labor, and it consisted basically in producing two vehicles a day. Industrial sociology suggests that the employer's analysis was sound; any attempt to push further would have been subject to the law of diminishing returns.

Thus, quite similar forms of job control originate in very distinctive control processes and have very different effects on the performance of the organization. Whereas the process of control observed in the Canadian factory could satisfy the competing rationalities of management and labor, such a social arrangement did not exist in the British factory. The next section discusses the main structural and institutional factors that might help understand this difference.

Structural and Institutional Factors

Workplace relations evolve in a particular structural and institutional environment. This section considers the characteristics that appear to have an impact on the different trajectories studied here, first technology, then forces outside the workplace. These forces include the economic environment within which the factory is located, in other words, its position in the product market and the local labor market, as well as the national institutions of labor regulation.

Technology

The idea of technology should be understood in a broad sense, namely, as the configuration of different characteristics that make up a technical organization of production. Although some aspects of technology account for the similarities, in the sense that it fostered job control in the two factories, other aspects may help explain the differences. First, the type of machine being used had similar effects in the two plants. The presses in the Coventry factory were nonautomatic machines; the operator had to intervene at each cycle. This control over work pace can be considered the main technical basis for these operators' autonomy. In the Quebec factory, the workers worked primarily with hand tools, which also gave them much control over the rhythm of production.

Second, the integration of production, or the link between different work stations, also contributed to the development of job control in both cases. In the case of the manufacturing of car components, social cohesion was often assisted by "working in line," when a variable number of presses were linked by conveyor belts, automatic "catchers," and chutes. The whole issue of the effort bargain for every specific type of component was a matter to be discussed with the group as a whole, and collective discipline was assisted by this technical arrangement.

Although the organization was different in the subway car factory, the effect was similar. The assembly process was designed according to a clearly determined set of tasks that had to be completed in one shift. Although job assignments were given on an individual basis, this production technique induced employees to work as a team voluntarily. Moreover, the assembly line moved along only once per day, at the end of each shift,[8] another factor that fostered group cohesiveness.

Despite their very different characteristics, the technical organization of these two factories can be distinguished from the ideal type of the Fordist labor process, in that there was no moving assembly line. This relative absence of technical control highlights the importance of the introduction of the mechanized assembly line at the Ford Motor Company, from 1913 onward, because it had the immediate effect of regulating work intensity throughout the duration of the shift (Lewchuk 1987, 47–52). In the factories under study, not only did the workers control their work pace, they were also able to increase greatly the work intensity at the beginning of the shift in order to accumulate a considerable reserve of free time.

A third factor, however, appears to represent a major source of difference between these two factories. This is the production system, as defined by Joan Woodward (1980). Since its position had declined on the product market, the British company was reduced to manufacturing a great number of small batches of components. Such a production system generated a great deal of uncertainty on the shopfloor, as Woodward's theory suggests, and also meant that the production lines had to be reorganized repeatedly, leading to instability in the makeup of the work groups and to the determination of different production standards. This system put a great deal of pressure on middle management and the foremen, who tended to make concessions at any cost to fill the specific orders. The work groups and their representatives were in a very good position to exploit these bargaining opportunities.

In contrast, it was sometimes possible for the Quebec enterprise to develop the engineering and know-how for a single product that would be manufactured over the course of several years. The manufacturing of a large series of identical subway cars enabled the standardization of production, from the fabrication of components to the assembly line, and delivered great regularity and predictability, conditions highly appreciated by managers (Osterman 1987, 55–57).

Of course, these technical features were not wholly decisive; the outcome could have been very different had the power relationship been different. It should also be acknowledged, however, that the social cohesion among the work groups in both factories was founded in the technical arrangement described here. While rejecting technological determinism, it must nonetheless be emphasized that technology is not neutral. If job control practices are explained mainly by work relations, they nevertheless take root in the technical organization of production, which foster them or make them possible at all.

Economic Environment

Factors outside the workplace are also very important in explaining the contrasts in the labor regulation processes. The two companies operated in very different economic spaces, in terms of both their products and labor markets. The position of the British company had declined over the years. When fieldwork was conducted, it was producing to the orders and specifications of a few large customers, which completed the assembly of the components and then dealt with the car manufacturers. Thus, the Coventry factory had developed a relationship of dependency on a few large end users. Obviously, this was exacerbated because British industry was losing ground in the face of international competition during this period, especially in the motor vehicle sector.

In contrast, not only was the Quebec enterprise very competitive, but this huge export contract had consolidated the company's leadership position in the public transport sector. Since 1987, it had experienced very rapid growth, as a result of the acquisition of several manufacturing companies in Europe and North America and more recently in Mexico.

The local labor market obviously represents a highly important structuring condition. The Coventry factory had been located on the same site since 1930. Craft and industrial unions have a long and rich history in this important industrial city, marked by the evolution of British manufacturing. The Quebec factory was located in a rural region. Although the labor market for craft workers was tight during our fieldwork, most employees were rather dependent on the company, since employment opportunities in manufacturing were limited in the area. For many of these workers, it was their first factory job; a good number of them had grown up on farms in the immediate area. Although such questions are highly complex, these two very different economic environments likely played a role in their development of different patterns of workplace relations.

Labor Relations Institutions

Although the position of the two companies in the economic sphere represents a major source of difference, this chapter seeks to examine in greater depth the influence of national labor relations regimes. Our interest is not particular aspects of each of these two different models of collective bargaining but rather the founding principles that give them coherence and exert distinctive influences on workplace relations. It is only in this sense that it is possible to compare the British and North American models of labor relations.[9]

Since 1944, the principal foundations of the Canadian labor relations regime have not been modified substantially. It is a regime highly regulated by state action. Among other elements, the notion of exclusive jurisdiction, usually in a single establishment, is a cornerstone. So is the legally binding nature of the collective agreement. The law prohibits the use of sanctions throughout the duration of that agreement, thus granting crucial importance to the grievance procedure.

In contrast, labor regulation in Great Britain has a profoundly voluntarist tradition, wherein labor and management alone developed mechanisms of joint regulation. The state does not elaborate a legal framework that shapes workplace relations in any detail, which means that workplace industrial relations reform at this level has to proceed on a voluntary basis.[10] Hence, during the 1970s, the effort to reorganize workplace bargaining did not find much legal support, and its impact was limited by sectionalism. Such a pattern of work relations then leaves much room for customary regulation and informality. Indeed, it is in this process that the shop stewards perform best, since the local union structure remains very decentralized in comparison to the North American model. Although the importance of the collective agreement has been increasing in Great Britain during the last fifteen years, its regulatory function is not comparable to the North American collective agreement. As explained by Burawoy (1985), this difference has much to do with state regulation.

In the introduction to this chapter, I discussed a major trend in the North American literature that portrays the collective agreement as a major source of rigidity in the organization of production, as a serious impediment to labor flexibility. My contention is that the impact of the collective agreement as a source of rigidity in North American work organization has been exaggerated in recent industrial relations literature, which is still dominated by the institutionalist tradition. Without minimizing the importance of the collective agreement as a major principle of regulation within the New Deal compromise, it also has to be recognized that, whatever its length and technical complexity, the formal agreement is mainly concerned with the general terms of employment. Coming back to Allan Flanders's useful distinction, its focus is on "market relations," as opposed to "managerial relations," which refer to the actual use of labor (1975, 88).

There is a major exception to this general distinction, and it relates to the broad sphere of labor mobility, on which many of the substantive rules of the collective agreement have something to say. This complex set of rules on the internal job structure and seniority regulates a whole range of issues associated with assignments and with movements of labor within and even outside the factory gates. But beyond this, the complex set of arrangements related to the effort bargain, which ethnographic studies show to be the key issue, has to be settled on the shopfloor. In other words, even in the context of a unionized workplace and once a collective agreement has been struck, shopfloor management and employees still have to make arrangements on the contours and the nature of the numerous tasks to be included in a given job, as well as on the volume and quality of actual work to be performed on every shift. Clearly, the day-to-day management of work has to be dealt with by a different mode of regulation, in which, as in the Quebec factory, workers may have a fair deal of influence.

Of course, a major reason the North American collective agreement does not go into these issues of work organization is simply that it would be technically impossible, considering the complexity of day-to-day production, characterized as it is by uncertainty and short-term adjustments. But there are also more fundamental reasons. Indeed, it is relevant to recall that collective bargaining was not designed for managing work organization.

At the risk of being too schematic in discussing complex historical processes, it is worth insisting on some of the general principles of the Fordist social compromise. The central principle was to institutionalize conflict by giving legal status to a long-term agreement and settling grievances according to the "due process of law." The Fordist social compromise also established a formula for raising wages and living standards in a planned and systematic way and, with the seniority principle, gave wage earners some social status and career prospects within the ranks of supervised workers. But this can only be considered a social compromise because there was also something left to the employers in the process. Thus, the New Deal compromise consolidated managerial prerogatives in the labor process, including most issues related to work organization (i.e., issues other than the deployment of labor) and the choice and development of technology. Indeed, the logic was that, by giving a relatively free hand to the employer in managing production and by limiting the manifestations of spontaneous resistance that had developed between the world wars, the companies would have benefits to share with their employees.

This is not to say that nothing has changed in the conduct of collective bargaining over the last fifty years or so. The working of collective bargaining has evolved over time, and the agreements have been adjusted more or less successfully to the changing nature of work. They have also gained in technical complexity. But the founding principles of this institutional framework have not been altered, and they have to be kept in mind in contemporary analysis, and particularly in international comparisons.

There is another reason recent accounts have exaggerated the rigidities associated with the collective agreement. It is simply that formal rules on issues related to the deployment of labor should not be associated too closely with rigidities, or to undue constraints upon efficient management. Indeed, collective agreements are creatures of *joint* regulation, on issues for which rules have to be established anyway. To illustrate this important point, it is relevant to consider in some detail the actual workings of some of the rules defined in the eighty-page collective agreement covering all manual workers in the Quebec factory. This rather typical agreement has provisions for all the various aspects of remuneration, including numerous fringe benefits, and specifies the terms and conditions of employment (work schedule, vacation, and so on) as well as the usual procedural rules (union rights, grievance procedure, and so on). But to support our argument, it is relevant here to focus on the rules that relate directly to work organization. Indeed, it is useful to study the very issues that are portrayed by so many commentators as most detrimental to organizational efficiency. Three of these will be considered here, namely, job classifications, internal transfers, and layoff procedures.

On the issue of job classification, an important distinction has to be made between the high number of formal classifications and the actual distribution of the workforce within them. In this agreement, a first glance at the large number of classifications in the internal progression hierarchy may give the impression of excessive complexity. But the other side of the coin is that, in a very large department such as equipment installation, the great majority of the 176 manual workers were concentrated in only three classifications. Above the grade for unskilled labor, semiskilled workers were classified either as "électricien monteur" or "assembleur mécanicien," and all earned the same wages.

A second observation is that the wage scales were remarkably uniform. The elaborate hierarchy of classifications had significant repercussions concerning the transfer of personnel but very little impact on earnings, a phenomenon already emphasized by Haiven in his comparative study of Canada and Great Britain (1989, 27). For instance, in the equipment installation department, the wage differential was very small between unskilled ($12.73 per hour as of October 1, 1988) and semiskilled workers ($13.37). Craft workers, at the top of the wage scale, earned $13.89 per hour. One concrete advantage of these small wage differentials was that temporary movements on the job ladder, as a result of bumping, for instance, had little effect on real earnings. Another advantage was that monetary concerns did not interfere with the cooperation among workers at different grades, who often worked inside the same subway car.

Although job classification, as such, was not considered a critical matter in the Quebec factory, the second issue, internal transfers, by which I mean temporary movements of labor between sections of a large department, was the object of tight regulation. This was one of the issues covered in a long (ten pages) and complex article simply entitled "Seniority." The logic of the rules on temporary transfers was that management had the freedom to transfer workers during the course of one shift but had to proceed on a voluntary basis and according to seniority for movements of more than one and fewer than twenty-eight working days and follow the usual job-posting procedure based on seniority for any movement of more than twenty-eight days.

Each of these basic principles was spelled out in much detail, and these complex rules on internal mobility really represented potential sources of rigidity. In this case, however, their application was not so much of a problem for management because work organization was remarkably stable and short-term absenteeism was usually covered on an informal basis by shopfloor arrangements that reduced the effect of seniority rules regarding overtime. Indeed, I observed a common practice that consisted of offering overtime to the other members of the group affected, at lunchtime. Such an arrangement, which went against the spirit of the collective agreement, was advantageous for all sides, and especially for management, considering the extent of tacit skills that were shared only by those working with the absentee on a regular basis. Of course, in a different social context, such local arrangements might have been out of order and the seniority rules much more of a problem for the employer. Notably, when a method of production requires more frequent changes in the organization of work, the application of seniority rules often becomes a more salient issue. And when union-management relationships are more tense, these same rules give the workplace union many ways to resist change, from a defensive position.

My observation period took place toward the end of production for a huge contract. It therefore corresponded to the first stages of a program of mass layoffs, which is the third issue considered here.

Even though a layoff does not invariably put an end to the employment relationship, no one could predict when the factory would again reach such a high level of employment. Despite the scale of this phenomenon (several hundred layoffs were gradually announced over a period of a few months) the rules of the game were agreed upon by all, so that no basic problem was raised by the employees. For the union, it was a question of procedure, and it made sure that the seniority rule was adhered to in all respects.

In informal talks with the factory's executives, I confessed to being very impressed with the small amount of tension involved, given the issue at stake. They dismissed the comment, emphasizing instead the complexity of the exercise from an administrative viewpoint. The mechanisms defined in the collective agreement were indeed complex to administer. In the context of a mass layoff, each worker exercised his seniority right within one of the eight promotion sequences, depending on the department to which he was assigned when he first entered the factory. Thus, a more senior worker might displace someone in a department other than the one he had been working in for the last few years. This led to a series of bumpings, until everyone reached his proper position in the grade structure and only the most senior workers remained in the factory.

The complexity of such a succession of movements at this factory should not discount the real importance of the regulatory function, considering the potential source of conflict. Above all, it should be emphasized that this regulatory function allowed for the maintenance of cooperative relationships in the workshops until the very end of the contract. The drastic reduction in the workforce did not affect at all the social arrangements studied in this chapter. And it is only recently, several years after the end of the very large contract discussed here, that the factory reached again almost full-production capacity.

These examples clearly illustrate why the regulatory mechanisms of the collective agreement and the internal labor market should not be seen only as constraints upon the free management of labor. Indeed, like all rules, they also represent resources, in that they make things possible for the actors who elaborate and interpret them. Work rules are ways of dealing with problems arising from production. This section has shown that, instead of considering the collective agreement as a source of rigidity, even with respect to the specific rules that are widely referred to as irritants in current debates on North American industrial relations, the interaction between these rules and shopfloor regulation can evolve into productive relations. Indeed, in the specific case of the Quebec factory, the regulation by the collective agreement of many of the difficulties arising from the employment relationship opened up the necessary space for the development of accommodative arrangements at the point of production.

Problems stemming from the employment relationship have to be regulated one way or the other, a point illustrated more sharply by international comparison. Actually, job demarcation, internal transfer, and redundancy were issues of serious conflict in the British plant, where they were regulated in such a way that major constraints were placed on management. In comparison with the Quebec factory, the number of job classifications was limited and the progression hierarchy much less formalized; however, a complex array of customary regulations, which could only be documented through direct observation, limited management freedom quite significantly. In addition to demarcation rules based on the craft tradition, another form of job demarcation had developed among noncraft workers in the press shops. Among them, the technical division of labor was quite sophisticated, and there were clear distinctions between the types of tasks. For instance, in the largest of the press shops, ten "classifications" could be differentiated, including three for quality control. Insofar as shop stewards' constituencies were defined according to these distinctions, they were enforced and reproduced over time.

The issue of internal transfer had also been one of the most serious matters of contention for many years in this factory. This was subject to the domestic dispute procedure, which incorporated a status quo clause. Whenever shopfloor workers wished to resist a managerial proposal to transfer labor from one section to another, they insisted on the issue being put through the procedure. In practice, this gave a veto power to the shopfloor. Management saw this as one of the most serious obstacles to their developing a more flexible response to customer demand.

Finally, considering the financial instability and decline of the company, several programs of redundancy were implemented in the late 1970s. Their operation was the object of much bargaining and tension between senior management and the various unions involved, which nevertheless had to accept them as inevitable. In short, it would be plainly wrong to assume that British managers have a free hand on the various matters that are dealt with by seniority rules in the North American context.[11]

Conclusion

Despite the similarity of job control practices observed in the two factories, further analysis showed how these forms of behavior were part of very different processes of social regulation. The patterns of job control had opposite effects on productivity because they developed in contrasting historical and social contexts. To understand these processes, it was necessary to distinguish between different levels of analysis and to consider the various structural and institutional constraints that shaped the strategies and behavior of management and labor. After underlining the factors related to technology and the position of the company in the economic environment, this chapter placed particular emphasis on the patterns of labor relations and their impact on work relations.

Although all actors had the opportunity to develop their own strategies and orientations, it is also important to emphasize that their actions and relations evolved within very different social structures in Britain and Canada. Clearly, the structural and institutional context was more conducive to cooperation and efficiency in one case than in the other. Thus, if each of the companies studied developed according to its own particular dynamic and with a relative degree of autonomy, this dynamic must be understood in reference to a particular national context.

In the Quebec company, management and labor operated on the basis of social conventions that allowed them to adjust their competing rationales in order to mitigate the contradictions inherent in the employment relationship. In the other firm, management and labor were not in a position to accomplish as much, since neither had enough control over the situation to fulfill its own objectives. In particular, my analysis suggests that the social dynamics related to labor relations regimes were quite influential in shaping these different trajectories. These institutions better facilitated the regulation of tensions generated by the labor process in the Quebec factory, after several sources of conflict were smoothed out by the legal framework of the collective agreement.

The approach adopted in this chapter consisted in analyzing the distinct circumstances that allowed shopfloor controls to emerge in each case. Although the Coventry factory presents many of the salient features of the "average" British engineering plant—considering a methodological point made earlier, I would not use the word *typical*—some critics might emphasize the dominant influence of the product market conditions in the Quebec plant. Indeed, it was underlined that operating with fixed contracts reduced external market pressure, at least in the short term. Nevertheless, the production of public transport equipment is by no means isolated from market forces; it remains a highly competitive market, which now operates on an international and even global scale. But, more fundamentally, such economic factors do not wholly determine workplace relations. Indeed, one might argue that the Quebec case is interesting precisely because, in contrast with the British factory, even under favorable conditions, aggressive shopfloor bargaining did not emerge. In fact, once the interrelated influences of product markets, technology, and social relations have been acknowledged, it is extremely difficult to disentangle the distinct influence of each. This would be very demanding from a methodological viewpoint. The idea here was to analyze further the influence of labor relations institutions, a major theme of this book.

A possible objection to such a comparative perspective could be that the situation has changed significantly in Britain since the fieldwork described above, which was conducted at the very beginning of the Thatcher regime. Considering that the method and object of study have to do with the general principles underlying labor regulation and not with current developments in each country, such an objection, if granted, would not completely invalidate the analysis presented here. More to the point, there is much debate about the extent to which the adverse economic and political environments have altered in fundamental ways the dynamics of labor regulation in British workplaces. Productivity increased in manufacturing over the 1980s, and there was much debate about the extent to which workers had really been "working harder" in the process (Elger

1990; Guest 1990a; Nichols 1991; Edwards and Whitston 1991). This debate on change is stimulating, but not yet conclusive. Indeed, not many publications deal with institutional change at the workplace over the same period. A notable exception is the systematic account presented by Bruce W. Ahlstrand (1990), who found that the deep-seated problems observed at the Esso oil refinery at Fawley by Flanders had persisted, in spite of more than two decades of "change."

This chapter tends to emphasize the contrast between North American and British models of labor relations. Its analysis goes against the argument advanced by Tolliday and Zeitlin (1989), which has a lot in common with that of the MIT school. In that it asserts itself as the new orthodoxy, it deserves more detailed scrutiny.

By looking in some detail at the interaction between formal collective bargaining and shopfloor relations, this chapter seeks to offer a fuller picture of the way noncraft labor is managed in a unionized manufacturing setting. Using material on the Quebec factory as an illustration, the idea was to define more precisely the contours of the collective agreement, which leaves much freedom to management on decisions related to technology and the organization of production.

At least two general points should be made from the empirical material and analysis presented in this chapter. First, it is clearly an exaggeration to suggest that North American employers are not free to organize production and manage labor under the collective agreements that have developed on the basis of the Fordist compromise. Second, it is important to consider the actual working of job classifications, seniority rules, and, more generally, the internal labor market and to conceive such rules not only as constraints upon management but also as ways of regulating labor utilization that have been developed jointly with the union.

Once the regulatory function of the North American collective agreement is properly considered, the contrast with the British situation is not in doubt. A fair number of ethnographic studies have shown that the high degree of job control that had developed over several decades in British factories was a form of both resistance and adjustment to managerial authority (Terry and Edwards 1988). As a general rule, work groups and shop stewards imposed these discretionary powers from a defensive position, and sectionalism was such that even the workplace union could not channel these manifestations of shopfloor autonomy and develop broader and more positive strategies.

The rigidities ascribed to the North American collective agreement do not have the same effect as a weakness of the labor relations institutions. The Coventry study shows clearly the multiple ramifications of a situation where these mechanisms cannot master, in Flanders's (1975) now-famous phrase, the "challenge from below." By comparison, the rules of the North American collective agreement constrain management's rights on issues that inevitably will be, in one way or another, the object of regulation.

Indeed, recent analyses too often ignore this unavoidable obligation to establish criteria and rules on issues such as the technical division of labor, internal mobility, and layoffs. While reducing management's discretionary power, the collective agreement follows a wider logic (Edwards 1986, chap. 5), a coherent model that leaves the decisions that are most crucial to organizational efficiency within the range of managerial prerogatives. This is so for technology and for most work organization issues.

Such a pattern of labor relations thus lays the necessary foundations for the possible development of cooperative relationships on the shopfloor, and the case of the Quebec factory is a particularly good illustration of this dynamic. More generally, it opens the way for the innovations in work organization and the forms of worker involvement that have been advocated in recent industrial relations literature. Indeed, the literature on human resource management underestimates the regulatory function of this labor relations regime, which, in fact, deals very well with the challenges posed by conflict and thus enables new managerial approaches to develop on these crucial matters. Clearly, the real challenge is not to weaken the collective agreement but to move beyond the Taylorist principles of work organization, which are also associated with the Fordist model of economic development.

3

Workplace Discipline in International Comparative Perspective

Larry Haiven

This chapter compares the systems that have been designed to handle labor-management disputes over workplace discipline in Britain and North America. To many on both sides of the Atlantic, the system of arbitral review of discipline appears to be the jewel in the crown of dispute resolution in North America. Several British commentators (Dickens et al. 1985; Concannon 1980) have championed an arbitral, rather than a judicial, review of such disputes. Hugh Collins (1982) in particular espouses North American Arbitration as a method of disciplinary dispute resolution far preferable to British Industrial Tribunals.[1]

Indeed, as will be seen later in this chapter, Arbitration appears to have many advantages. But appearances can be deceiving. For not only must the vaunted North American arbitral review of discipline be compared to the British disciplinary Tribunal system per se, but an appreciation of the role of disciplinary structures in the generation and resolution of conflict can be gained only through a comparative analysis of the *whole* system of handling such disputes in the two countries. And that invariably involves investigating a domain ignored by most commentators on the subject—the workplace.

In both countries third-party adjudication plays a role that cannot be ignored. But we must look beyond the formal confines of the respective Forums, however, at the entire process of disciplinary dispute handling, from its origin on the shopfloor, to the more formal aspects of procedure, to the Forums, and finally to the impact of these Forums back at the shopfloor.

The author wishes to thank the Social Sciences and Humanities Research Council of Canada and the Committee of Vice Chancellors and Principals of the Universities of the United Kingdom, which helped finance this work.

This chapter combines a review of available secondary sources and statistics on discipline in Canada and Britain with a more detailed analysis of the operation of discipline in a matched set of four workplaces in the two countries. The chapter begins by describing the main industrial relations features of the two countries and the four workplaces where fieldwork was undertaken. It then moves on to a delineation of the theoretical approach to industrial conflict on which the chapter is based. Next comes a review of various intellectual approaches to questions of industrial discipline and the spectrum between more punitive and more corrective schemes. The next section looks at a fascinating debate on the political and industrial efficacy of the two national systems of disciplinary adjudication.

In the spirit of this debate, the chapter then performs its own analysis of the disciplinary Forums in the two countries, considering rates of success by applicants, the involvement of trade unions, the conduct of hearings, procedural fairness, substantive fairness, and the structure and scope of legal appeal.

Penultimately, the chapter turns away from the Forums themselves to a consideration of their *actual* impact *at the workplace*, including the case study workplaces—how often they are resorted to by the parties, their impact on management, and their impact on unions.

Finally, a more detailed investigation of discipline at the workplace is organized under three of the most important grounds for discipline—poor attendance, insubordination, and incompetence—and lessons are drawn from the case studies.

Two Countries, Two Workplaces

As mentioned in the introduction to this volume, Canada has recently emerged from its former obscurity on the world industrial relations scene as the "other country" in the "North American model" of industrial relations. Even as the United States declines in union density and industrial conflict, Canada's union movement remains robust and fractious. This robustness provides plentiful instances for fruitful study of the "North American model."

Since 1943, Canadian governments[2] have sought to regulate industrial conflict by a distinct formula that includes legally enforceable collective agreements, the outlawing of strikes during the term of those agreements, and the substitution of grievance and Arbitration procedures. Dispute resolution is formal, collective agreements are comprehensive, and arbitral jurisprudence is encyclopedic.

In Britain, by contrast, strikes on issues related to the workplace are generally not illegal at any time. Collective agreements are not legally enforceable and are much less formal and comprehensive than in Canada. Dispute resolution is much more informal and is left almost entirely to the parties themselves. Arbitration, while available, is entirely voluntary and seldom used by the parties. One might then expect a higher level of industrial conflict in Britain, but the opposite is the case.

In fact, what makes the Canada-Britain comparison truly compelling is that although strikes are much more *tightly* regulated in Canada and more *loosely* in Britain than in practically any other pair of countries in the world, Canada has regularly equaled or surpassed Britain in industrial conflict indexes over the past thirty years (Haiven 1988; Lacroix 1986).

The research for this chapter comes from a larger comparative study of industrial conflict (Haiven 1988). As well as comparing Canada and Britain at the aggregate level, that study looked specifically at matched pairs of workplaces in the two countries. Four unionized workplaces, two in each country, of similar size (approximately four hundred manual employees) were examined. This size is sufficiently large to generate enough union-management "business" (grievances, records, strikes, Arbitrations, and so on) to study, yet sufficiently small to be in the range where a crucial threshold of union power (e.g., continuity of shop stewards, organized and regularly convened shop steward committees, full-time conveners, and attendant bureaucratization) operates (see Turner, Roberts, and Roberts 1977; Brown, Ebsworth, and Terry 1978). Exactly where the threshold lies depends heavily on the technology, product markets, labor costs, and profitability (and on the *stability* of the last three elements). Within each industry chosen, the plants were matched cross-nationally as closely as possible according to these factors. Nonetheless, the two industries chosen contrasted dramatically in those same features.

The two industries chosen were aluminum fabrication and brewing. The style and militancy of the trade unions in the two industries contrasted accordingly. The breweries had among the strongest workplace union organizations for their size in both countries. The aluminum plants had much weaker unions. Hereafter, the British and Canadian breweries will be referred to as BRITBREW and CANBREW, respectively. The British and Canadian aluminum plants will be referred to as BRITMET and CANMET respectively.

Political Apparatuses of Production

The study of international variations in industrial conflict has been revolutionized in recent years as the old institutionalist approach has been replaced by an interest in the political economy of industrial relations. This approach seeks to explain industrial conflict according to the organizational capabilities of labor and capital and their ability to mobilize and assert their interests in the various spheres of struggle, especially national politics (Shorter and Tilly 1974; Korpi and Shalev 1979; Cameron 1984). Yet this approach has several problems (see also Chapter 1, this volume). First, it fails to discuss differences among the many countries (such as

Canada and Britain) where workplace struggle is still the dominant form of working-class self-expression. Second, by treating institutions as mere intervening variables reflecting the balance of power between labor and capital at a macro level, it assumes an inordinate fineness of tuning between that balance of power on the one hand and the institutions of regulation on the other. Third, the macro focus ignores how the struggle between labor and capital is played out at the crucial level of the workplace. Fourth, it portrays the state as a neutral in that struggle, which it most definitely is not.

More recently, there have been attempts to address these problems. Invariably informed by Braverman's *Labor and Monopoly Capital* (1974), they have investigated management of the "labor process," that is, the techniques and strategies managers use to extract labor from the labor power they have purchased on the labor market. Burawoy (1979b; 1985) has pioneered what might be called a "politics of production" approach, suggesting that the tools used to generate and resolve day-to-day disputes at the level of the workplace may hold a hitherto untapped power to explain differing patterns of industrial conflict across countries. Burawoy calls these tools, or workplace microinstitutions, "political apparatuses of production." This approach is similar to what in this volume is called a "regulation of labor" approach.

I (1988) have defined four apparatuses whereby unions and employers construct and reconstruct their relationship along the frontier of control—interests, rights, adjustments, and enforcements. The first two are well-known terms in industrial relations parlance; the last two are new but quite distinct and important. The *interests* apparatus concerns itself exclusively with the setting of written substantive terms and conditions of employment, formally and usually at regular intervals. The *rights* apparatus concerns itself exclusively with claims against these formal terms and conditions.

The third apparatus, *adjustment*, is necessary because the parties cannot make rules to fit every situation. Yet the exigencies of production demand the improvisation of unwritten and informal provisions. Because they are not reduced to writing, these provisions are often overlooked. Nevertheless they are exceedingly important. Adjustment is the apparatus wherein the most dramatic difference between North America and Britain can be observed and the one that may hold the greatest explanatory power for the differences between the two regions. For although adjustment is very feeble in North America, it is a vibrant part of British industrial relations (see Haiven 1991). The ability to make adjustments, it is argued, allows for a dispute resolution system that is much more flexible and much less conducive to open conflict on a large scale.

One further apparatus, distinct from the others and important in its own right, is *enforcement*. Given the exact same provision in two different workplaces, the combination of the vitality with which a claim is pursued and the sanctions that can be applied (or threatened) will have a tremendous effect on whether the claim is realized.

The larger study examines how these four "microinstitutions" for conflict handling articulate with three key loci on the frontier of control where conflict can erupt (discipline, regulation of the internal labor market, and job control). Insofar as this chapter is about the first of those loci, we turn to a consideration of the role of discipline in workplace industrial relations.

Theoretical Considerations of Workplace Discipline

If a fundamental dialectic in the employer control of production is between the coercion of employees and the generation of their consent, then the handling of discipline is the most special of special cases. The power to discipline employees is an essential employer tool, no matter what system of production or what production regime exists. The power of the employer to "mobilize sanctions" (Offe and Wiesenthal 1985) comes naturally from the law of property and from the power differential between capital and labor. Whether this power is frequently used or merely sits in the background, it is an essential backdrop to all methods of compelling compliance (Lukes 1974). Several factors make it increasingly difficult for employers to wield discipline arbitrarily without inviting operational inefficiency, industrial conflict, or state sanctions. These factors are: the increasing complexity of work organization (Gersuny 1973); the increasing power of trade unions to organize resistance to such arbitrariness; the intervention of the state to limit managerial discretion; and the need, in many sophisticated industries, to obtain not only passive employee compliance but active employee cooperation and use of their "tacit skills" (Manwaring and Wood 1985) in the production process.

It is by now quite common to describe labor control mechanisms on a continuum from "direct" or "coercive" on the one hand, to "responsible" or "cooperative" or "hegemonic" on the other (Friedman 1977; Edwards 1979; Burawoy 1985). Correspondingly, the handling of discipline is widely theorized as ranging from the more "punitive" or "punishment-centered" approaches to the more "corrective" or "representative" approaches (Gouldner 1954; Ashdown and Baker 1973; Anderman 1972; Adams 1978). Inevitably, the tendency is toward periodization from one end of the continuum to the other. In less subtle approaches, punitive discipline is seen as almost invariably clumsy, immature, and autocratic, while corrective approaches are seen as sophisticated, mature, and democratic.

The stages seem to divide along three essential elements: (1) the formality of rules, (2) the consensuality of the disciplinary process, and (3) the progressivity of the sanctions themselves. "Punitive" discipline is characterized by managerial peremptoriness in the ad hocery of the rules, by a greater severity of discipline (the use of dismissal in preference to less harsh forms), and the lack of consultation with employees or their representatives. Corrective discipline is characterized by greater codification of rules; by the involvement, through multistage disciplinary and grievance procedures, of the employee and his representatives; and the use of "an arsenal of calibrated punishments" (Glasbeek 1982, 75) up to and including dismissal, with all, except dismissal, seeking to rehabilitate the employee. The corrective approach is theorized as not only humane for the employee but also "good business sense," because it reduces the costs for the employer. Together with the construction of an internal labor market, it serves to increase job security and secure employee commitment.

By providing clear and reasonable rules and procedural involvement, the employer secures legitimation, or as George W. Adams (1978, 19) puts it, "voluntary compliance . . . avoids the cost to management of having to surveil the workplace in an extensive manner and to commit substantial resources to rule enforcement . . . [and has] a positive impact on workplace morale and productivity." By providing a range of punishments short of dismissal, corrective discipline helps the employer avoid "capital losses" which have been spent in recruiting, training, and accepting suboptimal productivity in the employee's early days at work (Adams 1978, 27–28).

Securely based in pluralist thought, the corrective approach is the engine that drives most liberal industrial disciplinary practice. But it has met some serious criticism from more radical commentators. M. Mellish and N. Collis-Squires (1976) suggest that the punitive/corrective dichotomy is overly concerned with procedural as opposed to substantive reform, accepts uncritically the advantages of increasing formalization, and is almost exclusively management-oriented.

Stuart Henry (1983, 1987) proposes a more subtle evolution of styles, with "representative-corrective" as only a second stage beyond "punitive-authoritarian." In this second stage, the "voluntary compliance" of workers and their representatives is illusory:

> In spite of its claim to provide fair justice there are considerable grounds for the view that justice by formal procedural equality of treatment delivers less justice than it delivers legitimation and less legitimation than is generally perceived. By assuming a formal equality it ignores the marked substantive inequalities in conditions and opportunities between employer and employee. . . . Because the employer's fundamental power base is never threatened they can concede a number of points on procedural matters, allowing union representatives to win what are localized and contained victories so long as the substantial and material conflicts of interests remain suppressed. (Henry 1987, 291)

Henry propounds a third style, "accommodative-participative," wherein disciplinary outcomes are more truly bargained between management and labor. Management's attitude is similar to that of the earlier stage, but because the union's attitude is different, "any notion of fixed penalties is not feasible since the penalty arrived at is itself the outcome of negotiation" (1987, 299). At one end, smaller transgressions are tolerated, while at the other, both management and the union cooperate in discipline, engaging in a sort of "mutual moral training" (312).[3] One impetus leading to this stage may correspond to Burawoy's concept of "hegemonic despotism" (1985, 150), wherein the relentless forces of international competition compel labor, out of fear for its survival, to take on the aims of the corporation.

P. K. Edwards and Colin Whitston (1988) take issue with the periodization implicit in Henry's (1983) and others' discussion of these issues, pointing out that coercive and participative methods of discipline have coexisted across enterprises at various stages of capitalist development and even coexist within single enterprises, and that in the free labor market regulatory environment of the 1980s and 90s, more coercive measures are by no means absent. They correctly criticize Henry for failing to reconcile his macro approach to "micro approaches" of workplace sociology, such as in Gouldner (1954), Lupton (1963), and Mellish and Collis-Squires (1976). Henry himself (1987) appears to have moved away from a temporal evolution and suggests that disciplinary styles may appear in combination.

Yet the more competitive atmosphere of the 1980s and 1990s has not made it a simple matter for managements to claw back concessions. The justice and legitimation provided by the corrective approach may well be illusory, but a ratchet effect is at work here. Unions often fight hard to keep what they have come to consider their only shield against the onslaught. Despite the temptations of a looser regulatory environment and high levels of unemployment, mainstream managements on both sides of the Atlantic are still wary of abandoning the legitimizing institutions that they and the unions have grown comfortable with. Likewise, despite some nibbling at the edges, governments have been loath to destroy institutions they have been set in place to encourage and disseminate more liberal disciplinary approaches.

Collins-Glasbeek Debate

On the robustness of those institutions, a most interesting debate has emerged comparing British industrial Tribunal and North American (and particularly Canadian) arbitral treatment of discipline. The debate is especially interesting in that it is not between pluralists insisting their own system is better than the other fellow's but between radicals intent on knocking the stuffing out of their own systems (Collins 1982; Glasbeek 1984). As such, the debate revolves around the limitations of the two systems and the question of just how much they deny workplace justice. It will be argued that both of these authors overstate their case because they look only at the adjudicatory aspect of discipline handling in the two countries and ignore discipline at the level of the workplace.

Collins suggests that in the 1960s the British polity was suffering from a crisis of pluralism, in which unions exercised their market power to wring unacceptable compromises from capital and created much industrial conflict, especially on the question of dismissal. The state responded by establishing Industrial Tribunals, but in so doing "bypassed the structures of joint regulation between management and union" (1982, 82) by specifying that the parties to the dispute would be the individual employee and his or her employer. Collins rejects suggestions (e.g., Elias 1981) that pluralism has been enhanced by the project, insisting that the regulation employed was "corporatist" in the sense that it "marginalize[s] the significance of collective bargaining for the regulation of the workplace, [establishes] systems of compulsory arbitration of collective disputes and [severely curtails] the right to strike"[4] (1982, 82).

Collins insists that the courts and Tribunals responded naturally to their order-restoration mandate and their neutral "above-the-fray" position by using their powers to define a doctrine of fairness that focused on reviewing management's procedure rather than on the substantive merits of the discipline imposed. This response neglected the power relationship between the parties and, in so doing, accepted the status quo of management hegemony. From this, it was then a logical step for the Tribunals to begin to interpret the "reasonableness" of management's discipline in the most conservative way possible.

To this Collins compares favorably the arbitral system in North America. Not only does the North American system provide a higher degree of substantive equity and greater job security to employees, he insists, but the process is also firmly rooted in the collective bargaining relationship. Rather than a mere rights apparatus, says Collins, it is an interests apparatus, fully accommodating the power positions of the parties.

Collins echoes Harcourt Concannon, who, comparing voluntary British arbitrations to unilateral Industrial Tribunals, praises the former for their flexibility, emphasis on compromise, and acknowledgment of the collective power dimension—in short, for their ability to appear legitimate to both parties—calling them "essentially the product of collective relations" (1980, 15) and "a reflection of the application of the union's power" (16).

Dickens et al. sum up the position well:

The more tribunals have to treat a dismissal as an issue between an individual worker and an individual employer without regard to the industrial relations context of the dispute and the possible collective implications of it, the less attractive will the system be to the organised sector. The more reluctant tribunals are to overturn employers' decisions because of the broad nature of the "range of reasonable employer responses" test . . . the less likely are they to be seen as efficient from the point of view of dismissed workers (1985, 217–18).

These authors suggest that the introduction of an arbitral system of dismissal review in Britain would do much to eliminate such deficiencies.

Harry Glasbeek agrees with Collins's general approach, but finds that many of the latter's remarks about the North American arbitral system do not correspond to reality and berates him for taking the claims of "conventional North American industrial relations" scholars at face value. Using the case of Canada, Glasbeek submits the North American system of dismissal review to close scrutiny. He insists that system affords employees no qualitatively greater job security, allows employers no smaller a list of grounds on which to dismiss employees legitimately, imposes severe penalties on many employees in place of dismissal, closes off lawful access to the strike weapon, forces employees to "work now and grieve later" rather than arguing their case to the employer immediately, forces the union to "filter" grievances and thereby "educate" the workforce on "acceptable" work conduct, and juridifies the entire process of discipline handling so that, despite its pretensions to rough justice, it is "a cumbersome, dilatory, highly technocratized system of dispute settlement" (1984, 149).

But while Collins vastly overstates the efficacy of the North American system, Glasbeek engages in his own share of exaggeration. Although most of his points are incisive, he ignores the workplace practice, as opposed to the law, of Arbitration. More important, in seeking to temper Collins's adulation of dismissal Arbitration, Glasbeek goes too far. Indeed, a comparison of British Tribunal to Canadian Arbitration would inevitably compel a dismissed worker *with no recourse but to adjudication* to prefer the Canadian over the British body.

In purporting to explore the wider effect of the two mechanisms on pluralism, collectivism, and industrial conflict, both legal scholars Collins and Glasbeek, make the fundamental error of restricting their scope to third-party intervention only and ignoring its place in the entire context of discipline handling between the parties. The present study, as an investigation of workplace industrial relations in which third-party intervention has played a part, is in a unique position to evaluate this debate and correct some of the deficiencies. To assess just how well the two systems work in managing conflict and delivering justice, it is necessary not only to undertake a selective comparison of third-party adjudicatory bodies, but then to place them in their context and finally to explore how various substantive discipline-generating issues are handled by the parties in each country and across the industries studied.

In light of the preceding discussion of the theoretical issues, the following questions must be asked: To what extent do the two systems of discipline treatment advance the legitimation of managerial control, obscure exploitation, and generate consent? To what extent do the two systems advance or retard collective bargaining and collective action? And to what extent do they deliver equity to individual workers?

Tribunal and Arbitration Compared

While we fault Collins and Glasbeek for their disregard of the primacy of the workplace, it would be remiss to ignore the formal disciplinary Forums entirely. Indeed, both Arbitration and the Tribunal *were* designed precisely to take certain disputes *out of the workplace* to a less volatile venue where they could be resolved not by force and economic coercion but by due process and juristic deliberation. The success with which the respective Forums do that will help determine the confidence the parties have in them and their impact at the workplace.

What "Winning" and "Losing" Mean

If the results of only those cases coming to hearing are compared, then Canadian Arbitration is by far kinder to the dismissed employee. Canadian Arbitrations overturn slightly more than 50 percent[5] of dismissals, while British Tribunals overturn less than 30 percent (Dickens et al. 1985). Yet, before pronouncing Canadian arbitrators more liberal than their British counterparts, it should be noted that Canadian Arbitration has the power (which British Tribunals do not) to reinstate the complainant with a lesser penalty than the employer-imposed dismissal. In about two-thirds of the Canadian reversals of the employer's decision, Arbitration imposes a penalty of its own. Between 25 and 57 percent of the reinstatements carry penalties greater than three months off work with no pay (calculated from Adams 1978, 57 and 61; Barnacle 1991, 109[6]).

Comparing complete reversals of dismissal (or exoneration), the British Tribunals actually come out ahead. With exoneration in only one-fifth of the cases, the Canadians trail the British by one-third. If those employees without union representation[7] are deducted from the British total, resulting in a sample more comparable to that for Canada (where all grievors are union-represented), the British exoneration rate looks even better. Certainly, with only a yes/no choice confronting it, the Tribunal may be like the jury faced with imposing the death penalty: very careful about upholding what has come to be known as "industrial capital punishment." Yet the difference in exoneration rates between the two countries is still wide enough to shake seriously Collins's contention that "the standards by which management discretion is reviewed" (1982, 85) in North America offer greater job security.

By far the greatest difference between the two Forums is in their power over the penalty. Canadian arbitrators can and do reinstate both exonerated employees and those found culpable but deserving of lesser penalties. This has been arbitral practice since the earliest days.[8]

An order of reinstatement is enforceable by the union in the courts, and companies are liable for contempt of court for refusal. Canadian employers have come to accept reinstatement. Almost three-quarters of reinstated employees in Adams's survey chose to return to work, and about 60 percent remained employed (Adams 1978, 63). Adams declares that "these results appear to vindicate the corrective approach to discipline forged by arbitration tribunals" (66).

British Tribunals can either find a complainant fairly dismissed or quash the dismissal (although some degree of culpability may be recognized in the compensation award) but do not have the legal power to substitute a penalty. Although the Tribunal does not have the power to impose reinstatement or reengagement, it can recommend such remedies but seldom does[9] (Dickens et al. 1985), preferring a compensatory award, which in about 85 percent of cases is worth less than one month's pay (calculated from the *Employment Gazette* 1986). Tribunals are supposed to take the employee's and not the employer's views on reemployment into account, but because they must also decide on the practicability of reemployment, the employer's views (usually negative) prevail.

Who Uses the Forums

The parties of record at a British Tribunal are the individual employee and the employer. The majority of applicants (68 percent[10]) are not union members. Of the trade unionist applicants, only half are represented by their unions, and a quarter (27 percent) have been refused such representation. The reason for these refusals will be examined presently. Unions, then, are marginal to the process of the British Tribunal.

Moreover, although application to the Tribunal is unilateral by the aggrieved employee, fewer than a third of all cases submitted ever reach a hearing, since the prehearing assessment process and the involvement of Advisory Conciliation and Arbitration Service (ACAS)[11] conciliators result in the rest of claimants dropping their cases or settling "out of court" (Dickens et al. 1985[12]).

In Canada, by contrast, the union is central to the process of Arbitration. Dismissal Arbitrations, like all Canadian Arbitrations, arise from grievances over the interpretation of collective agreements, and although the dismissed employee must ask her union to take up her case, the parties to the dispute thereafter are clearly the employer and the union. Application to Arbitration is unilateral by the union.[13] Yet, although Arbitration springs formally from the collective bargaining relationship, Collins (1982) is quite wrong to assume that the collective bargaining strength of the parties has more than the faintest effect upon the arbitrator. A key tenet of Canadian arbitral jurisprudence is that neither the past practice of the parties nor their intent in collective bargaining can be considered by the arbitrator in fashioning an award (Haiven 1991; Palmer and Palmer 1991, 74–84). And, although arbitrators are usually appointed by mutual consent and can become unpopular if they are perceived as biased over a range of many cases,[14] in the real world their decision has virtually nothing to do with an "attempt to adjust the result in accord with the bargaining strengths of the parties" (Collins 1982, 90).

Concannon (1980) contends that "[the] possibility or reality of industrial action is a significant factor in the Arbitration of dismissal cases [in Britain]," and this may well be the case where Arbitration is voluntary.[15] But it is most definitely not the case in Canada, where Arbitration is compulsory and meant to preclude, not solve, industrial action. Whether a grievor's fellow employees are apathetic or burning with anger over his dismissal is totally irrelevant to the Canadian arbitrator. And even if the employees conduct an (illegal) strike in support of the dismissed employee, that will have no impact on the eventual decision.

Glasbeek is mistaken in assuming that because the union has carriage of the dismissal case, it can take a ruthlessly expedient attitude such that "the pursuit of a grievance is not likely to be undertaken unless the union believes it to be important to its long range bargaining position and/or is winnable" and thereby engages to any extent in "educat[ing] the rank and file into what is acceptable or, more importantly, defensible work conduct" (1984, 146). Although Canadian unions definitely do carry on such filtering and shaping activity in *nondismissal* grievances (see Haiven 1988), dismissal is perhaps the one area in which the grievor is almost invariably given the benefit of the doubt.

At CANBREW, for instance, practically every dismissal that the union is unable to mitigate in the grievance procedure is taken to Arbitration, partly because the union is so diligent and partly because union members are unlikely to find a better job anywhere. Even cases of misconduct that CANBREW union members privately view with distaste are taken up, rather than deprive the employee of her "day in court." Thus, the union has defended employees disciplined for dangerous drunkenness at the wheel of a truck, for racial slurs against other union members, and for widely acknowledged lapses of competence. The union has won several of these cases simply as a result of procedural errors by the employer. The union does not apologize but sees its role as relentless challenger in a fully adversarial system.

At CANMET, a much smaller percentage of the cases involving dismissal reach Arbitration, not because the union agrees with management's decisions any more than at the brewery but because the union lacks diligence and because of the two very different labor markets in which they operate (or, as the convener says, "because there are lots of similar jobs 'out there' to the ones they do in here").

All labor law across Canada contains provisions that unions must represent their members in a way that is not arbitrary, discriminatory, or in bad faith. The "duty of fair representation" (Adams 1985, 710–69) is not so stringent that a union cannot refuse to pursue a case it has investigated thoroughly and found weak. Nevertheless, unions seldom refuse to challenge dismissal at Arbitration. It is far less risky politically to go to Arbitration. If the union wins, it looks good. If it loses, it was the arbitrator, not the union, who agreed with the employer (and there is no provision in Arbitration for costs against the union for vexatious claims). Given the union's limited scope of action and low success rate with most other workplace issues between rounds of interests bargaining, representing its members at Arbitration is one of the only and one of the most important things a union can do to justify its existence to its members.

The Hearing and Procedure

Although the hearing in the Forums in both countries was originally intended to be informal and open to the pleadings of lay practitioners, and the more formal trappings of the courts are absent, Collins and Glasbeek correctly observe that they have developed into formalistic and legalistic arenas, removed from the ken of most nonpractitioners. A veteran Canadian trade unionist claims bitterly that

> the whole system has become so legalistic that a layman has to be a linguist. You have to know your Latin very well in order to know what's being said. Here's an example from one case: *ejustem generis* [sic] rule. Well, who knows what the *ejustem generis* rule is? If you don't know, they tell you it's very much like the *noscitura associus* [sic] rule. Now if you have a legal dictionary beside you, you might find out what your opposition is talking about, but the poor fellow who's got the grievance and who's listening and who's waited six or eight months to get justice—*he* doesn't know what's going on. And this often drags on for four or five days. (quoted in Roberts 1983, 20–21, emphasis in the original)

Although only about half of British Tribunal applicants are represented by lawyers or full-time union officials (Dickens et al. 1985, 45), virtually all dismissed grievors in Canada have such counsel. And although the quality of this representation is usually excellent, grievors are little more than spectators or witnesses to a clash of legal or paralegal titans from beyond the workplace. Technical and procedural complications abound, preparation is often meticulous, and cross-examination is frequently withering. Both workers and first-line supervisors at CANBREW tell horror stories about "folding" or "making fools of themselves" and thereby "kissing the case goodbye" under cross-examination at Arbitration.

Thus, Collins is incorrect to imply that North American dismissal Arbitration is in any sense an interests apparatus (1982, 89) or closer to the shopfloor than British Industrial Tribunals. Although the arbitrator has much greater power to "second-guess" management, especially in the quantum of discipline, Arbitration as a forum is light years removed from the workplace. As Ronald W. Schatz says of seniority rights, so it is of disciplinary procedures in North America: they are "collective achievements which protect individual liberties" (1983, 117).

Burden of Proof

In Canadian discipline Arbitrations, the burden of proof is on the employer to establish "just cause" for the discipline.[16] This used to be the case in Britain. But although the record of applicant success in British Tribunals should hardly have warranted their concern, British employers lobbied and in 1980 secured a change so that employers now need only prove they had a reason (as opposed to no reason) for the onus to shift equally to both parties on the question of reasonableness (Anderman 1985, 107). Although this may seem a small change, many observers of Tribunals echo the dour assessment of the BRITBREW union's shop stewards' handbook that "in practice, this shifts the burden of proof on to the dismissed worker and can make it harder for him/her to win a claim."

Procedural Fairness

In both countries, a major concern in dismissal Forums is the procedure the employer used in disciplining the complainant, not just from the point of view of equity to the individual complainant but in light of the interests of industrial relations as a whole. Thus, in Britain, part of the public policy rationale was "the importance of restoring order to industrial relations by insisting that proper procedures should be followed by employers before dismissing the employee" (Collins 1982, 87). This includes the right of the employee to know the charge against him, the right to answer to it, the right to representation by an appropriate champion, and the right to be warned that a mode of conduct would lead to discipline. Not only would a dismissal executed without such procedural solicitude insult the complainant but, more important, it would outrage fellow employees, and even precipitate (quite unnecessarily from the point of view of the policy makers and courts) industrial conflict.

But even though a preoccupation with proceduralism initially characterized the Tribunals, these bodies have become so managerialist in their orientation that even this concern has begun to break down. Thus, in several cases,[17] procedural omissions by the employer, failure to involve a trade union official, failure to warn, and failure to give the employee an opportunity to be heard, *even in contravention of a collective agreement*, have not kept Tribunals or the Employment Appeals Tribunal (EAT) from upholding dismissal. They have done so on the grounds that such procedural niceties would not have altered the employer's decision in any case. Not all Tribunals or EAT panels have been so cavalier, but the above cases have received much publicity. The credibility implications for workers and trade unions of such decisions need only be imagined.

Since Arbitration cannot be set in motion in Canada without the completion of a grievance procedure specified in a collective agreement, many of the preconditions for procedural fairness will already have been satisfied automatically before the hearing. In most cases, failure to follow the procedure or to give proper warnings will result in the discipline being overturned.

Because Canadian arbitrators have the power to alter penalties, even if the procedural defect is not sufficient to overturn the discipline in itself, a procedural defect may well result in serious mitigation of the penalty.

Substantive Fairness

In both countries, the legislation setting up the Forums provides little guidance and few standards to judge the substantive fairness of dismissal. Other than certain circumstances under which dismissal is automatically unfair (if the dismissal is connected to union activity, pregnancy, sex, race, and so on), the British legislation directs fairness to be determined by "whether the dismissal was reasonable in the circumstances (including the size and administrative resources of the organisation) and in accordance with equity and the substantial merits of the case" (Dickens and Cockburn 1986, 421, paraphrasing the Employment Protection Act).

In Canada, the overwhelming majority of collective agreements specify nothing more than "cause" or "just cause"[18] as the test of substantive fairness. In fact, many arbitrators and courts have found such a provision to be implicit in collective agreements that are silent on the matter (Palmer and Palmer 1991, 230–32).

Yet Forums in the two countries have gone in very different directions in fleshing out these indeterminate prescriptions. While British Tribunals and the EAT have opted to give managerial prerogative wide rein, Canadian Arbitrations (in the area of discipline) take a much more critical view of the actions of employers. And the courts have allowed them to do so. This is not an attempt, it will be shown, to seriously question the right of management to make rules and enforce them, but rather a way to assist management in handling the potentially explosive results of an unpopular dismissal.

One serious limit on the British Tribunal's powers to second guess employer action relates to the facts on which the employer based its decision. The employer need not prove on the balance of probabilities that the employee was guilty of the alleged misconduct, only that it reasonably believed there was such guilt after as much investigation as was reasonably warranted[19] (Anderman 1985, 117).

A second important limit relates directly to the reasonableness of the dismissal. The British Tribunal errs in law if it asks itself what it would have done if it were the employer. Rather, the test is whether the dismissal falls outside the action that might be taken by "a range of reasonable employers" (Dickens et al. 1985, 103; Anderman 1985, 149).

Dickens et al. (1985) criticize this test and cite a judge who warned that Tribunals should "not impede employers unreasonably in the efficient management of their business." They point out that "by subsuming the interests of employees in general under the 'needs of the business' the interests of any individual employee in retaining his or her job can be overridden" (106).

Yet it is not merely the willingness to subordinate personal job security to "business interests" that allows the Tribunal to override the interests of the employee; it is the entire context of the Tribunal and especially its inability to substitute a different penalty. The ability to substitute a penalty in Canada allows the arbitrator to fashion a "workable compromise between the interests of the individual and the demands of efficiency" (Adams 1978, 29). In *nondisciplinary* cases, the argument of "legitimate business interests" is admittedly a powerful one in Canadian Arbitration. But in the field of discipline, Canadian arbitrators are more likely to assume that the harm to the employee, and especially dismissal, can seldom be outweighed by the harm to the employer. So, with no less attention to "business interests" than in Britain, this rationale in Canada is turned on its head. The mainstream view, supported by the Canadian courts, is clearly that arbitrators have the right to substitute their judgment for management's. As a leading Canadian arbitrator has said:

> When an arbitrator selects a penalty different from that selected by an employer, he is really saying that the employer has ignored some relevant consideration, proceeded on some misunderstanding, acted from some illicit motive, or otherwise affronted the arbitrator's sense of what is "just." . . . In other words, the arbitrator is not only judging the grievor; he is judging the employer as well.[20]

Because of the leeway of substantive review and the ability to reinstate with lesser penalty, the concept of corrective discipline is powerfully cast into workplace industrial relations by Canadian Arbitrations, and the doctrine of a "culminating incident" takes on great importance. Except in cases of gross misconduct, arbitrators will simply not allow dismissal unless the offense leading to the dismissal has been preceded by several similar transgressions and progressive warnings have been given. Arbitrators do not consider this position as one that impinges on management's rights but rather that

> the doctrine simply purports to accommodate the employer's legitimate interest in being able to terminate the employment of someone who, but for such a doctrine, could with impunity commit repeated infractions of diverse company rules and policies and generally perform in an unsatisfactory manner without fear of being discharged, so long as she did not commit a serious offence or did not persist in misconduct of the same type (Brown and Beatty 1993, 7:4310).

The mirror image of the doctrine of culminating incident is the ability of the arbitrator to look at the grievor's record of employment and disciplinary history to find cause to mitigate any penalty imposed. Thus, the following factors will be reviewed[21]: previous record, service to the employer, whether the offense was an isolated occurrence, whether the grievor was provoked, whether the offense was a momentary aberration, the hardship of the penalty to the grievor in her circumstances, the uniformity of employer enforcement of the rule(s) transgressed, the intent of the grievor, the overall seriousness of the offense to the employer, and several other factors, including the grievor's degree of remorse.

Yet, though Arbitration may differ from the Tribunal in its freedom to consider substantive fairness, more radical Canadian trade unionists find the process still stacked heavily against the worker because of the yawning class gulf between arbitrators and most trade unionists:

> I have some questions for these arbitrators who adamantly proclaim their neutrality in judging labor-management disputes.
>
> How can you, in all honesty, pass judgment on an aggrieved employee who has been suspended or even fired for lateness and absenteeism when you yourselves regularly arrive late for arbitration hearings? Or, as so many of you do, let months go by before rendering your decisions?
>
> . . . How can you claim to understand the family difficulties imposed on shift workers and families with working mothers when, as recently happened to us, you arrive at a case, late I might add, and announce that you would like to leave early as your wife has gone skiing for the day and your children will be at home alone?
>
> How can you comprehend the financial problems of a discharged, suspended or laid-off worker with a family to support when you receive several hundred dollars[22] for one day's work? (Taylor 1977, 9)

Appellate Structure and Power

While both Tribunal and Arbitration have become highly legalistic, the British courts have had a far greater impact on restraining the Forums in that country. The EAT has generally taken on the role of coordinating and setting standards of fairness for Tribunals to follow. Although it is not a Tribunal de novo, and can only review points of law, the EAT has interpreted this restriction quite liberally. The EAT is a court of specialized jurisdiction, but in the absence of the privative clauses that prevail in Canada,[23] its activity comes under the scrutiny of the Court of Appeal. The particular combination of appellate bodies has resulted in the courts exercising a high degree of second-guessing and a correspondingly limited ability of Tribunals to develop their own law (see Dickens et al. 1985, 209–12).

Although the Canadian courts have shown a fondness to rein in arbitral activity in nondisciplinary cases, they have left arbitrators relatively free to nurture their own law of just cause in discipline. Earl E. Palmer and Bruce M. Palmer, marveling at its comprehensiveness after a mere forty years, say (1991, 227): "There has been no decisive outside influence which has shaped the work of arbitrators in this area. The courts have only intruded to a minimum, and then largely on procedural points; their intervention has been episodic and, on the whole, of limited duration." Thus, the credibility of Canadian Arbitration as an "expert" body and its distinctness from the judicial system is far better developed than its British counterpart.

Impact of Tribunals and Arbitrations in the Workplace

A comparison of the finer points of Tribunals and Arbitrations, although essential, can be dangerously misleading. For only by examining the impact of each upon workplace industrial relations can a true picture be put together. This is why an ethnographic approach is especially useful. It is quite difficult to make definitive statements on this subject from aggregate data. In Canada, workplace industrial relations remains a domain well hidden from aggregate investigation. Much more is available in Britain from the Workplace Industrial Relations Survey (WIRS) and similar sources (Millward and Stevens 1986; Brown 1981). Yet, even so, one can only approach a true picture by intelligent inference from the aggregate data and the careful examination of the day-to-day operation of specific workplaces. In our discussion henceforward, we will be relying heavily on these two techniques.

Comparative Use of Third-Party Adjudication

The first, and perhaps most important, question to be addressed is, Just how much use is made of these Forums in the two countries? To be sure, Arbitration is an intimate part of discipline handling in unionized Canadian plants such as the ones in this study. Tribunals, by contrast, have only marginal impact on similar British plants.

Although figures are not available for an exact comparison, it can be roughly estimated[24] that, in any year, the number of Industrial Tribunal hearings where British unions represent dismissed members is about 10 percent lower than the number of dismissal Arbitration hearings in Canada (proportional to the number of unionized employees in each country[25]). In Britain, such union activity is highly concentrated among employees in smaller workplaces and very much rarer in workplaces with more than one hundred employees (Dickens et al. 1985). In Canada, by contrast, dismissal Arbitration activity is more evenly spread across the range of workplace sizes, and some evidence indicates, as might be expected, it is slightly higher in larger workplaces (Gandz 1978).

A look at the rate of discipline in our four plants[26] may help put these figures into perspective. It is remarkably similar along industry lines. Expressed as a percentage of the workforce per year, both the British and the Canadian aluminum plant dismiss approximately 0.7 percent of their workers. Both breweries dismiss 0.4 percent. Aggregate figures on dismissal rates in the two countries as a whole are meager. The best estimate for Britain as a whole, obtained from survey data, is just above 1 percent per annum (Brown 1981, 116), with a range between .04 percent for workplaces with more than one thousand employees and 1.8 percent for those with fewer than one hundred (Daniel and Millward 1983, 171). So the range of dismissal rates in our plants fit within these parameters.[27]

The evidence of external dismissal adjudication in our plants shows dramatic differences. In the ten years previous to this study, BRITBREW faced only two Tribunal applications and BRITMET faced only one. In the Canadian plants, disciplinary Arbitration is far more common. In the eight and a half years preceding this study, CANMET faced five discipline Arbitrations (four for dismissal and one for suspension), and CANBREW faced twelve (four for dismissal, seven for suspension, and one for disciplinary demotion).

Unlike British Tribunals, however, Canadian Arbitration also deals with complaints of discipline other than dismissal (suspensions, demotions, and disciplinary notices). These cases account for slightly more Arbitration hearings than those on dismissal, so that there is actually more than twice as much third-party adjudicatory activity on discipline in Canada as in Britain.

The rate of nondismissal discipline is much higher in the Canadian plants. Although in both British plants it is almost the same as for dismissal, CANMET's figure is 2.2 percent (more than twice its dismissal rate) and CANBREW's is 4.4 percent (more than four times its dismissal rate). Two somewhat contradictory reasons can be posited for this: First, the rate reflects a major preoccupation with progressive discipline, in response to the signals given by arbitrators, especially at CANBREW, where a sophisticated management is concerned with the cost of depleting an internal labor market in which it has invested considerable resources. Second, the rate reflects a less paternalistic, more punitive orientation toward the disciplining of the workforce in Canada. To be somewhat glib, the motto of Canadian managers might well be "punish them, but be careful and methodical about how you do it."

At first glance, it appears that the corrective approach to discipline is not nearly as well developed in the British plants as it is in the Canadian. Though there is some concept of progressive discipline at BRITMET— (several dismissals came after a series of smaller warnings or suspensions)— none of the dismissals at BRITBREW was the result of a culminating incident. Those dismissals that did occur were mostly a result of gross misconduct, such as theft or dishonesty. As we shall see, however, further consideration will yield quite different conclusions.

On a more qualitative level, the differential impact of third-party adjudication in the two countries is even more striking.

Impact on Management

In the disciplinary activity of the British managers, third-party adjudication has some discernible impact, but it pales in comparison to Canada. In keeping with a pronounced national trend (Millward and Stevens 1986, 169–80; Dickens et al. 1985, 232–38), the introduction of Tribunals, the publication of the ACAS Code of Practice, and its propagation by the Institute of Personnel Management (IPM) all promoted the growth of disciplinary procedures and the development of published workplace rules in our plants. But in our British plants, and especially at BRITBREW, formal procedures often fall apart or are suspended in cases of serious misconduct or when the collective implications are ominous. What takes over is a throwback to pre-Donovan[28] days when informality and sectional bargaining reigned supreme.

Although the personnel managers in our British plants have a nodding acquaintance with some of the broad Tribunal precepts of substantive fairness (one manager remarked favorably on the leeway that the "range of reasonable employers" test gives him), these precepts have very little to do with the way in which they administer discipline from day to day. Their personal experience with Tribunals is very limited, so in considering discipline, they generally "play it by ear," as they have always done.

The impact of Tribunals on line management is even more vague, and direct familiarity with Tribunals is nonexistent. Immediately after the introduction of Tribunals and subsequent procedures, both plants echoed a national trend in manufacturing (Daniel and Stilgoe 1978, 41; Brown 1981, 32; Dickens et al. 1985, 264–65) whereby authority over disciplinary matters was shifted from line managers to personnel managers. Yet BRITMET has more recently made efforts to pass responsibility for discipline back down the line, and BRITBREW managers talk about doing the same thing. In summary, although Tribunals have been in operation for several decades, their jurisprudence has very little impact on British management in day-to-day disciplinary decisions. This is, of course, a relative assessment and is validated when compared with the situation in Canada.

The situation in Canada is very different. Thomas R. Knight (1984) reports that arbitral decisions have a major impact on the employer administration of disciplinary policies, including such areas as progressive discipline for absenteeism, the question of intent in theft cases, employer procedure in insubordination cases, leniency in alcohol and drug abuse cases, and the importance of disciplinary procedures. Our Canadian plants confirm this. Not only do personnel managers have considerable personal experience with Arbitration both in their own plants and in those of sister plants, they have a broad knowledge of arbitral jurisprudence and the comments of legal and academic commentators on it. Many have copies of *Canadian Labour Arbitration* and *Labour Arbitration Cases* on their bookshelves. They often communicate news of and their own commentary on recent Arbitrations to their colleagues, including line managers.

The familiarity of Canadian line managers with Arbitration is also much greater than in Britain and is especially pronounced at CANBREW, where line managers not only have been called upon to testify at Arbitrations but are expected to attend them as part of their training in how to discipline.

The following splendidly apposite tale is an example of the impact of discipline Arbitration on CANBREW managers.

The grievor was a fully licensed maintenance mechanic with four and a half years' seniority who, according to disciplinary documents,[29] was suddenly found incapable of performing up "to the high standards of craftsmanship expected and required of a qualified skilled tradesman." Acknowledging the grievor's lack of intention to do wrong, and employing a "nondisciplinary" approach,[30] the employer demoted him to the position of production worker (which the union estimated would cost him $15,000 in salary per year).

The grievor's professional mediocrity was widely acknowledged by managers and workers alike so as to be almost legendary in the plant. But justifying the demotion was quite another matter, especially when the union swung its legal guns around to defend the grievor. Several supervisors testified to major and costly errors directly caused by the grievor that had led them to assign him simpler tasks or "work around him." He was told about these errors but had *never been warned that failure to improve his performance could result in discipline or demotion.*

The union's witnesses testified that the grievor was able to do a wide range, indeed most, of his maintenance tasks with acceptable competence. The union further argued that "elemental fairness demands certain steps to let him know he is in jeopardy . . . If a mechanic is incompetent, that is serious for the Company in terms of cost. It should be important enough to document and tell the employee about.[31] The union also argued that the employer was attempting to make the grievor a scapegoat for the lack of supervisory competence in his department.

The case went on to Arbitration, and the grievor was reinstated to his old position with full back pay. In his decision, the arbitrator ruled (1) that the evidence did not convince him that the grievor was so bad at performing the range of tasks expected of him as to be classified "incapable," (2) that even if the grievor was incapable, the evidence did not prove he was incapable of improving, and (3) that even if (1) and (2) were proved, the employer's neglect to warn the grievor of the consequences of his performance rendered the discipline null and void.

At first the decision hit the employer like a thunderbolt. Fearful of its impact on managerial prerogative, top managers sought a legal opinion on the chances of quashing the award in the courts. While arguing that the decision would seriously "fetter or circumscribe the discretion and mandate that the Management Rights Clause provides to the company," the lawyer retained by management reminded his clients of the very narrow scope of judicial review in Canada (the arbitrator had written his award so that it did not seem "patently unreasonable"[32]) and put their chances at "less than even." The employer did not challenge the arbitrator's decision.

Yet, after a period of reassessment, a top corporate industrial relations manager sent a memo to other top managers, in which he took a different view of the award's effect on managerial prerogative:

> I think the arbitrator is right. We made the age-old mistake of *knowing* [that the grievor] is incompetent, but being unable to *prove* it in a just cause sense . . . (emphasis in the original)
> *The result of the arbitration is not unmanageable but (as usual) it makes the process longer and harder to administer* (emphasis added).

This is an example of what could be called "management education effect," whereby even losses at Arbitration act not to restrict management's freedom of action but rather to educate management in the proper methods for carrying out necessary tasks such as dismissal with due regard to proper procedure. The corporate manager indicated he was sending a copy of the memo to all personnel managers (in all of CANBREW's sister plants across the country), recommending they treat similar situations in the future in the following way:

1. We will document every incident where an employee completes a work assignment in a manner which is unacceptable to us, and we will impose appropriate discipline if circumstances warrant.
2. If the employee has a history of such documented incidents and we feel we must remove him from his job, our options are open. If we feel we can prove incapacity we can use the non-disciplinary approach, and if we cannot prove incapacity we will simply follow the disciplinary approach through to its logical conclusion.

The memo is highly significant in the insight it gives into the interplay between Canadian Arbitration and management practice. The Arbitration had different effects at two different levels of management. To many line managers, it was further proof that, as one supervisor said, "Arbitrators won't let us manage" and that "once probation is over, there's a problem getting rid of the poor performer." But to some line managers and to those higher up, the Arbitration was a slap on the wrists of lazy managers and a lesson in how to manage better. As one manager said, "We tried to take the easy way out and demote him. It would have taken a lot longer to build a case against him and we didn't. We colluded with him by putting him on the easy jobs. It's a symptom of a larger problem here."

Thus, what at first appeared to be a major victory for the union, an example of the arbitrator "bending over backward for the worker," actually became a great boon to management, a learning experience, an opportunity to use the arbitrator's knowledge of "good industrial relations" to fine-tune its practice of control. The arbitral award undoubtedly does make the "process longer and harder to administer" but more efficient in the end.

Impact on Workers and Trade Unions

In the comparison of Tribunals and Arbitration, it is the legitimacy of the two Forums to trade unionists that is most striking and most determinative of their differential impact in the workplace.

In the eyes of Canadian trade unionists, disciplinary Arbitration is employed and highly regarded not just because it is the only method of seeking equity in the absence of the right to strike during the term of the collective agreement (although that is doubtless a powerful impetus). Nor is it favored because it actually delivers a high quality of equity. The comparison with the dismissal reversal rates of the beleaguered British Tribunals, the fact that almost half of all dismissals are upheld in Canada, and the fact that trade unionists are ill equipped to form evaluative assessments of the equitable quality of Arbitration in any case makes the whole question indeterminate.

Arbitration is favored because it *appears* to deliver equity, especially compared with its poor record for trade unions in nondisciplinary cases.[33] What cannot be overlooked is that in more than half the dismissal cases put before arbitrators, management is slapped on the wrists in some way. An employee earlier seen emptying his locker is now seen returning triumphantly to work. In just less than half the cases of discipline short of dismissal, there is a similar slap on the wrists. Just as this has a demoralizing effect on some supervisors, it has an encouraging effect on workers and trade union officials, who seldom consider that the arbitrator has acted essentially as an arm of management's disciplinary apparatus. In their rush to welcome the dismissed colleague back to work, they seldom ask the prodigal son if he has lost his inheritance.

Yet, for all its popularity, disciplinary Arbitration is not seen by trade unionists as something integral to the workplace, something they themselves have accomplished by their power, mobilization, or ingenuity. It is something apart from them, a sometimes benign yet always distant deus ex machina, not the result of collective action. The full significance of this relationship becomes clearer when we consider the impact of Tribunals on the British trade unionists.

In the British plants, Industrial Tribunals quite simply have little or no credibility. Even at BRITMET, where the union is not able consistently to mount a workplace challenge to management's disciplinary activity, Tribunals are seen as a forum for losers, a desperate last resort for the employee in which the union's participation is far from certain.

The only Industrial Tribunal to take place at BRITMET within the period encompassed by our study involved an employee dismissed for excessive absenteeism. The union declined to represent him.

Of the two Tribunal cases at BRITBREW, the union represented the complainant in one case only. The convener explained that this was only because of extraordinary circumstances. To set an example, the company was determined to fire a woman canteen worker accused of unauthorisedly taking leftovers home. The union felt that, in light of the overall high level of pilferage in the area, there was sufficient uncertainty about her guilt to give her the benefit of the doubt. The union won the Tribunal case, and the complainant received compensation.

In a second Tribunal case, however, involving pilferage of product by a drayman (a worker who delivers casks, kegs, and bottles of beer to pubs and other drinking establishments), the union refused to help the complainant, and his case was dismissed. The BRITBREW convener believes (whether or not it is true) that "the first question Tribunals ask [when a union member appears before them] is whether the union is backing the case. If it isn't, his case is as good as lost."

Thus, the BRITBREW union's refusal to represent a claimant is more than mere indifference but a conscious act of collusion in his dismissal. The difference between this situation and the one in Canada could hardly be more pronounced. Why is this so?

This union (and, of course, this company) in Britain prefer to handle disciplinary matters within the bounds of the workplace. In this case, by unspoken agreement, the union participates in the policing of its members, while the company keeps discipline to a minimum. In return for its willingness to withhold serious support for the few employees who cross the bounds of acceptability (especially in cases of egregious absenteeism, theft, and larcenous fiddling), the union is able to protect the jobs of others (see Haiven 1988). Both management and the union have ways of "signaling" the degree of their concern about the issue and of reading the other party's signals. Thus, discipline at BRITBREW is a shared activity, to an extent that separates it not only in degree but in kind from the other three plants.

A look at the disciplinary statistics at the two breweries proves the case. They have the same rate of dismissal, showing a similar propensity for ridding themselves of employees with unacceptable behavior. But the Canadian brewery has four times the nondismissal disciplinary rate of the British one. If the BRITBREW union were weak or not vigilant in defense of its members, the paucity of nondismissal discipline might indicate a less progressive, more punitive model of discipline. But given the union's strength, a different conclusion must be drawn, that is, that more than any of the other three unions, this one participates in the disciplinary process. This is not simple co-optation but rather a process in which the union has much to gain for its members.

This process is repeated in many British workplaces. The Institute of Personnel Management reports that in 14 percent of workplaces with more than one hundred employees and 19 percent of workplaces with more than five hundred employees, "all disciplinary matters [are] agreed between trade union and management" (1979, 96).

Henry's (1983, 87) move beyond the simple punitive-corrective model is useful for analysis here. In essence, while the three other plants are at different places on the "representative-corrective" approach, BRITBREW has advanced into the "accommodative-participative" sphere, wherein (1) worker participation is not limited to "advocacy or appeals roles" as it is in the "representative-corrective" approach but (2) the collective nature of the disputes is fully acknowledged by both parties and (3) discipline is more fully subject to negotiation. Henry implies that with this approach, management "institutionalize[s] the collective bargaining process by incorporating representatives from both management and unions in a joint disciplinary procedure" (1987, 298). Yet it can be argued that the process is not quite as overt as this, that the approach works better in the British context if, as at BRITBREW, the collaboration is not formalized into a joint disciplinary procedure but rather operates informally. The implications of this process on levels of industrial conflict can be readily inferred.

Space does not permit canvassing the full range of causes giving rise to discipline. However, I will investigate the handling of three of the most important grounds and ones that permit comparison between Canadian and British workplaces: poor attendance, insubordination, and poor work performance. Orientations and reactions toward these issues vary significantly across the two countries and two industries, especially in the two breweries, and shed valuable light on the question considered in this chapter.

Attendance

Attendance is a major cause of discipline in both countries and the major cause they share (Barnacle 1991, 121; Adams 1978, 45; Edwards and Whitston 1988, 3). Certainly, a common major problem in all four plants is controlling lateness and absenteeism by employees. What is acceptable attendance? Edwards and Whitston (1988) justifiably criticize attempts at simplistic construction of differential "cultures of absence." Nevertheless, it is undeniable that in tackling absenteeism, managements themselves make assessments based on a perceived "acceptable" level of attendance, which differs from work area to work area and is closely bound up with the nature of control in those areas. Managements are aware of attendance levels in their industry and, having established an acceptable plant norm, assess different departments on their deviance from that norm and different employees on their deviance from the departmental norm. Thus, on the one hand, BRITBREW management, while admitting that the tough manual work of their draymen and staging unit workers contributes to high rates of absenteeism, also concludes it has an absenteeism problem. On the other hand, BRITMET management points to its foundry workers as having a record of absenteeism well below the plant norm.

Management in all four plants, as in most modern industrial workplaces, has moved beyond a purely punitive approach to absenteeism. At one time both managements might not have distinguished between the legitimately incapacitated and the malingerers. Today, collective bargaining and a corrective approach have introduced sick pay schemes meant to protect those with "legitimate" absences. Nonetheless, the following questions must still be addressed: What is to be done with malingerers and those whose incapacity, though blameless, does not allow them to fulfill their obligations of service? How is the scheme to be managed to prevent it from both encouraging absenteeism and becoming too costly? And to what extent can the sick pay scheme itself, as opposed to direct disciplining of employees, be used to address these problems? The level of participation of the union is crucial to the answer.

In Canada, the union is both structurally and attitudinally precluded from participating in disciplinary actions.[34] The coverage and payout level of the schemes is bargained and set in the interests apparatus and is subsequently "locked in" as an employee right. The policing of attendance is off limits to joint regulation. Neither party would dream of fettering its discretion to impose or oppose sanctions as the case may be. Most attempts by management to use the sick pay scheme itself to curb absenteeism are resisted by the union, using the grievance procedure.[35] Thus, management is forced to resort to straight discipline to police attendance. At both Canadian plants, then, management uses written warnings, suspensions, and dismissals (or warnings, counseling sessions, and final discharge where a "nonpunitive" policy exists[36]), even as the sick pay scheme continues to give monitored employees their day's pay.

In the British factories, where bargaining structures are less rigid, there is room for a more flexible approach to absenteeism (i.e., more room for "adjustments"). Management at both plants has attempted to involve the union in policing absenteeism, holding out the promise of a better sick pay scheme if the "abusers" can be isolated. It does this because an ounce of the union's cooperation in discouraging abuse is worth several pounds of company-initiated punitive action.

Like the Canadian unions, the BRITMET union is highly distrustful of management's initiatives in this area. Significantly though, unlike the Canadian unions, it cannot fall back on its "rights" because of the indeterminacy and lack of legal enforceability of the collective agreement. The union either continually renegotiates and enforces its rights or it loses them. For example, management proposed a progressively punitive scheme for reducing lateness. Recidivists would eventually lose access to the sick pay plan. When the union refused to negotiate, the employer acted unilaterally and, according to a personnel manager,

> we ended up imposing a harsher procedure than we had proposed to the union. Because we couldn't get their agreement to our proposal or even some compromise, we had no guarantee of compliance. I think the union lost out in this instance as in many others by its behavior in negotiations.

The BRITMET management offered the union improvements to the sick pay scheme if the union would stop disputing all suspensions as a matter of course. This the union would not do. Says a personnel manager,

> They have two faces. They privately admit the legitimacy of discipline for offenders but publicly defend them. The union sees cooperation as selling their members out, but their own members support our scheme. Why, even the abusers admit they deserve to be suspended from the scheme!

A union steward agrees:

> We're in an uncomfortable situation. We're expected to represent the members. But we'd like to get the number of waiting days [an obligatory period of absence before the plan goes into effect] down. It's a job to know how to do it.

Eventually though, after a year in which the company unilaterally suspended acknowledged abusers from the scheme, the union began to accept the company's goodwill and agreed to an improved scheme, while tapering off its automatist opposition to the treatment of abusers.

The BRITBREW union, by contrast, more readily enters into negotiations, not only on the payout of the scheme but on the method of identifying abusers. The jointly agreed-upon discipline procedure involves the following sequence: (1) a verbal, then a written warning, (2) a six-month suspension from the sick pay scheme, and (3) dismissal from employment if, during suspension from the scheme, the level of attendance remains unacceptable. The union retains the right to appeal each case on its merits and stops short of joining with the company in actually disciplining offenders. But a personnel manager says the company would not have it any other way: "It's the union doing its job. If the union didn't do it, then it would have a problem of credibility with its members and the whole procedure would start to fall apart."

Another manager, however, says the disciplinary system works so smoothly because the union is seen as "coauthor." Though it can intercede in absenteeism disputes, the union seldom does so except to ensure employees have union representation.

By participating in the regulation of absenteeism, the BRITBREW union may be abandoning the defense of some of its members in the short run. But by doing management the favor of helping to castigate them, it is building up IOUs that it expects management to repay at some future date.

Only in this plant does the union have the strength or confidence to participate in regulating absenteeism. In most Canadian workplaces and in British workplaces with weaker unions, such activity is barely possible.

The BRITBREW union's arsenal contains favors as well as industrial action, while the arsenals of the other three unions contain only industrial action.

In one case, BRITBREW sought to dismiss four employees for abuse of the sick leave plan as well as other offenses.[37] But, ironically, once the union had achieved its purpose of preventing the dismissal of the four employees concerned, it proceeded to help convince three of them that they would be better off quitting voluntarily and taking redundancy pay (which they did). The fourth employee transferred to a new job within the company and was, with union acquiescence, suspended from the sick pay scheme for six months. A further irony is that it is the strongest of the four unions at BRITBREW that participates most intimately in the discipline process.

Insubordination

Adams defines insubordination as a "direct challenge to authority such as refusing to obey an order and swearing, fighting and insolence where a supervisor is involved" (1978, 43). It is in the area of insubordination that we see some of the most dramatic differences in workplace industrial relations in the two countries.

In Canada, insubordination is an issue of gravity. Adams's survey of dismissal Arbitrations (1978) finds it is the chief cause of dismissal,[38] even ahead of attendance. Surveys suggest that between 14 and 24 percent of dismissals are for insubordination (Adams 1978; Barnacle 1991, 119), and Palmer and Palmer insist that

> unquestionably, insubordination is *the most common type of disciplinary action found in the field of labour arbitration*. Equally, it is considered by most arbitrators to be "one of the most serious industrial offenses." The reasons for this is that it strikes at the heart of an employer's prerogatives: the right to manage. It is felt that the right to order employees to carry out orders without extended debate and without a loss of respect is central to the role of management (1991, 315, emphasis added).

In the Canadian plants, although it lags behind attendance, insubordination is a prominent cause of discipline, especially at the aluminum plant, where the industrial relations climate is often bitter. In Britain, however, insubordination ranks much further down the list of causes of discipline. In the IPM survey, only 2 percent of the employers listed "refusal to obey reasonable instructions" as the major cause of discipline, and only 25 percent listed it in the first four causes of discipline (IPM 1979, 31–33). Even Tribunals are careful in finding "a refusal to obey a legitimate instruction" a reasonable cause for dismissal (Anderman 1985, 158–59).

Managers and trade unionists in both the British plants are somewhat nonplussed by the concept of insubordination. Few cases of outright disciplinary action result from this cause in either plant.

The reason for the great difference between the countries on this matter should be fairly obvious. In the Canadian regime, where such great pains are taken to ensure that "the industrial plant is not a debating society" and that employees "work now and grieve later," much behavior outside these norms inevitably becomes a challenge to managerial prerogative, even if it is not specifically intended as such. To be sure, a certain amount of "shop talk" between employees and supervisors is not only unavoidable but also necessary for the smooth functioning of any regime. Indeed, Canadian arbitrators have ruled discipline for insubordination too severe when swearing did not connote insolence (Palmer and Palmer 1991, 334), when the supervisor was not clear in an order or in the consequences of disobedience (316–18), when there was provocation of the employee (332), and when the order was illegal, dangerous, or patently unreasonable (319–29). Yet, in this environment, it could be said that management neglects to discipline for insubordination at its peril.

Because most of the causes of discipline for insubordination relate directly to the forum of what might be called "job control"[39] (i.e., issues dealing with the actual work to be done, the pace of work, and methods of work) (Palmer and Palmer 1991, 334–35, 340; see also Haiven 1988, 282–303, for a fuller elaboration), it is inescapable that many of the high number of disciplinary disputes in the category of insubordination have been displaced from that arena. Many cases that begin life under job control and cannot find legitimate expression there are serious enough that they will not be suppressed. Thus, they inevitably find their way through to the disciplinary forum. By contrast, in the British regime, which not only tolerates but invites debate on the shopfloor, and where strikes are considered only "those stoppages which seriously impair our ability to trade,"[40] it is little wonder that insubordination per se is of far smaller import than in Canada.

BRITMET supervisors claim no more than two disciplines for insubordination in ten years. One involved unusual rudeness, unpleasantness, and verbal aggressiveness to supervisors. The other involved a shop steward telling an employee to slow down. The personnel manager says, almost apologetically, "We know it goes on but it's never done openly. In this case he did it right out in the open. There was no way we could let it go."

Discipline for insubordination is even rarer at BRITBREW. From observation, a far higher degree of irreverent and often scatological "shop talk," especially by shop stewards toward line managers, is tolerated than in the other three plants. With small-scale departmental stoppages always a possibility, mere argument, even if vigorous, can seem like a blessing next to a strike. Being confronted by an angry steward (or one pretending to be angry) is quite common in many departments at BRITBREW. Almost all of the few cases of insubordination have involved an ongoing dispute between the management of the shipping department and the draymen.[41] One such case is illustrative of the general approach taken to discipline by the company.

A departmental agreement specifies that draymen who are unable to rouse a pub proprietor to accept his delivery may lose bonus earnings if they fail to telephone a supervisor and accept his instructions (to wait, revisit, reroute, or return the beer to the depot). One dray crew openly refused to obey the supervisor's instruction to attempt redelivery and were disciplined by a written warning and the loss of bonus pay for their entire truckload. Eventually, the parties agreed to a verbal warning and the loss of the bonus pay for the particular delivery only (a drop from £9 to £3). The company realized that more severe punishment might well *invite* rather than *prevent* violation of the agreement if workers felt they "may as well be hanged for a pound as a penny." A personnel manager said: "The union accepted the final result as just. Neither the company nor the union feels it was compromised by the deal. [The company] sometimes goes in higher than it might otherwise in discipline if we feel it might be reduced on appeal."

What is unique about BRITBREW is not that management often sets discipline high and reduces it on appeal. The three other managements, indeed all managements, do that. Where BRITBREW differs qualitatively is in the fact, and the readiness to acknowledge the fact, *that discipline is a negotiable item*, even when direct management orders have been flouted. Refusals to follow orders, then, can seldom be classified as insubordination. They are not as much willful challenges to managerial prerogative (as they are in Canada) as positional tactics in the gestalt of continuous collective bargaining.

Work Performance

Adams defines culpable work performance problems as "carelessness; negligence; breach of company rules [involving] no direct affront to authority . . . most cases relat[ing] to how the work is done" (1978, 44A). Managements in all four plants have used discipline when employees, through their negligence, have been found to be culpably responsible for substandard or damaged product. Yet, again, the Canadian plants use a far heavier hand than their British counterparts in the same industry.

Nowhere is this more evident than in the brewhouse of the two breweries, which are similar in all major respects. In both countries this unit employs process production in large batches, is capital intensive, and uses high technology. Work tasks are primarily monitoring and intervention at key junctures to expedite flow and prevent disruption or contamination of the process. Morale and self-discipline in these areas are higher than plant norms because of the job content and high degree of responsibility.

Despite (or perhaps because of) the high degree of automation, errors by operatives can result in considerable loss of or damage to product and consequent loss of profit. Quality is of primary concern and negligence a very serious offense.

Although it is impossible to quantify the concept of product quality (and no attempt is made to disparage Canadian beer), the importance of quality may be slightly higher in Britain, especially in the ale (as opposed to the lager) market, where consumer loyalty depends more on taste distinctiveness and less on marketing techniques.

Yet the number and seriousness of disciplinary penalties handed out at CANBREW for negligence and carelessness in brewing is significantly higher than at BRITBREW. Verbal warnings, written warnings, suspensions, and disciplinary demotions for slipups have been handed out over a long enough period that the contrast with BRITBREW is noticeable.

In a typical case, a CANBREW employee with some twelve and a half years' seniority was disciplined after committing four performance errors, over a two-year period, that resulted in product loss. The first offense (pumping uncompleted product prematurely) netted a two-day suspension and a letter that said:

> Based on this incident and your employment record . . . which is completely unacceptable, you should be fully aware that if you fail to follow procedures or disobey Company rules and regulations you could subject yourself to further progressive discipline up to and including discharge. As you know, working in the Brew House requires a high degree of diligence. Should you fail to follow proper procedures again, you may be removed from the Brewing Department.

The second offense (allowing the concentration of product to fall below acceptable levels) resulted in a verbal warning. The third (allowing ingredients to drain onto the floor) also led to a verbal warning. In neither of the latter two cases was the union formally notified. The fourth offense (overfilling a tank and hence spilling large amounts of product) resulted in the employer finding the grievor "unsuitable for work in the Brewing Department" and permanently demoting him to the packaging unit (a much more difficult and tedious job).

The union grieved the demotion and carried it through to Arbitration. According to the collective agreement, it argued, the middle two offenses were not disciplined formally and hence were incapable of being relied upon in support of the company's claim of a "culminating incident."

The arbitrator agreed with the union, finding the middle two offenses incapable of being part of the grievor's disciplinary record. As a result, there was not enough conclusive evidence that the grievor was incapable of performing his job and deserving of demotion. Finding that "the culminating incident was an incident of blameworthy conduct," the arbitrator imposed a three-day suspension.

Without making any judgments on the grievor's degree of culpability, there is one aspect of this case and most of the others examined thus far that is particularly striking. That is the extent to which procedural and technical, as opposed to substantive, considerations dominate the union's arguments in Canada.

With few weapons available to defend its members other than third-party adjudication and trapped by its own and the employer's unwillingness to engage in any more active approach, the union inevitably becomes a *prisoner of proceduralism*. With nothing to "trade" with, it responds with a passive/aggressive, automatistic adversarialism that spins it and the employer into a vicious circle of formal but often inconclusive confrontation. Because of the importance of the concept of "culminating incident" in Arbitration, each incident becomes a separate battlefield and credibility counts for little in the ensuing scrap. Indeed, the union's practice is to challenge even letters of warning for fear that they will later haunt the employee. In this vortex, both conceding that the employee deserved discipline and mobilizing members for collective action to resolve the dispute (two sides of the same coin) are equally unthinkable to the union. Invariably, it focuses on the narrowest and most proceduralist grounds to build its case.

At BRITBREW, by contrast, the union is able, and far more willing, to bargain discipline, both within the context of a single incident and overall. Within the incident, it may (but does not always) "trade" on anything from the threat of industrial action to petty blackmail (such as the responsibility of members of management for performance errors, drunkenness, and other misdemeanors[42]). Overall, it may rely on its willingness to concede the guilt of its members in certain cases to trade for employer leniency in others. Because third parties are mostly irrelevant to discipline, more than a minimum of attention to proceduralism (to ensure a fair hearing of the issues) is unimportant, and the substance of the discipline comes to the fore. In this setting, it is impossible for the union to avoid making value judgments on the incidents provoking discipline, and thus its credibility to management is very important. This credibility can be maintained only by a process of give and take, by conceding guilt in some cases in order to defend union members better in others.

Summary

The beginning of this chapter promised to test the proposition that Canadian Arbitration is a "jewel in the crown" of industrial dispute resolution in that country and a major contributor to assuaging industrial conflict, especially compared with Britain's Industrial Tribunals. Contemplation of theoretical debates on discipline helped provide a framework for the analysis. More than any superficial win/lose rate, deeper considerations of the quality of equity provided, of the legitimation of managerial control, of the obscuring of exploitation, and of the importance of collective action are necessary to address the issue.

A comparison of Tribunals and Arbitration per se indicated (1) that the superiority of the latter in protecting job security has more to do with its ability to effect reinstatement than its propensity to encroach on managerial prerogative to discipline; (2) that, compared with Tribunals, the credibility of Arbitration is enhanced by its power to reinstate, by its greater flexibility and procedural solicitude, and by its greater reluctance to "second-guess" managerial decisions; (3) that collective considerations have little more effect on Arbitration than on Tribunals, both of which individualize disputes; (4) that in "second-guessing" managerial action, Arbitration threatens managerial prerogative little more than Tribunals do but actually restrains, guides, and teaches those employers sophisticated enough to appreciate such assistance and (5) that, in substituting its own discipline, Arbitration does not usurp but collaborates in management's role.

Notwithstanding these findings, an investigation of the differential effect of third-party adjudication on the shopfloor in the two countries revealed its impact on unionized workplaces in Canada as far greater than in Britain. Because of the minimal relevance of such adjudication in Britain, workplace apparatuses take on a far more important role in dispute handling. Where the union has the requisite strength (including the ability to back up its position with collective action) and confidence to breathe life into those apparatuses (and where management is strong enough to respond in kind), a transition to something like Henry's "accommodative-participative" mode of discipline handling results, offering a higher degree of collective action and participation and arguably at least an equal degree of substantive equity to that found in the Canadian workplace. What is more, in these circumstances, the apparatuses can be very effective in conflict management. Where the union lacks the requisite strength and confidence, a vacuum results that Tribunals, ACAS codes of practice, and considerations of "good industrial relations" can only partially fill.

In Canada, the efficacy of third-party adjudication in handling industrial conflict can only be partial. For within the system itself lies not only a barrier to more collective forms of conflict management but the seeds of conflict itself.

4

Shopfloor Relations at U.S. and Canadian Plants of an Automotive Parts Supplier, 1936–1988

Stephen Herzenberg

U. S. industrial relations scholars' interpretation of shopfloor relations in U.S. and Canadian manufacturing from 1950 to 1980 emphasizes the rule-based, procedural character of dispute resolution. According to this interpretation, nascent industrial unions, faced with deskilled jobs and a Taylorist division of labor imposed by managers during the development of scientific management and mass production, adapted to this division of labor by attaching wages and job rights to the narrow classifications previously defined by corporations. In the resulting system, which they call "job control unionism,"[1] Thomas Kochan, Harry Katz, and Robert McKersie maintain that "work and disciplinary standards are clearly defined and fairly administered and disputes over the application of rules and customs are impartially adjudicated through the grievance procedure" (1986, 29). In the description of U.S. unionism in Kochan, Katz, and McKersie (1986) and in Katz's 1985 analysis of the auto industry, collective action plays no systematic role in the process of shopfloor dispute resolution or in substantive outcomes, including effort levels.

Given mainstream U.S. industrial relations scholars' neglect of the shopfloor, their analysis rests on little empirical foundation, even in the auto industry (Katz 1985). Studies by more critical scholars, such as Steven Jefferys (1986), Donald M. Wells (1986), and Craig Zabala (1989), have begun to fill the gap, but even these focus primarily on machine-paced assembly line workers at General Motors, Ford, and Chrysler. To increase empirical knowledge of postwar North American industrial relations, and to shed light on the historical context of contemporary work reorganization in the United States and Canada, I conducted a detailed case study (1991) of labor relations at U.S. and Canadian plants of the Budd Company, a diversified auto supplier.

The Budd case suggests that conventional interpretations exaggerate the exclusively procedural character of North American shopfloor relations during the post–World War II period. In the process, they overstate the uniformity of U.S. shopfloor relations and underestimate the continuing importance of collective action in the process and outcome of negotiation in many plants. Rather than a single pattern of shopfloor relations captured by the notion of "job control unionism," the evidence from Budd suggests that North American labor relations spanned a range of qualitatively distinct patterns of shopfloor relations distinguished by the extent and character of collective action.

Underlying the differences observed between shopfloor relations at Budd and the Big Three were fundamental differences in management labor strategy, technology, and the effort control system. At GM, at least among assembly line workers, management relied on centralized, bureaucratic personnel policies, close supervision, and machine-pacing to maintain high effort levels (Lichtenstein 1982 and 1986). At Budd, until around 1960, by contrast, engineering-oriented top managers relied on highly decentralized personnel policies, low supervisor-worker ratios, and piece rates or fixed quotas to induce self-supervision among self-paced work groups. Thus, while GM tried to eliminate work stoppages as a regular feature of assembly line life, slowdowns and brief stoppages remained an integral part of effort determination and shopfloor regulation in general at Budd. Overall, Budd's labor relations were more reminiscent of what Wayne Lewchuck (1989) calls "the British system of mass production" than of job control unionism.

Even after 1960, when financial difficulties precipitated an attempt to modify practices at Budd's Detroit plant in line with those at Ford and General Motors, work group control over the pace of work and Budd's reliance on quotas and piece rates to increase effort levels sustained more collective patterns than typical in Big Three machine-paced production.

The rest of this chapter presents the Budd case in more detail. The second section describes the study methodology. The third section reviews the origins of the company and its labor policies between 1910 and 1960. The fourth section presents the history of labor relations at the Budd-Detroit plant from its opening in 1924 to the mid-1980s. The fifth section describes events at the Canadian plant during its first twenty years of operation. The sixth section addresses the broader implications of the Budd case. It reconceptualizes postwar North American shopfloor relations in the auto industry in terms of a three-part typology based on the role of collective action in shopfloor regulation and discusses whether the Budd case—with its echoes of British experience—represents an aberration. This section then considers whether the relative strength of collective traditions at Budd's Canadian plant in the 1970s and 1980s generalizes to other Canadian plants and uses the Budd case and other evidence to speculate about the roots of shopfloor militancy among Canadian auto workers.

Methodology

The Budd case study combined ethnographic and historical research methods (see Herzenberg 1991, 41–47 and 470–477, for more detail). Analysis of contemporary shopfloor dynamics was based primarily on one- to six-hour open-ended interviews in 1986 with at least ten managers, fifteen union officials, and twenty-five hourly workers at each plant. Follow-up interviews were conducted with critical informants at each plant by telephone and in return visits in early 1987 and November 1988. Interviews were conducted one-on-one in offices off the shopfloor. All but a few of the interviews were taped and then transcribed. A crude index of the Canadian workers' opinions on critical issues was created by hand; similar information was extracted from worker interviews conducted at the Budd-Detroit plant, using software designed for that purpose.

At each factory, the workers who were interviewed were drawn primarily from three small groups in different parts of the plant, rather than randomly from the plant as a whole. The focus on particular work groups at each plant enabled repeated discussions to take place of the same events from the perspective of different workers. Within the small groups from which workers came, the individuals interviewed mirrored the plants' demographic profiles and included participants and nonparticipants in new participation and quality programs. With the exception of one group at the U.S. plant, most of the workers who were interviewed were direct production workers. All the interviews began with a series of demographic, occupational, and personal background questions. These were followed by deliberately general questions (e.g., what do you like most/least about your job?) intended to solicit views of life on the shopfloor without imposing a particular set of analytical categories on the discussion.

To amplify the historical dimension of the study, a number of interviews were conducted with key managers and union officials who had been at the two plants earlier in the postwar period. These included the chief executives of the Canadian subsidiary in its early years and in the period of peak labor-management conflict in the late 1970s; a labor relations executive who helped bring to an end the tradition of frequent work stoppages at the Budd-Detroit plant in the 1960s; the UAW regional director with jurisdiction over Budd-Detroit during this period; and Erwin Baur, a radical activist and skilled worker employed at Budd-Detroit from 1942 to 1977. Baur was president of the UAW local at Budd-Detroit from 1963 to 1966 and a committeeman for much of the rest of his time there.

Interviews about contemporary and past events were complemented with a detailed examination of company work stoppage and grievance records, as well as other company documents. In addition, corporate managers, local managers, and union officials reviewed a draft of the Canadian plant case study for factual and conceptual accuracy.[2]

The Budd Company

Budd's position in the auto industry and its competitive strategies and fortunes provide the context in which its labor policies have evolved.[3] German immigrant Edward G. Budd founded the Budd Manufacturing Company in Philadelphia in 1912. Like many automotive pioneers, Edward Budd began his career as a shopfloor engineer and skilled worker. His company's success in its first half-century was based on two competitive strengths: engineering innovations, such as the all-steel body, and Budd's ability to produce parts in volumes too low and uncertain to suit its customers' dedicated, high-volume components operations. When Edward G. Budd died in 1946, company employment had grown to 21,751. The Detroit "mini-Rouge," where hourly employment ranged from 4,300 to 7,500 between 1943 and 1961, included a foundry, hub and drum operation, brake assembly area, stamping, chassis, and wheel production (fig. 4.1).

The engineering orientation of Budd's managers went along with an autocratic and decentralized approach to labor relations. Its autocratic aspect was evident in Budd's efforts to prevent the AFL from organizing its Philadelphia operations in 1933 and 1934 (Fine 1963, 197–202). Faced with this organizing campaign, Budd created a company union and then replaced one thousand workers who struck for recognition on November 13, 1933. Despite being directed to reinstate the strikers by the National Labor Board, Budd refused. The company insisted on retaining authority over who would be rehired so that it could screen out militant strike leaders that, in the words of Budd's attorney, would "stir up further trouble" if reemployed. It took the UAW until 1945 to organize Budd-Philadelphia.

Although autocratic, labor relations at Budd were also highly decentralized. Even after unionization, shopfloor relations varied considerably as superintendents and foremen retained more authority than analogous figures at GM. In part, this decentralization reflected the engineering emphasis of the company's founder and of Edward G. Budd, Jr., CEO of Budd from 1946 to 1967 and himself a four-year machine shop apprentice. While financial analysts and business school graduates rose to power in GM, Budd's top managers remained "product men," many like Budd, Jr., second- or third-generation offspring of company founders. Consistent with the personalized and nonbureaucratic nature of the company, industrial relations managers only belatedly gained the authority and stature at Budd that they had at General Motors. The decentralization of labor policies provided the space within which shopfloor negotiation backed by the threat of small-scale collective action could become entrenched.

In association with its decentralized approach to labor relations, Budd did not adopt the combination of day rates, machine-pacing, and close supervision used to control effort levels among machine-paced workers at the Big Three. Especially in Budd's physically demanding production jobs,

*Figure 4.1 Employment Levels at Budd's Detroit and Kitchener Plants, 1937–
1987*

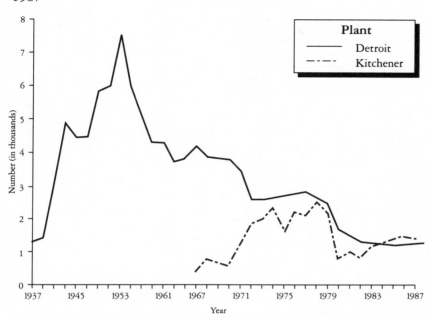

Note: Annual employment in Detroit for 1937–79 is estimated based on the voting strength of Local 306 at UAW conventions (locals receive one vote for each one hundred members). Estimates for 1980 forward are based on newspaper accounts and company records. Missing figures are interpolated from surrounding years.

Employment figures for Kitchener equal "average hourly employment" as reported in company records. Kitchener's peak hourly employment, reached in 1978, equaled approximately 3,100. The lowest hourly employment in the last decade, in 1980, equaled 590.

Note that employment is reported every two years from 1937 to 1967 and every one year thereafter.

attempting to force work groups to maintain a steady pace throughout the day for a fixed hourly wage would have given them a common interest in slowing down production. As a result, Budd managers operated most of their plants on piece rates. In Detroit, faced with UAW opposition to piece rates, the company opted for a fixed quota system. With a low enough quota, workers had an incentive to work at maximum pace early in the shift so that they could "make out" (finish the quota) one or more hours before the end of the day.[4] In addition to securing high effort levels, the self-supervision and peer pressure to maintain output induced by piece rates and quotas enabled Budd to hire fewer supervisors.

Taking into account the functional similarities between quota and piece rate incentive systems, what Lewchuck (1989, 35) says of British auto industry managers early in the twentieth century was also true of Budd's managers for most of the post–World War II period. Budd's managers could not envision a production system without a direct link between wages [or work hours] and output as a check on labor behavior and as an aid to factory coordination. The Fordist notion that both could be embodied in a system of machine operation did not suit the particular needs or the general world view of British [or Budd] managers.

Labor Relations at Budd-Detroit

The historical evidence indicates that there were four eras in labor-management relations at Budd-Detroit from the time of its organization by the UAW in 1936 to the mid-1980s: the consolidation of the union, between 1936 and the immediate postwar years; a period of relatively stable shopfloor bargaining, from after the war to 1960; a period from 1960 to 1978 in which industrial relations managers forced supervisors and workers to channel formal conflict resolution into the grievance procedure, with varied results in different parts of the plant; and a period from 1978 to the mid-1980s in which economic and political factors produced a further qualitative decline in collective action.

In the first of these periods, Budd Local 306 used union protection and the wartime boom to establish sectional collective action as a regular feature of shopfloor conflict resolution. Even after unionization, Budd remained a "loose-run outfit."[5] Superintendents in the wheel, foundry, and other major production units operated virtually independent "fiefdoms." Especially early on, when many ethnic stewards neither read nor wrote English well, the grievance system played a small role. Since shopfloor managers retained considerable autonomy, stewards, who represented an average of about forty workers (table 4.1), and work groups could win concessions by employing slowdowns, work stoppages, or other pressure tactics.

The development of collective traditions enabled the Budd-Detroit plant to establish quotas that provided workers with time to take cigarette or restroom breaks or to have a couple of hours off at the end of the day. "In the best of departments, they had half [time] on and half time off jobs." Collective action also gave employees the power to discipline supervisors selectively. Worker influence on supervisory behavior reinforced floor managers' partly shared structural interest in having easily attained standards. Low standards reduced the pressure on supervisors when downtime, absenteeism, or drinking problems eroded performance. Low standards and cooperative relations with workers also made it easier to gain cooperation when upper managers or customers put on the squeeze.

Indicative of the tendency among supervisors to identify with workers as much as with upper management, the majority of foremen at Budd-Detroit joined a special chapter of Local 306 before Taft-Hartley stripped them of the protections of the Wagner Act in 1947. Especially after Budd changed its labor policies, around 1960, the absence of union protection for supervisors made their cooperation with workers fragile and open to

Table 4.1. Ratio of Stewards to Hourly Workers at Budd-Detroit and Budd-Kitchener

Detroit

Year	Number of stewards	Hourly workforce	Ratio
1944	107	4,650	1:43
1946	123	4,475	1:36
1948	111	5,150	1:46
1950	125	6,750	1:54
1958	103	4,700	1:46
1971	60	3,500	1:58
1973	52	2,600	1:50
1977	50	2,800	1:56
1983	36	1,222	1:34

Kitchener, 1986

Work Group	Number of stewards	Workforce	Ratio
Skilled workers	4	318	1:80
Press shop	4[a]	370	1:93
Assembly	7	450	1:64
Nonproduction Workers	3	318	1:106
Entire plant	18	1,456	1:81

Source: The number of stewards at Detroit was estimated from local union contracts, various years. The number of stewards at Kitchener in 1986 was obtained from the company's seniority list.
[a]Two of the press shop stewards at Kitchener work half time.

disruption by higher managers, who viewed such cooperation critically. A foreman seen as too solicitous or protective of hourly workers could always be demoted or reassigned.

The entrenchment of work group bargaining at Budd helped a core of about twenty politically conscious radicals establish themselves within the plant leadership. Steward-supervisor bargaining gave radicals opportunities to demonstrate their value to other workers, including nonpolitical militants. The close ties developed with nonpolitical rank-and-file leaders during daily conflicts, in turn, protected left-wingers from red-baiting in the late 1940s and 1950s.

The end of World War II marked the approximate beginning of the second era in the history of Local 306. When the economy and demand for Budd's products permitted, Detroit management sought to tighten work standards and shopfloor customs loosened under permissive wartime conditions. Despite management's goals, the basic structure of the effort control system and the dispute resolution process remained unchanged. The chance to rest at the end of the shift induced high effort from workers earlier in the shift. Negotiation between floor managers and workers or union representatives remained the dominant form of dispute resolution. Work stoppages and disciplinary suspension or discharge remained the final arbiters when shopfloor negotiation proved unable to resolve disagreements.

In this period and the previous one, the strength of collective traditions enabled Local 306 to negotiate an unusually good collective agreement. Wages at Budd-Detroit remained at or above pattern until the late 1950s, and the local retained the right to strike during the collective agreement on any issue. By contrast, at General Motors, Ford, and Chrysler by the late 1940s, the UAW had renounced the right to strike during the contract over all issues except health and safety and work standards.[6] Overtime was voluntary at Budd-Detroit during the week unless the union gave the company the right to operate departments for nine or ten hours. The 1940 collective agreement prohibited overtime if workers were on layoff.[7] In 1947, after foundry workers walked out in support of skilled trades workers, the union also won one of the first UAW collective agreement provisions against outside contracting of skilled work. After 1947, the steward and supervisor would sit down and plan production in a way that permitted as much as possible of the work to be offered to in-house skilled trades.

At Chrysler plants with strong shop steward systems, financial pressure in the mid-1950s provided an occasion for eliminating collective action as a regular feature of shopfloor conflict resolution and for setting work standards. Despite declining employment in Detroit, the Budd Company remained profitable from 1953 to 1960 as a result of the huge success of the Ford Thunderbird. Stamping, assembling, and painting the Thunderbird body employed between two and three thousand workers at Budd-Detroit in this period. By 1960, the Thunderbird was selling in too high a volume for Budd's good. Ford decided to produce the Thunderbird body in its own plants. From $12 million in 1959, Budd's profit slipped to $6 million in 1960. Its losses equaled $1.7 million in 1961. In 1962 and 1963, the company earned only two cents profit for every dollar in sales.

Financial pressure and the example of other companies that had substituted the grievance procedure for continuous shopfloor negotiation led Budd-Detroit management to attempt the same transition. The attempt to use GM's approach to resolving labor disputes at Budd-Detroit came partly at the instigation of the UAW's international headquarters. Compared with his own experience as a GM employee, UAW regional director George Merrelli interpreted what he saw at Budd-Detroit as "utter chaos."

> In the GM circuit . . . everything was precision, according to rules, . . . I perhaps had an advantage on those in other plants . . . GM ran their plants . . . There was utter chaos in labor relations in Budd. . . . It was amazing how they did well with the loose labor relations that they had. It was not unusual for management to make a decision which the supervisors completely ignored. They had hundreds of personal agreements in departments [between] individual stewards and supervisors.[8]

"The end result," Merrelli continued,

> was that there were some practices that were out of this world. Concessions
> not by the corporation but by individual supervisors and superintendents
> . . . People thought nothing about walking out. Walkout, or the threat of a
> walkout, usually would obtain your concession, no matter how outlandish
> it was.

When the union officers heard that the company was considering closing
the Detroit plant, they prevailed on Edward G. Budd, Jr., to come to
Detroit to meet with Walter Reuther; Norman Matthews, head of the
UAW Budd department; Merrelli; and the Local 306 president. Budd
argued that the stoppages at the plant demonstrated that workers did not
want to work. The UAW officers responded by saying that the repeated
stoppages stemmed from the lack of set policies and discipline among
supervisors at the plant. As long as the company would, in Merrelli's
phrase, "cave at the mere suggestion of a wildcat," the union could not
fulfill its collective agreement obligation not to interrupt production.

In exchange for a commitment from the company to reinvest $50
million in the plant over five years, the UAW head office agreed to try to
help the company persuade workers and the local union to resolve disputes
through the grievance procedure. In early 1963, Local 306 also agreed to a
series of cost-saving concessions: a reduction in foundry wash-up time from
thirty to twenty minutes; the elimination of the fifteen-minute paid lunch
periods for those workers who received them; a recognition of the company's right to "introduce new standards based upon revised and/or new
methods of equipment"; and a pledge to negotiate "new approaches to
seniority and job classifications."

According to Bob Wangbichler, Budd's vice president of employee
relations in the mid-1980s and a Detroit manager in the 1960s, the change
in job classifications at Detroit represented a literal attempt to impose
Fordist work organization: "We used to have employees change over their
own jobs. . . . We made the decision that was inefficient because we'd
gotten some people in . . . that came from Ford. They had job set-up
people. If it was good for Ford, it was good for Budd."

By assigning die transition in hub and drum, wheel, and stamping areas
exclusively to job setters, managers would free up production operators—
who had previously assisted the set-up man during changeover—to be
assigned temporarily to other production lines. In retrospect, Wangbichler
viewed this application of Fordist principles as a mistake:

> We established a whole cadre of people whose sole purpose was to change
> over jobs. . . . We took people whose jobs it had always been to run those
> lines and change them over, and then said, "No longer can you change over
> the new tooling." And we put these inexperienced set-up people . . . on the
> job. . . . We were losing money hand over fist because of that.

After its negotiations with the union headquarters and the decision to reinvest in the plant, Budd-Detroit managers began their efforts to channel disputes into the grievance procedure. In association with this change, the labor relations department restricted supervisors' authority to negotiate on the shopfloor when workers filed grievances or stopped work. In 1963,

> manufacturing personnel were advised . . .[that] all Grievances are referred by the Department to Labor Relations prior to processing. This step . . . resulted in Management being immediately advised of impending issues and of a more factual and beneficial method of disposition of Grievances, and more efficient operation with Plant operations in line with Contract Agreement. (yearly statistical report of the Detroit labor relations department, 1963)

Symptomatic of the centralization of responsibility for dispute resolution, Budd-Detroit managers around this time began to keep detailed records on work stoppages. From 1954 to 1960, the company's work stoppage files contain records of only six incidents. In the 1960s, the details of some stoppages are outlined in memoranda as long as twenty pages.

One example of the attempt by the labor relations department to reduce the role of shopfloor negotiation after work stoppages took place on September 24, 1963. The union claimed that foundry supervisors had promised the foundry workers a pay increase if the number of silicon bricks they placed in the foundry charge increased. A labor relations department memorandum on the dispute noted that "management stated to the Union that not only in the Foundry but throughout the plant, Supervision did not have the authority to make any commitment relative to the rate of pay, standards, or change in practices, procedure, or the Contract without this being approved by Labor Relations."

While restricting supervisory authority to make concessions to the union, the company simultaneously sought to affirm workers' obligation to follow supervisory orders and to require that, if workers felt managers' actions violated the collective agreement or plant custom, their only recourse was to file a grievance and follow the instructions while the grievance was being processed. Thus, in a 1963 dispute involving some foundry workers who refused to follow a supervisory order that would have saved only "20 or 30 minutes total time" over the course of two weeks,

> it was recognized by the Company that Management's principle of having the right to make temporary changes and work assignments was at stake. Because Management has been making an all-out effort within the last few weeks to reestablish Management prerogatives within the Foundry, it was evident that this principle could not be compromised. (company work stoppage files)

The effort to shift dispute resolution to the grievance procedure coincided roughly with a generational change in the labor relations department. In their dealings with union officials, the young professionally trained managers combined a refusal to "cave" in to pressure tactics with a new emphasis on persuading the union of the legitimacy of company demands. In addition, the bureaucratization of dispute resolution coincided with the hiring of college graduates and management training course graduates as supervisors. As the proportion of supervisors promoted from the ranks declined, their identification with hourly workers loosened and their ties to labor relations increased.

Over the course of the 1963 to 1966 period, Local 306—particularly the foundry, wheel, and skilled trades areas—vigorously defended shopfloor bargaining traditions. The plant had its first two sanctioned strikes, one of them at mid-contract. On two other occasions, the workforce overwhelmingly authorized mid-contract strikes. Between 1963 and 1967, twenty-nine illegal work stoppages took place, and the plant's strike frequency per one thousand workers equaled more than half that at Chrysler during its most volatile period from 1956 to 1959 (tables 4.2, 4.3, and 4.4). Disputes centered on a range of substantive issues: the changes in classifications and work rules associated with the reorganization; works standards, especially on new technology; the company's ultimately successful attempt to introduce a progressive discipline policy to help control absenteeism; and, in the skilled trades, seniority, jurisdictional questions, and outside contracting.

Despite the union's militancy, this period produced the last large-scale defiance of the company by production workers at the Detroit plant. After a transition period, Budd managers succeeded in suppressing the use of work stoppages in the resolution of shopfloor disagreement. In 1969, in negotiations during the last nontemperature-related plantwide wildcat in the plant's history (not itself over a health and safety issue), the bargaining committee tried to salvage a limited right for representatives to countermand a foreman's instructions when they "thought a bona fide health and safety condition existed" (company work stoppage files). Although making it clear that the company hoped supervisors would not jeopardize employees' safety, company negotiators emphasized that "under no circumstances did a Committeeman or a Steward have the right to countermand instructions of a Foreman." Backed into a corner, the committeeman involved in the wildcat promised that he would not countermand a foreman in the future. Indicative of its now more sophisticated approach, the company did not press its advantage (for a similar case, see chap. 3). It suspended the committeeman for four days and the worker involved for three days.

The company's success at getting the union and workers at Detroit to abandon work stoppages had more gradual and varied consequences for shopfloor patterns of relations than Jefferys (1986) describes at Dodge Main. Unlike car assembly workers, Budd workers retained control over

Table 4.2. *Work Stoppages at Budd-Detroit, 1961–1987*

Year	Illegal stoppages	Nonweather-related illegal stoppages	Total workers involved	Hours lost in illegal stoppages	Legal mid-contract stoppages	Contract strikes	Hours lost in legal strikes	Total work hours lost
1961	3	3	5,794	29,792				29,792
1962	1	1		9,504				9,504
1963	7	7	1,240	8,123				8,123
1964	9	9	5,113	56,598	1		72,823	129,421
1965	4	4	5,347	11,769		1	354,298	366,067
1966	6	6	895	11,778				11,778
1967	1	1	2,254	14,811				14,811
1968	1	0	207	652				652
1969	5	4	5,444	33,097				33,097
1970	9	7	1,506	6,202				6,202
1971	3	3	695	4,317				4,317
1972	3	1	514	3,352				3,352
1973	5	1	352	2,229				2,229
1974	2	0	1,181	1,998				1,998
1975	2	0	63	381				381
1976	3	2	79	188				188
1977	6	0	454	2,230				2,230
1978	4	0	73	374				374
1979	1	1	107	0				0
1980	0	0	0	0		1	406,000	406,000
1981	0	0	0	0				0
1982	0	0	0	0				0
1983	0	0	0	0				0
1984	0	0	0	0				0
1985	0	0	0	0				0
1986	0	0	0	0				0
1987	0	0	0	0				0

Source: Aggregates for hours lost in 1961–71 and for the number of stoppages in 1961–68 are from company records. Other aggregates were estimated by the author based on company records on individual stoppages. Although there are no heat walkouts listed in the 1960s, some probably took place but went unreported because larger strikes were still occurring.

Table 4.3. Strike Frequency per 100 Workers at Budd, Chrysler, and General Motors

Year	Chrysler	General Motors	Budd-Detroit	Budd-Kitchener
1956	1.5			
1957	5			
1958	8			
1959	0.7			
1960	0.25	0.17		
1961	0.28	0.1	0.86	
1962	0.15	0.07	0.29	
1963	0.25	0.08	2.00	
1964	0.4	0.09	2.70	
1965	0.23	0.08	1.11	
1966	0.45	0.07	1.33	
1967	0.6	0.3	0.22	
1968	0.85	0.35	0.22	
1969	0.4	0.25	1.11	
1970	0.8	0.12	2.00	
1971	0.7	0.06	0.86	
1972	0.5	0.15	1.00	
1973	0.75	0.09	1.67	
1974	0.5	0.17	0.67	0.43
1975	0.25		0.67	3.75
1976	0.55	0.085	1.00	17.27
1977	0.9	0.08	2.00	8.07
1978	0.15	0.01	1.33	27.21
1979	0.17	0.03	0.37	12.57
1980	0.07	0.055		
1981				6.09
1982				
1983				
1984				
1985				
1986				0.67.
1987				0.69

Sources: GM and Chrysler data from Jefferys 1986, 10, fig. 2; calculations for Budd plants based on company data.

the pace of production. The effort control system also helped maintain collective patterns of shopfloor relations. The declining authority of supervisors did reduce the frequency of cases in which workers and stewards had influence over many aspects of production management. Interviews in the 1980s indicated, however, that significant steward influence and cooperative relations with worker-allied supervisors persisted in the truck wheel department until it closed in early 1983.

Table 4.4. Work Hours Lost per Manual Worker during Unauthorized Stoppages at Chrysler and Budd-Detroit, 1955–1979

Year	Chrysler	Budd-Detroit
1955	13.5	
1956	18	
1957	20	
1958	100	
1959	6	
1960	0.8	
1961	1.5	8.5
1962	0.55	2.7
1963	0.6	2.3
1964	2.5	15.3
1965	0.55	2.6
1966	1.5	2.6
1967	10	3.3
1968	4	0.1
1969	2.7	7.4
1970	4	1.4
1971	1.5	1.2
1972	2.5	1.1
1973	5	0.7
1974	1.7	0.7
1975	0.12	0.1
1976	5	0.1
1977	8.5	0.7
1978	0.06	0.1
1979	0.65	0.0

Sources: For Chrysler data, Jefferys 1986, 9, fig. 1. Jefferys 1986, 7, table 1, indicates that unauthorized man-hours lost between 1955 and 1959 equaled 63 percent of total man-hours lost. Between 1960 and 1964, unauthorized man-hours lost equaled only 22 percent of total man-hours lost. Budd-Detroit figures are calculated from company data and author's employment estimates.

In centers of union strength throughout Local 306 after the open conflict of the mid-1960s, workers and supervisors found ways to reconstruct their historic relationship that escaped the notice or had the silent approval of labor relations. One worker maintained that wheel workers reverted to changing over their own jobs. More generally, cooperation across classifications and between workers and supervisors reemerged based on a common interest in finishing quotas. This cooperation was punctuated by occasional slowdowns or other collective action as an alternative to both work stoppages and the frequent use of the grievance procedure. Formal grievances played little role in fractional bargaining in these areas, presumably because supervisors had no official authority to make concessions to workers.[9]

Although pre-1960 patterns of shopfloor relations reemerged in pockets of former union strength, economic and political forces combined with changing management industrial relations policy to produce a gradual decline in collective action and workforce cohesion at Budd-Detroit. As at Dodge Main, one critical economic force was the decentralization of production. In the mid-1960s, Budd began shifting pieces of its diversified Detroit operation to single-product small plants in rural areas and then the South. The closing of the Detroit foundry and the passenger wheel area shrank employment by almost 40 percent from 1967 to 1972 and took with it two of the most militant parts of Local 306.

The shrinkage of employment at the Detroit plant coincided with a change in the demographics of the workers as those hired after 1964 took the place of those hired before 1955 (table 4.5). In the 1940s and early 1960s, first-generation migrants from the South made up a large part of the Budd production workforce. Like Sabel's (1982) prototypical "peasant" workers, many of these migrants had modest expectations and self-conceptions rooted in their place of origin rather than their status as semiskilled industrial workers. This background plus their pride in having helped build the union contributed to worker solidarity and support for the union.

By the second half of the 1960s, young blacks raised in Detroit entered the workforce in increasing numbers, bringing with them a northern native's view of the bottom rung of the industrial ladder. This transition helped fuel the Detroit riots in 1967 and the emergence of rank-and-file autoworker movements—most prominently, the Dodge Revolutionary Union Movement (DRUM). These militant groups challenged black workers' relegation to the dirtiest, most arduous jobs, the petty abuses of some white supervisors, and the UAW's eschewal of direct action on the shopfloor. No rank-and-file protest movement emerged at Budd-Detroit in the late 1960s; the racially integrated local union was still fighting to preserve its shopfloor power and was perceived by workers as their advocate. Nonetheless, the young workers' frustration on the job expressed itself at Budd in rising absenteeism and drug use.[10] The change in the world view of young blacks exacerbated generational and racial divisions and made it more difficult to incorporate workers generally within orchestrated slowdowns or other subtle collective action.

Racial and generational heterogeneity did not by itself destroy workforce cohesion at Budd-Detroit. Indeed, workers' reminiscences about the truck wheel area suggested that solidarity across race, generational, and skill lines existed into the 1980s in parts of the plant where pre-1960s patterns of shopfloor relations were restored after the wildcats of the mid-1960s. Where collective traditions had broken down, however, racial, sexual, and generational resentments found fertile ground.

By the mid-1970s, external political and economic factors and Budd's emphasis on the grievance procedure meant that work stoppages no longer took place over issues such as works standards, job assignments, seniority,

Table 4.5. Seniority Profile of the Workforces at Budd-Detroit and Budd-Kitchener

| | Budd-Detroit | | | Budd-Kitchener | |
Time period	Number hired	Percent of 1986 workforce	Time period	Number hired	Percent of 1986 workforce
Pre-1955	161	13.0	Pre-1968	272	18.5
1964–66	189	15.2	1970–73	641	43.6
1968–70	149	12.0	1974–77	271	18.4
1972–74	204	16.4	1983–86	266	18.1
1975–77	233	18.8	Other	20	1.4
1985–86	239	19.3			
Other	66	5.3			

Source: Company records.

or attempts by union officials to countermand supervisors. Work stoppages had become confined to small numbers of workers and to protests about hot or cold temperatures in the plant.[11] Worker influence over standards, supervisory behavior, and working conditions became more dependent on the traditions of individual work groups. As stoppages involved fewer workers or became less frequent, the company could easily isolate participants. For workers who joined weather walkouts in the 1970s, a letter entered into a file one year sometimes became a two-week or indefinite suspension a year later.

Reflecting the evolution of patterns of shopfloor relations, the rate of grievances changed radically over time (table 4.6 and fig. 4.2). In the first half of the 1960s, the union annually filed one grievance per four production workers to protect against the weakening of collective agreement provisions and customary rights. By the mid- to late 1970s, production worker grievances to enforce the collective agreement or to pressure supervisors were filed at about a quarter of that rate. Disciplinary grievances represented more than 60 percent of total grievances.[12]

Combined with the decline in collective action, the changing composition of grievances soured many production workers on the union. Rather than enforcing grievances that preserved shopfloor protections for workers in general, union officials spent increasing fractions of their time defending workers with poor attendance records on the verge of losing their jobs. In many cases, after the progressive discipline procedure became institutionalized, the union knew it would lose cases it pursued to arbitration. It ended up pleading with management on behalf of individual workers. Concern about provoking management into recalcitrance on discipline issues meant sacrificing more collective gains in other areas.

The late 1970s marked the beginning of the fourth stage in Budd-Detroit's labor history. After rising in the expansion of the late 1970s, discharges for walking off the job without permission, insubordination, and refusing a job assignment virtually disappeared after 1979. The last heat walkout took place in 1978. In 1986, a press operator contrasted a heat walkout in the mid-1970s, when such walkouts were still accepted practice, and one several years later: "[Earlier,] it was enough people that . . . there wouldn't be no firing . . . The majority of people left out of here." After such occasions, if it was hot, the company would give out free drinks, repair the fans, and try to keep the plant cooler. A few years later, the worker continued, "about thirty people" initiated another heat walkout. "As far as they got was downstairs, and they realized wasn't nobody else coming." A second worker said, "We used to go when we got too hot. But after the last walkout management said, 'You walk out, we fire you.' "[13]

By the mid-1980s, a metal finisher at the Detroit plant maintained that workers stayed on the job even when "it's like ovens in here." In winter, with no heat in the building, workers performed assembly welding jobs "in overcoats and gloves." Speaking generally, he said,

Table 4.6. Grievances per 1,000 Workers at Budd-Detroit, by Aggregate Groupings of Grievances, 1962–1987

Year	Discharges and discipline	"Skilled" (SJ + OC)	"Production" (SW + P&NPJ + JR + OT)	Wage- or pay-related	Health and safety
1962	78	100	144	52	55
1963	74	147	225	55	45
1964	83	126	209	36	60
1965	121	76	190	30	33
1966	95	118	190	20	26
1967	61	63	72	39	17
1968	96	25	45	17	6
1969	88	40	69	14	11
1970	102	71	107	28	12
1971	85	67	80	21	9
1972	87	76	77	22	11
1973	155	58	51	9	7
1974	144	52	56	8	10
1975	128	106	80	9	10
1976	152	36	24	7	4
1977	250	41	34	11	8
1978	258	30	34	12	5
1979	178	29	38	7	11
1980	91	91	62	13	8
1981	71	59	53	9	3
1982	95	39	118	11	4
1983	84	65	35	8	5
1984	67	71	175	7	6
1985	142	220	109	33	61
1986	128	76	43	10	13
1987	110	138	78	16	36

Source: Author's calculations from company records.

> You have people here who are really afraid of losing their jobs. . . . You can't get that unity that you need to make a . . . strong statement—about anything. . . . They say, "We walking out today? Man, I can't afford to walk out." If there's a good reason, you can't afford not to leave. But . . . these people [are] not leaving here.

In the 1980s, the labor market, in which Budd's middle-aged workers faced little prospect of gaining equivalent jobs, helped ensure workers' compliance on the job. A once-militant press operator with seventeen years seniority and a sixth-grade education explained:

> You got to have a high school education now to get a job. You got to have work experience now to get a job. You ain't got work experience and all that other stuff, they don't want you. You be out there on the streets on the welfare rolls or behind a gun. And they're neither one of them no good.

Figure 4.2 Grievances by Major Type at Budd-Detroit, 1961–1987

Source: Author's calculations from company records.

Job security fears were particularly great at Budd-Detroit among moderate-seniority workers who had been laid off for extended periods of time in the early 1980s recession. More educated and ambitious workers in this group expressed the strongest antagonism toward the local union. With a perspective similar to Sabel's (1982) "would-be craftsmen," these workers felt that the union jeopardized plant survival by protecting poorly performing workers and that the union hurt them as individuals by enforcing seniority principles that made it harder for them to obtain more challenging and secure positions in a restructured workplace. Some moderate-seniority blacks were caught between the collective, protective responsibilities of an informal leader and more self-interested support for work reorganization that might help them as individuals but threaten higher-seniority workers. Overall, would-be craftsmen were now more prominent in the plant than the informal leaders and shop stewards who had historically orchestrated the imposition of collective constraints on the company.

The erosion of collective action and the emergence of would-be craftsmen did not mean that Budd-Detroit managers had things all their own way as they sought to establish teamwork and worker cooperation in response to competitive pressure and new demands from their customers. As indicated by the rise in nondisciplinary grievances filed by production workers in the

1980s, workers and union officials resisted what they saw as company attempts to change longstanding work rules and customs unilaterally (table 4.6). Collective action, including slowdowns, continued in some departments over quotas and other matters, albeit in more covert forms and with the cooperation of smaller fractions of affected workers.

In summary, the history of the Budd-Detroit plant differs fundamentally from standard interpretations of postwar U.S. auto industrial relations. Until the early 1960s, Budd's highly decentralized management structure and quota system nurtured cohesive work groups and frequent bargaining between workers and their representatives over work standards and a wide range of other subjects. After that date, industrial relations managers forced production workers to abandon the use of work stoppages to gain shopfloor concessions and to process their complaints through the grievance procedure. Although industrial relations managers sought to mimic General Motors and Ford, however, the result in Budd's technological and historical context was different. Budd's continued reliance on quotas to induce high levels of effort in physically demanding production jobs sustained a tradition of periodic slowdowns and struggles over the establishment or revision of the quota.

Only in the 1980s, in an unfavorable economic and political context, did collective action get driven underground. As this change occurred and the plant's technology aged, some groups ended up working until the end of the day: downtime, the perception that the quota was unattainable, or conflict and discontent among the workforce impeded finishing early. Consistent with Bélanger's (1989) analysis of the efficacy of group quota systems, however, that workers were on the job a higher proportion of the time may have done little to improve plant performance. On days or in groups in which the goal of finishing early seemed elusive, productivity lagged early in the shift, as did cooperation to solve downtime problems among workers and between them and supervisors.

Labor Relations at Budd-Kitchener

Labor relations throughout Budd's smaller and less diversified Kitchener, Ontario, plant have always been more uniform than in the sprawling, multistory Detroit complex. Budd-Kitchener's labor history divides roughly into three periods: 1967 to 1974; 1975 to 1979; and late 1979 to the end of the period discussed in this chapter (1988).

Kitchener opened under an extremely aggressive production management team that sought to intimidate workers into increasing their effort without demanding higher piece rates. By the mid-1970s, this approach helped breed a militant shopfloor union and precipitate a rash of work stoppages as the balance of power shifted toward workers. Despite company attempts in this second period to remove grievance settlement from the shopfloor and take a firm line against pressure tactics, economic expansion and a major sole-source contract made management vulnerable. Workers learned that procedural channels produced little response but that direct action yielded immediate attention. The auto recession brought on the third stage in the plant's labor history. As the workforce began a decline from three thousand to a low of six hundred, and the plant faced the possibility of closure, management and the union agreed to a shopfloor cease-fire. Wildcats, walkouts, and sitdowns dwindled. By the mid-1980s, stable collective patterns of conflict resolution had evolved that included occasional use of less drastic collective action.

Budd's plant in Kitchener, Ontario, was the first major investment in Canada after the signing of the U.S.-Canada Auto Pact in 1965. The pact eliminated tariffs on most auto products crossing the U.S.-Canada border and fully integrated the industries in the two countries.[14] As a result of the labor problems at its existing quota and piece-rate plants, Budd-Canada's first president, American Jim McNeal (later Budd's CEO), advocated operating the new plant on a day rate and trying to impose a steady work pace technically and managerially. The company's older, production-oriented management, however, continued to favor piece rates because they were "somewhat self-regulating and needed less supervisors and less sophisticated management" (interview with McNeal, Nov. 1988). Using piece rates had also enabled company operations in Philadelphia and Gary, Indiana, to achieve high levels of output on physically-demanding frame jobs.

Plant management combined incentive pay with other strategies designed to induce high effort and output levels that reduced fixed costs while containing labor costs per part. Though few in number, supervisors—selected in part because they were physically intimidating—and the threat of suspension, firing, or being placed on more difficult or less financially rewarding jobs reinforced the attempt to ensure high output at modest rates per piece.[15] Hourly lead hands assisted supervisors and dealt with minor maintenance and other problems that threatened to slow down production.

The plant hired a strong, young workforce to perform its stamping and assembly jobs. A third of these workers were immigrants, and another 15 percent were internal Canadian migrants. The immigrants' interest in maximizing their short-term earnings helped the company achieve high piece rates. Especially at a plant that soon had among the highest-paid manufacturing jobs in the area, the immigrants were also less likely to challenge the company's autocratic management. In the short run, despite a top corporate decision to recognize the UAW voluntarily,[16] autocratic local management and workforce fear and inexperience discouraged workers from challenging the company collectively.

Budd-Canada's first manufacturing manager, Darwin Clay, set the tone of labor relations at Kitchener in its early days. On the one hand, Clay did the job for which he was hired. He helped establish high production norms that surprised even top company management. Filtered through two decades of shopfloor conflict and rising union strength, the norms established initially helped make Kitchener Budd's most profitable North American operation even into the late 1980s. On the other hand, even after two decades, the collective memory of Clay's aggressive approach sustained solidarity against management among Kitchener's workers.

For high-seniority workers interviewed in 1986, one incident involving Clay symbolized the nature of plant management in its early years. The incident surrounded a dispute about overtime pay on Sunday. When the union refused to concede the issue, Clay instructed a foreman to take the plant chairman, a committeeman, and a third official outside the plant. At that time, union officials did not have the right to spend full-time on union business and could be reassigned to different jobs daily. They could not refuse a direct order without the risk of being fired. Clay instructed the three men to use shovels sawed off at the handle to clear snow three feet deep from plant walkways for two and a half to three days.

Clay's approach shaped that of plant supervisors before and after he left in 1971. Several production workers hired before the union grew strong in the mid-1970s had personal stories of intimidation. A union steward described his first day of work:

> I went on line 13, right from Newfoundland, didn't know what a press was.
> . . . I worked with guys working here for six months, eight months, that
> knew how to work. . . . So [the foreman] says to me, "listen, Newfy,
> you better keep up." . . . I worked so hard that I couldn't open my eyes, I
> was just soaked in sweat . . . I'd force myself to get them open enough to
> get the part in. He walked over, he said, "Listen, you stupid Newfy.
> You can't work any better than that, I'll fire you."

While Darwin Clay's departure ushered in an era of more liberal plant management, the hostile character of shopfloor relations established during his tenure continued. By 1973 and 1974, as the influx of workers hired during a 1971 expansion started to get to know one another, the balance of power on the shopfloor began to shift. Piece rates and self-pacing nurtured the same collective traditions that they had at other Budd plants. The youth of the workforce also made it more willing to resort to collective action. Many of these employees were single or without children in the mid- to late 1970s.

At first, the workers' reaction to the tight rates and autocratic management was confined to slowdowns or other hard-to-detect actions by individuals or small groups of workers, undertaken to pass the day, vary the work pace, or increase their earnings.[17] By 1973 and 1974, however, worker frustration about supervisory harassment, favoritism in the allocation of overtime, violation of seniority-based job rights, and an ineffective grievance procedure broke out into small-scale sectional work stoppages.

By August 1974, according to company records, local action snowballed into the plant's first major wildcat, an eight-day stoppage the proximate cause of which was a dispute over health insurance deductions. After this, sitdowns, walkouts, and wildcats became more regular events (table 4.7).

In 1976, to help it reestablish control at Kitchener, corporate manage-

Table 4.7. *Work Stoppages at Budd-Kitchener, 1974–1987*

By Source of Dispute

Year	Humidex[a]	Discipline	Incentive	Safety	Other	Total
1974	0	0	0	0	1	1
1975	0	3	0	3	3	6
1976	8	3	14	0	10	38
1977	2	0	13	0	2	17
1978	22	7	14	6	19	68
1979	0	1	12	4	10	27
1980	0	0	0	0	0	0
1981	0	0	4	1	1	6
1982						
1983						
1984						
1985	0	0	0	0	0	0
1986	0	0	0	0	1	1
1987	0	0	1	0	0	1

By Type of Dispute

Year	Sitdowns	Walkouts[b]	Wildcats	Total
1974	0	0	1	1
1975	5	0	1	6
1976	26	11	1	38
1977	15	1	1	17
1978	34	30	4	68
1979	23	3	1	27
1980	0	0	0	0
1981	6	0	0	6
1982		0	0	
1983		0	0	
1984		0	0	
1985	0	0	0	0
1986	1	0	0	1
1987	1	0	0	1

Sources: 1974–81, company records; 1982–87, author's estimates.

[a]Stoppages over the temperature and humidity in the plant.

[b]Incidents in which a group of workers left the plant over a dispute with management.

[c]Incidents in which workers picketed the next shift and therefore the whole plant went on strike.

[d]No entry indicates lack of data.

ment at Budd hired Steve Nash, who had earned a reputation for toughness at the McDonnell-Douglas plant in Malton, Ontario, with its militant UAW local. Nash sought to impose a version of the GM approach. He deprived foremen of the power to settle grievances on the shopfloor. He also issued a series of labor relations bulletins emphasizing plant rules on tardiness, relief time, reading newspapers in the plant, making emergency phone calls, and the like.

At least until 1979, the conditions under which Nash's approach would work did not exist. Heavy demands for frames and other stampings translated into high profits, which made the company reluctant to leave customers short of parts and able to afford concessions on rates. From 1975 to 1979, Kitchener was the sole supplier of the Ford Torino frame. Extensive overtime to meet high demand further reduced the money worries of the young workforce. Low unemployment in Kitchener-Waterloo and the plant's expansion to 3,200 employees contributed to the escalation of shopfloor conflict in two ways. Workers fired could find jobs across town at Lear-Siegler, Butler Manufacturing, or other plants. In addition, as one worker reported, Budd "was just desperate for people and would hire anybody. Some of these people were pretty weird and wonderful." A substantial number of motorcycle club members joined the plant. So did workers attracted by both Budd's area-high wages and by its reputation for confrontation on the job. Drugs, some of them hard, also entered the plant in volume for the first time in the late 1970s. During the spate of stoppages in this period, Kitchener's workforce became known locally and throughout the Canadian UAW as "the Budd animals"—a badge of honor or dishonor depending on who used it.

The basic issue underlying the spate of work stoppages at Kitchener in the last part of the 1970s recalls events at Detroit in the 1960s. As at Detroit, the labor relations department insisted that supervisors should pass grievances on, rather than negotiate, a settlement. In this way, Nash sought to avoid setting undesirable precedents and to reestablish consistency in shopfloor customs throughout the plant. Unlike Detroit managers, however, when workers did follow procedure, Nash rarely made tactical concessions. As a result, workers often found the grievance channel slow and backlogged. While grievances brought few results, workers found that halting production got their problems addressed quickly. Budd's economic situation and the collective confidence of the workforce left plant managers reluctant to use the ultimate sanction for interruptions of production. Firing employees for leading direct action risked prolonged battles that the company could ill afford.

Managers did suspend workers on occasion for their role in precipitating stoppages.[18] As at other plants, during wildcats, the company formally refused to bargain until workers went back on the job. But experience taught workers a different lesson. Work stoppages led the company to take seriously demands that otherwise went unaddressed. Despite Canada's legal prohibition on mid-contract strikes, workers learned, as one press operator said, that "the only way the company listened is when you're talking from Homer Watson [Boulevard in front of the plant gate]. Then they'd listen real good."

Company records indicate that a variety of substantive issues contributed to the spate of work stoppages: incentive rates,[19] heat and humidity in the plant, safety, discipline, and "supervisory harassment." As work group leverage grew, some supervisors began to use more cooperative approaches to achieve output goals. Any tendencies toward pragmatic cooperation, however, were overwhelmed by the general atmosphere of hostility. More than at Budd-Detroit in the mid-1960s, open warfare superseded structured bargaining. By 1978 and 1979, routine factory events could reignite the smoldering feelings of rebellion on the shopfloor. The official union leadership had progressively less control over shopfloor eruptions.

The recession that began in 1979 and Budd's loss of contracts as their customers started using unitized bodies instead of frames for large cars brought the conflict at Budd-Kitchener to a head. On three occasions after wildcats between October 31, 1978, and September 1979, the company asked the Ontario Labor Relations Board (OLRB) for a cease-and-desist order and to find the union in violation of the collective agreement and the Ontario Labor Relations Act. On the third occasion, the OLRB recommended that the two parties participate in a four-and-a-half day mediation effort called Relationship by Objectives (RBO). Faced with the prospect of workers losing jobs and union officials going to jail, the local and regional leadership of the union agreed. Forty-three members of the formal and informal union leadership and forty-three floor and staff managers—all the "power centers" in the plant, according to Hugh Sloan (of Watergate fame), then Budd-Canada president—attended the RBO.

Attendees say the RBO established some mutual understanding between foremen and supervisors. In 1981, however, the ongoing labor-management committees set up at the RBO stopped meeting. With employment recovering slightly, six sitdowns took place. They stopped again after a further decline in employment. Together with the aging of the workforce and the permanent layoff of some of the wilder young militants, this decline ushered in a more enduring stability.

By the second half of the 1980s, conflict resolution at the plant was characterized by less volatile struggles over rates. All three of the production areas from which workers were interviewed in the summer of 1986 had recently experienced a fairly explicit slowdown concluded by a renegotiation of the rate. In a truck frame assembly area, the slowdown lasted a year. In March 1987, workers on one press line sat down during a dispute about the incentive rate and about safety. In the course of the dispute, the workers exercised their right to stop work under 1976 Ontario health and safety legislation—a right the Detroit union had unsuccessfully attempted to assert in 1969 as management forced local officials to accept that disputes be channeled through the grievance procedure.

A series of attempts by management to tighten in-plant customs—on relief time, leaving early for breaks, working "bell-to-bell," or the temperature and humidity at which workers could work a short day—also precipitated periodic conflict, including brief sitdowns. In one case a few weeks before the 1986 interviews were conducted, a sitdown took place when management attempted to stop workers from spending a customary twenty-minute personal relief time in the plant cafeterias. At a meeting in one assembly area in which management sought to explain the change, according to one worker present,

> There were . . . five or six guys out of . . . fifty huddled around. They were the vocal people. Say, "Hey you guys, where you going? You ought to just get [the production manager] down here." . . . Then all of a sudden . . . there's fifty guys sitting down. There's actually a handful of guys speaking for fifty here. But in this instance, all fifty guys felt they were right.

Within the workforce in 1986–88, informal leaders who had close ties to shop stewards and helped orchestrate collective action in rate fights or conflicts over customs remained a highly visible group. Asked if some workers had more contact with stewards than others, interviewees uniformly responded with their own perspective on the more outspoken workers, often describing outspoken workers using one of the following terms: "shit disturber," "whiner," "spokesman," or "5 percenter."[20] Antiunion would-be craftsmen were not prominent.

The early 1980s recession and increasing competition in the auto industry had somewhat weakened workforce cohesion and collective confidence. Many workers expressed ambivalence toward union officials and toward militant workers, who frequently asked for their steward or complained to supervisors. This ambivalence stemmed from a combination of the diminished benefits that collective action now delivered to workers generally, from a perception that some union officials and informal leaders used their position or social confidence to avoid their share of the work, and from anxiety about long-term job security and lack of confidence that the union's traditional approach would adequately address this issue.

Some workers saw the company as self-consciously attempting to marginalize militants who challenged the company and as depicting them as threats to plant survival. According to the local union president at Kitchener in 1986:

> Well, now they're the whiners, whereas years ago they were the guys that you would have liked to be a steward . . . They're the guys that don't put up with any bullshit and they want to stand up for their rights. And sometimes they'll nitpick. But you can see where they're coming from. It's like the battle of Verdun . . . You've got to fight for every inch of ground.

In this context, conflicts over plantwide customs, such as relief time or the heat and humidity in the plant, reunited the workforce behind militants and in opposition to management.

In sum, despite cracks in the workers' solidarity, Kitchener retained significantly stronger collective traditions than Detroit. Operation under piece rates—which determine workers' incomes as well as effort levels—rather than quotas may be one reason for this difference. Contextual factors also played a major role. While employment at Detroit had been declining since 1950, Kitchener reached its employment peak only in 1979. In part as a consequence, the early 1980s recession hit Detroit after collective traditions had already decayed substantially; it hit Kitchener when the local was at its most militant. The plant's employment histories contributed to the relative youth of the Kitchener workforce and to its narrower age distribution (table 4.4).

In the early 1980s, the youth of the workforce meant that fewer middle-aged workers with families endured long periods of unemployment at Kitchener than at Detroit. The relative youth of the oldest Kitchener workers also meant that in the mid-1980s there was less conflict between seniority and perceived merit—potential would-be craftsmen did not tend to see seniority or the union as an obstacle to their obtaining better jobs at Kitchener. In addition, Kitchener had a more racially and sexually (virtually all male) homogeneous workforce. Although there were some ethnic tensions, there was less visible evidence than at Detroit that they eroded workforce cohesion.[21]

The broader economic context also contributed to the maintenance of collective confidence at Kitchener. In contrast to the Detroit worker who viewed his alternatives as welfare or crime, one Kitchener steward acknowledged worrying about his family but added that if he lost his job, it would not be the end of the world. The relative generosity of Canadian unemployment compensation, the availability of national health care, and the much smaller gap between autoworker and average wages in Canada than the United States made job loss less costly to workers at Kitchener. In the late 1980s autoworkers' wages were roughly 50 percent higher than the manufacturing average in the United States but only 20 percent higher in Canada (Herzenberg 1991, 206, table 4.1).

The overall strategies of the unions in each country may have contributed to the preservation of collective confidence at Kitchener. At Kitchener, workers did not accept that they would have to make major shopfloor concessions to keep their jobs. A national union education campaign in Canada against concessions reinforced this view, particularly among local activists. In Detroit, by contrast, the UAW's decision to cooperate with work reorganization—manifested in a "modern operating [team] agreement" the UAW signed with a Chrysler plant one block away from Budd-Detroit while the 1986 interviews were being conducted—made most workers expect (correctly as it would turn out) that they too would soon have teams. This expectation led Detroit would-be craftsmen to think about how they might gain security and better jobs.

Finally, Canadian national leaders and local Kitchener union leaders appeared to regard direct action as more legitimate than did their counterparts in the United States. At Budd-Kitchener, despite the legal prohibition on work stoppages, local union leaders regarded the direct actions that escalated in 1978 and 1979 as legitimate responses to management provocation.[22] Reflecting this view, the local leadership refused a company offer to drop charges against union officials and let only informal leaders face the legal consequences of violating the OLRB's cease-and-desist order. Instead, the local union hired a bus to take one hundred people to the OLRB's hearing—an unprecedented tactic that contributed to the OLRB's decision to get the two parties to seek mediation. The regional union leadership also regarded local actions as legitimate and encouraged local leaders to accept the mediation effort only for the practical reason that it would help keep them out of jail. This contrasted with the UAW intervention in the United States in which the union helped Budd put an end to the tradition of decentralized worker-supervisor bargaining.

Implications of the Budd Case

Reinterpreting Postwar North American Shopfloor Relations

The history of Budd underlines the incompleteness of Katz's (1985) account[23] of postwar U.S. and Canadian industrial relations in the auto industry because it ignores wide variations in patterns of shopfloor relations based on the extent and purpose of collective action.[24] Confining discussion (for the moment) to direct production workers, evidence from Budd and the major auto assembly companies suggests a need to distinguish between three patterns of relations. Which pattern emerged in a particular group of workers depended most on managerial labor strategy, the effort control system, and broader economic, political, and ideological conditions. Although the typology here emerged out of field research at Budd, it corresponds closely to the heuristic framework described in Edwards (1986, 226–36). The names of the three patterns, introduced below, are taken from Edwards (1986).

The first, or *organizational*, pattern, emerged in the context of highly decentralized labor policies and self-paced work groups under incentive or quota systems—it approximates the state of affairs in many Budd-Detroit departments before 1960. The combination of supervisors or superintendents to whom broad authority over labor matters was delegated, workers' shared interest in raising their income or lowering effort levels, and the vulnerability of an auto supplier to work stoppages or other pressure tactics gave workers and union officials at Budd broad influence over many aspects of work: not only work standards but also job assignments, discipline, hiring, and the allocation of overtime.

The second, or *collective*, pattern emerged in contexts where responsibility for labor relations was more centralized, at the plant or corporate level, but incentive pay or group quotas continued to be used to induce high effort levels. Here, although the effort control system promoted sectional solidarities, limits on supervisory discretion impeded worker and union attempts to make broad inroads into managerial prerogatives. Shopfloor conflict concentrated on the specifics of the effort bargain, rather than on a broader set of managerial controls. This describes relations at Budd-Kitchener from the mid-1970s forward and at many Budd-Detroit departments after the mid-1960s.

The third, or *individualistic*, pattern typically emerged among machine-paced assembly line workers in companies with centralized labor policies. Here, workers shared an interest in lowering job standards but learned that open, large-scale work stoppages would not be successful.[25] Unlike self-paced work groups, machine-paced assembly line workers had no easy collective alternative to shutting down the line—they could not organize slowdowns. As a result, conflict over work standards rapidly disintegrated into individual struggles, which sometimes reinforced rather than overcame individualism. In reallocations of line work, for example, the gains of workers who fought for reduced workloads might come at the expense of workers in neighboring jobs (for one example, see Zabala 1987).

Understanding the role of collective action in different patterns of shopfloor relations in the American auto industry does not deny the critical importance of narrow job classifications, detailed work rules, and the grievance procedure. It does indicate that the role of these defining institutions of "job control" unionism varied with the prevailing pattern of shopfloor relations. In the organizational patterns fostered by Budd's decentralized management before 1960, the collective agreement and grievance procedure were secondary to the process as well as the substance of shopfloor dispute resolution. In the collective patterns at Kitchener and Detroit after 1960, the collective agreement, grievance procedure, and arbitration determined many individual job rights but not the wage-effort bargain. In addition, workers' interest in maximizing output and eliminating downtime made them more willing to perform outside their job definition and to cooperate with one another and with supervisors, making work-rule conflicts less important than in machine-paced settings.

More generally, under collective as well as organizational patterns, collective traditions enabled workers to use pressure tactics to force managers to deal informally with the substance of their complaints or to resolve formal grievances more quickly. In individualistic settings, work rules and the grievance procedure played their largest role. But even here, effort levels and worker and supervisor rights emerged from the interplay of individual worker actions and formal dispute resolution;[26] outcomes depended on the particular leverage of workers and managers as well as the merits, according to the collective agreement and precedent, of particular grievances.

Although shopfloor relations at Budd fell primarily into the collective and organizational patterns, the case leaves open the possibility that individualistic patterns—which most resemble Kochan, Katz, and Mc-Kersie's (1986) analysis—were more common in the postwar North American auto industry. Is the Budd case an exception that proves the rule? On the one hand, the Studebaker and Chrysler cases demonstrate that the decentralized management approach that gave rise to organizational patterns was not unique to Budd, at least through the mid-1950s (on Studebaker, see Amberg 1989). On the other hand, the same cases, as well as Budd-Detroit's own history, indicate that organizational patterns became less common in the United States after that. Although they may have survived in smaller companies, and isolated, autonomous plants of large companies, organizational patterns were probably rare among U.S. direct production workers after 1960.

Collective patterns persisted more widely because managers in a significant but unknown portion of the industry still relied on group quota systems to control effort levels.[27] This was true not only at Budd-Detroit but also at some subassembly operations in Big Three assembly plants (Lippert 1983), in many Big Three captive parts operations (Thomas 1986), and at the rail car manufacturer (and Budd competitor) Bombardier (chap 2).

Whatever the prevalence of group quota systems, it should be kept in mind that assembly workers and self-paced work groups together account for only about half of hourly workers in the auto and parts industries. Like workers in self-paced quota production, most of the other half—primarily indirect production and skilled workers—had more control over their work pace and methods than machine-paced workers. In the case of skilled workers, interviews at Budd indicate that this fact expressed itself collectively and gave workers and stewards the autonomy and control characteristic of organizational patterns of shopfloor relations even into the 1980s (Herzenberg 1991, 407–11).[28] In sum, the collective and organizational patterns are not mere footnotes in the context of largely individualistic patterns of relations.[29]

Having argued that a framework similar to Edwards's (1986) typology, developed from studies of British factories, applies to North American auto production, it becomes possible to contrast U.S. and British shopfloor relations based on how common individualistic, collective, and organizational patterns were in each country. The insistence of U.S. managers on eliminating mid–contract work stoppages and minimizing supervisory discretion to bargain in response to pressure tactics did make it harder for workers outside the skilled trades to climb to the organizational peak of Edwards's typology. The elimination of large-scale work stoppages also forestalled the development of collective patterns among most machine-paced U.S. workers. In Britain, the absence of central union or legal support for firm discipline against wildcatters permitted the development of collective patterns among machine-paced workers even in U.S.-owned auto assemblers such as Ford (Beynon 1984).

Collective Action and the Divergence in U.S. and Canadian Industrial Relations

Is the difference in the strength of the collective traditions at Budd-Detroit and at Kitchener in the 1980s indicative of greater militance in Canada generally? The tentative answer appears to be that generalizations can be made but that the difference in the strength of the collective traditions between the United States and Canada was small—significantly smaller than the variation in the strength of such traditions within each country. Evidence that the Canadian collective tradition is somewhat stronger comes from national strike data: the number of strikes per worker in the Canadian transport sector increased relative to the number in the U.S. motor vehicle and equipment industry from roughly 4:3 in the 1950s, to 2.5:1 in the 1960s, to 3.5:1 in the 1970s (calculated from Herzenberg 1991, table 2.4, p. 134 and table 1.2, p. 38).

That Canadian collective traditions were not qualitatively different is to be expected given that the same corporations dominated the auto industry in both the United States and Canada. Consistent with this expectation, the number of Big Three mid–collective agreement strikes reported in national strike statistics for Canada dropped substantially after the first half of the 1950s, roughly following the pattern Jefferys (1986) observed for Chrysler in the United States. Interviews with ex-union officials at Local 444 at the Chrysler plant in Windsor, Canada, confirmed that the tradition of short work stoppages and departmental negotiation with supervisors ended in the 1950s, as it did at Dodge Main, across the Detroit River. The drift toward individualistic patterns of shopfloor relations did take place more gradually at Chrysler in Windsor. In addition, Chrysler's persistent demand for more production in the mid- to late 1970s led to the partial reemergence of departmental deal-making between supervisors and union representatives in parts of the Chrysler-Windsor engine plant.[30]

To the modest extent that one can generalize from the Budd case, and that collective traditions did endure in Canada more than the United States, managerial labor strategy, technology, and the effort control system were probably not the primary reasons. Compared with the United States, Canada had a disproportionate share of machine-paced assembly production conducive to individualistic patterns, in part as a consequence of Auto Pact assembly company commitments to produce in Canada. Before the Auto Pact, it is true, Canada's small, tariff-protected industry, had older technologies and produced large numbers of autos in low volume, which may have facilitated the preservation of collective patterns of workplace organization. In addition, Canadian nationalism, and a shared resentment of high-level U.S. managers, may have led, in some circumstances, to informal alliances between Canadian managers and union officials and to the preservation of negotiating room for Canadian workers.

More important than technology and management strategy in explaining the apparent persistence of collective traditions in Canadian auto plants were the external factors relevant in the Budd case. From the late 1950s onward, the decentralization of production in the United States reduced employment in the militant core of the auto industry and powerfully reinforced the dampening effect of management's procedural emphasis on collective traditions. By contrast, employment expanded in Canada after the signing of the U.S.-Canada Auto Pact (fig. 4.3). This employment remained concentrated in southern Ontario, often in established locals with strong local unions. The three flagship locals of each of the Big Three in Canada (Ford-Windsor and GM-Oshawa, as well as Chrysler-Windsor) all had more working members in the late 1970s and 1980s than in the late 1950s. As at Budd-Kitchener, Canadian employment expansion in the 1970s and recovery in the 1980s meant that fewer of the workers laid off

Figure 4.3 Employment in the Auto Industry in the United States and Canada, 1926–1990

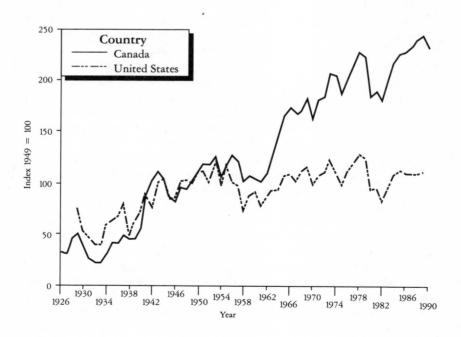

Source: Herzenberg 1991, 38.

for long periods in the early 1980s were thirty-to-forty-year-olds with family obligations; it also reduced the tension between seniority and merit. The racial and sexual homogeneity observed at Budd-Kitchener relative to Budd-Detroit also generalizes to the rest of the Canadian and U.S. auto industries.

Other differences in political and economic context contributed to the persistence of collective traditions in Canada generally as well as at Budd-Kitchener. Such differences include the overall strength of the labor movement in Canada, the smaller gap between autoworkers' wages and average wages in Canada, the existence of a labor-allied political party in Canada, and the relative generosity of social programs (including medical care and unemployment insurance) in Canada.

A final contrast between the United States and Canada that is informed by the Budd case concerns the attitude of union leaders toward direct action. Union leaders in the United States seemed to have a deeper normative commitment to following the grievance procedure. In the Budd case, this was clearest in regional director George Merrelli's pejorative description of Budd-Detroit in the late 1950s as "chaos."

One possibility is that the attitudes of Canadian and U.S. union leaders toward direct action grew out of the process of UAW formation in each country and, in particular, differences in state policy and the character of the workforce in each country in the 1930s and 1940s (Herzenberg 1990). In the United States, the government initially facilitated union formation through the passage of the 1935 Wagner Act. During World War II, the War Labor Board's promotion of union security in exchange for the no-strike pledge gave a generation of labor leaders experience in applying the grievance procedure and arbitration process to the resolution of shopfloor disputes. In Merrelli's case and more generally, the commitment of UAW leaders to the grievance procedure grew in part out of their role in inventing it.

In Canada, by contrast, the federal government did not enact its equivalent of the Wagner Act until 1944 (Huxley, Kettler, and Struthers 1986). While the U.S. government encouraged employers to make a tactical retreat from staunch anti-unionism, Canadian government policy prolonged the period of open conflict preceding the regularization of collective bargaining under industrial unions. As a result, Canadian union leaders did not go through the incorporating experience of applying the grievance and arbitration process during the war. In addition, the role of political mobilization and direct action in winning legislative support for union formation, and in winning union security in a critical postwar strike at Ford-Windsor, taught Canadian union leaders an enduring lesson in the importance of direct action to union power.

The lessons that U.S. and Canadian unions took from the wartime experience reinforced a preexisting difference that reflected the relative importance of British and Irish leaders within their ranks. Recent Anglo-

Gaelic emigrés to North America had often had contact back home with radical politics and the efforts of British shop stewards to wrest more control from management, and more autonomy within their unions. Based on his study of the formation of the UAW in Michigan, Steve Babson (1989a, 712) contrasts their views with those of American-born leaders.

> American-born leaders . . . generally put more trust in procedural actions . . . while Anglo-Gaelic leaders favored disciplined Direct Action. This did not mean that Anglo-Gaelic leaders counterposed Direct Action *against* procedural action [but] . . . something more subtle: a recognition that Direct Action could strengthen the union's position in procedural action, while procedural action could protect and ratify the gains of Direct Action. Imbalance in either direction could weaken the union. Excessive reliance on procedural actions could attenuate the capacity and will for Direct Action, and make the union overly dependent on a legalistic process where lawyers and government regulators defined the issues . . . Excessive use of Direct Action could exhaust membership and public support, and provoke extreme countermeasures from employers and the State. (see also Robinson 1990, 374–76)

In the United States, first-generation Anglo-Gaelic immigrants make up only 2 percent of the Michigan workforce, but as Babson (1989a) demonstrates, they had a powerful impact on the structure of the UAW within plants and at the national level. Nonetheless, over time, the influence of these experienced unionists, often skilled workers, was diluted by the influence of American-born leaders and rural European "peasant" immigrants seeking more limited checks on management in the plants. In Canada, there were six to seven times as many Anglo-Gaelic first-generation immigrants as in the United States. Together with a wartime experience that reinforced the importance of direct action, this phenomenon helped root a much more pragmatic view of procedure within Canada. This view was more conducive to the preservation of the kinds of traditions observed at Budd-Kitchener. In sum, if Canadian unionism is shifted slightly toward the British norm in the strength of its collective traditions, it is partly because it was more heavily influenced by British traditions at the outset.

5

Bargaining Regimes and the Social Reorganization of Production: The Case of General Motors in Austria and Germany

Karen Shire

The uneven diffusion by the General Motors Corporation of its team concept for reorganizing production is typically explained by reference to a "dual strategy of management" thesis, based on differences in labor relations at old and new factories (Katz 1988; Kochan, Katz, and McKersie 1986). European scholars and trade union officials have picked up the same thesis in explaining the contrast between the model teamwork organization introduced at the Austrian subsidiaries of General Motors–Europe and the more conflictual and protracted negotiations for a similar teamwork organization at the older German subsidiary (Kohl 1988; Malsch 1988). In the European cases, however, the fact that the production facilities are located in different countries raises the question of how national context influences firm-level organizational change, a question obscured when firm-level characteristics such as "old versus new factory" become the center of explanation. A related problem with the "dual strategy" thesis is that it implies that understanding management intentions is the most important key to explaining differences in workplace organizational change. Yet in most advanced industrial countries managers are not free to reorganize production as they or their headquarters please but must do so through varying degrees of negotiation with local or industry-level labor representatives.[1] The reorganization of production is never the direct result of a management strategy but mediated by a process of negotiation and adaptation within different national and institutional contexts.

In this chapter I compare the introduction of teamwork at General Motors' subsidiaries in Austria and Germany. This choice of cases is unique in that the firms share an unusually wide range of environmental characteristics: there are strong similarities in works council legislation, collective bargaining practices, vocational training systems, and the occupational structure of labor markets. All these institutional factors seem to present management with a similar context of opportunities and constraints in reorganizing production. What makes a comparison of General Motors in Germany and Austria particularly worthwhile is a cleavage of another sort—in the *network* of institutions of trade union bargaining. By examining how the corporate-level team concept of General Motors is filtered through two different societal networks of industrial relations, this study explores how the connection of workplace representation and bargaining to the structure of industrial relations shapes new organizations of production.

Most industrial relations research on the reorganization of work has tended to focus on the primarily technical dimension of changes in the division of labor, especially the integration of indirect (craft, skilled) and direct (un- or semiskilled) production jobs (Jürgens, Malsch, and Dohse 1989). Teamwork also has implications, however, for the structure of authority in production and the balance of power between labor and management. From management's perspective, the expected social contributions are the rationale for many of the details of a new work organization. For example, in a presentation to a group of Austrian trade unionists, one General Motors manager explained the company's teamwork strategy in explicitly social terms:

> It is now clear that competitive success is fundamentally secured through social innovations, i.e., through people, the employees. That means that without participating employees, without employees who are included in running the company, it can't be done since no company, especially in the automobile industry, can expect to hold any advantage over the competition with technological or economic measures alone.

In this chapter the focus is on the social dimension of innovations in the reorganization of work; in other words, how changes in production organization affect the structure of relations between managers, local labor representatives, supervisors, and workers. In the first part of this chapter, a model of industrial relations bargaining regimes in Austria and Germany is developed in order to conceptualize the context within which the negotiation of teamwork in the two countries can be compared. In the second part, three elements of teamwork relevant for social relations are analyzed: the formation of teams with a degree of autonomy from supervision, the creation of joint labor-management consultation committees, and the introduction of pay-for-knowledge wage systems. The last dimension is often a topic of studies of changes in the technical division of labor, particularly the integration of direct and indirect labor through new production concepts. But pay-for-knowledge wage systems also have consequences for worker mobility within and between firms and for who controls and receives production knowledge, and thus for union regulation of labor markets and the balance of labor and management control over the terms and conditions of employment. The social consequences of technical innovations in wage structure are complex, and the pay-for-knowledge wage system as part of the social organization of teamwork is given more lengthy treatment for this reason. The final part of the chapter discusses how variations along all these elements of the teamwork design—team autonomy, joint consultation, pay for knowledge—are related to differences in union regulation of workplace bargaining in Austria and Germany.

Social Democratic and Industrial Democratic Regimes

More than any other pair of European trade union movements, Austrian and German labor organizations share a sequence of historical developmental characteristics. From the late 1800s through the first republics established after World War I, similarities in Austrian and German political formation and industrialization conditioned the emergence of similar ideological and institutional legacies, most importantly the idea of economic democracy and institutions of works council codetermination. After 1945, both labor movements reorganized according to a model of politically inclusive and industrially concentrated "unitary trade unions" (*Einheitsgewerkschaften*) (Pelinka 1980). Austrian and German works council laws are nearly identical, and rather than introducing "dualism" into workplace representation (trade union and legal representation), works councils in both countries have developed into "quasi-union bodies" (Pelinka 1980; Streeck 1984a). In the post–World War II period, however, differences in the foreign occupations of these countries, and coinciding developments in industrial structure and political structure, led to a pivotal difference in how trade unions became institutionally integrated.

The most important aspect of institutional networks for the negotiation of work reorganization is the presence in Germany of an integrative mechanism between workplace bargaining and industry-level collective bargaining. By comparison, there is no such institutional link between these levels in Austrian industrial relations. German union officials have a legally guaranteed right to be represented on company boards of directors (*Aufsichtsräte*) of all large enterprises.[2] Though union officials on company boards have not been able to exercise much actual influence over company decisions, this level of representation is important nonetheless because it gives the external union in Germany autonomous access to company information and intensifies communication with local labor representatives, who also sit on the board. Representation on company boards of directors thereby contributes to the ability of German unions to regulate local workplace bargaining actively.

In contrast, Austrian union officials have no such mechanism, but, as has been well documented by studies from the neo-corporatist perspective, union officials are directly represented within the Austrian party system (especially in the Social Democratic party) and political institutions (through the Chambers of Labor in federal and national state administrations and parity representation of chambers within ministries) (Marin 1982; Lehmbruch 1967). Although Austrian unions are relatively detached from workplace bargaining, their participation at the societal level in macroeconomic policy-making is far more extensive than has been possible in Germany.

The contrast between institutional networks of industrial relations in Germany and Austria can be conceptualized as two models of industrial relations *bargaining regimes*: social democratic regimes and industrial democratic regimes. Figure 5.1 illustrates this model by contrasting the levels of bargaining and the networks linking levels for the cases of industrial relations in Austria and Germany.

This contrast in bargaining institutions and networks has its origins in alternative developments in the structure of trade union representation in politics and industry, in norms generated about the role of trade unions in society, and in practices of collective bargaining developed within the bounds of legitimate representation and participation. The German and Austrian cases display mutually reciprocal limits to the extension of trade union bargaining into unconnected levels of representation and participation. In the Austrian case, union political representation has so far depended on a social consensus that union codetermination not extend to private enterprise. The extension of German union participation into the political sphere has been limited by the social democratic party's failure to enter government until the mid-1960s and thereafter by norms regulating private-interest representation in government. Austrian union executives

Figure 5.1. Model of Social Democratic and Industrial Democratic Trade Union Bargaining Regimes, Applied to Austria and Germany

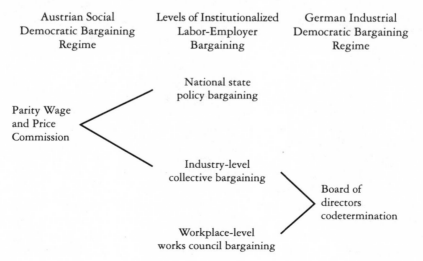

wield direct political influence by wearing a number of official hats, including those of party executives, parliamentarians, ministers in government, and officials of the federal or state-level Chambers of Labor (Lachs 1976). In Germany, overlaps in party and union offices are not legitimate, and the German *Parteidemokratie* does not afford to labor anywhere near the internal party influence enjoyed by Austrian trade unionists. German unions have instead focused on extending representation at the company level, where their claims to codetermination at the board level have never been fully accepted by employers and where, as a result, workplace negotiations are more overtly conflictual.[3]

Events in the 1970s served to sharpen the contours of the postwar social accommodation of trade union political power in Austria and company-level representation in Germany.[4] After the German Social Democratic party entered a coalition government in 1966, German trade union officials invited to fill political posts were expected to resign their union titles. But the inclusion of even ex-union officials in government posts provoked accusations of building a "trade union state" (Markovits 1986).

A similar but reverse situation occurred in Austria when a reform of labor law was proposed that would have allowed for the election of union officials to company boards of directors in the private sector. Immediately, employers protested that unions were attempting to extend their influence over national economic policy into the workplace. Rather than risk the balance of power at the societal level, the Austrian union federation withdrew this labor law reform demand (Misslbeck 1983). By the end of the 1970s, it was clear that codetermination in Austria meant societal-level participation, whereas it signaled greater enterprise-level participation in Germany.[5]

The development of collective bargaining in Austria and Germany since 1945 also differentiates these cases of social democratic and industrial democratic bargaining regimes. In Austria, collective bargaining is embedded in an institutional structure of political exchange wherein the Austrian union federation has acted to regulate economywide wages set at a rate that can accommodate the cost restraints of the high proportion of small and medium-sized firms in the private sector of industry. Wage bargaining is nationally regulated through the bipartite wage commission within the Parity Wage and Price Commission, which also operates as a mechanism for linking industry-level collective bargaining with union participation in state macroeconomic and social policy-making. Yet, despite the seemingly centralized appearance of wage determination in Austria, wage supplements negotiated at the local firm level play an important role in wage determination, and high wage drift reflects this relative decentralization in wage bargaining (Marin 1982, 1985; Traxler 1982).[6]

German collective bargaining appears less centralized than the Austrian structure, since the national federation has no formal legal bargaining authority. Wage increases are coordinated horizontally, however, through

the "vanguard" role of IG Metall (Markovits 1986), and within industries
and regions by strong industrial unions whose wage proposals are aimed at
average firms, not the weakest. Local supplements are common, but wage
drift is kept to a minimum through the imposition of discipline on labor
representatives in more competitive firms. Furthermore, industrial unions
in Germany emphasize normative goals in wage determination far more
than do Austrian unions (Swenson 1989).[7]

The dominant interpretation of the contrast between the Austrian and
German trade unions focuses on the superior strength of Austrian unions
in political exchange, based on factors such as the high centralization of
wage bargaining, the "closeness" of unions to social democratic parties,
and the frequent participation of these parties in government: in other
words, based on a "societal bargaining" pattern of industrial relations
(Cameron 1984; Korpi 1983a). The German case has not been easily
interpreted within the neo-corporatist paradigm, and different authors have
ranked German union strength inconsistently.[8] The concept of bargaining
regimes, however, suggests that German unions, though lacking in indexes
of social democratic bargaining strength, have a greater capacity for
industry-level coordination of workplace bargaining, forming an alternative
model of industrial democratic bargaining strength.

One additional aspect of workplace-level labor representation in Germany, trade union shop representatives (*Vertrauensleute*) intervenes in shaping and adapting work organization strategies, but, as the case study will
demonstrate, in ways consistent with the overall regulatory model of
industrial democratic bargaining. On the basis of this model, it may be
expected that unions in Germany would be more willing and successful
than Austrian unions in influencing workplace negotiations over the
reorganization of production. In the next section this hypothesis is explored
from the perspective of workplace negotiations covering the social dimensions of a new teamwork organization at General Motors' subsidiaries in
Austria and Germany.

Studying Work Organizations

The data for this research were gathered through a total of twenty-one
lengthy open-ended interviews of local works council representatives,
managers active in planning and negotiating the reorganization of work at
General Motors' subsidiaries in Germany (Opel) and Austria (GM-Austria
and Rochester Products Austria [RPA]), trade union representatives, and,
in the Austrian case, government staff and officials.[9] Interviews were
conducted during two time periods, throughout 1988 and in March 1991,
and less extensive follow-ups done in the intervening period.[10] Questions
addressed the negotiation of details of the new teamwork organization: the
autonomy of teams from supervision, the new wage system and how it
would encourage "continuous improvement," and the inclusion and function of a joint labor-management committee.

At the time of the first round of interviews in 1988, a preliminary agreement covering teamwork had been reached at the German subsidiary, but management was in the midst of retracting from several key points. The Austrian teamwork organization had been in operation for four years already. In 1988, the second Austrian plant had just opened and negotiations were still under way over a teamwork design.

By the time of the second round of interviews, in 1991, a company-level agreement on teamwork at Opel-Germany had finally been negotiated and was about to be signed by management and labor representatives. Training of in-house foremen (*Industriemeister*) for their new role under the teamwork organization had begun, and it was possible to observe one training session and to interview several participants informally. Also, a series of decisions concerning a new investment by General Motors in the eastern German town of Eisenach had just been reached, and even at this early stage a number of contrasts were emerging between Eisenach and the Opel and GM-Austria teamwork organization (Shire 1993). In Austria, the teamwork organization at the Rochester Products subsidiary had been in operation for more than two years and it was possible to confirm the course of developments begun at the time of the first round of interviews in 1988. The interval between the two interview periods contributed to producing a more dynamic picture of the negotiations over the social dimensions of teamwork.

Interviews were conducted at a total of four General Motors facilities, two each in Austria and Germany.[11] Age, size, and production information is summarized in table 5.1 for each of the sites. Although important differences in size, age, and production are evident, there was no evidence that these firm characteristics affected the operation of unions or industrial relations or that they were relevant in explaining observed variations in social aspects of teamwork.[12] Size, age, and production are relevant in explaining the timing of social innovations, but the contention here is that variations in the type of innovations eventually introduced is not explained by these factors. Further, both the Austrian and German subsidiaries of General Motors have kept pace with technological developments in automobile manufacturing; both use computer-supported manufacturing systems and electronically guided transport vehicles in some areas of production.[13] At the German plants, information technology is used to guide the production of several different models on one production line. A central computer monitoring system at the GM-Austria engine plant is used to track and diagnose machine downtime.

Managerial Change

According to management's ideal, the General Motors teamwork concept should enable workers from all job and skill classifications within a designated area to work in a team that collectively services and maintains a machine set or process segment of production. Teams are assigned collective

Table 5.1. Basic Information on General Motors' Facilities in Germany and Austria, as of 1992

Location	Subsidiary	Facility	Age	Number of employees	Number of trainees	Number of vocations offered	Production information
Germany	Opel	Rüsselsheim	1862 founded; 1898 begins auto production; 1929–31 becomes 100% subsidiary of General Motors	30,000			full-range of automobile sub- and final assembly
		Bochum	c. 30 years	18,000	(1,400 total)	(22 total)	same as above
Austria	GM-Austria	GM-Austria	12 years	2,700			transmissions and motors
	Rochester Products Austria	Rochester Products Austria	6 years	210	(140 total)	(3 total)	fuel-injection components

responsibility for certain production tasks, for the flow of materials, and for monitoring immediate costs and point-of-production quality and have a degree of autonomy from direct supervision to meet these responsibilities independently in that they figure job rotations and coordinate material supplies and production schedules by themselves.[14] Team meetings, moderated by team leaders, are seen as forums for enhancing internal coordination. Foremen, managers, and anyone else from outside the team attend team meetings only by invitation.

Team autonomy is also supported by changes in the job definition of foremen. Instead of supervising production directly, foremen are in charge of interteam coordination, leaving the teams to oversee direct production matters themselves. For an interim period, foremen remain responsible for team performance, but eventually the teams are expected to internalize responsibility to such an extent that foremen are consulted only in extreme circumstances. In the long run, team autonomy and responsibility should make direct supervision redundant.

The General Motors teamwork design also includes an incentive system to encourage less skilled production workers to extend and deepen their range of expertise by learning the operation of more machines and simple servicing tasks. This element of teamwork is supported by a new pay-for-knowledge wage system and is tied to the goal of integrating direct and indirect work to increase the flexibility of the workforce. Not unlike Japanese employment relations, pay-for-knowledge systems affect skill acquisition in the Austrian and German contexts by transferring the mode of training from formal and externally valid certifications to on-the-job and firm-specific skill learning. In Japan, it has been shown that internal and firm-specific training is a key factor in generating the company loyalty of workers by limiting the transferability of skills and thus providing a powerful material basis for identifying with company goals (Koike 1987). If coupled with recruitment practices oriented toward hiring young, inexperienced, and relatively untrained workers, as is the practice in Japan, the shift to company-specific training may also limit the mobility and thereby strengthen the loyalty of workers in Austria and Germany. At General Motors in Europe, management expects the shift toward on-the-job training to reduce the overall cost of skilled labor and to expand the productive capacities of at least some direct production workers while securing the control of management over the development and flexible deployment of skilled labor.

Another aspect of the General Motors teamwork concept is a change in the institutions of labor-management communication. In most European countries, the multinational has no choice but to fit its teamwork organization into the existing structure of labor-management relations. Instead of attempting to change the existing structure of labor relations directly, under the management teamwork concept, an addition is made to the repertoire of negotiation bodies at the workplace. The General Motors teamwork strategy includes the introduction of joint committees to oversee the reorganization of production and to channel labor's support in the implementation and improvement of the design. In concept and in practice, however, consultation is expanded into other areas and in this sense reflects a strategy for making labor relations more cooperative at a subnegotiation level. This strategy closely resembles joint consultation as it is used in Japanese enterprises: most issues that would come to collective bargaining are first introduced at joint consultation (Inagami 1988, 24–27). Business information may also be made available to lower echelons of the firm, and issues may be discussed that are formally outside the areas covered under collective bargaining. The intention of General Motors management, like that of Japanese managers who use joint consultation bodies, is to intensify the communication between labor and management representatives, but by preempting the formal and legal institutions of enterprise bargaining.

The negotiations and final agreement on these three social relational aspects of teamwork—team autonomy, pay for knowledge, and joint consultation committees—are compared in the following sections for the Austrian and German subsidiaries of the General Motors Corporation in Europe. The differences in the designs of teamwork agreed upon at the German and Austrian subsidiaries are analyzed from the perspective of how management and labor strategies are shaped during negotiations by the context of industrial relations bargaining regimes, in particular, by the degree of external union regulation of workplace bargaining.

Team Autonomy

A fundamental element of the teamwork design is an attempt to delegate responsibility and accountability to teams for a range of immediate production tasks and services. At the core is an adjustment of supervisor-worker relations aimed at gradually minimizing direct supervision by encouraging self-responsibility by production teams for their collective work. The idea, according to an Opel management study, is to try to ensure "that responsibility for plant tasks can be transferred as far as possible toward the bottom" of the organization.

Teamwork also involves a changed role for foremen in production; instead of performing direct supervision, they are gradually resocialized into a "coordinator" role. An autonomous sphere is created for teams within the chain of supervision, to make team members collectively accountable for the functions delegated to the team level.

Managers at the Austrian and German subsidiaries faced similar constraints in developing strategies for reorganizing the foreman's role. Industrialization in Austria and Germany carried with it vestiges of craft-based production organization, not the least important outcome of which was the integration of master tradesmen (*Meister*) into large industrial production organizations. In contrast to North America, foremen in Austria and Germany are the most skilled workers in production, and this role coincides with their function as the first line of supervision. Despite the "newness" of the Austrian factories, the attempt by managers to alter the supervisory role of *Meister* is not made any easier. Nor do German managers have an advantage. An Opel management study makes clear that the teamwork organization will create redundancies among the *Meister*.

The *Meister* role is one-half of the equation for encouraging team autonomy; the other half involves the social design of teams in production. Here there is some contrast between the negotiations in Germany and Austria. Since the beginning, teams at the GM-Austria plant have elected their leaders and have enjoyed an hour a week of official "team meeting" time to plan and coordinate the work in their production areas.[15] At the time of the first round of interviews in 1988, it had already been agreed that teams at the new RPA division would also elect their team leaders.

In contrast, interviews at the German subsidiary revealed a great deal of conflict over the issue of team leader elections. In 1986, tentative agreement had been reached to allow team elections, but in 1988 management was in the midst of retracting in favor of the appointment of supervisory personnel to lead teams and govern team meetings. The turnabout in management's position at Opel was predicated on a difference in the structure of labor representation in the German automobile industry—the practice of electing union shopfloor representatives (*Vertrauensleute*), which number in the hundreds at large plants like Opel's.

Union shop representatives have no formal role in labor relations in Germany, but they do cement communication between workers and works council and between internal and external union representatives. Several Opel management studies warned of the disadvantages to management of employees attempting, "out of purely ideological interests, to nominate *Vertrauensleute* as team leaders." Having already been elected as shop representatives, *Vertrauensleute* were likely to be elected to team leadership positions. The external union and the works council supported this practice[16] (Muster 1988a).

Management conceded this point as part of a series of compromises made during the negotiations, but it balanced its loss in another manner. In 1991, Opel managers agreed that at the new subsidiary in Eisenach, where the same managers were involved in designing a teamwork production organization, team leaders would be appointed by management. According to an Opel manager, two teamwork designs would then be allowed to "compete with each other" on German soil.

Joint Consultation

The implementation of General Motors' team concept is supported through the intensification of labor-management communication, the mechanism for which is the institution of regular joint consultation. Nominally, joint labor-management committees are charged with oversee-ing the implementation and development of team autonomy and the flexibility wage system described in the next section. According to man-agement, however, the committees should sidestep existing forms of labor-management communication by excluding company executive officers and the works council president (i.e., those who engage in formal company-level bargaining under the provisions of works council legislation) from membership on joint committees. Rather than formally extend the role of local works councils, joint committees are designed to intensify labor-management communication at lower echelons of the organization.

Joint committees at the GM-Austria subsidiary have become the corner-stone of labor-management cooperation over the implementation of team-work, but also over a range of other issues. Virtually all local matters that management must eventually negotiate with local labor representatives are first taken up through joint consultation. In effect, final agreements between the works council president and company executives have become ritualized, with the heart of negotiations displaced to consultation at joint committee meetings.[17]

Opel managers refused to create a similar committee at the German subsidiary, despite tentative agreement to do so in 1986. An internal company study recommended that labor representatives be allowed to participate only in management-selected areas, but not necessarily in the formal planning and implementation stages. In response to management, an IG-Metall document proposed that a "steering committee" be included to improve the participation of the local works council in the reorganization process (Muster 1988a). The final agreement, signed in 1991, provides for a series of ad hoc joint committees but nothing comparable to the joint consultation meetings at the Austrian subsidiary (Opel AG 1991a, 1991b).

In the Austrian case, the planning for teamwork organization began well before a works council could be elected. Yet, during the earliest phases of planning, a team of General Motors executives, including Opel managers, visited the headquarters of the Austrian metalworkers union in Vienna to seek the support of labor officials for the teamwork idea.[18] The union sought assurances that teamwork would not undermine the legal rights and responsibilities of the new works council, in exchange for its approval in principle to teamwork. The details were left to be worked out at the enterprise level. Opel managers did not seek the cooperation of IG-Metall, which, according to one manager involved in designing the teamwork organization, already had too much of a voice at the company. Indeed, union officials had involved themselves in the details of the negotiations and had developed a strategy that aimed to transform elements of the teamwork design into a means for extending labor representation and codetermination at the workplace. Austrian works council members and union officials indicated that a similar strategy was never contemplated there, where instead labor representatives described their position as one of accommodation so long as the legal rights of collective bargaining and works council participation were not infringed by teamwork.

Throughout the mid- to late 1980s, the German IG-Metall was engaged in developing an alternative set of *group-work* proposals for the reorganization of production.[19] In communication with the Opel works council (which was also an important participant in union group-work proposals), the union drew up a point-by-point comparison of its group-work proposals and management's teamwork proposals. This union document was first brought to my attention not by the works council but by an Opel manager, who pointed to its existence as the core reason for management's retraction at Opel-Germany of elements of teamwork already implemented at the Austrian subsidiary. The document called joint consultation "the organizational form of works council codetermination" (Muster 1988a) and provoked management to view such a new committee as serving to strengthen the "trade union orientation of the workforce" in a situation where "trade unions have too much to say already."[20] Unlike the Austrian situation, teams and the aspects of production they oversee could fall under too great a trade union influence in Germany.

Pay-for-Knowledge Wage System

The General Motors teamwork idea includes a new wage system, aimed at encouraging job rotation and learning within teams by "paying for knowledge" learned primarily on the job. The consequences for increasing the flexibility of the workforce are obvious. Less attention has been paid to possible consequences for worker and supervisor and labor and management relations.

In the Austrian and German contexts, the GM pay-for-knowledge idea aims at improving management control over the acquisition and distribution of skills among the workforce, thereby sidestepping the more costly practice of depending on formal vocational training as the source of skilled labor. Two versions of the pay-for-knowledge concept have been implemented in Austria. That at Rochester Products Austria comes closest to management's ideal. German managers never attempted to negotiate a similar system, but the 1991 teamwork agreement collapsed forty-two wage categories into ten and standardized the form of payments to skilled and unskilled and semiskilled workers.

There are great complications in comparing the negotiation and introduction of wage systems cross-nationally because forms of remuneration touch upon a wide range of factors that vary at firm and industry levels: union wage determination, vocational training and skill acquisition, personnel policies and recruitment. The Austrian and German cases make an especially valuable comparison in this light because of a number of similarities between most institutional factors. In both countries, wages are determined for each worker through the intersection of broadly defined skill differentials set by industry-level bargaining, company-level cataloging of jobs, and the assignment of jobs to wage levels. When hired, workers receive a job description (connected to a wage group) in the form of an individual employment contract. Furthermore, skills are acquired through a "dual system" of vocational training. In Austria and Germany, adolescents are tracked into the system during secondary school, with the result that nearly everyone except school dropouts receives some form of vocational certification or a university entrance diploma.

Another important similarity is in the recruitment of workers in the automobile industries of these countries. Although GM-Austria was the first large-investment automobile production company in Austria, its recruitment practices resemble those in Germany. In the beginning, metal industry tradespeople were hired from among those rendered unemployed by the closure of a steel firm. Since then, skilled workers have been recruited from the pool of apprentices trained at GM-Austria's internal training facility and are certified by public bodies. Direct production workers are recruited first from the surplus of in-house apprentices for whom no skilled position is available. These workers receive the job description and wage of a semiskilled production worker, and this is put in writing in the individual work contract given each recruit by the employer. If a skilled position becomes available, certified tradespeople waiting in direct production jobs are promoted into it, and their individual contract with the employer is changed accordingly.

The rest of the demand for unskilled and semiskilled production workers is met by recruiting workers from other trades, firms, or industries who are attracted to jobs in the automobile industry because of the lucrative pay and benefits. Without an appropriate certification (which would require a return to vocational training), this last pool of workers cannot advance into skilled jobs; their prospects in the internal labor market are thus limited (Muster 1988b).[21]

These similarities translate into very similar sets of opportunities and constraints for introducing pay-for-knowledge systems at the Austrian and German subsidiaries. Industry-level collective bargaining and the works constitution acts limit the scope and nature of variation at the workplace level. Industrial agreements become the baseline from which supplements may be voluntarily added by management, but there is flexibility in the constitution of wage categories at the firm level, especially when compared with the United States, where obstacles are posed by numerous union-regulated job classifications (Jürgens, Malsch, and Dohse 1989; Katz 1985; Kochan, Katz, and McKersie 1986). Nonetheless, skilled workers have a lot of influence within the German and Austrian trade union movements, and their opposition to collapsing wage rates for skilled labor into the same scale for unskilled and semiskilled workers has only been partially averted at Rochester Products Austria and not at Opel or the GM-Austria engine factory. Yet in both countries, works councils and union leaders are sympathetic to measures that would improve the promotion opportunities and working conditions of unskilled and semiskilled direct production workers. For this reason, labor has accommodated managements' demand that more on-the-job training, minor repairs, and inspection work become tasks for production teams.

Similarities aside, variations were found in the introduction of the pay-for-knowledge wage systems at the Austrian and German subsidiaries. Differences have emerged too between the two Austrian subsidiaries, implying an even stronger shift toward deregulation of workplace bargaining within the context of social democratic industrial relations. At the GM-Austria engine factory where the first agreement on a "pay-for-knowledge" system was reached, the works council opposed a system that would collapse skilled labor into the knowledge wage scale. There are thus separate wage systems for tradespeople and less skilled direct production workers.

At Rochester Products Austria, a pay-for-knowledge system negotiated in 1988 goes beyond the innovation at the first facility and begins to integrate skilled labor into a unitary wage scale, opening the possibility for workers without the appropriate vocational certification to move into skilled jobs through a combination of on-the-job training and short courses. In Germany, management was not committed to a pay-for-knowledge scale, and labor opposed it altogether; instead, an alternative adjustment has been negotiated.

In the place of a pay-for-knowledge system, the German teamwork agreement simplifies the structure of wage grades at the local level by making them congruent with the ten wage grades used in industry-level collective bargaining. As with the other aspects of teamwork, the management at Opel was the first to call into doubt the introduction of a pay-for-knowledge system in the German context. The reason in this case was that tighter external union coordination of wage determination had outpriced the ability of the company to add knowledge premiums to the collectively bargained base wage. Conversely, under the Austrian social democratic bargaining regime, collectively bargained wages are minimums, with the result that there is more maneuverability at the local level for adjustments. German collective bargaining, however, is not over minimums; nonetheless, it may have been possible to adjust local wage supplements at Opel to achieve some knowledge-based wage steps.

This possibility was blocked, however, by the Opel works council, which bargained hard to prevent wage differentials on the basis of team internal knowledge promotion decisions. To begin with, it argued that on-the-job learning should be formally recognized by attaching it to the system of formal vocational education. Management opposed the idea of linking on-the-job training with the traditional system of vocational qualification and certification, complaining that unions want workers to have a certificate for everything they learn. But the central point of the union and works council's opposition to a pay-for-knowledge system was the threat that inequalities would be introduced between team members in violation of trade union norms of wage solidarity. German managers responded by arguing that equal wages for team members would dissolve an important rationale for pay-for-knowledge: the encouragement of peer supervision through the development of a "knowledge" hierarchy within the teams, and with it competition among team members for "knowledge" promotions. In the words of one Opel manager interviewed:

> Wage equality is the most ridiculous thing of all times. . . . What (the trade union) wants is for all members of the group to be paid the same. This is very damaging for the groups because then, namely, they no longer have this pecking order, this internal differentiation, like it is very nicely expressed in Austria in these different wage levels. . . . I'm very against treating everyone equally.[22]

In the end, the new wage system agreed upon in 1991 actually tightened union regulation of wages at the local level, while leaving unresolved the question of on-the-job learning and vocational certification, and it deferred the type of intrateam hierarchy intended by management (Opel AG 1991a).[23]

In Austria, the successful negotiation of two different pay-for-knowledge systems provides a unique opportunity for observing management intentions within a European context of industry-level bargaining and works councils. At the Austrian subsidiaries, management has made clear that the pay-for-knowledge system does not give workers a right to demand further training. It is also not the goal of management to train as many workers as possible to the highest knowledge levels. Rather, management would like to control the number of workers who will be permitted to reach the top skill and wage level, according to the needs of production. At the low-knowledge end of the wage scale, the aim of management and labor is the same: to improve the knowledge of all workers. But the gate would be closed nearing the high-knowledge end, blocking advancement for most workers beyond the "middle-knowledge" range.

The works council at both Austrian facilities has negotiated with management over a "flexibility distribution," a curve of skill levels for the workforce and has, in effect, won the right to codetermine the local skill distribution. According to the GM-Austria works council, the skilled tail of the distribution has been filled out higher than the levels negotiated because there has been a strong demand for workers in the higher "knowledge" brackets. It remains to be seen, however, what the effects will be for those who remain at the "middle-knowledge" level once this demand tapers off.

There is an important difference between the GM-Austria and new

Rochester Products Austria factories that points to the longer-term goals of management regarding the social effects of the pay-for-knowledge system. At the former, the local works council followed an industrial union directive that "skilled work must remain skilled" and refused to subsume indirect production jobs into a pay-for-knowledge system.[24] Thus, there are two separate pay systems in operation: one traditional system, covering skilled tradespeople, and a second pay-for-knowledge system, applied to unskilled and semiskilled workers in production teams. But a concession to management has been made at the second Rochester Products Austria plant, where skilled tradespeople and direct production workers belong to the same teams. This is reflected in a knowledge wage scale that encompasses wage groups at all skill levels and contains a mechanism for allowing unskilled and semiskilled workers to be promoted into the skilled labor wage group. The system has obvious advantages for competent direct production workers, and it is on this basis that the works council at Rochester Products Austria supports the plan.

Longer-term social implications of the Rochester Products system are apparent in the way in which it has affected the recruitment of certified tradespeople. Already in 1988, Austrian managers were planning to halt the hiring of any tradespeople other than those initially employed at Rochester Products and to meet all new demand for skilled labor by upgrading the skills of the unskilled and semiskilled sector of the workforce. Since 1988, no new skilled tradespeople have been recruited, and a select number of the most ambitious and competent members of the unskilled and semiskilled workforce have been promoted into a new occupational category, "skilled production worker" (*Produktionsfacharbeiter*), created at the plant. At the time of the second round of interviews in 1991, about 9 percent of the RPA workforce had become skilled production workers, and, as promised three years earlier, no new skilled tradespeople had been hired.[25]

Skilled production workers at RPA are partially trained on the job and also attend short courses for which they receive documents of completion. Their repertoire of skills, however, is tailored to the company's needs. Unlike tradespeople whose vocational qualifications are certified, skilled production workers at RPA are unlikely to be hired into skilled jobs at other firms. Thus, the central difference between RPA skilled production workers and skilled tradespeople at the same knowledge wage level is that the latter have formal vocational certification, guaranteeing their eligibility for similar jobs at other companies, and preserving their option to exit to the labor market. Quite similar to the situation of Japanese workers trained primarily on the job in firm-specific skills, there is a strong material incentive for RPA skilled production workers to remain loyal to the company. No one in this small pool of skilled production workers had left the firm at the time of the second round of interviews in 1991.

Were on-the-job skill acquisition of this sort generalized, the consequences might be the marginalization of formal vocational education and certification and a reduction in the dependence on external labor markets by workers beyond the point of entry at the lower-knowledge end of the wage scale. This is precisely the sequence that the works council in Germany has, in effect, avoided by arguing that on-the-job learning be integrated into more comprehensive and certified vocational training. For General Motors managers, the success of the pay-for-knowledge system at Rochester Products is measured in economic terms and in the reduction in the ratio of direct to indirect production workers (projected to be from 1:4 to 1:7) and, with it, a labor cost savings estimated at 10 percent. From management's perspective, tying knowledge acquisition to formal vocational training and certification would essentially make all workers "indirect" and highly paid. The works council at GM-Austria has been under pressure from the six hundred skilled tradespeople at the plant not to follow Rochester Products' lead. But, citing the benefits to the low-skill sector of the workforce and the most competent of the semiskilled, the works councils at both plants are united in supporting the integrated pay-for-knowledge system.

Industrial Relations and the Social Reorganization of Work

Despite what they agreed were successful results at the Austrian subsidiary, German managers retracted from each of the dimensions of teamwork related to changing social relations at the workplace: team elections, the use of a joint consultation committee, and the pay-for-knowledge wage system. The "greenfield" character of the Austrian factories was to some extent a more suitable setting for introducing change. But in many respects—the change in the role of foreman, the use of a unitary wage system that combines skilled and unskilled workers—the Austrian subsidiary faces obstacles not unlike those in Germany. Furthermore, even though the German factory is much older and larger, the local works council was overwhelmingly in favor of key elements of the general teamwork concept, including team autonomy, joint labor-management committees, and improving the mobility of less skilled production workers.

By all accounts, German managers were on the road to transferring the Austrian teamwork design as of 1986 when a draft agreement was reached for a new production organization. Thereafter, company studies reveal that at the heart of management's rescission was a careful consideration of a unique "environmental" factor: the greater regulation of company affairs by German trade unions.

The research reported here can contribute to a more nuanced approach to studying how management strategies of organizational change might reshape such environmental factors as industrial relations. To move beyond some of the old debates about the cultural compatibility of organizational structures and practices, it is necessary to develop an understanding of environmental susceptibilities to change affected by the introduction of new production organizations. Where trade union regulation is institutionally embedded in an industrial democratic bargaining regime, managers will have less opportunity to reshape the environment, and the chances are they will be shaped by it. The contrast of the Austrian case suggests that social democratic regimes of bargaining, whose contours have long been considered models of labor strength, may in fact pose fewer constraints on deregulation because of their relative neglect of workplace regulation.

Throughout the study, Austrian and German managers often referred to the contrast between union bargaining in the two countries in explaining their own perceptions of the constraints and opportunities for reorganizing social relations through teamwork. German managers opposed team leader elections and joint committees because they might have extended the ability of external unions to regulate production as well as the terms of employment. Such a threat was not posed in the Austrian context, because of the decentralization of workplace bargaining within the structured network of industrial relations. Works council legislation governing bargaining at the workplace level in Austria and Germany contains very similar provisions. The key difference, however, is that unions are more willing and able to regulate workplace bargaining in Germany than in Austria. Characteristic of bargaining under an industrial democratic regime, the attention paid by external union officials to company affairs in Germany, institutionally supported by the election of union officials to company boards of directors, by the organization of union shop representatives, and by collective bargaining practices, tend toward a regulatory network of industry and workplace levels of labor representation and bargaining. In the case of social democratic bargaining regimes such as the Austrian one, this study suggests a rather ironic conclusion: that managers aiming to reorganize social relations according to their own design may find social democracies more accommodative contexts because of a relative neglect of industrial democratic workplace regulation.

At the time this research was being completed, Austrian managers had begun to overlay a comprehensive "continuous-improvement" suggestion scheme onto the teamwork organization. The works council expressed a great deal of exasperation with "all these new management philosophies" detracting attention from the job of nurturing the autonomous development of production teams. Although Austrian management had gone on to the next step of reorganizing social relations, the works council felt itself alone in its concern for the state of the teamwork organization. Meanwhile, at the societal level, key elements of the Austrian social partnership were disintegrating, calling into question the very basis of union and employer cooperation at the level of the national economy. One Austrian manager interviewed in 1991 speculated on a near future of conflictual labor relations as the balance of power between labor and management at the societal level begins to give way to a new focus by industrial trade unions on the company level. The immediate future will be decisive for the Austrian labor movement, involving a choice between industrial democratic regulation and an Austrian version of Japanese-style enterprise unionism.

6

New Technology and the Process of Labor Regulation: An International Perspective

Anthony E. Smith

During the 1980s, a key theme in workplace relations was the debate on the impact of new technology. This chapter concerns that debate, particularly the effect of national industrial relations on the process of labor regulation at the workplace. It reports the results of studies of technological change in Britain, Canada, Germany, and Italy.

The implications of new technology are generally seen to be considerable; indeed, many commentators argue that they constitute a new industrial revolution. The precise nature of that revolution is the subject of considerable disagreement, however. Labor process writers emphasize the class-based conflict between capital and labor as the driving force behind technological change and identify technology as one means by which management seeks to extend its control over the shopfloor. Writers such as Harry Braverman (1974) tend to see management strategy in one-dimensional and mechanistic terms involving the progressive deskilling of job content through the application of scientific management forms of work design and control. Other contributors to the labor process debate, such as Andrew L. Friedman (1977 and 1990), Michael Burawoy (1979), Richard Edwards (1979), Peter J. Armstrong (1988), and Paul Thompson (1990), offer more sophisticated models, emphasizing the alternative choices that are available to managers in controlling the labor process and the way management strategies are shaped by the "contest for control" between capital and labor. Little significance, however, is attached by labor process writers to the problems of formulating and implementing management strategies. The approach tends to assume that strategies to control the labor process flow unproblematically from overall business strategy and that managements act in unison to pursue a single objective.

In contrast, contingency theory writers advance the proposition that there is no "one best way" to organize and manage production. Rather, different approaches are appropriate to particular situations, depending on a range of "contingent" factors such as product markets, labor markets, organization size, and technology. The work of Joan Woodward (1980) is a classic example of this approach in which "technology" is accorded a primary role as an independent explanatory variable. Woodward's analysis of the relationship between technology (the production system), organization structure (management control systems), and commercial success provides little analytical space for the idea that managerial choice or negotiation with the workforce might be significant influences on the outcomes of change. Rather, the logic of technological progress and commercial requirements means that managers are required to adapt their organization's structure to suit the production system if the organization is to be commercially successful. Similarly, the idea that technological change might involve a conflict of interest between management and labor is not seen as significant.

Still another approach, strategic choice, provides an antidote to the weaknesses of both labor process and contingency perspectives. It is based on the idea that the outcomes of technological change are the products of choice and negotiation. This approach suggests that it is the actions of organization actors—managers, unions, and workforces—at critical junctures in the process of change that are critical in shaping outcomes and not exclusively technological, commercial, or capitalist imperatives.

An important early contribution to this action-based approach is that of John Child (1972), who uses the concept of "strategic choice" as a means of emphasizing the role of managerial choice, rather than technology, in shaping work and organization. This action-based approach has had considerable influence on recent research concerning the introduction of new computing and information technologies (see, for example, Sorge et al. 1983; Wilkinson 1983; Clark et al. 1988; Smith 1991).

Many researchers who have adopted this approach view it as an essential corrective to the inadequacies of the labor process approach and what is seen as the "technological determinism" of writers such as Woodward. In other words, the changes that result from the introduction of new technology are seen to be profoundly affected by the decisions made by managers and the way these are contested by unions and workforces within organizations. (For further analysis of this discussion on the historical context of technology and work, see Clark et al. 1988; Gallie 1988).

Technological change tends to be incremental and piecemeal (see Bijker et al. 1987). For this reason, it obliges management to bring about usually quite small changes in working methods but to do so with inconvenient frequency. In spite of this approach, technological innovation poses a far greater challenge to established controls, with which much industrial sociological study is concerned. Technological innovation requires not the maintenance of existing regulation but a constant process of *reregulation*.

The central challenge for management in achieving economic success is thus to persuade workers to abandon competencies in which they have come to earn their self-esteem at work and to undertake the intimidating challenge of acquiring new competencies. Workers have to learn, repeatedly, to work with new colleagues, to adapt to new work rhythms, and to develop new career and work expectations. As this chapter shows, these adjustments can be made only if management can offer plausible guarantees of successful reregulation in terms of comparable protections.

This chapter attempts to show how fruitful the international comparative approach can be in addressing issues surrounding technological change. Technological change knows no frontiers. Consequently, the way in which it is digested through work regulation in different countries reveals much about their institutional strengths and weaknesses. The chapter traces the processes at work in human interactions. By providing insights into the perceptions and rationales of the actors, it considers much that is crucial in understanding social change, especially the power and dependency relationships that impede or facilitate innovation.

The focus of analysis is a "matched set" of workplaces in three sectors (chemicals, engineering, and finance) so as to identify similarities and differences between the four countries analyzed in the use of new microelectronic technologies. In the first section, the case studies are discussed in the context of a review of the nature and extent of corporatist arrangements, which have been a feature of recent economic and sociological studies of advanced capitalist societies. The second section outlines the salient features of the cases and their national contexts. This section also comments on the methodology adopted. The third and main section discusses the conditions for different types of change. A key factor suggested here is the nature of existing relationships between labor and management. Where participatory mechanisms have prevailed, management is often willing to make concessions to sustain consensus. In light of this empirical material, the conclusions provide a critical review of developments in the new technology debate. Of particular significance is the way in which workers and managers develop specific relationships against a backdrop of capitalist dynamics and pressures.

Labor Regulation in International Perspective: Toward an Analytical Framework

Technological change in the workplace does not occur in isolation from the wider industrial relations environment. In particular, as several chapters in this book show, national frameworks of regulation have major effects on developments at the workplace level. For the present purposes, the likely connections regarding technological change need to be indicated. This is best done with reference to recent theories of corporatism. The key argument is as follows. Where trade unions have high levels of density, and particularly where they are industry-based and strongly centralized within a single confederation, they represent all-encompassing organizations that are able to act in strategic or class terms. Moreover, where such unions also have close relations with social democratic or labor parties that achieve power, they can use political means to achieve many of their demands. The nature of the arguments advanced by various writers varies, however.

Corporatists frequently see the initiative for such developments as emanating from the state, often in terms of a functionalist argument concerning the presumed "needs" of a modern capitalist economy (Poulantzas 1973). That is, "the state may adopt strategies that conflict with those favored by dominant corporate interests but ultimately it acts to reproduce extant economic relationships" (Frenkel 1991, 49). Class analyses typically emphasize the development of union-government relationships as a result of a class or labor movement strategy. A common view propounded by Burawoy (1983), P. K. Edwards (1986), and Hyman (1989a) is that variations in the nature and effective implementation of state policies are explained by reference to changes in class relations and state dynamics. But although some writers claim that such "corporatist" arrangements work against the interests of union members and endanger political democracy (e.g., Panitch 1981), others argue that such arrangements constitute an important vehicle for the advancement of workers' interests (Zeitlin 1985; Hyman 1989a). Thus, involvement in corporatist arrangements need not lead to a dissipation of union organization and power (Korpi 1983a; Frenkel 1991).

Three weaknesses within this literature need to be confronted. These concern the details of national-level union organization, the links between national and local levels, and the tendency to assume that the gains workers achieve from corporatist arrangements emanate directly from the political process.

First, if corporatism is defined as meaning that there are close relationships between the state and union confederations, then it is clear that neither a high union density nor a unified union movement is a necessary precondition. For example, much of the literature ignores the fact that there are a number of union confederations in Germany. Competing views over optimum wage differentials, the shift in the occupational structure in favor of nonmanual groups, and the growing confusion between what constitutes manual and nonmanual work have increased the tensions between the various confederations, although a fairly high degree of cooperation remains. Nevertheless, the four major confederations wield a great deal of influence, and the German Trade Union Federation (DGB) in particular has a close relationship with the state.

Similarly, close relationships between the state and the union confederations exist in Italy, even though union density is low and the union confederations are divided along religious and political lines. The confederations cooperate closely with each other, however, and the union movement has access to the state no matter which party is in power.

In short, what is important is that union confederations should be fairly centralized, and, if there is more than one confederation, the various bodies should cooperate with each other to a significant degree. In these circumstances the confederations become "all-encompassing" organizations capable of acting strategically.

Second, there is the question of the links between national and local levels of trade union organization. While writers such as Alessandro Pizzorno (1978) and Charles Sabel (1981) have noted the tensions that may arise in centralized trade unions involved in corporatist arrangements, the bulk of the corporatist literature subsumes the dynamics of the internal negotiation of order within the blanket notion of centralization. It therefore fails to consider not only the question of the nature of national policy formulation, in which local representatives may play a role, but also the way in which centralized unions may shape lower levels of union organization. Most important, it fails to take into account the coordination of various levels of bargaining.

Third, the corporatist approach focuses on direct outputs of political activity, which bear little direct relevance to the employment relationship. Hence, for example, the issue of structures of authority in the workplace is totally ignored. It is, however, possible to modify the analysis to take account of this and the other weaknesses noted.

It is argued here that centralized and cooperating union confederations can structure the nature of workplace activity, and hence how new technology is addressed, in a number of important ways. The first way is by establishing legislation, national-level agreements, or both that lay down rights concerning local-level bargaining and information relating to such specific issues as new technology and work organization. This approach is more likely to be used when there are centralized rather than decentralized unions. First, it is only in centralized organizations (particularly where employers are organized on a similar basis) that power is located at a level that permits such central agreements and meaningful bargaining with the state. Second, with this type of union structure, there is a long tradition of a wide range of legislation and bargaining at central levels. Thus, new technology tends to be subsumed under conventional patterns of regulation or the distinctive features of technology issues are handled by making relatively small changes to the conventional pattern of labor-management relations. Third, such centralized unions typically have a relatively high degree of coordination between the different levels of union organization, which encourages local representatives to relate their local activities to the general policies of the wider union.

Although centralization and cooperation are important, union density is also important, since it affects the degree of integration between different levels of worker representation. What is particularly striking here is that where union density is high, as in the Scandinavian countries, workplace representation is union-based. Where union density is lower, as in Germany, formal structures tend not to be union-based. Although it is true that key works council positions are held by union activists, their primary commitment within the workplace is to their role of works councillor. This includes an obligation to further peace and also encourages them to adopt a parochial approach to many matters. Of equal importance is that the structure of works councils provides relatively fragile links between the company and establishment levels, and weak relationships between works councillors and the membership.

Relatedly, national-level agreements and legislation tend to be more supportive of trade union or worker influence at local levels where centralized unions have a high level of union membership. Hence, in both Britain and Canada, where union organization is relatively decentralized and the authority of the confederations over member unions is very limited, national agreements are very rare and legislation provides few rights for local negotiation over new technology except for relatively vague rights to information. At the other extreme, in countries such as Sweden and Norway, which have high union densities and centralized trade unions, there is a wide range of legislation and national agreements that provide not only worker and union rights within the workplace but also principles to be followed in the organization of work. In countries with relatively centralized union organizations but with low union densities, as in Germany and Italy, the situation tends to be midway between that of, on the one hand, Britain and Canada and, on the other, Sweden and Norway. Legislation exists, but it primarily provides rights to nonunion forms of representation within the workplace.

In summary, this section has developed a framework to connect theories of the state with workplace and national union organization. Where unions have a considerable degree of central control and union density is high, union confederations are likely to have a more strategic approach to the pursuit of members' interests and to be able to secure national agreements and legislation that provide a basis for local union activity. At the same time, the different levels of union organization are likely to be relatively well integrated, permitting coordinated bargaining at various levels. Consequently, local unions are more likely to achieve greater influence over the strategic aspects of technological change, as well as over its more immediate and direct implications for the wage-effort bargain. Where unions are relatively centralized but have low union densities, the effect of their strategic actions is constrained by their more limited ability to achieve such favorable legislation and by the fact that the key formal workplace institutions are not union-based. Where unions are decentralized, national agreements and legislation are likely to play a limited role, so that the degree of establishment- or company-level union development is likely to be of much greater importance. (For further analysis of this framework, see Batstone and Gourlay 1986).

Twelve Case Studies in Four Countries

This chapter draws on two research projects. In the first, the research was carried out by teams based in Britain, Germany, and Italy; this ensured that an understanding of the national industrial relations background was integral to the analysis. In each country, research was conducted in a process industry (chemicals), small-batch engineering, and finance. The second project "matched" this set of workplaces in Canada. The two research projects were undertaken in the mid-1980s and late 1980s respectively. (The first project also included case studies in brewing or a similar production process, and in the Netherlands and Sweden; but it is beyond the scope of this chapter to discuss these cases. For a detailed description of the European case studies see Hugo Levie and Roy Moore 1984, and for a discussion of the constraints on the selection criteria see Batstone and Gourlay 1986.)

New Technology in Different Environments

A basic assumption of both projects was that technological and organizational change involves a process of choice and negotiation that, within certain constraints, offers scope for managers, unions, and workforces to play a significant role in determining whether change occurs and, if it does, its implementation and outcomes. In the early 1980s, various trade unions in Europe had published policy statements on the importance they attached to worker involvement in the introduction of new technology. The first project set out to examine the activities of trade union representatives and other means of worker representation, such as the works councils in Germany and Italy, in technological change. The selection of industries in the second project was the result of a desire to carry out a detailed comparison of "matched" workplaces based on the work of Maurice et al. (1986). Table 6.1 gives an overview of the twelve cases.

Although the exact criteria of selection of case study sites varied, as did the precise nature of the technological change investigated, a common core of data was collected in each country. In the selection of the cases, an important criterion was that the research might facilitate a comparison of the process of change in particular industries that would therefore provide for commonality on, for example, the labor process, skill requirements, and type of products.

First, a description was made of the enterprise, management, and unions. Second, a reconstruction was made of the actual processes of technological and organizational change. What were the aims and options, who made the decisions, and why? Third, an effort was made to compare the technology and work organization before and after the process of

Table 6.1. Overview of Twelve Workplaces in Britain, Canada, Germany, and Italy Undergoing Technological Change

Case	Company size	Size of site	Technological change investigated
Britain			
Chemicals	62,000	90	Electronic process control
Engineering	7,600	700	Computer numerically controlled machines
Finance	3,400	1,800	On-line systems
Canada			
Chemicals	8,000	1,500	New, automated plant
Engineering	3,500	350	Computer numerically controlled machines
Finance	3,800	3,400	On-line systems
Germany			
Chemicals	3,500	670	Automated packing
Engineering	78,000	3,200	Computer-aided drawing equipment
Finance	3,000	3,000	On-line systems
Italy			
Chemicals	100,000	3,000	New catalyzers
Engineering	3,000	1,500	Computer numerically controlled machines
Finance	12,000	12,000	Counter terminals

Note: Data on the European case studies are based on Levie and Moore (1984).

change. In each of the cases, technological change had taken place in the previous five years.

The main techniques employed were structured and unstructured interviews, but extensive use was also made of observations of meetings and analyses of documentary sources. Given the focus of interest of these studies, the bulk of the structured interviews were conducted with line managers and worker representatives. The questions covered specific information relating to the organization of work within the workplace and labor-management relations. In addition, structured interviews were undertaken with senior managers to gain a knowledge of the organization's background: size, labor and product or service markets, management structure, and so on. Managers with "labor" responsibilities were also interviewed. These interviews covered the managers' tasks, discretion, and attitudes and behavior concerning industrial relations, worker representatives, and particular issues in which they had been involved. Subsequent unstructured interviews with managers and worker representatives consisted of "open-ended" questions guided by a detailed list of points about work situations and technological change.

To understand the roles played by individuals, it was essential to attend meetings. Both formal and informal meetings were attended during the research, including local union and works council meetings and regular and ad hoc joint union-management meetings. Although observing relevant joint union-management meetings was allowed, observing meetings between managers was not. Occasionally, however, informal "meetings" developed in the presence of the researchers, especially between lower-level managers, and these, more than formal interviews and meetings, clarified the various interests and power positions of different groups of managers.

In an attempt to enrich the data gained from the interviews and observations of meetings, minutes of the various meetings were analyzed. Although the detail in the minutes varied considerably, full sets of minutes and other union and management documents dating back to the late 1970s were obtained, and these provided valuable insights into processes taking place and the historical development of technological change in the workplaces.

As indicated above, technological change was accompanied by changes in many other areas: company organization, employment, degree of automation, choice of equipment, health and safety, division of labor, skill requirements, autonomy and cooperation, pace of work, working hours, training, recruitment and promotion. Although changes did not occur in all of these issues at each of the case study sites, job content and work organization did change, often dramatically.

In some cases worker representatives limited themselves to attempting to influence only some of the changes. In other cases the representatives tried to influence all changes that affected the position of the workers involved. In fact, a pattern seemed to emerge. In four cases, involving the British and Canadian chemicals and finance firms, the unions tried to influence only five or fewer of the areas of change. Here, the unions limited themselves to the more traditional issues, such as employment, health and safety, and pay. At the other end of the scale, unions in the German engineering firm and insurance company and in the Italian chemicals firm and bank, attempted to influence nearly all the changes. In these cases the worker representatives tried to intervene not only when the issues were traditionally trade union concerns but also when the changes involved job content and work organization (see Levie and Sandberg 1991). Indeed, the difference between these two groups was significant.

The overwhelming reliance by the unions in Britain and Canada on collective bargaining meant that they could influence the *consequences* of changes on, for example, pay grades, working hours, and the physical working environment. Concerning these "traditional collective bargaining issues," there were well-developed union goals and often quantified demands. To exert influence concerning these traditional issues, however, required little knowledge of possible changes in work and work organization, and the unions did not have to be involved during the period of planning and implementing the changes.

In the German and Italian cases, more formalized and explicit arrangements existed for worker representatives to be involved in the process of technical and social change, which was complex and took several years. In these cases the unions became involved in extended areas of decision-making concerning "sociotechnical issues," such as the quality of the product and work (see Sandberg 1986 for a discussion of sociotechnical systems). "Worker participation" in these new matters therefore changed the balance of decision-making within the firms.

There are a variety of definitions of what the concept of participation entails (for a review, see Poole 1986). The important point is whether, and to what extent, workers influence decision-making within their firms. Within this definition, collective bargaining is a form of participation since it entails negotiating with worker representatives on matters that otherwise would be management prerogatives. Thus, collective bargaining can be said to be the major form of worker participation in the British and Canadian cases. Negotiations resulted in the unions accepting technological change in exchange for certain trade-offs, frequently related to how the change was implemented. Where more formalized and explicit arrangements for worker participation exist, they assume a wide diversity of forms of either a legal or voluntary nature.

In Germany, "collective bargaining provides the basic pattern of working conditions on a regional or industry-wide level; co-determination fills out this pattern on the plant and firm level" (Adams and Rummel 1977, 20). In Italy, trade unions have traditionally viewed collective bargaining as the primary way to regulate labor-management relations (Treu 1981). Nevertheless, worker participation gained momentum in the 1980s not only through an extension in the subject matter of collective agreements but as a result of the increasing institutionalization of procedures and joint committees (Negrelli 1988, 93–94). In both the German and Italian cases, however, participative involvement occurred through input into decisions about work and work organization.

In none of the cases were the unions as such involved at the design stage, although union members in their role of workers had varying degrees of involvement. Unions became involved at the stage at which management deemed it appropriate. The case studies suggest that an important factor influencing the timing was the pattern of labor-management relationships in the period before the current period of technological innovation.

To illustrate this point, the cases can be subdivided into two groups: six cases of "participative" workplace relations and six cases of "collective bargaining" relationships. The "participative" group was characterized by a history of stable interunion and union-management relationships, a well-developed union organization, potential conflict avoided by informing and consulting, and concessions to facilitate changes. The common feature of the "collective bargaining" cases was a lengthy history of mutual antagonism between unions and management. Interunion relationships in these enterprises also tended to be tense and occasionally hostile. The feelings of antagonism were reflected in frequent use of the grievance and disputes machinery, the existence of few or no consultative mechanisms, and constant disagreements about union rights and the "style" of management. The following section reviews the broad pattern of labor-management relationships that emerged from these studies and proposes a number of reasons for the variance in the evidence.

Labor-Management Relations and the Conditions for Change

The formal structures of negotiation and consultation in the enterprises in the "participative" group were, of course, very varied. The common feature, however, as indicated earlier, was the existence of a reasonably long-standing consultative system or body alongside the grievance and bargaining machinery. In the German cases, for example, the codetermination law provided the unions at the local level with rights to a relatively high degree of involvement and planning of major changes. In practice, however, in all the cases, the limited definition of information rights constrained worker representatives' access to information.

The Italian experience provides an interesting contrast to the German situation. Though the legislative support found in Germany was lacking, a combination of negotiated industry-level information rights with precise workplace-level strategies of worker representation was an effective alternative. Although the extent to which this approach was reflected in formal institutions was limited, it led to regular consultative meetings on the enterprises' development and planning objectives.

Rather than extend this set of illustrative descriptions, the question of effectiveness should be addressed. What did these arrangements actually mean in practice? Were the worker representatives able to use them to find new strategies and procedures for dealing with sociotechnical issues?

Participative Workplace Relations

In the German cases, the unions tried to develop their own resources (including detailed demands regarding both technology and work organization and new procedures), but they were related neither to participation (in the sense that worker representatives formally take part in management's decision-making or in project groups that are involved in development work) nor to negotiation, in which case a compromise is reached in accordance with the traditional pattern of labor-management relations. These cases indicate that the development of union resources that is not rooted in the local process of change does not further worker representation on sociotechnical issues. Or perhaps it requires a negotiating power that the worker representatives at the workplaces lacked. Two of the Italian case studies demonstrate a mix of participation and negotiation, as well as a degree of independent trade union work, that led to worker representatives using these processes more effectively in the interest of their members.

To summarize broadly from these six case studies, two conclusions can be drawn. First, new technologies obviously emerge in established bargaining environments. Thus, in addition to formal information-disclosure agreements, informal assumptions and modes of behavior have developed that put a premium on a consultative/participative style of management. It is completely unremarkable in such a climate for new technology to be handled in the same way, particularly where its introduction is on a fairly gradual and piecemeal basis. Second, the consequence of a relatively mutually nonantagonistic industrial relations environment, coupled with often quite elaborate participative systems, is that the process of debate on new technology can lead to a wide degree of agreement.

German chemicals. The German chemicals case study site was a detergents plant of the subsidiary of a major American concern. The plant employed 670 workers. The technological change was the introduction of two highly automated units for the filling and packing of detergents. After a time-consuming struggle, the works council received the relevant information about the new packing line. Management provided the information, however, only because the works council threatened legal sanctions.

Late in 1980, the plant works council heard rumors about the planned automatic filling units but did not act on these rumors. It was officially informed in mid-1981, only one year before the units were to be introduced and more than one year after management had started to plan the operation. The proposed loss of twenty jobs allowed the works council to use its legal rights to demand more information and to visit a similar filling unit at another plant. The works council objected to the fact that information was provided only after all crucial decisions had been made but, because its members were subject to a legal "peace obligation," felt unable to inflict any sanctions (see Tallard 1988 for an outline of the legal framework in Germany).

Because the company was highly centralized, the works council was constrained in its acquisition of information about management plans by the minimal functioning of the central works council. It was also management's strategy to disclose as little as would avoid conflict and to break down large projects into smaller projects.

Having been forced to accept that it could not influence the design of the new filling system or the intended introduction of an advanced form of teamworking at the new units, the works council concentrated on protecting the workers who stood to lose their jobs through redeployment and guaranteed earnings; limiting line speeds to avoid additional stress; and negotiating minimum staffing levels, working time, and breaks. By pursuing these demands, the works council became strongly involved in the work organization for the new filling lines. A major problem for the works council members was that they had to deal with a plant management that had very limited autonomy, little freedom to negotiate, and no knowledge of the various options for the work organization that had been considered by the company's research and development staff in Brussels.

The works council did not influence the basic staffing level per shift.

But it did achieve an overall increase in employment by insisting on replacement workers to allow time for breaks and to reduce the stress of greatly increased productivity. It also influenced employment during the transition period by insisting on the use of more temporary workers for a longer period. Other than delaying it, however, the council had little influence on the introduction of the company's new concept of teamwork. This was because the workers on the first teams, who had received extensive training, appreciated the new work organization.

By delaying test runs on the new lines, the works council restricted the line speeds and achieved additional break times. After protracted negotiations on an additional night shift and management threats of dismissals, the labor court endorsed the works council's rights to codetermination. On this basis, the works council was able to influence staffing levels and break times and to ensure shift premiums for the shift workers. Because it was not involved in the design and development of the new units and the concept of teamwork, however, it had no influence on job composition and job rotation.

German engineering. The German small-batch engineering company was a large subsidiary of a major steel, pipes, and engineering concern that produced large lifting and conveying equipment. At the time of the field research the site employed 3,200 workers. The focus of this case was the introduction of computer-aided design (CAD) in the drawing office.

The use of CAD was first investigated in the late 1970s by company headquarters and the engineering department. In the following years a project group drew up the specifications. Workers in the engineering and design department on site were involved in this process, aimed at selecting the appropriate hardware and software. The works council, however, was not informed about management's intention to introduce CAD until 1980, three years after investigation and planning of the system had begun. Indeed, information about changes in the work organization was received only after the equipment had been ordered.

Routine financial and economic information did not point the works council to the development of CAD because the equipment was to be leased by the company and therefore was not one of the investments about which it received information from plant management every six months. Events also point to a lack of exchange of information between members of the metal workers union in the department and the works council members. This situation was not improved by the presence of approximately one hundred shop stewards. The union works council members and shop stewards were well integrated into the wider union, and the works council was well integrated into the company. But this did not help to anticipate the introduction of CAD.

Since 1978, the works council, informed by the increased emphasis of the union on the humanization of work, had tried to negotiate a site agreement on the use of visual display units (VDUs). The local works council had hoped that the central works council would deal with this, but it had failed to negotiate an agreement. It was distracted by VDU guidelines, which had been drawn up by the company's ergonomics department. The local works council then hoped that the introduction of CAD would make it possible to conclude a site-level agreement after all. Essentially, it considered that the introduction of new technology would be to the workers' benefit because it might improve the company's competitiveness. The works council also thought that the introduction of CAD should be negotiated, however, particularly issues concerning health and safety, the number and quality of jobs, training, and work organization. But management succeeded in restricting the works council to negotiations far removed from the actual design of the new system.

In 1981, the local works council presented an innovative draft agreement on CAD to management. The draft included many substantive points, covering sociotechnical as well as traditional collective bargaining issues. The draft had been written by local works council members, however, in collaboration with experts from their union headquarters, with little information about management's exact plans and without involvement in management's planning and development process.

The substantive demands of the works council did not influence the new system. There was no job loss, but productivity increased. There were also indications of loss of drafting skills among draftsmen. Furthermore, the company began to move toward a flexible manufacturing system. By the time the first terminals were installed, management still denied the works council codetermination rights on the issue and rejected a proposed site agreement. Thus, the right to be informed and to negotiate technological change, and not the draft agreement, became the sole issue. In a subsequent legal case, the works council made some progress. This was a partial victory, however. Information about management's plans concerning CAD had lost its relevance by the time the works council had gained the right to use it because the new system was already in operation.

German finance. The German finance case study site was a medium-sized insurance company employing nearly three thousand workers. In recent years the relevant union had gained a strong foothold, although with approximately 10 percent density, the degree of unionization here was lower than at any of the other firms studied. The technological change at this insurance company was the introduction of on-line computing in area offices together with the reorganization of administrative procedures and the closure of some offices. The associated job loss was nearly three hundred.

In the late 1970s, management informed the central works council that management consultants would examine the structure and strategy of the company. Little further information was provided until 1980, when the works council received the final report of the consultants. In subsequent negotiations the works council was gradually informed of how management planned to implement the consultants' report. The central works council decided it was too late to influence the direction of area and branch office reorganization. Instead, it concentrated on the timetable and scale of changes, the form of job loss, redundancy payments, and working conditions at the remaining offices. A general agreement on these issues and procedures for implementing changes was reached in late 1980. The same pattern applied to a subsequent change toward centralization of premium payments, which had also been suggested by the management consultants: late information, followed by negotiations over procedures and safeguards.

During this period the nonmanual members on the central works council, then in a minority, tried to complement the scarce information from management by drawing up a detailed checklist of technological and organizational changes in the short and longer term and their impact on the workers. This approach was not accepted by the professionals, then in the majority, on the works council. Although in following years the nonmanual representatives gained control of the works council and received some support from their union, they decided against trying to bring in outside experts as an additional source of information. This was because of the inevitable further conflicts with management that such an approach would have caused. Partly because the nonmanual representatives received details about the reorganization and job loss too late and partly because they had no alternatives, they decided to accept the direction of the plans.

Through protracted negotiations between 1980 and 1984, the nonmanual representatives were involved in the implementation of the management consultants' report, forcing considerable concessions. The involvement of the worker representatives should be considered in the context of a battle for the "hearts and minds" of the insurance workers, who were traditionally loyal to their superiors. The nonmanual representatives were able to influence the process of change only as far as they succeeded in developing and gaining acceptance of their concept of independent representation. Although membership growth stagnated after 1980 and remained about 10 percent of all employees, the gains made in elections for the central works council in 1981 and the supervisory board in 1983 signified considerable acceptance of the process of change by the employees. The negotiations over centralization of premium payments in 1981 showed that management had to accept increasing involvement of the works council in shaping the actual changes.

The works council influenced the number of area offices to be closed. Originally, management had planned to close eighteen area offices, but in the agreement of 1980, this was reduced to eleven. In this and the even stronger subsequent agreement of 1981, the works council influenced the timetable of reorganization, training for new functions, the qualifications required of workers at the remaining branch offices, staffing levels, rules for redeployment, the timing of redundancies and redundancy pay, and guarantees for training. Finally, it achieved the right to additional local agreements before any changes were made.

Italian chemicals. The Italian chemicals case study site was an important plant of a major private sector company. In addition to being a vital research center, the site produced polypropylene and in the early 1980s employed nearly three thousand workers. The technological change studied was the introduction of high-output catalyzers. This resulted in a reduction of about half of the production jobs and considerable savings in plant, energy, and material costs. The interesting aspect of this case is that these changes were in fact actively encouraged by the worker representatives, who feared the alternative: closure of the production areas. They used both their influence on regional and local authorities and contacts with scientific, managerial, and technical staff at the research center to obtain the necessary investment and to help shape the work reorganization.

The three chemical workers' unions worked closely together in the federation of chemical workers. At the plant level, representation was organized in the works council. Four major sources of information were available to this council: the national agreement for the chemical industry, which obliged the company to provide detailed information at corporate and establishment levels; the information the company provided to the government to obtain financial assistance; the research and development department, which had a strategic function in the company; and the regional and local authorities, which assisted in making decisions about planning permits and environmental control. As a result of these sources of information, in the period prior to the decision to invest in the future of the plant, the union representatives were well informed about the company's structural problems and the possibility of modernizing the polypropylene production.

Between 1979 and 1983, the works council was closely involved in discussions about the future of the plant. Management proposals to reduce employment were discussed, with the knowledge that a strategy of outright resistance to the reduction of the workforce had been unsuccessful at other plants in the company. The works council was also aware of the work of the local research and development department on a new technology for polypropylene production involving high-output catalyzers.

The involvement of the works council was based on internal discussions among technicians and operators and on extensive negotiations with local management. Instead of rigidly defending every job, the works council accepted some job loss with three provisos. First, there would be sufficient investment in the new production technology to guarantee that the plant would continue as the smaller polypropylene facility of the company. Second, the work reorganization would increase the autonomy and expertise of work groups. Third, a loss of working hours would be distributed between all workers by rotating monthly layoffs rather than targeting individual workers for redundancy.

At the end of 1983, there were still nearly three thousand employees on site. After the changes in the production process in 1984, this was reduced by seven hundred jobs. The trade unions had influenced the company's decision to modernize the plant, however, instead of closing it. By applying pressure on the regional and local authorities to provide planning permission, the unions had also influenced the speedy construction of the new plant. Furthermore, the changes in work organization toward more autonomous work groups, upgrading for some of the operators, as well as closer contact between maintenance operators and research and development staff were coordinated by the trade unions.

An interesting aspect of this case was that detailed participation in the design of the new work organization and subsequent negotiations were possible because of the independent work by the trade unionists in improving their understanding of chemical and technical issues and providing training courses for the technicians and operators, so that they could do likewise (Levie and Sandberg 1991, 246).

Italian engineering. The engineering plant investigated in Italy was a major site of one of the largest Italian manufacturers of capital equipment primarily for the automotive industry. The company employed 3,500 workers, of whom 1,500 were at the plant. Between 1977 and 1980, the company had experienced a complex process of mergers, and this study focused on the introduction of computer numerical-controlled (CNC) lathes as part of this reorganization.

At this plant there was a traditional basis for trade union involvement in sociotechnical issues as a result of the high skill levels of the production workers and their representatives. In addition, management relied heavily on shopfloor workers' and supervisors' technical knowledge. The difference between this and the chemical plant should be noted at this point. The existing technical competence was an important starting point when the trade unions were faced with major proposals for reorganization. For example, the trade union representatives studied questions such as subcontracting, capacity utilization, the specifications of different CNC equipment, and the type of work most suited to CNC and conventional machines. This knowledge was used both at formal annual information meetings between corporate management and regional management and more frequently at plant-level meetings. As at the chemical works, the basis for this tradition was the 1979 national agreement (see Levie and Sandberg 1991).

The formal structure for information disclosure was an annual meeting at the regional union headquarters where the company provided information on production prospects, investment, and employment. This flow of information was augmented by more frequent meetings at the company level at which management provided detailed information to try to gain consent for its plans for the mergers and reorganization of the various facilities. Because of the nature of the company (for example, managers came mainly from production areas and were promoted because of their technical expertise), information on orders, production planning, technology and work organization overlapped. Consequently, this made it easier for the union representatives to deal with this information.

Using these resources, the union representatives engaged both in participation and negotiations, although they were not involved in any formal project work. The interests of the workers were the advancement, or at least the maintenance, of skill levels; control over the internal labor market, partly through an informal system of seniority; and negotiated changes in staffing levels and in the proportion of production contracted out. During the technological change studied, this involvement meant that initially difficult decisions regarding the organization of the department were postponed.

In 1980, detailed negotiations over the future organization commenced. One indication of the detailed involvement of the union delegates was that they no longer dealt with personnel management. This function was taken over by production managers, who were more inclined to utilize workers' competence.

The union representatives had considerable influence on the process of change, within the boundaries of the general reorganization program, which had already been accepted. Employment in the department had decreased by 40 percent since 1980; however, the union had considerable influence on the improvement of capacity utilization, the organization of the production process, and the amount of subcontracting. The latter was partly determined by the success of the union in influencing which CNC machines were bought and for which processes they were used. Finally, the union protected and improved the skill levels and grading.

Perhaps the major success was that the introduction of CNC machinery led to a development instead of an erosion of skills and to a strengthening, rather than a weakening, of the position of the unions locally. One interesting measure of their increased development of resources was that, as noted above, during the process of change the unions for the first time met regularly with production management instead of with personnel management, which traditionally had been their main counterpart.

Italian finance. The Italian finance case study site was one of the largest banks in the country. It had expanded from five thousand employees in 1975 to twelve thousand ten years later. Thus, the introduction of a branch office network of terminals connected to the computer center was not accompanied by attempts to reduce employment. At the national level the trade unions were involved in discussions with management regarding the goals of the decentralized on-line systems and the changes in work organization. These included the integration of the previously separate functions of clerk and teller. This integration resulted in more varied work for the employees involved and improved service for customers.

In this case the picture of a unilateral process of decision-making by management and a separate bargaining process in which it was the strategy of the union to "uncover" all the information that the other side was trying to conceal does not apply. During the various phases of the design and introduction of the on-line system, the unions were provided with all the information they requested, and more could have been provided. The main body of worker representatives received the first information about the planned on-line system in 1980, before even the outline of the system had been finalized.

This study, compared with the industrial cases, pointed out differences in worker representation. The main differences were the greater formality, stricter adherence to the law that defined the basic rights of workers and trade unions at the workplace, the strained relations between the four unions that constituted the banking unions' confederation, and the greater emphasis on individual interests such as training, careers, and transfers. The central representatives were involved in discussions about the objectives of the new on-line system and changes in work organization. In particular, they shaped their involvement and that of the local representatives by ensuring that the new system would be introduced flexibly so that the bank employees would not be forced into particular career patterns.

The central worker representatives helped shape the decision that the system would serve to expand the service and improve the personal contact between front-office employees and customers, rather than reduce employment. One of the means of doing this was to integrate the previously segregated functions of bank clerk and teller. Another was to have one extra employee for every two terminals and have the three clerks rotate between the terminals and the function of general assistance. The new system considerably reduced balancing time at the end of the day, which made it easier for both the unions and management to accommodate a national agreement that banks be open longer. The whole process of change, however, including the influence of the worker representatives, must be seen against the background of an expanding bank. As noted above, employment had risen between 1975 and 1984 from five thousand to twelve thousand. This made it much easier to reach the goals of the new system.

Summary. One of the most striking characteristics of the German cases was that the limited definition of information rights under codetermination legislation constrained worker representatives' access to information. Considerable time was spent negotiating the procedures for codetermination. These case studies also illustrate the difficulties of coordinating general trade union demands in relation to new technology and the potential influence of works councils on specific processes of change. (For an analysis of works councils' problems in intervening in the process of change see Michael Gold and Mark Hall 1992). Nevertheless, the German case studies indicate a fairly wide range of worker representative influence even though that influence was of a "bureaucratic" and positive-sum nature. Moreover, it involved significant trade-offs, such as an increase in shift work or effort levels in return for greater job security. For some, this might indicate serious weaknesses in the role the worker representatives played, suggesting an incorporated workplace organization. For others, while recognizing these were significant costs, the gains achieved, particularly in job security, would appear to outweigh the costs.

The Italian experience provides an interesting contrast to the German situation. In the chemicals and engineering cases, the unions achieved a relatively high degree of influence. Though there was not the same legislative support as in Germany, other characteristics appeared to play an important role. First, in these cases union density was high, workplace organization was well developed, and there was a high degree of contact with other parts of the labor movement. Moreover, the unions cooperated closely at the industry level and had developed a fairly wide range of approaches to bargaining with the employers. In large part this appeared to reflect changes in the approach of the unions, which were also found at the national level. Members' interests were increasingly defined in terms of the maintenance of employment, and, to this end, the unions had been increasingly prepared to cooperate with employers, recognizing that company viability was a precondition of job security. Although the extent to which this approach was reflected in formal institutions was limited (reflecting its evolving nature and relatedly its relative insecurity), it did mean that the employer accepted union involvement in the planning of technological change (see also Batstone and Gourlay 1986).

Collective Bargaining Relationships

The six firms categorized as exhibiting a traditional collective bargaining relationship had markedly different experiences surrounding the introduction of new technology. The common element in the development of industrial relations was an oscillation between "constitutionalist" and "standard modern" approaches, reflecting complex and shifting blends of unitary and pluralistic perspectives (Fox 1974).

In two cases, however, a quite different relationship was found. In the British and Canadian small-batch engineering plants, no participation or advanced negotiations took place. Here, the existing well-developed union organization relied on traditional patterns of collective bargaining and, in particular, on management's need for the workers' technical competence. The trade unions' influence in these cases depended on their strong position at the plants. This position was evident in the formal frameworks of procedural agreements on work and work organization, which had been developed over many years, and in the strong informal relations between the senior union representatives on site with both personnel and production management.

Influence without specific development of union resources and fluid lines between participation and negotiation typify these two cases. Arm's-length collective bargaining, often not until the implementation phase, was the dominating procedure. The organization of the discussion here diverges from that of the previous section, in which all three plants in each country were discussed together. Because of the special features mentioned above, the British and Canadian engineering plants are discussed first and together.

British engineering. The British engineering firm was one of two spares division sites of a company that made specialized production machinery for processing and packaging. The site employed 600 out of a total of 7,600 workers in the company. All production employees were members of a craft union, which represented the major source of worker influence exerted on the technological change being implemented. This change involved the introduction of CNC machine tools for milling and turning, aimed at providing enhanced quality and customer service and improved productivity and cost effectiveness.

The earliest evidence of the company's intentions to introduce CNC machines came during the 1979 wage negotiations. Information based on more detailed planning did not emerge until a 1981 communications meeting (when all employees were addressed by senior managers), by which time negotiations over a "new technology agreement" had been proceeding for a year and the first CNC machine had been introduced. The works committee, consisting of senior managers and senior shop stewards, addressed this new technology as a regular agenda item only after this agreement was signed, early in 1982. The trade union's attempt to secure information was limited by the "reactive" strategy so typical of British unions. Rather than seeking early influence over managerial plans and decisions, the shop stewards' committee preferred instead to await announcements of intentions and implementations and to seek the best deal for its members at later "crucial" stages. There was no joint union machinery either on the site or within the company; little or no wider union or external assistance was either sought or apparently available; and there were no legal rights to which the union could have referred.

The aims of the stewards thus did not really challenge the recognition of unilaterally determined company management plans and implementations other than as a subject for collective bargaining at arm's length. At works committee meetings, discussions of the company's plans were informative rather than consultative, let alone participative. Moreover, the original initiative for a new technology agreement was simultaneously supported by production management, although this was later to be controlled by personnel management. Nevertheless, the shop stewards' committee made its own version of a new technology agreement an aim of negotiations and matched management's plans for the introduction of CNC machines with a three-year plan of its own. Union distinctions and priorities could be identified in the attention it gave to rights of consultation over the choice of machines, principles of the payment system, employment and job security, overtime and hours of work, outside subcon-tracting, and training.

In most of these areas, the union was successful in establishing "spheres of influence" that took it beyond the scope of collective bargaining's conventional coverage. The new technology agreement provided for rights of consultation over the choice of machines, short- and long-term plans for their introduction, and health and safety issues; for operator programming of the CNC machines, with consequent entitlement to access to training; for employment- and earnings-level guarantees; and for the distribution to all operators of any benefits derived across the payment system.

There are two important qualifications to be made in what appears to be a rather impressive catalog of union achievement. First, neither the union's claims nor the negotiating procedures used as a vehicle for promoting them amounted to any real challenge to unilateral managerial prerogative in planning and implementing changes in technology and work organization. Second, there was no evidence that any of the outcomes mentioned represented conflicts with or departures from what management itself (albeit for its own reasons) would have advocated or agreed to in terms of "custom and practice."

Canadian engineering. The plant where the Canadian engineering case was carried out was the service division headquarters of a multinational company specializing in production equipment for manufacturers in the food and drink sector. New machines were produced at other plants, and the separate spares facility had only been established in the early 1980s. This move heralded the start of a strategy of improving customer service to compete more effectively. Senior management saw the function of the spares plant primarily as providing a rapid response to customers' needs. Recently, some production of parts for new machines had also been undertaken in the plant. Three hundred and fifty workers were employed at this site.

In 1981, a joint union-management production committee agreed to modernization plans for key production equipment. There was a close working relationship between local management and union stewards, which meant that throughout the period 1981–84 information about manage-ment's plans to invest in CNC machines and their problems in convincing senior management of the necessity of such investments was available. The main use of such information by the union stewards was to support local managers in making their case to senior management and in expressing their preference for the CNC machines.

The basis for the union's involvement was its agreement with local management on the best strategy for retaining jobs at the plant. This strategy was to improve profitability by increasing the throughput of the plant, strengthening the plant's ability to adapt products to specific customer requirements, and accepting work that was previously done by subcontractors. Early on it was accepted by the union that a double-shift system would be introduced to improve the utilization of the expensive CNC system and reduce the payback period.

Trade union involvement consisted mainly of cooperation on a project team, which had been instigated by the union via the health and safety committee late in 1982. Further involvement developed from the management group and in the departmental production committee. The union stewards strengthened their involvement by attending courses on new technology organized by the union nationally, which they repeated themselves locally. At no time, however, was their involvement based on independent demands about the future of the plant and its work organization.

The union's agreement with management on the definition of the workers' interest meant that specific input in the various joint committees was limited to matters of detail. Their involvement particularly gave the union stewards the opportunity to learn about CNC and the associated choices in work organization. The actual influence of the workers and their representatives took place on two levels. First, they helped local management ensure that the investment in new technology took place without job losses but with the introduction of shift work. Second, they helped choose the most important CNC system and the way it was integrated into the production department.

On the basis of this influence, the union stewards developed their ability to influence further choices about technology and work organization. Before 1989, no separate production engineering department existed at the plant. In 1989, such a department was set up, but it is not at all clear that it constitutes a division of labor that eventually will lead to the loss of control over the production process by the skilled workers.

Events at these small-batch engineering plants are not typical of worker involvement in technological change in Britain and Canada. Indeed, the other four cases showed considerably less influence.

British chemicals. The British chemical company employed some sixty-two thousand people, of whom fewer than 1 percent worked in its chemical manufacturing sector. In the late 1970s, the design and construction of a manually operated, remotely controlled chemical plant was undertaken. Capacity was soon expanded and advantage taken of new construction work to computerize the process-monitoring and control systems. The centralization of process control was subsequently extended with the installation of a computer to control three of the four plants constructed.

The union organization in the plant was well resourced with respect to office, telephone, and flexible "time-off" procedures. Management was organized in a relatively rigid hierarchical and bureaucratic fashion and clung firmly to the notion of managerial prerogatives and the need to defend them from what was seen as an aggressive union continually seeking to encroach on management rights. All formal union-management contact was within the grievances and disputes machinery; informal conversations and telephone contact tended to relate to issues that had already gone into the machinery. There was no forum for worker and management representatives to meet regularly to discuss company activities. Union and management representatives would grudgingly accept each other's legitimacy but lacked the mutual respect and trust needed to advance beyond the adversarial, distributive aspect of collective bargaining. Management criticized the stewards for conveying partial and biased information about negotiations to their members, thereby not doing justice to the company's case. The stewards criticized management vigorously for failing to provide information, for distrusting the union, and for not seeking to stimulate union or worker input regarding company decisions.

This pattern of mistrust and hostility was exemplified by the introduction of new production facilities, which used computer control and associated changes in machine staffing and plant layout, in the older buildings on the site. Automation took place in three phases, two in the late 1970s and one in the mid-1980s. There was no consultation on the design of the new facilities, or on the jobs to be created in it.

The process workers' union on the site focused its attention on wages and other conditions of work as they affected its members generally, most of whom worked outside the chemical production sector. As far as the new technology was concerned, the union as a whole, and the chemical workers' section, were primarily concerned with its effects on members' job prospects. Negotiations on the changes in the existing buildings took place over several months against a background of management assurance that staff reductions would be handled by natural wastage and early retirements.

At the end of this period, with agreement still some way off, the company declared there would be fifty redundancies. Not surprisingly, the union representatives felt that they had failed to influence management. But despite the apparent strength of the shopfloor organization, they feared that a call for industrial action would not be well supported.

The perspective and strategy of the process workers' union prevented it from exerting influence on the design of any of the stages of innovation. It also appeared that working practices in the new facilities conformed entirely to management's plans. "Productionization" occurred on management's terms, and the union had no influence on how the plant was run.

British finance. The British finance company employed 3,400 workers, and of these, 1,800 worked in area offices. The focus of study was the development of on-line inquiry and endorsement systems for personal household and auto insurance and the introduction of these systems in the area offices.

In the mid-1970s, executive management asked the data-processing department to investigate the potential for reducing the administration costs in the personal insurance area by using teleprocessing. During 1975 and 1976, some first choices about the shape and location of the new system were made, including whether investment in a teleprocessing network would be coupled with increased centralization or decentralization of personal insurance. In 1976, the union, then still a staff association, was informed about the planned initial on-line system. Throughout 1976–81, once outline decisions had been made, further information about the new systems and the associated streamlining of insurance procedures and area office reorganization was provided either by its members in the data-processing department or through informal contacts with management.

This information was at times used to mobilize the membership with regard to ongoing negotiations. The actual changes, however, were not negotiated until 1980. Since the company offered upgrading to many of the workers remaining in the personal insurance departments, the only real issue negotiated was one proposed compulsory redundancy, which was withdrawn. During this period the union tried, but failed, to negotiate the level of employment at area offices. There was no attempt to use the early information to try to influence system design and work organization.

The union retained some of the characteristics of an in-house staff association and had a general interest in the economic well-being of the company. This led to a basic acceptance of the need for lower administration costs and higher underwriting profits by using new technology. At no stage did the union independently try to define the workers' interests in the face of the introduction of the on-line systems and the reorganization of area offices.

The strategy of the main union body, the divisional committee, can be explained by its history as a staff association and the possibly related relative overrepresentation of middle and higher grades among union representatives. Unless there was a clear threat of compulsory redundancies, the divisional committee would tend to wait for management to propose specific changes and respond to them on the basis of the following criteria. First, was it necessary and advantageous for the company? Second, did it unnecessarily harm union members? Third, how could the union limit any negative consequences and maximize any potential benefits?

Two further complications limited trade union involvement in the planning and implementation of the changes. First, though many of the staff developing the new systems were union members, their first loyalty was to the company. This made union involvement with the earlier stages of the process of change more difficult. Second, because industrial relations were highly centralized, local trade union activity was minimal.

The worker representatives had little influence on the design of the on-line systems and related changes in work procedures and area office reorganization. They welcomed the upgrading of the majority of the remaining personal insurance employees and tried to safeguard the health and safety of VDU operators and any individual members whose interests were threatened by the reorganization. Little progress was made in attempting to negotiate a new technology agreement in line with the union's model agreement. The main influence of the union on the process of technological change was that, because of its high membership and increasing independence, it reinforced senior management's strategy to introduce new systems at a slower pace than was technically feasible.

At least in part to reduce potential conflict with the highly unionized workforce, management approached the actual introduction of the on-line systems cautiously. Management's preference was to see most of the desired labor savings take place through "natural wastage" before the new systems were introduced. The upgrading of area office personal insurance staff was a management initiative that was confirmed by the joint job evaluation committee. Furthermore, the union had little influence on the changes in work procedures and organization or on the training in the new systems. (For further analysis of the British case studies, see Batstone et al. 1987).

Canadian chemicals. The company where the Canadian chemicals case study was undertaken was a multinational with 1,500 workers who were engaged in the manufacture and retailing of fine chemicals and related products. This study differs from the others in that it centered on the design and introduction some ten years earlier of an automated process plant. The decision to modernize the plant was taken in the late 1970s in the context of crucial decisions to invest in the manufacture of new products. The trade union was involved in these decisions, which guaranteed the reequipment of the plant. A trade-off was that the union agreed to allow the control room operators to work double shifts.

The initial discussions about the plans to automate were shrouded in secrecy, and a consultant's report on strategic choices was not widely disclosed. After that phase, however, all information about management plans to automate was available to all the union stewards and could be used freely. Studies by the main office of five possible machines used in the preparation of chemical solutions were revealed to the union stewards. The union influenced the decision about which machine to purchase through the central safety committee and was in full agreement with management.

At the company level there was some union involvement in the overall investment plan, which guaranteed the future of the plant, leading to the acceptance by the union of the further automation of process control tasks and double-shift working to increase the utilization of new machinery. On the basis of this acceptance, the union stewards became involved in a plant project group, consisting of department heads and senior shop stewards, which had been proposed by management.

Although there were some doubts about the real need for new machinery, the stewards on the project group saw this and the decision to implement double-shift work as outside their influence. That there was an a priori agreement that there was to be no job loss made involvement on this basis easier. Once it started, however, the project work appeared to be more extensive than expected. The group had to consider the whole production process. This made it more difficult for the stewards to participate in general discussions, and they concentrated on specific issues. Thus, union involvement was constrained by the boundaries of the scope of the project.

The stewards on the project group failed to anticipate the operators' unwillingness to engage in job rotation. They also failed to anticipate that the agreement that there would be no changes in employment levels but an extra shift and increased output meant that there would be no replacements.

The stewards on the project group influenced the choice of the chemical processing machinery, the process control tasks, and other tasks allied to processing, such as the requirements for checking records. The union's demand that all operators be trained both in the new system and in the more routine manual work was not accepted because of the workers' resistance to job rotation. Their resistance may be explained by the union's success in achieving small wage differentials. In fact, the project group had little influence on the degree of automation, the layout of the system and its skill requirements, the training, or the division of labor. Problems over the arrangement for shift work did, however, give the union some scope to improve the work organization marginally.

Canadian finance. The final example is the Canadian finance case study concerning the change from batch to on-line processing of personal insurance in a large and long-established company. In a similar vein to the other cases in this group, a complete on-line computer system was installed with merely perfunctory consultation well after all the important decisions had been made. This change had started in the early 1980s and by the time of the fieldwork research in 1989 had been largely completed, although some further developments were still occurring. The company handled all types of insurance and employed nearly four thousand workers, the majority of whom worked in a network of area offices. Partly through the takeover of two other companies, the company had increased its total employment considerably during the first part of the 1980s, but it had then fallen by about 3 percent as the company tried to reduce costs. Part of this job reduction was the direct result of the introduction of the new system of on-line processing.

Management considered the organizational weakness of the union, despite its strength in numbers, justified an arm's-length approach. The company ran a series of "propaganda" sessions about the new system but undertook no consultation or bargaining about its precise implications. The stewards viewed these sessions less as means to gain influence over the company's plans than as opportunities to be forewarned of possible effects on job security.

The stewards were very conscious of the fact that processing of a particular policy could end whenever a contract had been fulfilled or there was a downturn in the market. The end of orders meant that redeployment would have to take place, unless new insurance policies were brought in, and it was with this aspect of product and process changes that they were most concerned. The stewards and union members sometimes expressed concern about the deskilling of their work, which they felt accompanied automation and which they viewed as inevitable. That there was a new technology clause in the collective agreement did not seem to influence their perspective. The agreement was simply seen as a means of formalizing and strengthening their ability to obtain advance warning of changes affecting job security.

Compared with previous working practices, the new computer-based offices certainly did "deskill" the insurance underwriters' work by removing all but the most routinely simple tasks. But the computerization also created tasks for administrators and assistant programmers. These workers' conceptual skills were enhanced insofar as they had to be familiar with all the operation processes under their control, instead of only discrete parts of the offices. In addition, they were required to undertake elements of planning and to issue routine job-allocation instructions to the insurance underwriters.

The office automation seems to have been determined by the technical managers with little or no contribution from the workforce or the union. That the union had been recognized for only a few years when the first phase of organizational and technological changes took place partly explains its lack of intervention. The lack of information released by management also reduced the workers' ability to contribute to subsequent changes. More important than the lack of information, however, or the continuing organizational weakness of the union was the absence of any concern with "production" or work organization details on the part of either the workers or union representatives.

The stewards and union members were eager to receive early information about technological or organizational changes, but only to assess the likely effects on job security. Although there appeared to be some feeling that the new forms of work organization were undesirable in many respects, the prevailing attitude was that such issues were beyond the workers' competence or legitimate concern. With such a perspective, the provision of more detailed information about planned changes would have made no difference.

Discussion. It is interesting to contrast the experiences of the firms in Britain and Canada with those in Germany and Italy. In the former, there were frequent disputes over the rights of worker representatives to involvement and information, and invariably they were a good deal less involved in the planning process than the German and Italian unions. Similarly, in the chemicals and finance British firms, it was clear that there were significant problems of coordination between the various levels of worker representation. This resulted in a failure to collate information that was in fact available. Although worker representatives in the engineering firm did have some small influence over the broad nature of management strategy, it was confined to particular aspects of staffing levels and work organization.

Union influence appeared to be marginally greater in the Canadian case than in the British, but in neither did it approximate that found in the German and Italian cases. In many respects the British experience was quite similar to that of the Canadian firms, except perhaps that greater concern was demonstrated (but not necessarily with any result) over strategic issues, while the control over work organization was weaker. Again, this pattern reflects the weakness of legislative support in these two countries compared with Germany and Italy, the fact that management often did not accept a joint role for the worker organizations, the limited development of worker representation, and its weak links with the wider union organization.

There are thus marked contrasts between these six "collective bargaining" cases. Nonetheless, the common features are striking: high levels of union density but with weak relationships between the workplace and the wider union, mutual distrust between union and management representatives, limited joint consultative (far less participative) forums, and the absence of established systems of management-union-worker communications. In all six cases the trade union approach to technological change might have been formed by national union policies. Little evidence was found, however, of more specific national or regional trade union support of the local union activities studied.

In each of the cases, the trade union response was entirely up to the local representatives and no expertise or other resources were provided by the wider unions other than occasional discussions between senior local representatives and national officials and union training courses with some general emphasis on technological change (see also Levie and Sandberg 1991). Compared with the "participative" enterprises, technological change in this group was implemented with little deviation from the planned schedule of change. In both participative and collective bargaining groups, then, the preexisting patterns of institutions, styles of interaction, and sets of understandings seemed to determine the approach to the introduction of new technology.

Conclusions and Implications

This chapter has assessed the pattern of technological change in the 1980s at workplaces in Britain, Canada, Germany, and Italy. Of particular significance has been the effect of national industrial relations, as opposed to technology, on the process of labor regulation at the workplace. The process of assimilation has been traced within the four countries. Germany's works councils, established by law, and Italy's national agreements achieve much in this respect. But the very limited institutional representation achieved by the British and Canadian collective bargaining systems falls far short in achieving the framework of collaboration necessary for successful innovation. Thus, a key factor affecting technological change is the nature of the existing relationships between labor and management.

What do these two research projects suggest about the development of a specific union-management relationship? Three factors are of significance: the interplay between union structures and strategies, the effect of national institutions, and the need to gain workers' consent.

The cases have illustrated three different ways for unions to influence technological change. The first approach is the one pursued in the British and Canadian chemicals and finance firms. This involves confining bargaining to major employment issues, such as pay and job security, thus conceding to management most of the wider areas of decision-making over the introduction of technology.

The second approach is that adopted in the British and Canadian engineering plants. Here, unions seek to bargain over a wider range of effects of technological change, including both traditional employment issues and the more directly sociotechnical issues. Hugo Levie and Robin Williams (1983) describe this approach as achieving "external influence," since no attempt is made to become involved in management decisions over change but to bargain over them before, during, or after the process of decision-making. As illustrated earlier, with both approaches union influence on change is limited in terms of the stages at which bargaining takes place and the range of substantive issues involved. In addition, weaknesses in the links between the workplace and the wider union are exposed.

The third approach is direct involvement in strategic issues, which Levie and Williams (1983) refer to as exerting "internal influence" because, as a party to the decision-making process, unions directly influence the impact of change on the workforce. Germany has central trade union structures and a regulation by means of central agreements and legislation. There is a dual system of worker representation, however, in which works councils, independent of trade unions, are involved with a proportion if not all of the sociotechnical issues at the local level. With works councils the links between levels of representation are fragile, but local unions seem to interact more closely with the wider union. Local activity is supported by national regulation, while, at the same time, representatives at wider union levels learn from local experiences. The union confederations bargain with the state, and unions at the national level develop policies and expertise supporting local activity. At both the engineering and chemicals plants, the success of the local unions depended on help from the wider unions by way of expertise and resources. The interaction was less close and direct in the finance case.

In Italy, local union density is greater than in Germany. Although the unions are weaker centrally, there are clear indications that the interaction between the levels of union organization strengthen the position of the local activists. First, national agreements on the dissemination of information are mentioned in both the engineering and chemicals cases as important in strengthening the insight of the local unions concerning management's plans and options. Second, in both cases, the regional position of the unions involved was of major importance.

In chemicals, the regional unions increased the pressure on the company to safeguard the future of the site. Then, when the decision to invest in a new plant and new processes had been taken, they helped speed up the changes by persuading the regional authorities to give planning permission very quickly.

In engineering, the local unions' influence over the issues relating to subcontracting and the quality of suppliers depended on the influence of the unions in the whole regional engineering industry. Another difference from the situation in Germany appears to be that local works councils in Italy are less separate from the trade union organization at the plant level and much more an extension of union structures.

The conclusion is that local union activity and resources are the key to gaining influence on sociotechnical issues but that national and regional trade union resources can play an important part. Laws and national model or framework agreements, as well as knowledge of potential alternatives and their consequences, may support and coordinate local initiatives and stimulate contact between levels of trade union organization. Both the German codetermination law and the Italian agreements on information dissemination are good examples of measures that may stimulate contact and facilitate local initiatives. (This discussion of unions' direct involvement in strategic issues is based on Levie and Sandberg 1991.)

The case studies also show that the institutional framework of collaboration within each country has major effects on developments at the workplace level. The German codetermination system assumes a harmony of interest between labor and management. It is marked by a concern for consensus, and its legal characteristics require works councils and management to collaborate. The Italian national agreements embody consultative practices by involving unions to promote consensus. Joint committees are able to give binding and discretionary judgments on industrial and labor initiatives, which contribute to the right to information. Given the characteristics of sociotechnical changes, there are two important aspects of such procedural regulation. First, access to company information is available so that workers and their unions can take part in what is usually an ongoing process of change. (Although, as noted above, the German codetermination system does not lead to automatic involvement in the design of change.) Second, conditions are created for unions and their members to develop their own perspectives on the changes. In contrast, the institutional structures of collective bargaining in Britain and Canada are characterized by a traditional model of job control unionism at the workplace, periodic negotiations over a narrow agenda, and a clear separation of management rights to make strategic decisions. The research indicates that the possibility for British and Canadian worker representatives to gain influence over sociotechnical issues depends less on national institutions than in the other countries. Indeed, at the engineering plants the influence gained relied little on any form of outside support but was more a measure of the strength of the well-developed local unions involved.

Despite the similarities within each national system, then, some internal differences are apparent. Here, in particular, the case studies suggest that there are different reasons for and ways of gaining consent to technological change. In some cases, particularly those involving skilled workers, management may require the technical competence of workers to help make the investment decisions and plan the organizational change. For example, at the Canadian machine tools plant, no production engineering department existed, while at the Italian engineering plant, the reliance on the technical expertise of skilled machinists was traditionally high. In the British and German engineering cases, management also needed the considerable technical and organizational expertise of the workers involved, but, particularly in the latter case, this did not require consent from the worker representatives. Thus, even when management does not intend to foster participation, the employer will need the technical competence and tacit skills of its workers.

Another reason to gain workers' consent is to avoid potential conflict and minimize the opportunity for worker representatives to use the threat of technological change to strengthen their organization and the support of their members. In the British insurance case, a central management decision was made to inform the worker representatives relatively early, to adopt a cautious approach to the introduction of on-line systems, and to rely on "natural wastage" to minimize the impact of the subsequent reorganization and the reduction of employment levels. This example does not only apply to the British insurance case. More generally, a wish to preempt dissatisfaction and possible conflict inspired a choice to provide earlier and more comprehensive information than, for example, legal minimum regulations necessitated.

Yet another reason for management to seek early agreement with worker representatives on intended technological and organizational changes relates to a view of these changes as a package deal. In this case, trade-offs in jobs or work organization are needed to facilitate the proposed measures, such as an investment in continued production or the modernization of the facilities. Examples are the Canadian chemicals plant, where investment in a new product helped ease the way for changes in production methods and major job loss; the Italian chemicals plant, where job loss was traded off for investment; and the British engineering plant, where a new technology agreement was accepted against corporate opposition, with the knowledge that the actual input of the worker representatives in the process of change would be limited.

In conclusion, the diversity of the situations faced by the parties at the sites studied precludes simple comparisons. Nonetheless, this cross-industry material has demonstrated that although the sites across the four countries were similar in their technologies and products, they brought forth different processes of labor regulation at the workplace. According to John Kelly (1985), technological change should be modified through negotiation so that both labor and capital derive benefits as well as share costs. But the adversarial tradition of industrial relations in Britain and Canada "inevitably increases the salience of opposing interests in the distribution of costs and benefits" (Hyman 1988, 55). The German and Italian cases suggest that a collaborative process is more likely to be pursued where there is a tradition of cooperation. This process is more institutionalized and formalized in Germany, however, than in Italy. In the latter case, it is important to note that the collaborative process was achieved without formal institutions such as codetermination. Here, new methods to institutionalize negotiations with consultative procedures and joint committees are innovative ways of regulating industrial relations.

Since this material was collected, all the evidence suggests that in Britain the nonparticipative process documented here has been reinforced and certainly not halted (Gallie 1988). Similarly, recent literature on Germany and Italy does not suggest the emergence of a pattern that would be significantly different from the one developed here. (For a review, see Keller 1991). In Canada, where the evidence was collected more recently, none of the discourse on new human resource management perspectives has fostered a shift from the adversarial to an accommodative scenario (see Chaykowski and Verma 1992).

Locke (1992) has recently argued that the strategic choices of labor and management lead to outcomes that challenge the concept of national industrial relations. He suggests that the diversity within industrial relations systems will, in certain industries or sectors, be greater than the diversity across systems. National models of labor regulation, however, "should be understood not as homeostatic and self-producing systems of action but as complex and contingent historical constructions whose unity and coherence always remain open empirical questions" (Tolliday and Zeitlin 1991b, 277). Thus, the comparative experiences of the cases discussed in this chapter may portend the emergence of labor-management relations in which various institutional arrangements are in a state of continuing evolution. The propositions advanced here can therefore be interpreted as hypotheses to be tested in future international and comparative research.

7

Conflict and Compliance: The Workplace Politics of a Disk-Drive Factory in Singapore

Chung Yuen Kay

This chapter looks at the workplace politics of a "final assembly" station of a disk-drive factory in Singapore. The research on which this chapter is based was initially motivated by a desire to provide a "fresh" approach to certain research themes relating to women workers in Asian export factories. The problem, as I saw it, was that many of the better-known researchers in the field were so concerned with making theoretical points and abstractions that they often glossed over the actual lived experiences of the women they were generalizing about (Grossman 1979; Hancock 1980; Lim 1978). The women workers were often represented as "passive," "docile," and "submissive," unresisting of their exploitation and oppression. Dissatisfied with this essentially deterministic social scientific portrayal of the women as politically a-conscious (and I use the term "politically" in the broadest sense to refer to an awareness of power), I set out to do an ethnography that would explore the consciousness of women workers in Singapore, both in the workplace and out of it. For the factory phase of my fieldwork, I worked and researched full time as a production operator in a disk-drive factory, which will be known here as Sagetech.[1]

Sagetech is an American multinational company that, at the time of my research, had two factories in Singapore, one producing printed circuit boards, the other, disk drives. The company hires a total of 1400 workers[2] and is nonunionized.

Following an analysis of the wider socioeconomic and political context of Singapore, the chapter features an ethnographic depiction and discussion of management-worker relations in the workplace. Shopfloor relations were characterized by both conflict and compliance. Managerial strategies to control and manage the predominantly female workforce were met with a taken-for-granted acceptance on the one hand but also resistance, on the other. Although collective action was relatively uncommon, the women had knowledge of, and resorted to, a range of individual forms of action—from absenteeism to attempts to negotiate productivity both "covertly" and "overtly," to struggles to create "private" spheres within the workplace. The women interpreted their relationship with management in terms of "us" and "them," and at times, a nascent sense of "class" was detectable. This shaded into what I shall call a "factory consciousness." The dimension of "gender" runs through the whole discussion. Indeed, I argue that "compliance" may sometimes be read as a female strategy for wresting a small degree of power.

Throughout, the emphasis is on the terms of discourse used by the workers themselves. My theoretical orientation as a sociologist is toward interpretive/phenomenological sociology. By this, I mean that I use phenomenology as an organizing device for understanding and interpreting the social reality I study. I will briefly sketch some pertinent phenomenological ideas here.

The experience of the individual is pivotal to Schutzian theorizing. From the point of view of any such individual, the world that is experienced is her world. It is the world as it appears to her. And in this everyday lifeworld, the actor adopts the natural attitude. In contrast with the scientific attitude, in which anything can be questioned, in the natural attitude a policy of refraining from doubt is the norm. Thus, people/actors in their natural attitude generally suspend doubt that the material and social reality is anything other than it appears to be. Things are just as they appear. Factory workers, in their "natural attitude," accept and take for granted the nature of factory work, and the regimentation and control that goes with it. In the natural attitude, the actor's explication and understanding of the world is based on his or her "biography"—a stock of knowledge that comprises previous experience, immediate experience, and such experiences as are transmitted to the actor by other actors, parents, teachers, and so on.

This personal, taken-for-granted stock of knowledge does not form a closed, clear-cut sphere. There is a "kernel" of determinacy, "self-evidencies" (for example, it is "self-evident" within the world of the factory that managers and supervisors give orders, while workers carry out orders) that change from situation to situation, that are set against a background of indeterminacy (for example, the outer limits of supervisory control are indeterminate until "tested"). This indeterminate horizon is, however, capable of explication.

It is important to emphasize that the taken-for-granted stock of knowledge is considered adequate only until further notice. If a new experience in everyday life can be classified as a "type" (based on previous experience), then it confirms the validity of the stock of knowledge. When the new experience is incongruent with previous experience, however (as, for example, when factory operators consider that certain actions of a supervisor exceed the limits of what is "typically" acceptable), then the taken-for-granted nature of the actor's experience is breached. The chain of self-evidency is interrupted. Hitherto sufficient typification now appears insufficient, and the actor has to move on to new explications for that which is problematic (Schutz and Luckmann 1974). In turn, the very formulation of a problem determines what is to be taken for granted and what is to be questioned. Life process involves constantly shifting systems of relevance, so that we are "involved in the one topical and the many marginal topical relevances with layers of our personality on different levels of depths" (Schutz 1970, 120). Consciousness is thus seen as both a state and a process, and it can change and develop.

Actors also experience the social world as intersubjective. Other actors with whom I interact are taken by me to have a reciprocity of perspectives with me. This presumption of mutual understandability is essential to the production of everyday life. It is because I presume that others would see things as I do and would act as I do that there is reciprocity of perspectives, that I can proceed in the everyday lifeworld that I do. It is important to understand that Alfred Schutz is describing the natural attitude here, "not mounting a philosophical argument for its veracity, logicality, indubitability etc" (Sharrock and Anderson 1986, 37). It is in this sense that I use Schutzian phenomenology as a basis for understanding the social reality described in the rest of this chapter.

Singapore Context

Rapid industrialization since 1960 propelled Singapore into the ranks of newly industrializing countries. Singapore's economic growth has been characterized by its commitment to export-oriented industrialization and its heavy reliance on foreign investments. Industrialization via the multinational was chosen as the strategy for development because it meant instant jobs and access to world markets and technological expertise. Multinational corporations from the United States, Europe, and, increasingly, Japan were seen as the means for catching up with the developed world. This coincided with the period when multinationals from the industrialized countries were shifting the low-technology, labor-intensive end of the production process to "off-shore" sites in Southeast Asia, Central America, and South America. In particular, multinationals relocated whenever there was an abundant supply of cheap labor. The target group was young women and, quite often, young women entering the labor market for the first time.

Singapore was a favored location because of its strategic geographical position, relatively literate population (by the standards of colonial societies) and efficiently organized transportation and banking systems. The Singapore government also offered attractive investment incentives. By 1973, there were more than fifty MNCs engaged in manufacturing and which accounted for 83.5 percent of Singapore's direct exports (Heyzer

1983). The growth of the electronic products and components industry has been phenomenal, particularly since 1979, when U.S. disk-drive companies channeled millions into computer hardware, making Singapore a major world disk-drive exporter. Disk-drive companies are the largest employer in the manufacturing sector, accounting for 26.3 percent of the sector's employment (Chia 1989). Although the industry has been upgrading in recent years toward more sophisticated products and processes, it remains largely labor-intensive, involving primarily the assembly and testing of disk drives.

Central to the success of Singapore's industrial strategy has, of course, been the institutionalization of wage restraint and cooperative labor. The government took decisive steps to achieve this. Following the separation of Singapore from Malaysia, government leaders focused on the requirements for the survival of the small, independent city-state. The "ideology of survival" "insisted on the inseparability of economic and political survival and the necessary subservience of all other considerations. Above all else, survival demanded the internalization of an entirely new set of social attitudes and beliefs which embodied self-sacrifice for the 'national interest'" (Rodan 1989, 88).

Workers, in particular, would have to be very disciplined for Singapore to be successful in highly competitive world export markets. A succession of legislative measures whittled away at the traditional functions of unions. The National Trade Union Congress (NTUC) was henceforth to become a junior partner with the government in national development. In 1967, at the delegates' conference of the NTUC, the prime minister, Lee Kuan Yew, called for a change in the goals of trade unionism in Singapore—the unions were to give full support to the government's methods of industrialization (through the incursion of foreign capital), help contain any labor unrest, and keep a check on wage increases.

In response to this directive, the NTUC defined its new role as seeking to be "partners in production within an integral society" (to borrow a phrase from Heyzer 1983). Thus, in the National Wage Council (NWC) (set up in 1972 to ensure "orderly wage developments" and to promote national productivity), the NTUC became a partner in a tripartite relationship with the government and employers. Noeleen Heyzer has commented (1983) that "through this co-option of the NTUC national leadership, the government has been successful in regulating wage demands and also in defusing the capacity for organized labor to act as a locus for political opposition in the post-colonial period." (This did not mean that all workers necessarily identified with the national leadership then, and in 1974–75, when Singapore was in the grip of a recession, there was an occurrence of grassroots militancy involving retrenched workers at a shipyard.)

In keeping with the idea of a "New Society," new images emerged, and emphasized in these images was the need to be "modern," "disciplined," "rational," and "pragmatic." It is thus clear that "trade unionism" does not have the same meanings for many of the present generation of Singapore workers as it does for workers in Western industrialized countries.

Toward the end of 1980, however, the government addressed what it saw as the problem of workers' poor attitudes (as signified by the common practice of job-hopping) on a more conceptual level. In December 1980, the then prime minister, Lee Kuan Yew, prescribed that Singapore should model itself on the Japanese system of industrial relations, characterized by a cooperative relationship between employer and worker. Greater team spirit was identified as the key to success in the next stage of economic development, and Singaporeans were exhorted to learn to be team achievers. A comprehensive campaign to imbue the people with this message was carried out, largely through the media.

Despite government efforts, however, the results of a survey commissioned by the National Productivity Board in 1982 showed that Singaporeans had not yet internalized government discourse on the importance of cooperating. For example, about 70 percent of those interviewed felt that increasing productivity would be primarily to the company's benefit and not the workers'.

Garry Rodan has argued that the reason workers did not quickly take to teamwork was that, all along, the government had emphasized the need for Singaporeans to be competitive, and competition was very much part of the concrete reality (Rodan 1989). NWC guidelines, for example, rewarded the more meritorious workers. There was thus an obvious contradiction between the notions of "teamwork" and "meritocracy." Lim Chee Onn, then secretary-general of the NTUC, addressed this issue in his address to the Fourth Triennial Delegates' Conference in 1982, when he spoke of the need to maintain "a careful balance between developing individual skills and encouraging group performance" (Lim 1982, 3).

Lim also focused on the issue of new technology, pointing out that the advent of new production technology would greatly affect employment opportunities and that in order to maintain a competitive edge in securing more investments, the availability of a skilled, high-performance workforce was crucial. Hence the importance of training and upgrading workers at all levels.

The most serious test for tripartite cooperation was to come in 1985–86, however, when serious economic recession abruptly curtailed two decades of growth. The unions agreed to forgo claims for wage adjustments recommended by the NWC for that year. In 1986, the NWC recommended reduction of employers' contributions to the Central Provident Fund (CPF, a retirement fund for workers, based on monthly contributions calculated as a certain percentage of employees' salaries, by employers as well as employees) from 25 percent to 10 percent and a national wage restraint policy for two years. The unions accepted the "bitter medicine" as necessary for a quick recovery. In so doing, Ong Teng Cheong, NTUC Secretary-General said, "We have not only saved many fellow workers from retrenchment, but also helped the economy to turn around quickly" (Ong 1988). Trade union leaders, however, also reminded employers to remember the workers' sacrifices. The economy turned around from a -1.6 percent contraction in 1985 to an 8 percent growth in 1987. The labor market began to tighten again.

When employers were resistant to a 1 percent increase in employer contribution in 1991 to 17.5 percent, the NTUC responded sharply, pointing out that while workers' wages were now lower than those in South Korea and Taiwan, chief executive officers in Singapore were reported to be the highest paid in Asia, and if wage cost was a problem, more attention should be directed at executive and managerial pay (Wong 1992). The government came down on the side of the NTUC, urging employers to take the 1 percent increase in CPF contributions in their stride. At the seventh Triennial's Delegates' Conference in 1991, NTUC Secretary-General Ong Teng Cheong (who was then also the Deputy Prime Minister of Singapore) said, "If managements continue to interpret the patience and tolerance shown by our union officials as a sign of weakness, then they are wrong. Our unions will not hesitate to take tougher stands when their patience runs out" (Ong 1991, 9).

Notwithstanding Ong's firm stance in 1991, trade unionists themselves feel that they have some way to go in improving public perceptions of the constructive role that trade unions play in Singapore. As Evelyn Wong puts it,

> On the one hand, the conventional perception existed among many employ-
> ers that unions were adversarial and a hindrance. On the other hand, the
> union's cooperative approach and symbiotic relationship with the PAP
> resulted in some public perception, held by both employers and workers
> that unions were ineffective in representing workers' interests. (Wong 1992,
> 154)

Wong has also commented that the continuity of tripartism and the consensual mode of the industrial relations system cannot be taken for granted. As she sees it,

> Fundamental worker concerns on issues such as continued job security and
> adequate wage levels to meet the rising costs of living, as well as expecta-
> tions for a better standard and quality of life, will need to be effectively
> addressed . . . The challenge will be to translate consensus achieved
> through the tripartite relationship between labour, management and gov-
> ernment at the national level into cooperative labour-management relations
> and good human resource management, with an integral role for trade
> unions, at the enterprise level. (Wong 1992, 159)

What I have done in this section is to sketch some of the 'macro' issues that serve as background to the rest of the ethnography.[3] This section also shows that workers and management in the factory I studied are reacting to many of the same forces present in industries all over the world: new technology and new forms of work organization, such as teamworking. Thus, although this ethnography looks only at Singapore, it has comparative implications. The Singapore factory is not "unique." The Singapore experience is the outcome not just of a specific set of domestic but of international circumstances. Following a brief discussion of my research process, I will move into the ethnography "proper."

The Research Process

Three phases may be delineated in my research process: a first phase of participant-observation fieldwork in the factory and a second phase of interviews with supervisors and women workers, which shaded into the third phase of sustained interaction with the women. In July 1984, after months of trying to make contacts, endless phone calls to people connected with the electronics industry, and various false starts, I was finally able to carry out my participant-observation research at Sagetech.

In my earlier negotiations with the management of Sagetech over my entry into the company to do research, I had pointed out that I wished my researcher status to be known to the women and to the facilities manager with whom I dealt. Subsequently, however, my case was handled by the personnel manager, who, over several meetings, finally came to the conclusion that I should not reveal my identity as a researcher to the women. For all intents and purposes, once I entered the factory, I would be treated exactly like any other factory operator that Sagetech would hire; not even my supervisor on the shopfloor would know any different. The personnel manager also suggested that I not reveal my university connections but that, if asked, I should pose as an O-level school leaver.

I was unhappy with this position on various counts. First, I considered it ethically unsound that as one woman doing research on other women, I should resort to deception. Second, not only would I have to cope with the strange culture of the factory, I would have to cope with a new identity. Third, and finally, I did not see how I could pretend to be an O-level school leaver all the way through the research phase; at some point, I would have to reveal that I was a researcher.

The manager countered my protestations by saying that she thought it unlikely that the women I worked with would ask many questions about my background or my past and warned that if I was to do my research overtly, I might get nowhere because the women would not open up to someone so obviously an "outsider," and, worse, if it was known that I was in Sagetech with the approval of management, my motives and those of management would be suspect.

I was in a quandary over the question of presentation of self. Finally, when I entered Sagetech, I resolved that I would tell as much of the truth as I could without risking my chances of getting to know the women or falling out of favor with management. Thus, though I did not openly declare my researcher status, I let it be known that while I was working in Sagetech, I was also studying at the university and my studies were related to the nature of factory work. In fact, I faithfully and laboriously repeated this story to the women with whom I spoke. The women did not register much concern over my "university-educated" background except to remark, on days when overtime work was requested of them, that Kay would not be able to do OT (overtime) since she had to go for her "studies."

The part of my identity that aroused the greatest interest among the women was the fact that I was a Malaysian living in Singapore. For this, I was both envied and pitied; envied for being "independent" and living on my own, and pitied for being away from my family and home comforts. Thus, for the women, my being a "Malaysian living in Singapore" was more significant than my being a middle-class, university-educated woman. What was commented on, however, was that I spoke "good English," unlike the variety, or rather varieties, spoken by the women in the factory.

Every field "role" has its advantages and its problems. Starting off my research semicovertly as I did enabled me to experience for myself what it is like to be a production operator in a way that would not have been possible had my identity been known. Furthermore, as an incompetent novice—as one of the women—it was perhaps easier for me to "break the ice" and build rapport with the women. On the minus side, I was uneasy with the "cloak-and-dagger" secrecy that I had to engage in periodically. Meetings with management had to be managed in a stealthy manner without the women or the supervisor knowing about it. "Shorthand" field notes had to be hastily scrawled during trips to the restroom or when no one was around and I had a moment to myself. Additional notes were then made on the bus on my way home, and, finally, I spent each evening writing out the notes in full.

In my sixth week at Sagetech, I insisted that the supervisor and the women with whom I was working be told I was a researcher. Patrick, the supervisor of the station where I was working, was informed by management, and he in turn told the women at a meeting. The women took it calmly, more so than Patrick, who had been somewhat upset. There was curiosity as to what my research was about and perplexity that anyone should want to spend so much time writing about women and work in a factory, but no hostility, or none that I could discern. Indeed, many of the women remarked that they had gotten so used to thinking of me as "Kay, an operator," someone who worked alongside them, that it did not make much difference that I was also "Kay, a researcher."

Nonetheless, I believed that there was a shift in the women's awareness of me. The revelation of my researcher identity legitimated my tendency to be inquisitorial in the eyes of the women. I felt freer to ask questions that as just another (and relatively new) operator I would have been wary of asking. I would probably have been told off for being a "kay-poh" (Chinese term for a busybody). But the women now generously endorsed my appeal for information. On another level, some of the women felt that perhaps I could be useful in conveying their opinions about work and the workplace back to management, channeling their grievances as it were.

I withdrew from full-time work at the factory after my third month was up. In the interview phase of my fieldwork (amid continuing interactions with the women), I interviewed eight supervisors, one of whom was the only female supervisor in the factory. I also carried out "formal" interviews with twelve women operators in 1985. It was not always easy to arrange a suitable time for the interviews, given the busy schedules of the women, who had to juggle home and work responsibilities. Many women agreed to the interviews as an act of friendship, "helping Kay out with her project," as they put it. In the beginning, they were not convinced that they would have much to say, or that their stories would be of much interest to me. But then, in the course of the interviews, some of them seemed surprised by their own volubility. Some of them commented, when I asked how they felt about the interview at the end of it, that they had never talked so much about their lives before or knew that they had so much to say. None of the women interviewed found the experience disagreeable, and a few found the interview revelatory. Yen Lan asked to listen to her interview, and I made copies of their interviews for any of the women who were interested.

During this phase, I continued to interact with the women. It must be emphasized that these women were not just "subjects." Many had, over time, become friends, and, as friends, we continued to keep in touch. At the same time, merely saying that the women had become friends is simplifying a more complex relationship. The disturbing fact was that although they had become friends, they had not ceased to be sociologically interesting and relevant to my research.

A great deal of the women's lives, as communicated to me largely through telephone conversations, centered around the mundane and the ordinary. Given the demands on their time: a twelve-hour workday sometimes, on three or four days of the week, and child care and housework, the telephone was a very important way for them to maintain friendships and provide support. For my part, I made use of this medium to maintain relations with the women. Initially, I systematically called up all of them at regular intervals. Thus, I was kept informed of the latest happenings in the factory and among the women. I could also use the telephone to cross-check and verify information. Thus, when I learned from Siew Yu that Li Chiew was preparing to get married, I would call her up next to chat and gather information.

But although the telephone helped sustained regular interaction over time, it was not the only means of interaction. Sometimes, I went to the factory to meet some of the women for lunch, and even though these were necessarily hurried affairs, they helped me keep in touch and reestablish links with a larger group of women at one time.

For a long time after I left Sagetech, I continued to be regarded as a "Station 212 operator" and was included in all the celebratory events in the women's lives. Thus, I was present at birthday gatherings, I attended weddings, and I was invited to engagement parties. By these means I sought systematically to cover the lives of the women from the time I left Sagetech until March 1987.

Control at Sagetech

This section outlines the atmosphere of control that management sought to impose at the factory. It then discusses the major concern of management: controlling the target.

The hierarchy of authority in the company was as follows: at the very top was the managing director and under him various managers. Senior supervisors and, below them, supervisors were directly responsible for the running of their stations and in charge of the operators. A crew of technicians was responsible for the servicing of machines and tools. There was also an administrative network, consisting largely of clerical workers, and a personnel officer.

The sexual division of labor in the factory was as follows: All the top people, including the managing director and the various managers except the personnel officer, were male, as were the supervisors, with the exception of one, the supervisor in charge of the quality control (QC) operators. The quality control operators were more highly qualified than the other operators, and QC was seen to be prestigious work. At the same time, it was considered that the QC operators needed less control and discipline by virtue of their being better educated. This in effect meant that the other male supervisors considered supervising QC a "soft" option, rather than prestigious, and the female supervisor had lower status than her male counterparts. I gleaned this information from interviews with the supervisors.

The technicians, with the exception of one or two, were also male. So were the security guards. The operators, by contrast, were all female, with the exception of a few men who worked in the storeroom or handled bulky goods. The clerical workers and personnel officer were female. Thus, the people with the most authority were male and the ones without any authority were female.

The image management wished to have projected to its employees was that it was "open" and egalitarian. In reality, management was "open" only as long as there was no serious dissent or questioning of management's role. In meetings, the supervisors often said that "we are one big family" or, relatedly, "we must work together as a team." Heyzer (1986) has documented that this is a common feature of management ideology in multinational factories in Singapore and Malaysia. The operators would periodically be "thanked" for their hard work.

In principle, given the "open" channels of communication, even an operator could have access to the managing director. In practice, they very rarely did, since the women believed that it would serve "no use." The people with whom the operators were most in contact were the supervisors, who addressed the operators as "girls." The women preferred the self-definition of "operators," so that they would start a sentence "We operators."

An attempt by management to "feminize" the job of operator was seen in its adoption of the language of the domestic sphere as the vocabulary of the workplace. The term "housekeeping" was used to mean the tidying and clearing up of her work station by an operator. And memos sometimes deplored the "poor housekeeping" of certain sections and warned of the need to improve.

The egalitarian—"we are a team/family"—ideology was not borne out by the somewhat stern rules and regulations governing the behavior of the women. The "Uniform and Badge Policy" memorandum to new staff, for example, laid down that "you must wear the uniform together with the brown belt that we issued to you. Other belts are not allowed." Furthermore, "You must not alter the uniform shorter than 2 inches above the knees." Then, "If you fail to return the uniforms in good condition we will charge you for the uniform between $19 to $26 per set." As for the badge, "it must be displayed with the photograph facing outward, on the right side of the hook sewn on the uniforms." I can only conjecture that the ostensible reason for the uniform was to identify which women were production operators and not, say, clerical staff. Another possible purpose of the uniforms could have been to identify which women belonged to which factory, since there were many factories in the industrial area, each of which had its own uniform. There were no pragmatic reasons for some of the other rules, and they may be better understood as techniques of discipline and surveillance.

The security guards at the entrances to the stations further extended the system of control. Once the women had passed the guards and were on shift, they could not leave their floor of the building without informing the guard of their purpose for leaving. The guards could also reprimand the operators for not wearing their badges or refuse entry to an operator without a badge. Inside their stations, the women were not allowed to have any personal belongings except what they could put in their uniform pocket. Handbags and all other forms of carriers were forbidden because the company feared that the women would sneak components out of their stations.

The rules, regimentation, and depersonalization fulfilled symbolic and material purposes of "managing" people into accepting the "facticity" of social control within the factory. That is, the social world of the factory, with its control of the activities of subordinates by superiors, had to be reproduced daily until it became taken for granted and "thing-like" to the workers. It had to be experienced as a preconstituted and preorganized social setting that required neither explanation nor justification.

The Work Process at Station 212, Final Assembly

Station 212, final assembly, where I concentrated my fieldwork, occupied the front area of a huge room (fig. 7.1). The steady hum of machines

Figure 7.1. Plan of Station 212 at Sagetech

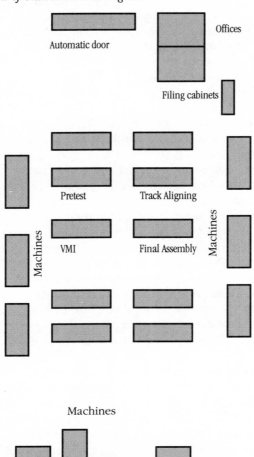

at the back of the room dominated. Overhead, a complex network of pipes, conduits, and vents traversed the ceiling. There was a wide pathway in the center of the station. Flanking the pathway on both sides were long worktables (also referred to as "stations"). There were computers on one row of the worktables, and track-aligning machines on another. There were also trolleys with disk drives on them.

There were ten operators in Station 212 when I first arrived. Our numbers gradually increased to fifteen. Li Chiew was the "lead" in our station.

The work in the final assembly station was organized into four consecutive tasks: track aligning, final assembly, VMI (visual and mechanical inspection), and pretest. The women also did rework and board changes when necessary, but these two tasks were not directly related to the main production flow. So, within Station 212, there were "stations" (consisting of a long worktable with the appropriate tools and machines) for each of the four operations, and the women were assigned to a specific station, although sometimes, when there was a "jam" (a common term and one spoken in English) in production flow, resulting in one station being particularly overworked, an operator from another station would be sent to help out.

The disk drives on which the women worked came from the "Clean Room," where they had been assembled. The drive was a rectangular, metal-framed object, rounded at one end. It was approximately seventeen centimeters long, thirteen centimeters wide, and four to five centimeters thick. The front was completely covered by a metal plate, screwed down with various big and small screws.

Back in Station 212, the drives would first be sent to the track-aligning station, which was run by Ritu. There were six track-aligning machines on the table, in a row. Ritu would hook on a drive and an E-Prom, which was a small metal tablet about two centimeters by one centimeter, with tines projecting downward, to one of the machines, switch on the machine that set the speed, then move on to the next machine, repeat the process, and so on. When the track-aligning process for each drive was completed, the sound from the machine, which had a jiggling rhythm, would stop. Ritu would then take down the drive and the E-Prom and attach an adhesive label with the number of the drive to the E-Prom to show that it had been tested and was compatible with the drive. Last, she would sign "TA" and her badge number on the traveler's card for that particular drive, to show that the drive had been track-aligned and that she had been the operator responsible for it, before returning the drive and the E-Prom back to the tray and putting it on to the trolley for drives that been aligned. It was clear that the traveler's card served as a basic means of surveillance of performance. In principle, the system kept operators under observation, and they became accountable for each piece of work carried out. It was a form of disciplinary power.

Seated behind Ritu were the final assembly (FA) women. The FA women worked on drives that had been aligned, fitting on printed circuit boards. Since this process involved more tasks and took a longer time to accomplish than track-aligning, there were at least two, and sometimes three or four, operators at this station, to keep up with the flow from the track-aligning station. FA was the process I was most familiar with, as most of my time was spent doing FA.

First, an operator had to check the drive, to see that the number on the drive tallied with the number on the traveler's card and that there were no obvious damages to the drive, such as a dented top cover, missing wires on the underside, or exposed wires (that is, wires with their protective covering chipped off so that the wires inside were exposed). Next, the various groups of wires on the underside of the drive had to be seen to. Some had to be tucked in neatly under the frame of the drive. P6 (the numbering for a particular wire) had to be crossed over a thinner wire and then trapped between two plastic pegs on the drive. A small piece of Mylar tape (no one could tell me why it was so named; it looked like ordinary tape to me) was then put over the capacitor at the corner of the drive. This completed the work to be done on the underside of the drive.

The operator would now unwrap a printed circuit board (PCB) from its bubble bag cover. Each operator would have a stack of PCB by her side. She next checked that the PCB had the correct "ec" number printed on it. For example, if the number she had been told to look for (and the criterion for which kind of PCB was deemed suitable for use varied and changed from time to time) was 1080 and the number on the PCB read 2360, she would then set the PCB aside and pick another one. The PCB would also have to carry the QA (quality assurance) stamp.

Next, the operator had to check the PCB to ensure that there were no missing components, that the coating on the components was intact, that the screws on the ground spring were flush, and that the ground spring was not bent. She then had to shorten some of the metal pins on the underside of the PCB (the side that would come in contact with the underside of the drive) so that they would not damage components on the drive. She would do this by snipping away with cutting shears, making sure that the PCB was well away from her eyes while she was doing this so that the snipped bits of metal would not injure her.

The next step was to fit the E-Prom onto the PCB, although some operators chose to do this last, after the PCB had been fitted onto the drive. This required that the tines of the E-Prom be fitted into corresponding apertures on the PCB.

The PCB was then fitted into the frame of the drive. The sets of metal tines on the edge of the PCB had to be inserted into the corresponding plastic sockets at the end of the P6, P7, and P8 wires in the drive. The metal tines for the P8 sockets were sometimes too long for the sockets and had to be shortened before insertion. After this was done, the operator had to check that the wires were not touching the PCB. If they were, this could be corrected by inserting a pair of tweezers into the space between the drive and the PCB to flatten the wires. The PCB could now be torqued into the drive at the edges.

After this, to ascertain that the ground spring was touching the spindle motor on the drive, the operator would have to peer into the space between the assembled drive and the PCB. If the ground spring was not touching the spindle motor, using the tweezers to press the ground spring down gently usually did the trick.

Finally, the operator had to check that all components on the PCB were level. This test was done by passing a ruler over the frame of the drive.

The operator then signed her operation, FA, and her badge number on the traveler's card. She would also mark her target sheet, to show that she had completed another drive. The drive then went back into the tray and on the trolley.

Across the aisle from the FA station was the visual and mechanical inspection station. The work of VMI in part duplicated the checking work that was carried out by the FA station. Using an overhead magnifying glass, the operators looked into the interior of assembled drives to check that there were no exposed or damaged wires, that wires were lying flat and not touching any component, and that the ground spring was touching the spindle motor. They also checked that the PCB was tightly torqued on to the frame of the drive, that the ground spring screw had the adequate numbers of washers, that the tines of the E-Prom were indeed fitted into the apertures on the PCB and not bent, and that the components were level. Finally, they checked the speed of the drive, using a small machine.

The women on VMI would rectify the lesser errors and oversights in assembly work, but if the rectification involved dismantling the drive, they would "reject" it and send the drive back to FA. Like the other operators, the VMI women would also sign their task and badge number on the traveler's card and mark their target sheet after working on each drive.

The pretest station was in front of the VMI station and the final stage in the process before the drives left Station 212. Pretest essentially involved testing the assembled drives to determine whether they "passed" or "failed." The job involved plugging in a drive to a machine with a computer; inputting the system, drive, and machine number; and then waiting for the readings. The crucial part of the job was knowing the ranges within which the different numbers (such as "long-term error") on the data readings were to fall. Which aspects of the data reading "passed" or "failed" determined whether a drive "passed" or "failed" overall. There were about twelve machines at the pretest, so that while waiting for the readings on one machine, the operator would either plug another drive into another machine or assess the readings from another machine. When the process of FA and pretest was completed, the drives would be taken away for the next step in the overall production process.

Two other jobs that were undertaken by operators in the station were "board changes" and "rework." Board changes involved drives that had failed pretest and needed to have their boards changed, after which they would go straight to pretest to be tested again. Rework involved drives that did not pass VMI or, if they did, were rejected by quality assurance and had to be "reworked" to have their faults corrected. On most "normal" days, we would have a small number of disks with faults, and these usually could be taken care of by one fairly experienced FA operator. Reworks and board changes were not popular with the other operators, who considered them "troublesome." There were times, however, when the flow of normal drives stopped and we all had to work with rework drives, burn-in drives, and so on.

Generally, the jobs were repetitive in nature. They were perhaps more complex than jobs in the semiconductor industry, but after an operator had assembled about eighty drives a day, five days a week, for some time, the monotony of the job got to them all the same.

Negotiating Target

A central focus of each workday at Sagetech is the "target." The target refers to the productivity of the operators and is measured, according to the particular task of the operator, on the basis of the number of drives that have been assembled, or aligned, or pre-tested in a working day. After completing her operation on each drive, the operator would mark this on her target sheet for the day. Since the length of time required for the completion of the operations varied between operations, the targets of operators carrying out different tasks varied as well. Thus, in my time, the target for the track aligner was about two hundred, while that of the final assembly operator was about eighty-five, on a "normal" day when production was flowing smoothly, when there was a continuous supply of the necessary components, and when we were not required to attend to other jobs.

My first intimation of the centrality of the concept of target occurred the day after I had been sent to Station 212. A man with a stopwatch was walking about watching operators at the station work. Li Chiew, the lead (the chief production operator, an assistant to the supervisor as it were, who transmits orders and sees to the smooth running of the station when the supervisor is not around), came to me and told me in a low voice that when "Kenneth" came to clock me at work I should do my work at a slower pace than I actually could.[4] I perceived the meaning of the account only later. Kenneth was the new second-shift supervisor. The second shift was newly started, and Kenneth was trying to assess what target he should set for the shift by studying the targets of the first-shift operators. This account revealed the essential tension, sometimes obvious, sometimes oblique, that existed between the women operators, on the one hand, and the supervisors and management, on the other, over the target that could be achieved.

Part of the typified knowledge the women shared about management was that management was never satisfied. Once an operator showed that her target could be raised a little, management would keep trying to raise it. It was therefore important for the women not to let that happen and to maintain what they considered realistic and achievable target levels.

In their everyday work, the operators paced themselves according to a kind of internal timing system. For example, after I had been at the station for some time and been socialized, I figured out (by observing other operators on the same task) that my quota of drives should be about ten to twelve an hour. If I had been assembling faster than usual in an hour, I would slow down, relax, and perhaps chat with the operator next to me.

On the one hand, the women felt that if they aimed for a much higher target, the quality of their work would be compromised and they would be blamed for this. On the other hand, if their targets were low, management came down on them. Many of the women said that they opted for "quality" work rather than target. Yen Lan expressed the contradiction between target and quality succinctly.

> Yen Lan had an argument with Patrick over the correct way to check the assembled drive. Patrick said that it was important that the operator work with "swift eyes and swifter hands" (said in Mandarin). Yen Lan argued that if she does it too fast, QA would reject, and that her way of using a plastic ruler to check the components level, although slower, is the correct way. After Patrick went off, she said, "What does he want, target or quality?" (field notes July 16, 1984)

Variations of this "target or quality" argument were often echoed by the women to clinch arguments with leads or supervisors about the speed at which they were working. It is possible to "read" this argument on two levels. First, it is possible to read it as a genuine expression of the operators' concern with the quality of their work, not so much because of their "dedication to the job," but because in the end, shoddy or flawed work would be returned to the operators in the form of "reworks," which were never welcomed. On another level, however, it is possible that the women use the "target or quality" argument as a form of leverage, that the argument is sometimes enlisted successfully to fob off demands to increase speed or complaints about the productivity level on a given day.

Work at Sagetech is considered highly technological in nature. New operators are constantly reminded by management that the disk drives they are working with are expensive and delicate products and are to be treated with care. Given these considerations, the women's reasoning that the quality of their work may be compromised by excessive speed is not one that can be easily deflected by the supervisors. This "mobilization of bias" thus uses the vocabulary of motives already existing in management culture. The women attempt to legitimize their practice by turning managerial ideology "against itself" (Armstrong, Goodman, and Hyman 1981, 43). This line of reasoning can be successfully resorted to only in certain circumstances. It is most effective when applied to demands or complaints from individual supervisors, rather than to dicta from on high. It also seems to be particularly valid on days when various technical problems have occurred in the production of drives, as often happened during my research phase at Sagetech. The particular model of drive that we were assembling in Station 212 had been newly introduced and there were many teething problems.

At Station 412 and at some of the other stations, the supervisors put a chart on the wall of the daily targets of individual operators. This public display was intended to exert pressure on the women to perform and perhaps compete with each other (See Nichols and Beynon 1977 for a description of similar pressure brought to bear on workers at "Chemco," a chemical production plant in England). The women did not like this practice, and some from our station felt that Patrick was more sympathetic because he did not adopt it in Station 212. Other women were skeptical and felt that this was merely a form of "cosmetic" sympathy. Underneath it all, and perhaps in "exchange" for his more sympathetic attitude, he expected compliance with the target he wanted.

> Ritu talks about her work. She says that all Patrick cares about is his target. That's why when she has done over 200 for track align, she relaxes, because if she does more, Patrick will only expect her to continue to perform likewise. Patrick is talking about getting another operator to help her manage the six machines, but if two people work six machines, then they would have more time on their hands and Patrick would expect them to do other things in between. Like that, might as well not, says Ritu. She did it before, with four machines, and other sorts of work, and target was low. (field notes, July 23, 1984)

This account is interesting not only for Ritu's analysis of Patrick but also because of its insight into the essentially ambivalent feelings the women had about target, that "Target was low." A lot of the women professed a lack of concern with target, because they saw that the central emphasis on target and on raising it worked against the women's collective interest. Adopting a disdainful attitude toward the matter was a form of disengagement from this central managerial concern. And, for a lot of the women, it was not just an attitude. Many women were not overly concerned about their target. Others had to take it into account. A temporary operator, for example, waiting for confirmation as permanent staff, knew that her productivity would be taken into consideration in the decision-making process. Thus, a new operator who consistently performed below expectations would be reprimanded by the supervisor. Should she continue not to improve, she could, as a penalty, be transferred to a station where the work was deemed less attractive (the noise level might be high, or it could be a very busy station). Likewise, if an operator was due for a wage increment, she would be aware that she would be assessed partially on the basis of her productivity and would not wish to jeopardize the situation by adopting a lackadaisical attitude toward her target. Thus, Ritu was merely echoing the contradiction that the women felt surrounded the target when she desisted Patrick's attempts to raise her target level, on the one hand, but did not want a "low target" on the other.

The women had a sense of what should and could be realistically achieved at work, so that Ritu would achieve a target of more than two hundred in track aligning, no less, because she judged that "more than two hundred" was what she owed Sagetech in a fair day's work. Sagetech, of course, did not concur. Management put pressure on the supervisors, who, because they wanted to be in favor with management, would try to get their "girls" to yield better targets. The women called Kenneth "target crazy" (spoken in English) because he was forever pushing for improved targets.

Nonetheless, a number of the women felt that the pressure for target was much less than it would be at a piece-rated factory. Lilian, who had worked in a garment factory, said that she had left because she disliked the atmosphere of fierce competition among the women. Sometimes there would be tussles among women who wanted more pieces to sew to boost their earnings. In contrast, since the women at Sagetech received a fixed fortnightly wage, and there were no monetary gains for individual women even if they were more productive (unless they put in a lot of overtime work, which was a different situation), "target-busting" by individual operators was frowned upon.

Pressure would be applied to an operator to toe the line if she was out-targeting other women in the station. There was an implicit code that no one should display overcompetence at work if by so doing she risked disturbing the collective target and caused hardship to the other women. (For American studies of similar "disciplinary" action against "rate-busters" in piece-rated factory work, see Lamphere 1979 and Shapiro-Perl 1979).

> Siew Yu was remarking disapprovingly of Joanna's careless ways at work. Sometimes, her drives are half hanging out of the trolley. Yes, but she's very fast, I said. But a lot of her FA gets rejected, says Siew Yu. Apparently Siew Yu said to her, "If you go so fast, you'll be the death of us. I can only manage one in five minutes." And the next day, [yesterday], she slowed down. She's over at VMI today. Aminah also asked me about the target here. Apparently, in the Grey Room [her former station], it's fixed at 180. What if the women don't reach it, I asked. All the women do, she said, or if they do not, maybe around 170. If they constantly reach only 160, the lead would query. But what if some women manage 200 then, I asked again. She said she didn't know. Sometimes, the leads of different sections would quarrel if one section attained a higher target than the other. Siew Yu

chipped in and said that in her former station, when they [sups] found that the women could attain a higher target, they would keep raising it until the women protested. (field notes, August 15, 1984)

At the beginning of this account, it would appear that Siew Yu's concern is with the quality of Joanna's work; she disapproves of her carelessness. When I comment on Joanna's speed, however, Siew Yu reveals another facet of her displeasure: Joanna is "doing harm" to other women who are assembling at a slower rate. That Joanna recognizes the validity of Siew Yu's complaint is evidenced by the fact that Joanna indeed slows down the next day. Aminah, who is new to the station, is immediately concerned with the target in Station 212. Her account of the work at her previous station, the Grey Room, also shows that codes about target and target-busting are equally valid in other stations and that the leads play an active role in policing targets.

As Armstrong has pointed out (1980), workers will often resist changes in management practices on the grounds of "fairness." Although workers undoubtedly have their own conceptions of fairness, it is also possible that its application to management action is an attempt to engage with that strand of managerial ideology that depicts management as being "fair" and impartial. Thus, in the preceding account, because a previous target of 180 had been established as a reasonable expectation of workers' efforts, workers may have contested the legitimacy of further increases in the targets by deploying arguments derived from managerial ideology of equity (Armstrong, Goodman, and Hyman 1981).

Some of the women's skepticism about Patrick's good intention in not installing a productivity chart in the station was later justified when relations between the women and Patrick reached an impasse. This happened after I had left Sagetech and was recounted to me by Suraya:

Patrick was in ill temper today, because when he asked the women to work OT the next day, nobody wanted to. They hadn't been told about it earlier on; it had been sprung on them. Furthermore, Suraya said, it's a public holiday, and we get paid for not working, so why should we work? Normally, if they work OT on public holidays, they would get 200% pay on top of normal pay, but now it's just treated as 200% pay in total (i.e., inclusive of the 100% normal) so why should they work? Anyway, it was so rare that they get a public holiday, and the women had all made plans. Patrick got pretty upset when the list was passed round and nobody signed up for OT (and here Suraya chuckled at the thought). He then called a meeting and asked them what reasons they had for not doing OT. Apparently, Suraya said cheerily, "It's Deepavali, and Devan Nair has invited me to his house. I am helping him to make tosay."[5] Patrick didn't think this was funny and looked hard at her, she said. He then wanted to know whether it was because of the money. Suraya said that she denied this. "If it's just about money, then what for we want to work on Saturdays and Sundays? We don't get that much money for it. Of course we want to help you when we can, but in this case we have already made plans with our family, etc."

Patrick stormed and turned nasty. Said he had never demanded a fixed weekly target for individuals before, but if they do not cooperate, he will take the target for all operators. Li Chiew later said privately to the girls, "Well, if he's going to be like this, fine. We'll give him his target by each Friday, but then we'll not work on Saturdays and Sundays at all."

Patrick then called each girl in and asked for a reason why they could not work OT. Some had to go for a barbecue; others were going away to Malaysia; on a picnic, etc. Suraya said to Patrick, "Look, Patrick, I've just got the keys to my new house and I am very busy, preparing and shopping for it." In the end only one operator changed her mind as she couldn't think of an adequate excuse why she could not do OT. The other women teased her about it and said, "You and Patrick can work together and have the whole station to yourselves tomorrow." (field notes, October 22, 1984)

Suraya's account illustrates that the control by supervisors and higher management over women is not absolute and is something that can be negotiated, depending on the circumstances. Also interesting is the way that both parties—Patrick and the operators—used "rules" in dealing with the situation. Writers studying organizational behavior have drawn on ethnomethodological insights in questioning the assumption that rules determine behavior (see Bittner 1973; Zimmerman 1973) Rather, rules are contingently applied and produced (Heritage 1984). The "competent use" of a given rule or a set of rules is founded upon members' perceptions of what specific actions are necessary on a given occasion to reproduce a "normal" state of affairs. Thus, competent rule use calls not just for compliance but for judgment, so that certain actions may be seen as essentially satisfying the provisions of the rule, even though the actions may contrast with precedent. Situational exigencies may, however, affect the production of desired outcomes, and the situation then has to be repaired.

I will now look at various features of the account. First, note that Suraya hints at the unreasonableness of Patrick's request and points out that the justification for women's refusal to accede is that they were not given sufficient notice of the overtime work; it was sprung on them. Suraya also admits that one of the reasons she and the other women do not want to work overtime is monetary. Usually, they are paid double wages for the day's work on top of the day's "normal" wage. On this occasion, they are to be paid only a single wage plus the "normal" wage. At the meeting Patrick called to deal with the women's collective refusal to work overtime, however, Suraya adroitly denies that their refusal has anything to do with the monetary rewards. She uses the occasion to disparage their wages; if it were only a question of money, they would not work on Saturdays and Sundays, because they are not well paid for it. She reminds him subtly that their working overtime "helps" him, does him a favor as it were. There is nothing in the "rules" of their work contract that says that overtime work is compulsory.

As I read it, Patrick detects the underlying meaning in Suraya's utterances and turns nasty. He in turn points out that he has hitherto been flexible with them and has not demanded a fixed weekly target. He will now enforce the target as a "rule" if the women refuse to cooperate.

Patrick's flexibility over an "official" target for the station may be construed as what Gouldner (1954) has called an "indulgency pattern," whereby supervisors may demonstrate flexibility or break certain rules in exchange for workers' greater cooperation beyond that required as minimal standards. In this case, Patrick expected compliance with requests for overtime work in return for his flexibility over a fixed target. When this was not forthcoming, Patrick's way of restoring the situation was to threaten to invoke the rule concerning the target, which he had hitherto eschewed. Li Chiew pitches her retaliatory gesture at the same level: if Patrick starts to demand an official target, the women will in turn play it by the rules. They will fulfill the target but will not cooperate with future demands for overtime work. This may be read as a form of "work to rule" or as a "restrictive practice."

This was one of the occasions when the women acted collectively and successfully in resisting authority.

Patrick then turns to the women individually, having failed to secure compliance on a collective basis. All except one operator stands her ground, and she is teased by the other women for not holding out. The occasion seems to be a source of glee for the women, or at any rate that is my reading based on the way Suraya told it. The next day, Janet circulated the tale that she witnessed displeasure with Patrick by higher management for his failure to exercise effective control over the women.

The term "negotiation" as used in organizational settings has been most closely associated with the work of Anselm Strauss and his colleagues on mental hospitals. The authors conceptualized negotiation as "the processes of give-and-take, of diplomacy, of bargaining" (Strauss et al. 1973, 304). These processes were present in the efforts of the women in my study to exert a degree of determination over the limits of their productivity and in their keeping track of their own speed of work, protesting against raised targets that seemed unreasonable, using the argument that the quality of their work would be compromised by excessive speed, and acting against target-busters. These strategies operated at both "covert" and "overt" levels and were central features of workplace relations.

Little Resistances

Beyond the central focus of the target, there were other ways in which the women's behavior on the shopfloor offered subtle challenges to or minimal compliance with company rules. It did not take me long to observe that the "Uniform and Badge Policy" was quite openly and widely flouted. When the rule concerning the compulsory wearing of the uniform was first instituted, many of the women came to work in their own clothes. Afterward, when the uniform became a must, probably because so many women violated the rule that management felt that it had to secure compliance as an act of discipline, many women registered their dissatisfaction by altering the uniform in various ways: instead of buttoning up the Mandarin collar, some of the women turned it down flat. Others rolled up their short sleeves so that the brown cuffs could not be seen, and still others wore their own belts. Many women wore cardigans and jackets on top of their uniforms. The operators also found different ways to wear their badges: some turned them around so that their photographs and badge numbers were not visible. Others wore their badges on their belts instead of on the top right of the bodice, as stipulated by company rule. Many also wore their uniforms shorter than they were allowed to.

Such issues as how the women altered their uniforms and badges might appear trivial, and it is certainly true that such little acts of resistance do not affect the essential balance of power in the organization, but they do show that order is something that has to be actively maintained because it is continually open to question. I would maintain that such games are actively creative. They may be read as the women's attempt to interpolate something of their own lives in the face of institutional authority. The same may be said for those occasions when the supervisor was not around and the women appropriated those moments for sociability. For example, eating was forbidden in the station, but it was general knowledge that this rule was contravened, and the leads turned a blind eye provided it was done discreetly. The eating of sweets and tidbits was not just a physical act; nor did the women eat because they were hungry. Rather, eating was an occasion for sociability.

Liz Stanley (1987) has persuasively argued that "the public" and "the private" should not be seen as physical places such that the private is equated with the domestic, the home, and the public is linked to places outside the home, the nondomestic, but rather as interactional products that can and do occur in any and all situations. Using this notion of the private as an interactional outcome, it is possible to see that the women, in various ways and means, seized control of moments of privacy, creating "private" spheres within the workplace. These moments occurred in "back regions," in Erving Goffman's sense of the term (1959), where individuals or groups could adopt patterns of behavior forbidden in the front/public regions.

Several forms of "private" activities were discernible. One such activity was to display an exaggerated reaction to anything slightly out of the ordinary, such as when an operator dropped a carton or pen. A chorus of mock protest and comments would be initiated, and wildly improbable stories would be spun to explain the event. One operator might initiate a mock insult or taunt another operator, who might retaliate verbally and/or physically (by hitting the initiator, for example), and they might chase each other around the station while other women laughed and made comments, encouraging one woman, deploring the other.

The Malay women at VMI—Hazizah and Suraya—spoke better English than many of the Chinese women, and they sometimes engaged in word play. There was a particularly subversive elegance about the way Suraya took the term "Clean Room" and the attendant sense of technological importance connoted, turned it on its head, and renamed it the "Dirty Room." This brought appreciative laughter from Hazizah, and they spent a while amusing themselves and listeners spinning variations on the theme: "This is not a clean drive, this is a dirty drive," "So what for you want to work with a dirty drive?" and "Do you know who's the dirty supervisor?"

Sometimes there would be singing sessions, particularly among the Chinese women, who would sing popular Mandarin songs. There were discussions too of "serious" topics, such as religion, marriage, and the position of women, the youth of the day, and so on. Operators from other stations who might be around on official tasks would linger to take part in the conversations or other play activities. In this way the private spheres in our station were a refuge for visiting operators taking disguised breaks. Thus, nonwork activities shaded into work activities. For some of the women, particularly Yen Lan, being sent on errands and chores was a welcome distraction from the monotony. The effect of such "private" spheres was that it subverted the dominant reality of discipline and control; it created an atmosphere of "play," as opposed to strictly "work."

Actually, work did not stop completely during "private" periods; rather, there was a decided slowdown. Nor did the creation of such "private" moments represent deliberate acts of subversion on the part of the women. Such moments had the immediate purpose of creating laughter, sociability, and relief from the tedium of the job.

The forms of interaction I have described are not new in organizational studies. I would, however, argue that the content of the playtime in this case was "engendered" (note the singing of Mandarin pop songs, discussions of men, marriage, and so on) and qualitatively different from that described in other studies. The activities were drawn from the everyday lives and relevances of the women as women. R.K. Brown et al. (1973) have called such activities as joking and horseplay "leisure in work." Donald Roy's participant-observation study (1973) of the creation of games and rituals within the work group of machine operators and the devising of a series of work breaks—"coffee-time," "peach-time," and "banana-time,"—is a classic on the subject. Burawoy too (1979b) has described the games workers play as mechanisms to make work more enjoyable, more tractable.

Although absenteeism in industrial sociological studies is often read as an individual act that reflects personal contingencies rather than as a response to control, I detected collective norms "legitimating" the behavior. There was a taken-for-grantedness about women "who wouldn't be coming in today" or "almost didn't come in today." It was part of the culture of the factory that a woman who was feeling "xian"—a Chinese Hokkien term used by the Malay and Indian women that denotes a state of being "fed up"—could "legitimately" (in the eyes of other women) take a day or two off from work. Such behavior, of course, runs counter to managerial ideology. Absenteeism was also resorted to strategically: if an operator was going to be absent from work, she would work it out so that her two days of absence would not fall in the same half of the month to avoid being penalized financially (wages were paid half-monthly).

"Us" and "Them" . . . : A Sense of Class?

So how do I conceptualize the women's actions? In what light do I read the gestures of defiance, the everyday acts of rebellion, the resistance to control?

Although "class" is a word that is often bandied about in the media and by policy makers in Singapore, there is, in fact, little social scientific evidence that people actually think about "class" or about how they think about it. In her critique of class and social stratification research in Singapore, Margie Hall (1982) points out that researchers have tended to use "socioeconomic status" and "class" interchangeably. Both terms have also tended to mean "prestige ranking."

I believe that the women in my study did possess an awareness of "class" as it related to the workplace. Once, the women were discussing a quarrel that had occurred between Ritu and the supervisor Chris and debating whether Ritu should have lodged a complaint with management. The women were generally skeptical that this would have had the desired effect. Li Chiew clinched the discussion on a note of antipathy: "Let's face it," she said in Mandarin, "we are the little people, and we are being oppressed by them [management], the rich and powerful." Later on, in an interview I had with her, she also said, "We are just like machines that can move, being made use of by others," and "they [management] treat you like a thing."

Li Chiew also expressed the closest understanding of the workings of capitalism. When I asked whether she thought she was receiving fair wages, she hesitated and said that yes, she supposed so, for the kind of work the women were doing. Then, after a moment's thought, she retracted and said, "But if you compare it with how much the company is making, then wages are low. Consider how much profit is made from the sale of one drive! But we are the ones assembling it, and they still time us and tell us that we must assemble one in so many minutes." Hazizah said, "They don't know the worker at Sagetech; they only know the work."

The other women might not have been as articulate as Li Chiew in expressing their sentiments about management, but their attitudes toward and relations with those in authority clearly showed an "us and them" approach. In speech too, the terms "us" and "them" were commonly used to define the women's relation to management, whatever was actually bound up in those categories. Generally speaking, the women had hazy notions about higher management, because their bosses were so seldom seen. The women were, however, generally skeptical about the motives of management. Thus, on the company's anniversary, when each operator was given a piece of cake and an umbrella with the company's logo, the women remarked among themselves that a piece of sponge cake and an umbrella cost very little compared with what the company was making, and it was no big deal.

Distrust of management was openly expressed when paychecks were issued. The first month I was there, Yen Lan carefully scrutinized her check, in case management had "cheated" her of her rightful wages for overtime. I thought she was doing this half in jest at first, but I later observed that each month a lot of the women went through the same ritual, looking for any signs of "fraud" concerning their paychecks. As far as I could discover, no one had actually ever been "cheated." Nonetheless, there was a belief that management could be unscrupulous and that workers had to look out for their own interests.

What of the women's relations with their supervisors, those figures of authority with whom they were most in contact? The women were generally unequivocal in their dealings with their supervisor: he was obviously one of "them." The women in my station generally agreed that Patrick was a relatively decent and understanding supervisor because he at least bothered to listen to the women's problems sometimes. Nonetheless, they appeared to have few illusions about whose side the supervisor was on and whose side management would be on if they should complain about the supervisor to management.

When I asked Li Chiew what qualities she thought a good supervisor should have, she said, "I don't think there is such a thing as 'a good supervisor.' If a supervisor is good, if he is nice to us, that will obstruct his work. If he wants to move up, he has to be crafty." As for Patrick, she said, "He's very devious" and "Patrick likes to give the impression that he is very good to us. But really is he that good to us? He's only making use of us."

It wasn't just Li Chiew who felt this way about Patrick. Some months after I had left Sagetech, the women were gathered in my apartment and the subject of supervisors came up. The women said that some of the supervisors were going from bad to worse, and Siew Yu said that at least Patrick wasn't too bad. I was rather surprised that Yen Lan, who I had always thought was rather fond of Patrick, rebutted this and remarked that Patrick was showing his true colors. Yen Lan also remarked, cunningly, that "Sometimes we even set the supervisors to quarrel and fight among themselves." I had observed this myself. One way of doing this was by refusing to carry out an order given by a supervisor from another station on the grounds that it would contravene instructions from one's own supervisor and that one had to seek prior permission before carrying out the task. Another approach the women used was to do as they were asked but then report to their own supervisor that they had been harassed into doing work for another supervisor and that as a consequence their target had been affected. This play seemed to be quite effective in setting the supervisors against each other. I witnessed quarrels among supervisors accusing each other of "poaching" on their respective "girls." I share Edwards's view (1986) that whatever may be the "class location" of supervisors as a group, at the level of the shopfloor, workers experience the force of capital through supervisors and this has consequences for everyday behavior.

There is no simplistic or automatic mechanism by which workers, by virtue of being members of the working class, don a working-class consciousness. Whatever perceptions of the nature of managerial authority the women have developed have evolved out of their concrete experiences, their day-to-day interactions with management, in the workplace.

A Factory Consciousness

In the previous section, I looked at the women's consciousness as it relates to "class," not so much as measuring how much or little there was according to conceptions culled from a theoretical framework, but exploring related notions of it as their consciousness emerged from behavior and discussions within the workplace. At the same time, one can go only so far in ascribing all feats of resistance, all everyday acts of rebellion, to a "class consciousness." To put it simply, people do not think and act in "class" terms all the time. In phenomenological terms, there are constantly shifting systems of relevances. At different moments in our lives, our consciousness is focused on different systems of relevance. Thus, although there may have been an overarching "ideological" element informing the women's actions at certain times, at other times, the women were acting in practicable ways to achieve personally desired, pragmatic goals.

I feel that "class consciousness" shades into something else, which I have called a "factory consciousness." A factory consciousness, as I conceptualize it, is a more pragmatic, purpose-oriented consciousness directed toward pushing back the frontiers of control within the factory. But my usage of the term bears little similarity to Beynon's conceptualization of it (1984). Beynon uses the term specifically to mean "factory class consciousness," whereas "class" is not necessarily present in my usage of it. A factory consciousness, as I see it, is a pragmatic response to the nature of factory work. As Graeme Salaman and others have commented in a similar vein

(1985, 1), "The structuring of factory work both reflects and is occasioned by, a basic paradox: the very circumstances which make factory work so tightly structured, also tend to undermine such attempts at structuring." Thus, employers may often deplore the instrumental and calculative approach to work of many employees, that employees are interested only in the monetary returns they can get from the job, rather than having an intrinsic interest in their work. But this is as much a reflection of the logic of employers' policies as anything else. So long as employees are given narrowly defined tasks to do, are closely supervised, and generally are treated as "factors" of production, employer-employee relations will be characterized by "low trust." Untrusting management policies and control techniques will be met with by resistance.

As I use the term, factory consciousness refers specifically to workers' actions within the workplace. A worker new to the factory soon learns about the nature of factory work. What hits the worker is probably an overpowering sense of hierarchial control. In observing how other workers around her cope with and attempt to resist managerial control, the new worker develops a factory consciousness. A factory consciousness may be viewed as a component of the wider "occupational culture" comprising ideas, values, attitudes, norms, procedures, and artifacts characteristically associated with the factory. Although the everyday resistances, the daily skirmishes, may not be collectively orchestrated or overtly confrontational, they should not be dismissed as sporadic, spontaneous acts of individuals which are narrow in scope. Factory consciousness, it may be argued, manifests itself in patterns of behavior which attempt to redraw the limits of control at the point of production. Hence, I adopt the "broader" concept of factory consciousness, rather than "shopfloor/factory floor consciousness."

A factory consciousness is thus about workers "not letting management get away with anything it wants" and about making life in the factory more tolerable (and maybe even enjoyable at times). And if factory work may be said to be a stereotypical form of work in industrial capitalist societies, it may be plausible to theorize that factory consciousnesses across cultures may even share some common features. This may explain why many of the resistive practices employed by workers in Western factories seem evident in the Singapore workplace I studied. In particular, I find parallels between the study by Armstrong and his colleagues of three factories and my own (Armstrong, Goodman, and Hyman 1981).

In introducing the notion of factory consciousness as a pragmatic resistance to management control within the workplace, I am saying that "class," or "gender" for that matter, should not be taken as the sole conceptual indicator for analyzing the complex material reality that can be found in a single workplace.

Gender: Collusion as a Female Strategy

Neither class phenomena nor factory consciousness can be understood in isolation. They tie in with, are sometimes underlined by and sometimes overshadowed by gender phenomena.

Within Sagetech, supervisors and higher management treated the operators in the way they did not only because they were workers but also because they were women workers. Likewise, the women reacted to the supervisors not just as figures of authority but as male figures of authority. Certain patriarchal practices can be clearly identified. There have been many controversies and debates in feminist literature over the conceptualization of "patriarchy," but in the context I am using it, I simply mean the rule of men (i.e., hierarchical relations of superordination and subordination in the factory are structured along gender lines). The nature of the control network is such that there is an attempt at gender subordination. Certainly it would be difficult to see how the rules relating to the uniform and badge fit into any one of the three elements of control that have conventionally been seen in industrial sociology to encompass the nature of control in the factory: technical control, control over workers' motivation to produce, and control of quantity and quality of output (Salaman 1985). These rules could instead be appropriately termed patriarchal control.

That they were dealing with female workers is very clear in the minds of the supervisors. One of the supervisors believed that "ladies, if you know how to talk to them, can be persuaded easily" and that, "women are easier to handle. You speak simple English to them and you crack jokes." To be fair, not all the supervisors I spoke with expressed themselves in such patronizing terms, but generally all agreed that female workers were more pliable than male workers, were less confrontational, and could more easily be handled if the supervisor showed that he was not insensitive to their problems and complimented them from time to time to show his appreciation of their "support." They pointed out, however, that if the women continued to be recalcitrant, sternness was called for.

Thus, in general, the supervisors saw the women workers under them as meek and docile, susceptible to cajolery and flattery, and occasionally irresponsible, whereupon strict measures were called for. The vocabulary the supervisors used to describe the women resembled the vocabulary parents use to describe their not-grown-up children, and one can see paternalism at work here. How did the women react to this treatment?

In their face-to-face interactions with the supervisors, the women seemed to collude by presenting an air of meekness, docility, and passivity. But what they felt or said or did behind the backs of the supervisors was quite different. Thus, the women often resorted to indirect means of achieving their purposes, preferring to circumvent than to confront.

Not long after I had been in Station 212, Yen Lan voiced a desire to be transferred back to Station 412, where her close friends were stationed. She raised the matter with Patrick, who apparently was reluctant to lose her, and fobbed her off with promises to think about the matter. Nothing happened. Feeling frustrated, she let it be known around the station that she was tired of working at Sagetech and was thinking of working in sales again. It was actually a calculated ploy to get Patrick to give her what she wanted—the transfer back to Station 412.

A few days later, Yen Lan was absent from work. The word went around that she had decided to resign and would be starting work in a Japanese department store in a few days. (I did not find out if this was true or a rumor intended to reach Patrick's ears only.)

Two days later, Yen Lan appeared triumphantly at Station 212 to chat with us. Patrick had asked Janet to telephone Yen Lan to ask her to return; he would have her transferred back to Station 412. And so Yen Lan was reinstalled.

I was relatively new to the factory then and was rather astonished at the complexity and artfulness that had gone into the maneuver. Later I became familiar with such machinations. In this instance, Yen Lan got what she wanted, of course, but she succeeded because Patrick valued her as a good worker, one who was intelligent and learned fast. A similar episode also occurred in 1984, when factories had difficulties getting workers.

When Siew Yu came to our station, she said that she had wanted a transfer earlier, because she could not get along with her lead, but her supervisor would not hear of it. Relations between her and her lead worsened, and one day they had a rather violent quarrel when the supervisor was around. When the supervisor reprimanded her, she said, "Well, I wanted a transfer, but you wouldn't let me." The result, of course, was that she was transferred. I don't know if Siew Yu actually engineered the quarrel to happen when it did, but I am quite sure that she was not displeased that it happened then, because she would have realized that it would have the effect she wanted.

The women were also aware that since they were dealing with male supervisors, sexual sexual politics[6] was a component of their relations. It was sometimes pointed out that a certain supervisor was "running after" a certain operator, and it was said of another supervisor that he would "see a pretty face and run after." The women sometimes made use of such knowledge. Yen Lan recounted how the supervisor, Steven, was known to be smitten with a very pretty operator, Chi Yuk, who was in Yen Lan's station. Yen Lan said that it was very difficult to get printed circuit boards from Steven—he would give them only a few at a time. When Chi Yuk was around, however, they would send her to get the boards from Steven. He would give her all the boards she asked for. In fact, said Yen Lan, he would bring boards up to them unasked, so that he would have a chance to talk to Chi Yuk.

Some of the operators openly flirted with supervisors. On one level, it is possible to see such acts as perpetuating sexist stereotypes about women, femininity, and sexuality. On another level, however, it is plausible to read that the women acted as they did because being "flirtatious" with a supervisor allowed them the license to "scold" him and resist his authority at times, without making it appear that they were doing so. That is, flirting gave them more leverage in their work dealings with their supervisor; it made their work lives easier and was a strategy for manipulating those in authority. Indeed, as Anna Pollert (1983) has pointed out, using sexual sexual politics as a form of management control is "a form of individual social negotiation based on gender not usually available to male workers but very common for women workers who are most often subordinated to men."

On the subject of passivity, it became clear to me that seeming passive did not necessarily mean thinking passive or being truly compliant. Thus, women who were being told off by a supervisor for doing something incorrectly, for example, often kept quiet in the presence of the supervisor but would act differently once the supervisor was gone. Janet recounted an occasion when Patrick told her off for placing some boxes where they should not have been placed. Janet said, "I thought to myself, you can say what you want, but this lady [meaning herself] is going to do as she pleases." Such stories were not unfamiliar; whether the women actually got away with their actions is another matter, depending on the circumstances.

My reading of such acts of collusion is that they were acts of accomplishment by the women. It is also possible to read them as pragmatic and common-sensical responses to situations in which the balance of power was clearly tilted in favor of management. That being so, the women decided that it was more strategic and productive to be circuitous than confrontational. It is a "So you think I'm dumb? Okay, I'll play dumb, so long as it gets me what I want" line of reasoning. Certainly the facade of docility and passivity hides a much more complex reality than some feminists have depicted. Heyzer (1981) concurs that the docility and subservience of women is not a "given," based on her study of a textiles factory in Singapore.

Further, the women did not always act docile and subservient, even in face-to-face dealings with supervisors. In a few instances, the more openly authoritarian a supervisor was, the more likely the operator was to be openly antagonistic. Thus, Kenneth, the second-shift supervisor, was initially known for his heavy-handed authoritarianism. Li Fen reported that when she worked overtime under him one day, he scolded her and said that an operator should not go to the toilet while working and should not walk about. Li Fen said, "After he said that, I deliberately walked here and there, just to see what he would do to me." Yen Lan said, "Does he know what he is doing? Who is going to obey him?" Later in the day, she taunted him when he walked by and she happened to be idle. She looked at him challengingly and said loudly, obviously intending him to hear, "I am going for my tea break," even though it was not the official time for tea break yet.

As conditions in the workplace became more repressive a year later, some women appeared to take a tougher, more confrontational stance toward management. This is compatible with the phenomenological notion that new experiences can breach the taken-for-granted stock of knowledge and cause it to be questioned by the individual experiencing it.

Biography, Experience, and Consciousness

Until now, I have looked at the women's work experiences within the factory. I have documented and discussed what I consider to be some of the salient features of women's consciousness, including their consciousness of "class" as bound up in ideas and actions about "us" and "them" (management), their resistance to managerial authority and control, and their consciousness of gender. It is also true, however, that factory work had a "taken-for-granted" quality for the women. By this I mean that although the women were not acquiescent and hapless subjects to be controlled and manipulated at will by management, by and large they accepted that factory work involves a certain amount of regimentation, control, and tedium. In this section I explore this issue in the wider context of the women's life experiences and conditions in Singapore. That is, I look at some of the features that help shape the "facticity" of factory work for the women.

First, there was a family "tradition" of factory work among many of the women I studied, so that the women had become "familiar" with factory work and the nature of factory work well before they left school and entered the labor market. Many of the women at Sagetech had sisters or mothers or female cousins who had or were still working in factories. In fact, many of the women had been initiated into factory work by relatives who brought them to Sagetech. Thus, the women's biography comprised a taken-for-granted understanding about the nature of factory work as transmitted to them by female relatives.

One of the questions I asked the women was whether they had much difficulty adjusting to factory work. Most of the women replied in the negative, which puzzled me, given my initial difficulties in adapting to the regimented environment at Sagetech. On reflection, however, it was obvious that my autobiographical experiences were vastly different from those of the factory women and this fact shaped our different reactions to the factory. Before I went to Sagetech, I knew about factory work only "theoretically." The women, by contrast, were much closer to it experientially through the accounts of female friends and relatives who were factory operators. As has been pointed out, workers often have a realistic expectation of the levels of intrinsic satisfaction to be derived from work, but this does not mean that they would not prefer to have more challenging and autonomous jobs (Brown 1980).

Many of the women also had a realistic awareness of the job choices that are available to young women who leave school at the age of fifteen. They pointed out that their choices were factory work or sales. Many of the women had been in sales before and had decided that working in a factory was preferable because at least they would not have to be on their feet all day, or forced to work shifts. It was not possible for these women, who had been educated mainly in the Chinese language, to work as saleswomen in the larger department stores. A prerequisite of working in such stores was a proficiency in English that the women lacked. Many women also felt that there was "nothing wrong" with factory work in that there was no social stigma attached to factory workers, as there was elsewhere in Asia. For example, Malay women who work in electronics factories are often described by their Kampung people as "sexy" and "jual murah" (cheap) and derogatorily called "Mina Karan" (Ackerman 1984). Lydia Kung, in her study of women factory workers in Taiwan, found that the women had negative self-images of themselves as factory workers, felt that factory work was work in which one could not "hold up one's head high," and that factory workers were seen as "frogs in a well" (1983). In this sense, factory work is more "acceptable" in Singapore.

A related and final point about women workers' consciousness is that it appears that the greater the repression at work, the more radical and militant women workers become. Linda Lim points out (1983) that especially in repressive states such as South Korea and the Philippines, women workers are militant and radical, have strong grassroots organization, and frequently initiate labor actions such as sit-ins and strikes. In Singapore, women workers in multinational corporations work under much more favorable conditions than in other parts of Asia. Singapore is often regarded as the "labor aristocracy" of Southeast Asia, and multinational factories tend to have higher wages and better working conditions (even if these are not aimed at making life better for the worker) than local factories. The women in my study were aware of this, pointing out, for example, that they had a better deal than Malaysian factory workers. The better conditions may also contribute to the "acceptability" of factory work in Singapore.

Conclusion

People who are in relations of domination and subordination react with one or several responses in managing their situations. They may submit; they may rationalize or legitimate their domination by adopting an ideological position that labels them as inferior and therefore deserving of subordination; they may become apathetic; or they may rebel and fight back (and there can be many ways of fighting back, including passive resistance, subterfuge, or militancy). There is thus a range of possible responses. The sociological lexicon for conceptualizing these phenomena is relatively undeveloped, however. For example, social science discourses have tended to treat power as a zero-sum effect of domination and denial, so that power and powerlessness become mutually exclusive polarities.

Yet different responses to control and domination will have different consequences for those who seek to dominate and for those who are being dominated. In the case of the women in my ethnography, it is clear that they did not just acquiesce. From efforts to restrict output, to wearing their uniforms in ways that went against company policy, to carving private spheres and moments, the women were resisting, sometimes successfully, sometimes not, the amount of control that management would have liked to impose. In so doing, the women were, I believe, wresting a degree of power for themselves and reducing their potential state of powerlessness. Likewise, although the women may sometimes have colluded in management's stereotypification of female operators as passive and docile, this collusion was itself a strategy for getting what they wanted, be it a transfer to another station or the successful manipulation of a supervisor. Kathy Ferguson has pointed out that to make direct demands when one is much less powerful is to risk refusal. Thus, women "fragment their demands into tiny pieces" and "employ a socially-learned verbal subterfuge in place of a direct command over resources" (Ferguson 1980, 166).

This is not to say that the women in my study were, in fact, powerful. But I would say that power in the workplace was contested, so that management sought "power over" the women and the women attempted to wrest some "power to be." The consequence of the women's actions was that, in not meekly acquiescing, they blocked the potential maximization of management's power. They did not let themselves be subordinated to the degree that management would have liked them to be. In so doing, they affected the quality of their lives on the shopfloor, for the better.

8

The New International Division of Labor and Its Impact on Unions: A Case Study of High-Tech Mexican Export Production

Harley Shaiken

The 1980s have witnessed a dramatic upsurge in the location of high-technology manufacturing in Mexico and other newly industrializing countries. Global manufacturing is of course not a new process. Transnational firms have long scoured the world in search of new markets, low wages, weak unions, lax environmental regulations, or all of the above. What is new, however, is that transnationals are increasingly siting high-tech production in Third World countries and using these plants as export platforms for global markets. Factories in which robots automatically weld car bodies are being built alongside labor-intensive plants in which workers still assemble toys by hand. Moreover, computers and telecommunications tie these new factories into powerful international production systems.

In this chapter I seek to define the underpinnings of this new international division of labor and then look at its implications for workers and unions in North America, with an emphasis on the United States and Canada. In particular, I probe the mobility of advanced manufacturing in the information age by addressing two interrelated questions: at what level of complexity and in what time frame can high-tech production be sited in a newly industrializing country? I argue that in industries such as automobiles, the most advanced Mexican plants—new facilities utilizing world-class technologies—are now capable of rivaling the productivity and quality of comparable plants in the United States, Canada, and even Japan. This argument challenges much conventional wisdom that low-wage countries do well with labor-intensive assembly but that high-tech production requires the skills and infrastructure found only in industrialized economies.

I anchor the argument in a case study of automobile assembly in Mexico. The plant I analyze is owned and operated by a U.S. firm I call Universal Motors and is located in a northern Mexican city I refer to as Azul. It is a

$500 million state-of-the-art stamping and assembly complex, one of the largest and most sophisticated manufacturing facilities in Mexico. After less than three years of operation, the plant produced the second-highest-quality subcompact car sold in the U.S. market—surpassing far better-known Japanese nameplates—at very high levels of productivity. Although a single case study can at best be suggestive, the complexity of this operation indicates that other plants would probably be easier to site in Mexico, and quantitative data underscore that this plant is part of a larger trend. Mexico's export of automobile engines, for example, more than quadrupled from 320,000 in 1982 to almost 1.4 million five years later (Asociacion Mexicana de la Industria Automotriz 1988, 167) and has remained at these high levels since.

The Universal Motors case is particularly fascinating because the plant employs new forms of work organization—elements of which Universal is seeking to introduce into its U.S. and Canadian plants—as well as state-of-the-art robots and computer systems. Building on techniques pioneered by Japanese auto firms, the Mexican plant combines two seemingly contradictory elements: participatory work teams and traditional Fordism—minutely subdivided jobs on a rapidly paced assembly line. In addition, Universal has sought to emulate the labor relations of the Japanese model by developing a compliant enterprise-based union. Despite these efforts, discontent over low wages and intense working conditions has resulted in high employee turnover and at times has flared into open conflict between workers and the company. Surprisingly, the plant has managed to perform well not only against a backdrop of high turnover but even during labor-management confrontations.

The final part of this chapter looks at the industrial relations implications of this new international division of labor for the United States and Canada. Although Mexican industrial development clearly does not have to come at the expense of workers and communities in the North, one possible scenario offers bleak prospects: the combination of First World productivity at Third World wages in Mexico will serve to depress wages and working conditions in the United States and Canada. I conclude by examining several cases in which this scenario has already unfolded.

I have chosen Mexico to explore these themes because of its economic importance—it is now the third largest trading partner of the United States and may soon move into second place—and because its skill levels and industrial infrastructure offer parallels to those found in other NICs. I have selected the automobile industry because it is at the cutting edge of technological and organizational trends and among the most international of manufacturing industries. The principal data for the case study were collected from July 1988—about eighteen months after the first model rolled off the assembly line at Azul—through August 1989, when the plant began a major changeover of models. I made a follow-up visit to the plant in February 1991.

In the 1980s, many analysts argued that new forms of automation would reverse the flow of high-tech production back to industrial economies. These critics advanced two complementary arguments. The first maintained that the lure of low wages disappears with automated production. Juan F. Rada, for example, contended that "labour cost is losing importance in the total cost" of production (n.d., 136). Peter Drucker concurred with Rada, maintaining that "wage levels for blue-collar workers are becoming increasingly irrelevant in world competition" (1988). As a result, Drucker asserts, "American manufacturers are slowly beginning to bring back to the U.S. operations they had moved offshore—precisely because they do not have to restore the blue-collar jobs they abolished when they moved offshore 10 years ago."

The second argument maintained that the complexity of new forms of automation—based on computers and microelectronics—is too great for the existing infrastructure and skill level in the Third World. Supporting this view, Robert Crandall argued that complex manufacturing found in industries such as automobiles requires "a considerable application of technology, production planning, and coordination that is not widely found in less developed countries and could not easily be transplanted there" (1986). Rada agrees, maintaining that "the complexity of production does not necessarily justify investment in developing countries" (n.d., 136).

Both strands of the "automation-as-agent-of-industrial-reversal" argument were combined in *The Future of the Automobile*, the influential final report of the International Automobile Program, a multiyear study of the global auto industry carried out at MIT. The index of the 1984 book contains only a single entry for the Mexican auto industry. The authors contended that "the advantages of low wages in the less developed countries do not offset the quality and coordination handicaps, the country 'risk', and the use of many more hours of labor for most production steps" (Altshuler et al. 1984, 192). As a result, "There is little economic advantage to Mexican production except in the cases of a few minor parts with high labor content" (193).

By the early 1990s, many analysts were acknowledging a far more important role for Mexico in the global auto industry. A *Business Week* cover story on Mexico's auto industry, for example, trumpeted that "a new big-league car producer is quietly rising south of the border" (Baker 1992, 98). In *The Machine That Changed the World*, promoted as a "5-million-dollar 5-year study on the future of the automobile" and a successor to the earlier MIT study, the authors found that the leading Mexican plant "had the best assembly-plant quality in the entire volume plant sample, better than that of the best Japanese plants and the best North American transplants" (Womack, Jones, and Roos 1990, 87).

The MIT study, however, like much of the recent research in this area, provides little discussion of the actual experience of siting high-tech plants in Mexico. As a result, the understanding of Mexico's full capabilities in operating advanced manufacturing is often skewed. Womack, Jones, and Roos, for example, argue that "cheap, entry-level cars and trucks" might become Mexico's specialty (1990, 266). Mexico clearly has significant production potential at the low end of the market, but Womack and his coauthors assume that technological barriers prevent more sophisticated cars from being assembled in Mexico. The widespread success in Mexico with even more challenging engine production contradicts this assumption. And, with more complex vehicles, the potential cost savings are greater because more labor hours are required. Rather than assume technological limits, this chapter seeks to define more accurately Mexico's industrial capability by analyzing the experience of Azul, the most advanced auto assembly plant in operation today in Mexico.

Mexican Auto Stamping and Assembly Plant

Universal's Initial Strategy

The 1.4 million-square-foot plant—filled with more than one hundred robots and other computerized manufacturing systems—has the capacity to produce more than 160,000 cars a year, all of which are currently destined for the U.S. market. It employs 1,600 hourly workers on two shifts. The facility combines a labor-intensive final assembly area with three high-tech production areas—stamping, the body shop, and paint— utilizing state-of-the-art technologies. Located in a northern Mexican desert, on the outskirts of an administrative and agricultural center of about 700,000 people, the plant is 160 miles from the U.S. border.

The company's strategy for setting up the plant depended on three key elements: a highly educated workforce, an intensive training program, and a cadre of seasoned managers, recruited from Universal's international operations. In addition, the company's Japanese affiliate supplied the car design and much of the production process—cloned from an existing model and plant in Japan—and Japanese suppliers provided about two-thirds of the car's parts. A proven design, manufacturing process, and supplier base reduced the potential for problems during the critical period in which the plant moved toward full production.

A key criterion for selecting the plant site was the strong reputation of the area's workers. After intensive screening, Universal hired a young, well-educated workforce with little previous manufacturing experience. The company was eager to mold workers to its vision of auto production and was therefore willing to sacrifice valuable on-the-job know-how as the price for obtaining a workforce with few preconceptions of how the plant should be run.[1] All the managers described the workers, often in effusive terms, as highly motivated and very competent. The workers average about twenty-three years of age and more than 90 percent have the equivalent of at least a high school education. Almost one-third have some university or professional training.

Given the combination of inexperienced workers and broad job responsibilities, training proved particularly critical. All workers receive four months of intensive classroom instruction, regardless of whether they ultimately wind up repairing robots or installing hubcaps on the final line. Once on the job, most workers attend advanced classroom sessions specifically geared to their work area. Moreover, Universal sent more than two hundred of the initial hires to Europe and Japan for one to four months of instruction.

The final part of the company's start-up strategy involved bringing in a group of veteran managers drawn from Universal's worldwide operations. Some of these managers were former skilled workers who had years of hands-on experience in auto plants. At peak, eighty of these foreign service employees were in the plant, and many provided on-the-job instruction to Mexican managers and hourly workers. As the Mexican workforce gained experience, these managers were withdrawn until fewer than twelve remained after three years of operation and only a handful of these on the shopfloor.

Organization of Work

The operation of the plant combines three seemingly contradictory elements: an innovative and participative form of work organization, traditional Fordism, and labor-management conflict. Consider first the way in which work is organized.

Although it is owned by a U.S.-based transnational, the plant has many of the characteristics of a "transplant"—a Japanese automobile factory located in the United States. The plant's unusual form of work organization, based on approaches pioneered by Japanese automakers, goes further than most transplants in emphasizing multiple skills, job rotation, and a single classification for all hourly workers. The most unusual feature of the plant's organization is the staffing of skilled maintenance jobs with line workers on a rotating basis, thereby dispensing with a permanent cadre of skilled trades workers.[2] The Confederacion de Trabajadores de Mexico (CTM) union represents workers in the plant but plays little role on the shopfloor. Despite its participatory rhetoric, Universal makes no attempt to include the union in any decision-making about plant activities.

Work teams of from ten to twenty-five workers comprise the heart of the system. Team members, called technicians, elect a facilitator every two months who coordinates production activities and relieves workers if they have to leave the line. All jobs within the team—skilled, production, and facilitators—are grouped into a single classification and paid the same. Workers are responsible for learning all jobs and in some departments rotate among them as frequently as every two hours. This cross-training gives the plant considerable flexibility and workers a broader awareness of the production system. "Since we rotate and many of us have been in each other's stations," one technician commented, "we all try to pitch in so that problems can be resolved quickly and efficiently. We give each other feedback."

In team meetings, held weekly for at least thirty minutes, managers transmit the company's perspectives concerning the operation of the plant and seek to harness workers' ideas about improving quality and productivity. A supervisor generally opens the meeting by speaking on themes ranging from local production issues, such as excess sheet metal scrap, to broader ideological visions, such as the company's position in the global marketplace.

After this opening talk, team members discuss ways to improve the production system. "The guy that is out there doing the job knows the little problems he has and how he has overcome them," the superintendent in final assembly maintained. Team members have collaborated on projects as complex as building new fixtures for the assembly line and restructuring the flow on a line of robots.

Workers make decisions in the teams that would be made by managers or defined by a collective bargaining agreement in a more conventional plant. The team, for example, determines penalties for absenteeism or tardiness. Under these circumstances, peer pressure can fuel the system. "When somebody is absent in the group, the work gets very overloaded," one worker complained. If the burden is more than the remaining team members can handle among themselves, the facilitator goes on the line and eliminates relief periods or pulls workers from training classes or both.

Groups vary in how they deal with absenteeism. In the body shop, they tend toward tough discipline. Some teams penalize absent workers by denying them overtime; other groups will not send workers with poor attendance records to sought-after training classes. "One of my friends was saying that we should get together and fire this guy who has missed a lot," one body shop worker recalled. "Each person in the group has raised [our complaints] with him." On the final assembly line, however, groups tended to excuse absentees, accepting whatever excuse was offered. As a result, the area superintendent instructed the supervisors to remove control over discipline for absences from the teams and restore it to the supervisors.

The plant's most unusual organizational feature is its integration of skilled and production jobs. Like many transplants, Universal has combined traditionally separate crafts such as machine repair and electrician into a single classification. Going well beyond this, however, the plant rotates production workers through skilled jobs, thereby eliminating permanent assignments to one or the other group. In the body shop, work teams elect two skilled workers for a nine-month stint repairing machinery, after which they return to the line and the team selects two replacements. This approach is equivalent to training bus drivers to fix their own busses, a particularly daunting task if the drivers have never been in a bus before, let alone repaired one.[3]

The company gains considerable flexibility through the integration of skilled and production jobs. Ultimately, the body shop could wind up with a production workforce that has an unusual depth of knowledge about how to maintain and repair the equipment. This know-how could prove important on a day-to-day basis, since production workers are responsible for minor repairs. It could prove especially beneficial during major breakdowns, since a large pool of experienced workers would be available.

Universal organizes work in this way not just to gain production flexibility but to make itself less vulnerable to the power of skilled workers. Outside the plant, this strategy shields the company from problems in the local labor market. If a skilled worker quits, a replacement can be found right on the line. Inside the plant, Universal hopes that by broadly distributing skills, the traditional power of skilled workers will be undermined. Skilled workers can often be the most cohesive and militant group on the shopfloor, because they derive considerable leverage from the scarcity of their skills and the constant necessity for judgment in carrying out their duties. "[U.S.] managers in this plant hate the [old] skilled trades," one manager related. "To them, the very mention of the term is like running your nails down a blackboard." Another manager commented that the "biggest benefit [of rotation] is you do not develop any prima donnas. Everybody is the same." The irony is that in its desire to undermine skilled workers, the company potentially makes everyone a skilled worker, pointing to new possibilities for organizing work in the process.

Fordism

Although Universal chose innovative ways to organize work, its new approaches rest on a traditional Fordist base. Further, although workers are organized into teams, the work they do is virtually identical to the jobs in more traditional U.S. auto plants. Cars move at the rate of thirty-two to thirty-five an hour down an assembly line, and the work is subdivided into small components, carefully defined and tightly timed. Moreover, there is considerable pressure to raise productivity by reducing the number of workers. A group of visiting managers from Universal's U.S. assembly plants were so impressed with the work pace that one commented, "I would take these workers up north anytime." Some of the pressure comes from industrial engineers, but much of it is integrated into the teams themselves. The ethos of the plant is to eliminate wasted seconds and excess staffing whether or not a compelling economic need exists to do so.

The extensive pressure—the heavy loading of jobs coupled with the fast pace—reflects the fact that the plant is measured against its North American and Japanese counterparts. The goal is to surpass the most productive Japanese plant producing a similar vehicle by the mid-1990s. But, given that wage rates are only a fraction of those in industrial countries, this pressure makes little economic sense. If labor productivity slipped by 50 percent—from twenty-four to thirty-six hours per vehicle—the assembly cost of the vehicle would rise by only about twenty-four dollars.[4] Moreover, the fast pace of the line is a key contributor to the plant's high turnover, a costly and disruptive situation. That there are nonetheless strong pressures to squeeze more production out of the system highlights Fordism as an ideology rather than Fordism as a response to competitive pressures. In a global production system, operating methods as well as technologies become standardized.

Not surprisingly, workers have complained extensively about the work pace. "The work is repetitive, and it drives you crazy," one worker charged. "And there is job overloading." Another worker agreed, commenting, "There are a lot of jobs that are really hard that you sometimes can't stand." He added: "The pressure is really high, and you can't stand it. The work is really, really hard." In the body shop, workers also complained about the smoke and sparks. "It is rare to see a guy who hasn't suffered and who hasn't gone to the doctor to get his eyes washed because of the sparks that he has gotten hit with," one worker recalled.

Conflict

The local union at the plant is affiliated with the CTM, the major labor federation in Mexico and a key pillar of the ruling Institutional Revolutionary party (PRI). Managers in the plant generally have a high opinion of the local and national leadership of the union. "The union is here, but it's almost as if they're not here," one manager commented. There are few work rules in the plant, and the union has little presence on the shopfloor. The primary role the union plays in the plant is to counsel workers who have personal problems and, at times, to bargain with the company for workers who have been discharged, generally for absenteeism or for infractions of plant rules such as drunkenness. At times, workers informally protest conditions in the plant, but this tends to be outside the official union structure. I attended one group meeting, for example, in which all members remained silent as a protest against an unpopular supervisor.

Despite this relatively warm relationship between managers and union leaders, there have been conflicts over wages and the intense work pace since the plant opened. The plant's low compensation—about two dollars an hour for wages and benefits at the start-up—reflect both the policies of Universal Motors and the Mexican government. The company has a policy of not paying more than the prevailing wage in the areas in which it operates. The Azul plant is already the highest-paying plant in the state, and the company's labor relations experts in Detroit see no reason to pay more. The plant's workers and managers, however, view the situation differently. The original plant manager—a North American—felt that the low wages were fueling the turnover and wanted to pay "enough so the workers feel they are being well paid," perhaps by doubling the prevailing wage in the area. In a two thousand–person plant, doubling the wages would add only about $8 million to the annual wage bill, still leaving it a small fraction of the compensation in the United States or Canada. The workers, long exposed to the rhetoric of global competition, feel they deserve a standard of living more in tune with the premier status of the plant. "A lot of people were trained in Japan and Spain and Belgium, and there the living standards are a lot higher," one worker commented. "I am not saying that I want the same living standard, but I would like something better."

Even if Universal were willing to raise wages significantly, the Mexican government would pressure the company not to do so. The government's austerity program—reflected in a pact with the official trade unions—is based on keeping a tight lid on wages. A significant raise at Azul, despite the plant's world-class productivity and quality—could fuel inflation elsewhere, in the minds of government planners.

On the day of the plant's form inauguration, with the president of Mexico and the chairman of Universal in attendance, the workers demonstrated that they had learned more than quality techniques in Japan. Imitating their Japanese counterparts, many wore red headbands, in silent protest against their wages. Conflict over wages erupted into a fifty-seven-day strike at the beginning of March 1987, led by the official union leadership, during the launch of the first car.[5]

In late summer 1988, conflict once again simmered to the surface, this time over working conditions and intraunion politics, as well as wages. The dispute reached a climax in a four-hour work stoppage in November. Four days later, a militant slate swept into office in union elections, winning by a vote of 801 to 169. During this period of heightened tension, 160 finished cars were deliberately damaged, according to the company.

Universal maintained that the new union leaders had organized the strike and been involved in sabotaging the cars. The company acted swiftly. It fired thirty-four people, including the entire newly elected union leadership, shortly before a planned holiday shutdown in mid-December. At the same time, the company announced profit-sharing bonuses and other contract changes intended to diffuse the potentially volatile situation. The union went into what amounted to a trusteeship, during which the more conservative national leadership appointed new local leaders. Despite the turmoil, the plant's productivity and quality continued to rise. Ironically, even the cars that were sabotaged were built to the highest standards.

Problems over wages and working conditions also manifest themselves in high turnover rates, one of the plant's most significant and enduring problems. Universal's turnover rate was 30 percent in 1987, 44 percent in 1988, and about 25 percent in 1989. One worker remarked that "you earn little and the pace is fast." Another stated these sentiments somewhat differently by saying people quit because of "working conditions, especially the overloading, but if they paid more it would be better." These turnover rates, while disruptive, have not been devastating since most workers who leave do so during their first six months to a year on the job, leaving a core of more stable and experienced workers in place.

Plant Performance

High quality is vital for an automobile sold in the fiercely competitive U.S. market. Many Big Three executives, despite a long history of operating manufacturing subsidiaries in Mexico, had serious doubts about Mexico's capability as an export platform to the United States and global markets. One senior executive recalled:

> "When we decided to assemble some of our models in Mexico for sale in the United States, I asked our lawyers if we were required to say on the car that it was assembled in Mexico. My own bias was that Mexican assembled vehicles were likely to have more 'fit and finish' problems than American vehicles and that the buying public would absolutely think this, even if it wasn't so. . . . To my amazement the Mexican cars have better assembly quality than those from our U.S. plants." (Womack 1989, 25)

Universal uses a wide variety of indexes to measure and compare the quality of its assembly plants. One of the most important is the New Auto Quality Study on Competitive Makes, which compares Universal products with other cars sold in the United States. The measure evaluates performance—after the cars have been driven for three months—on a scale of "things gone wrong" per thousand vehicles. The Universal car produced in the Mexican plant—the Stellar—moved from a strong tenth place showing among small cars in 1988 to a virtual first-place tie for the 1989 model year, improving its quality by 27 percent. The car's 1,406 rating narrowly trailed the 1,403 score of the U.S.-built Honda Civic. The Stellar surpassed all other Japanese-built cars in its class, including the Toyota Corolla (1,485), the Honda Civic/CRX (1,607), and the Nissan Sentra (1,904) (see table 8.1). Overall, the Stellar ranked ninth among all cars in 1989,

Table 8.1. Quality Comparison of Subcompacts Produced in the 1989 Model Year

Model	"Things gone wrong" per 1,000 vehicles
Honda Civic (United States)	1,403
Stellar	1,406
Toyota Corolla (Japan)	1,485
Toyota Corolla (United States)	1,490
Toyota Tercel (Japan)	1,565
Honda Civic/CRX (Japan)	1,607
Subaru	1,824
Nissan Sentra (Japan)	1,904

Source: New Vehicle Quality Study on Comparative Makes.

outdistancing the U.S.-built Honda Accord (1,419), the Buick LeSabre (1,738), and the Nissan 240 SX (1,829).

The plant also has achieved high productivity. Despite somewhat less automation than comparable U.S. plants, the Universal complex requires twenty-four labor hours to assemble and stamp a car, making it by one measure the seventh most productive assembly plant in North America.[6]

Suppliers

The Universal plant depends on a broad network of suppliers. Initially, it obtained 2,300 component parts from around the world: about 65 percent (by value) come from Japan (including the engines and transmissions), somewhat more than 30 percent from Mexico, and the rest from the United States.

Some analysts argue that offshore production becomes far less desirable in an age of just-in-time (JIT) inventory. JIT means that parts are delivered as they are needed—frequently every two hours—so that supplier plants are most effectively located within about a seventy-five-mile radius of the assembly plant. Clearly, Universal's managers would prefer nearby suppliers, and the plant does have five key suppliers in a neighboring industrial park. For the other suppliers, however, computers and telecommunications aid in adapting just-in-time methods to supply lines that straddle the globe. Japanese suppliers, for example, transport parts to a consolidation center in Japan as if it were the final assembly plant, and workers then pack these parts into oceangoing containers to build a day's quota of cars. As the ships cross the ocean, computers track their cargo electronically, transmitting the periodic reports via satellite to Detroit and Mexico. About two months later, Mexican workers install the parts on the line in Azul.

Broader Context

Low Wages and High Tech

How important are wages in high-tech manufacturing? That high-tech firms in Canada and the United States are in no rush to pay workers more or that collective bargaining over wages is often contentious indicates that wages remain key. Consider an auto assembly plant employing two thousand hourly workers. If they each work two thousand hours a year, the plant utilizes 4 million labor hours annually. At the time this study began, the total hourly compensation rate—wages and benefits—for autoworkers in the United States was thirty dollars an hour compared with about two dollars an hour in Mexico. Under these circumstances, if this assembly plant were located in the United States, its annual outlay for hourly workers would be $120 million compared with $8 million in Mexico, a difference of $112 million. Obviously, some costs are higher in Mexico, such as transportation and tooling. But other costs such as construction and natural resources, can be significantly lower. Labor savings of this magnitude could prove central in deciding where to locate a plant, although the final decision would depend on other factors as well, such as political stability, the strategic needs of the firm, and transportation costs.

Another way to evaluate the importance of labor costs is to look at the assembly cost per vehicle. The average assembly time per car in the Mexican plant is twenty-four hours. At this level of productivity and at the labor rates cited above, the assembly cost per vehicle in Mexico would be $48 compared with $720 in the United States, a difference of $672 per car. Put another way, a car would have to be assembled in little over an hour and a half in the United States to match the cost of labor in Mexico.

These labor cost differentials reflect only the cost savings on wages for hourly workers in the assembly plant. If other potential labor costs savings are included—salaried workers at the assembly plant and workers in the supplier companies—then far greater savings are possible. Ultimately, however, low labor costs must be matched with high quality and reasonable productivity if potential savings are to translate into low unit costs.

Mexican Exports in the 1980s: Maquiladoras and Automobiles

The Azul plant is part of a larger trend in Mexico toward more sophisticated export-oriented manufacturing. Although the domestic economy has gone through a period of severe trauma since 1982, exports have soared, making Mexico the third largest trading partner with the United States, after Canada and Japan. Two key economic sectors—*maquiladoras* and automobiles—have fueled this export growth.

During the 1980s, the automobile industry became Mexico's second largest exporter, after oil, accounting for $5.6 billion or 21 percent of total exports in 1991 (Banamex 1992, 278).[7] Much of this export growth was coming from a new generation of capital-intensive plants built in the 1980s, whose construction was spurred by Mexican local content decrees. These regulations mandated a minimum "national content" of vehicles, that is, that automakers domestically manufacture a percentage of every vehicle sold—36 percent according to the 1989 decree—and balance imports with exports. The success of early export plants, however, has led major auto companies to view expansion in Mexico as increasingly attractive.

Most of the export boom has been in finished vehicles and automobile engines—among the most difficult components to produce because of their tight tolerances and the need for complex manufacturing technology. Mexico's export of engines from these state-of-the-art plants soared from $30 million in 1989 to $1.2 billion in 1991 (Banamex 1992, 280).[8] Overall, the transnationals operating in Mexico had achieved an annual engine-making capacity of almost 2.5 million units by 1988. In addition, Mexico's exports of finished vehicles skyrocketed from 14,428 in 1981 to 359,000 in 1991—261,000 of which went to the United States (Banamex

1992, 276). As a result, Mexico is now the third largest exporter of passenger cars to the United States in terms of units, trailing only Japan and Canada (U.S. International Trade Commission 1992, 2).

Mexico could experience far-reaching growth in auto exports in the 1990s. A number of automakers have already announced extensive expansion plans. Nissan alone plans to invest $1 billion in Mexico in the first half of the 1990s, 400 million of which will go into a new 200,000-unit-a-year assembly plant in Aguascalientes, three hundred miles north of Mexico City. The plant plans to export upward of sixty thousand vehicles to the United States by 1995, with much of the remaining production split between Latin America and Japan.[9] Volkswagen is planning to boost its assembly capacity from about 220,000 annually to more than 300,000 in the 1990s. Chrysler, Ford, and General Motors all have expansion plans, and Honda, which operates a small-parts-making facility, reportedly is examining its export prospects. Even Mercedes is planning to open an assembly plant in Mexico, which may become an export platform for the U.S. market and among the first non-German bases for Mercedes exports.

The move toward more sophisticated manufacturing is also taking place in other sectors such as the *maquiladoras*. These assembly plants import parts and supplies duty-free into Mexico and export their production, largely to the United States, where duty is paid only on the value added in Mexico. The *maquiladoras* do not constitute an "industry" in the conventional sense of the term but rather group together assembly processes from a range of industries. Although still basically labor-intensive assembly operations, the most sophisticated categories have grown the fastest, and a "second wave" of *maquilas* have introduced far more automated techniques. According to Jorge Carillo (1989, 45), "The vision of the maquilas as assembly plants that exclusively use cheap labor in labor intensive processes is no longer correct."[10]

The labor remains cheap—averaging under two dollars an hour—but the production processes have grown more complex. In the 1980s, the transportation and electronic sectors grew rapidly, while the slowest growth was recorded in the more traditional textile sector. The three sectors employing the most workers are now electronics components, with 104,534; transportation equipment, with 93,656; and electrical machinery, with 66,661.[11]

The Impact of a New International Division of Labor on Workers and Unions in North America

The ability to site high-tech production in low-wage countries could well become a lever to lower wages and chip away at working conditions in Canada and the United States. This process has already taken place in low-tech, labor-intensive industries. The difference now is that far more skilled and highly paid jobs will be affected. The recently adopted North American Free Trade Agreement (NAFTA) between Mexico, the United States, and Canada will likely facilitate this trend.

In Mexico and other NICs, the dual structure of the economy—combined with restrictions against free labor organizing and often harsh government austerity programs—serves to depress wages regardless of the world-class productivity and quality of the industry involved. This "dual economy" is made up of a modern, increasingly high-tech sector composed of manufacturing plants such as Universal-Azul and a labor-intensive, often highly inefficient sector composed of small peasant farms, street vendors, and small-scale manufacturing. The labor-intensive sector contains large numbers of underemployed workers desperate to survive and willing to work for very low wages. Robert Blecker summarized an important aspect of this trend:

> In the modern sector, foreign capital and technology transfers have raised productivity relatively close to industrial country levels. But wages in the modern sector are held down by the pressure of the "surplus labor" from the backward sector which is constantly seeking employment in the modern sector. Thus the modern sector in a dual economy can potentially obtain an overall competitive advantage by combining cheap labor with high productivity. And if capital is highly mobile, there is a strong incentive for multinational firms to relocate production in the low-wage region.

The combination of high productivity and low wages in the NICs can set the stage for a global whipsawing of wages and working conditions in industrial economies. "Until we get real wage levels down much closer to those of the Brazils and Koreas," Stanley J. Mihelick, Goodyear's executive vice president for production, told the *New York Times*, "we cannot pass along productivity gains to wages and still be competitive" (Uchitelle 1987, D-7).

In the early 1980s, Ford and GM used the threat of increased global sourcing to pry open their contracts with the UAW more than six months before their scheduled expiration in September 1982. Peter Pestillo, vice president for labor relations at Ford, made it clear to the UAW that decisions concerning the location of seventeen thousand jobs would be made before September 1982, implying that unless the union reopened the contract and provided concessions to the company, many of these jobs would be shifted offshore. Roger Smith, chairman of the board at GM, was even more explicit, threatening that "unless we can get a handle on excessive labor costs in our industry, there will be more plants shutting down—and more auto industry jobs going offshore" (*Automotive News* 1981, 3).

One of the more dramatic examples of an operation that became "competitive" in this way occurred at General Motors' Packard Electric Division in Warren, Ohio, in the early 1980s. GM and Local 717 of the

International Union of Electronic Workers (IUE) agreed to slash the wages and benefits of new hires to $6.00 an hour, less than a third of the then-current compensation rate of $19.60. About 2,700 workers in Packard's Warren plants work assembling wire harnesses, which bundle together the wires of an automobile dash. This work is also done in three highly successful *maquiladoras* that Packard operates. "At the GM pay rate, these semiskilled [Ohio] workers cannot compete with the $1 per hour that Packard pays at three plants in Mexico," according to *Business Week* (1983, 54). To minimize the friction between employees doing the same work and receiving significantly different pay, the company planned to build new plants in Warren for the new low-wage assemblers. One Packard manager commented that "moving those jobs to Mexico didn't make sense when they could be kept here at a little more than the minimum wage" (*Business Week* 1983, 56).

Workers ultimately turned down these draconian cuts, but, little more than a year later, they accepted still drastically reduced wages for new hires in exchange for job security for existing employees. The new package allowed Packard to hire new assemblers for wages and benefits of about nine dollars an hour compared with twenty-two dollars for current employees.

This Packard Electric agreement is hardly an isolated scenario. Zenith Electronics Corporation workers in a Springfield, Missouri, color-television assembly plant, employing more than 1,600 workers, agreed to an 8.1 percent pay cut in 1987 to gain a company promise not to transfer more work to its Mexican *maquiladoras*. *Labor Relations Week* reported that "had IBEW [International Brotherhood of Electrical Workers] members rejected the company proposal, Zenith said it would have moved its plastics molding plant, which manufactures television cabinets and employs about 600, from Springfield to its plant in Mexico" (*Labor Relations Week* 1987, 268). The union gains, however, have proved to be short-lived. Zenith announced at the end of October 1991 that when its labor agreement expired in March 1992 it would eliminate one thousand jobs in Springfield by moving work to Mexico. Today fewer than 150 production workers remain in the facility.

In the early 1980s, transnational companies sought to put as low a profile as possible on their Mexican investments to avoid antagonizing their U.S. unions. Now, however, many transnationals take union representatives on tours of their Mexican plants to impress them with the productivity of these plants and to establish them as credible alternatives to production in the United States. As a result, the threat to move production to Mexico can play a central role in collective bargaining, intimidating unions and resulting in concessions.

The potential role of NAFTA in collective bargaining was underscored in a *Wall Street Journal* poll of 455 leading corporate executives. About 25 percent of the managers interviewed indicated that they were either "very likely" or at least "somewhat likely" to use the agreement as a " 'bargaining chip' to try to hold down wages in the U.S." (Anders 1992, R7). For many managers in the survey, the threat of moving production to Mexico is hardly an idle pronouncement. About 40 percent maintained that it is either "very likely" or "somewhat likely" that at least some production will be moved to Mexico within the next several years. Among companies with more than $1 billion in annual sales, 55 percent of the executives indicated that some production would be shifted.

Under the right circumstances, high-tech production can prove to be of significant benefit to a newly industrializing country, creating jobs and providing important new skills. But when the siting of production simply reflects the criteria of transnational corporations, then workers in industrial and industrializing countries are liable to pay a high price. The possibilities for industrial development exist, but the reality will require broader social intervention by those groups most affected in the United States, Canada, and Mexico.

9

Patterns of Workplace Relations in the Global Corporation: Toward Convergence?

Stephen Frenkel

R elations between management and employees have been of long-standing interest to scholars. This interest has been sustained by such diverse issues as informal groups and output restrictions, the behavior of work groups and fractional bargaining, industrial conflict, class consciousness and action, industrial democracy, the deskilling of work, and problems of organizational commitment and productivity growth. An important research issue today is the charting and explanation of workplace relations in the context of large, multiplant, global corporations (Bornschier and Stamm 1990). Do corporate subsidiaries pursue similar human resource policies? And what are the effects of such policies on workplace relations under differing institutional conditions? Are workplace relations converging on an organizational model, as proposed by Ronald Dore (1973, 1989) and supported by James L. Lincoln and Arne Kalleberg (1990), or does the trend toward divergence depend on whether workplaces are located in societies that are organized predominantly along corporatist or dualist lines (Goldthorpe 1984b)? Alternatively, are we witnessing the "disorganization" of labor as management reasserts its hegemony through the threat of capital flight coupled with policies designed to secure individual worker consent (Burawoy 1985)?

This chapter provides some evidence on the answers to these questions based on a detailed consideration of workplace relations patterns in four workplaces controlled by the same corporation but located in different countries. I shall show that different workplace relations patterns exist in the four countries but that there is a trend toward what I call cooperative

I would like to thank Kathryn Rawson for research assistance. The following colleagues made helpful remarks on a previous draft: Jacques Bélanger, Christian Berggren, Fred Deyo, Sandy Jacoby, Paul Marginson, and George Strauss. I would also like to thank several PH managers who took the time to read and comment on my research.

dependence. This is similar in some, but not all respects, to the organization-ideal type formulated by Dore (1989).

The plan of the chapter is as follows. The first section draws on the relevant literature to develop a framework for analyzing workplace relations. Comments are also provided on the research strategy and methodology adopted, including limitations of the research. The second section introduces the corporation and the workplaces that form the basis of the research. Workplace relations in the four plants are then compared in some detail. The third section discusses the pace and direction of change in workplace relations, while the fourth section attempts to explain the trend toward a cooperative dependent pattern of workplace relations, including the position of the plants in relation to this pattern. The concluding section considers the implications of the research in the light of the extant theories referred to above.

Workplace Relations: Theory and Research

The more competitive 1980s put pressure on management to increase productivity and profitability. This pressure spurred an interest among researchers as employers sought to recast their relationships with employees. Thus, Burawoy (1985) speaks of "hegemonic despotism," while Kochan, Katz, and McKersie (1986) note the development of strategies aimed at avoiding trade unions, reducing labor costs, and increasing labor flexibility. The mix of practices used to achieve higher productivity and labor flexibility has varied internationally, however, such that managements in the Anglo-Saxon countries tend to emphasize numerical flexibility while West German and Japanese employers have been pursuing functional flexibility (Lane 1989; Frenkel 1990a).

As several authors (Storey 1985; Edwards 1990; Littler 1990) have noted, Friedman's (1977) typology of labor control, which distinguishes direct control from responsible autonomy, is too simple a way of conceptualizing the complexity of management practice. P. K. Edwards (1990) seemingly argues that it is impossible to do justice to the nature of management's relations with employees through the reductionism involved in typologies, although one might add that this reductionism depends on the purpose of such constructions.

Arguably, taken as a *first approximation* of a more complex model, typologies such as those developed by Streeck (1987) (who distinguishes between contract-based and status-enhancing strategies) and Dore (1989) are useful. Nevertheless, more theoretical work is needed in the light of emerging empirical research to ensure a stronger fit between theory and practice, a point that applies particularly to the notion of variations in management style (Purcell 1987; Deaton 1985) and the concept of strategic choice. As elaborated by Kochan, Katz, and McKersie (1986), this research suggests that management chooses between alternative business strategies and then develops human resource (HR) strategies to fit its broader goals. This position is contested by some authors who see management as proceeding by "logical incrementalism," in a process of tactical shifts and partial solutions (Storey 1985, 202), or according to structural determinants, including prevalent notions of best practice (Lewin 1987). Others (Hyman 1987) argue that management can never succeed in implementing strategy because of contradictions inherent in the capitalist economy. According to David E. Guest (1990b), HR is in reality an extension of the American Dream.

The extent to which management develops and is able to implement business and HR strategies is an empirical matter that informs part of this chapter. But regardless of this issue, management research has been particularly useful in two respects. First, it has highlighted aspects of employment relations over which management exercises control. These include task or work organization, the control structure (i.e., the methods used to control labor), labor market relations (i.e., selection, recruitment, training, job security, and career opportunities), and lateral or interworker relations (Friedman 1990; Littler 1990). Second, it has yielded useful insights into the factors influencing management behavior. These include the impact of product, finance, and labor markets; forms of state intervention; the role of social institutions more generally; and the extent and nature of worker and union cooperation and conflict (Burawoy 1985; Friedman 1990; Edwards 1986; Grunberg 1986; Hyman 1989b; Frenkel 1991; Maurice, Sellier, and Silvestre 1986).

Research on worker responses to management initiatives has inspired a more comprehensive view of industrial conflict based on case study research. Edwards (1986, 226) uses the term "workplace relations" to categorize worker behavior according to three dimensions: the extent to which workers adopt a militant stance vis-à-vis management; whether they define their interests in collectivist or individualistic terms; and whether they are organized collectively within the workplace. According to their position in the matrix of possibilities, workers' behavior is manifested in various collective and individualized forms of conflict (effort bargaining, strikes, sabotage, pilferage, fiddling, absenteeism, and labor turnover). Edwards argues that it is largely the social organization of work—itself a consequence of management and worker interaction—that shapes worker behavior and that extra-workplace factors tend to play a less important explanatory role.

Edwards's framework is directed toward explaining patterns of conflict; the emphasis on worker behavior is insufficient for a model of workplace relations.[1] Other crucial aspects that comprise workplace relations include aspects of management practice and union organization that have been shown to vary systematically between similar workplaces in different countries (Dore 1973; Gallie 1978; Lane 1989) and to a lesser extent within the same society according to ownership nationality (Hamill 1983;

Purcell et al. 1987; Enderwick 1985; Jain 1990). A wider formulation is the notion of employment system, which although management-centered, distinguishes the different ways in which employees' relations with management are structured. Hence, Dore's reference to "organization" and "market" employment systems to delineate Japanese and British forms of work and industrial relations organization and George Strauss's (1990) characterization of U.S. arrangements as "unstructured" (market-regulated), "craft" (union-regulated), and "traditional internal" (jointly regulated) and of the "high commitment" (benign management–regulated) type.

These typologies are useful in suggesting the possibility of strategic choice and for drawing out the implications of different forms of organizing employment, but they include a long list of variables whose relationships to one another are left untheorized. Ideally, it would be desirable to work with fewer variables, all of which are grounded in theory.

In sum, two strands of research have been developed in recent years that are highly relevant in conceptualizing and explaining workplace relations: on the one hand, management research, and, on the other, new perspectives on worker behavior informed by Marxist and conflict theories of society. Neither perspective, however, focuses on the structured relationships between management and labor at the workplace level. To explicate these relations, it is useful to turn to Fox's (1974) classic analysis.

Fox distinguishes between work roles embodying differing degrees of discretion. Low-discretion roles (involving limited task range and low autonomy) are shown to have developed as part of the transition from status-based, preindustrial societies to contractual, market exchange–based industrial social formations. This process involved increased specialization in work roles, but manual employment in particular came to be characterized by low-discretion jobs, while the opposite was the case for managers and professionals. Fox shows that low discretion implies low trust (lack of confidence in realizing expectations), which tends to be reciprocated by manual employees through behavior indicating limited organizational commitment; hence, the low-trust syndrome (Fox 1974, 26–28), which includes close personal or bureaucratic control and coordination of the production process to counteract uncertainty arising from presumed worker recalcitrance.

Low-trust responses are not, however, an inevitable concomitant of low-discretion work roles. Prior socialization and benign management policies and/or the exercise of power by employees may confer superior rewards and status that compensate for the disutility of low discretion. But management's legal position as the shareholders' representative in the context of a market exchange system means that management typically uses its superior power to institutionalize inequalities of work. This approach encourages employees to respond collectively, especially through trade unions. Thus, Fox connects the organization of work, reward and status structures, the development of unions, and patterns of management-employee relations. He suggests that the most common management-employee pattern (the standard modern pattern) involves ambivalence and hence instability: only some employees accept management's claim to power, while the legitimacy of unions is only partially endorsed by management. Just how widespread this pattern is remains an empirical matter, bearing in mind recent trends in markets, technology, and the size of establishments (Piore and Sabel 1984; Sengenberger, Loveman, and Piore 1990).

Fox's framework can thus be used for defining and exploring workplace relations. The key concepts include work organization (which subsumes the nature of work roles); reward and status systems; trust; collective representation (unions); and industrial relations—the relationships between management and employees beyond the task level.[2] The starting point for an explanation are management and workers' ideology and action based on the distribution of power between the two sides.

There is one important point to add to these comments. It concerns the embeddedness of workplace relations (Granovetter 1985). As mentioned earlier, workplace relations are shaped by state and other institutions external to the workplace that affect management and employee behavior. Moreover, with few exceptions (Banaji and Hensman 1990; Beynon 1984), the observation that most large workplaces are units of multiplant, multinational companies has been insufficiently explored in empirical workplace research (Batstone, Boraston, and Frenkel 1977; Edwards and Scullion 1982; Gallie 1978; Maitland 1983; Sorge and Warner 1986; Lincoln and Kalleberg 1990). Yet there is now considerable evidence that workplace management practices are regularly monitored by higher-level managers and, although not constrained on operational matters, that such managers are subject to considerable control by corporate management in areas of strategic importance (Edwards 1987; Marginson et al. 1988). In addition, there is evidence that some multinationals, particularly American and Japanese companies, tend to be ethnocentric, introducing their home-based policies into foreign subsidiaries (Enderwick 1985; Oliver and Wilkinson 1989; Jain 1990; Florida and Kenney 1991). This evidence suggests the importance of examining relationships between higher-level managers and workplace management in explaining the human resource policies and practices of the latter.

Observations on Research and Methodology

If Fox's framework is to be used as the starting point in empirical research on workplace relations, we must ask whether his concepts can be readily operationalized. Further, what strategy and methods can usefully be employed to establish similarities and differences in workplace relations, identification of trends in such relations, and explanations for the research findings?

Two concepts presented difficulties for the work reported in this chapter. These were the concepts of status and trust respectively. Status, or the perceptions of relative position in a social structure, is probably best investigated using a survey methodology. For a variety of reasons, this was not possible in most of the plants. Data on the relative earnings levels of different types of employees in the same workplace, however—a reasonable proxy for status—were collected. Regarding trust, this concept was considered too difficult to operationalize. Instead, mainly behavioral indicators of conflict and cooperation were obtained, including assessments by managers and employees of the climate or quality of management-employee relations.

The research (which is ongoing) aims to provide a snapshot of current structures and practices and details of the direction in which workplace relations are developing in four workplaces in Britain, Australia, Taiwan, and Malaysia respectively. The choice of workplaces reflected three criteria: product characteristics, workplace size, and probability of obtaining access; often only the latter was a critical determinant.[3]

The research has entailed systematic interviewing of key personnel at subsidiary levels, including manufacturing directors, marketing and finance managers, middle and lower-line production managers, human resource managers, and union representatives (where relevant). At the largest plant an employee survey was administered to a random sample of shopfloor employees. The above information was complemented by detailed plant- and corporate-level documentary and statistical data, usually requested prior to engaging in the fieldwork. This information provided a basis for exploring issues in interviews, which were also conducted with HR managers at higher levels of the corporation, including senior officials at headquarters in the United States.

An advantage of studying a corporation with many formalized and standardized procedures is that comparable data relating to the framework mentioned above can be collected for each workplace. Cooperation by management and employees was for the most part exemplary. Although it was difficult initially to grasp the characteristics of the national system of labor relations in which the specific plants were embedded, this problem diminished as time passed.

Six limitations of the research should be noted. First, it proved impossible to select plants of similar size, a point that needs to be borne in mind in comparing workplace relations in these establishments. Second, limited time at each research site precluded comparative analysis of change dynamics and worker behavior. Third, as the research unfolded it became clear that corporate management exercised influence through a variety of channels; however, resource and access constraints made it difficult to explore this aspect adequately. Fourth, the research reported below is confined to production workers; the findings might have been different had I focused on employees in marketing or finance. A more general but separate point is that a workplace logic of comparison will tend to yield different findings from a study based on, for example, a product logic. In the latter case, contrasting social arrangements (hierarchy versus contracting) can be used to produce the same product and will therefore be the object of study, with the choice of arrangements depending on extant economic, industrial, and cultural conditions (see Nomura 1991). Finally, because of these limitations and the narrow scope of the study, generalizations about patterns and trends in workplace relations should be regarded as tentative.[4]

The Corporation, the Plants, and Workplace Relations

PH is a large U.S. multinational corporation that develops, manufactures, and sells pharmaceutical and allied products. Most of the R&D is conducted in the United States, and the basic chemicals are sourced largely from two facilities, one in the United States, the other, a smaller source, in the United Kingdom. Subsidiaries in various parts of the world produce and market similar items, although there are some important variations.[5] Table 9.1 provides further information on the corporation.

Table 9.1 shows that in the eleven years before 1990 PH shed nearly half its labor force but reduced the number of manufacturing sites by only about 18 percent. Some of the labor force reduction came from the sale of nonprofitable plants and divestitures arising from changes in legal ownership requirements in some countries, notably India. In addition, many nonprofitable products were discontinued. According to a senior corporate manager, there were very few compulsory redundancies. These changes did, however, alter the geographical distribution of manufacturing sites: in 1979, there were ten pharmaceutical plants in North America; by 1990, there were only two. From this standpoint, PH is a global manufacturing company. If we consider workforce numbers, this point is reinforced: in 1990, two-thirds of the corporation's total workforce was employed outside the United States.

The remaining data in table 9.1 indicate a strong improvement in the company's fortunes. Sales and profits per employee increased significantly, although the company did not improve its position relative to its competi-

Table 9.1. Key PH Corporation Data, 1979 and 1990

Characteristics	1979	1990
Number of employees	61,000	34,000
Number of manufacturing sites	97	80[a]
Sales per employee in U.S.$	53,000	137,000
Profit per employee in U.S.$	6,000	14,000
Cost of goods sold as a percentage of sales	48	32
Annual inventory turnover	2.4 times	3.8 times

Source: Company document.
[a]Estimate based on 1989 figure.

tors. Although these results reflect the impact of new products and effective marketing techniques, the reduction in cost of goods as a percentage of sales and faster inventory turnover point to improvements in manufacturing efficiency.

In sum, PH appears to have responded to the pressures of increased competition and the threat of corporate takeover as many other U.S. corporations have—by downsizing, streamlining, and consolidating (Useem 1990). By the mid-1980s, a new strategy was emerging, one that permitted greater operational autonomy of the subsidiaries from headquarters. Innovation rather than conservation was the new theme, with the emphasis on continuous improvement aimed at greater customer satisfaction. These values were disseminated in training programs and incorporated in management assessment procedures. In manufacturing, as described later, senior management encouraged the development of JIT and awards for manufacturing excellence based on results that included a wide range of indicators.[6] These awards were intended to convey corporate recognition of manufacturing improvements at subsidiaries.

Human resources was elevated in importance, so that a corporate HR vice president sits on the management committee (the highest internal management decision-making body) and the HR regional vice presidents responsible for the Americas, Europe, and Asia respectively are included in the corporate strategy process. These managers provide assistance and advice to the regional vice presidents of manufacturing while having a subordinate line relationship to the corporate HR vice president and a superordinate relationship with HR directors at the various subsidiaries.

Subsidiaries are expected to follow specific HR principles. These include retaining capable people and providing them with challenging work in an open and participatory environment where creativity is fostered and suggestions for improving the quality of working life are actively encouraged. Some HR management practices at the plant level are standardized—for example, the salary and appraisal system for supervisors and above—but for the most part local managers are free to devise their own policies consistent with the above-mentioned principles. The subsidiaries' HR practices are required to be audited every three years by a team that typically includes an HR corporate staff member and an HR director from another affiliate in the region. This process follows a well-defined methodology such that ensuing action plans are implemented by subsidiary HR directors and monitored by HR regional vice presidents.

The four workplaces are located on sites that are central to the subsidiaries located in the different countries shown in table 9.2. These subsidiaries produce and market approximately thirty different types of pharmaceutical products with many variations in item size, shape, and packaging. The latter stages of production are generally undertaken in three physically separate areas—fluids, dry, and sterile products—and workers are employed in one of these three areas. Production proceeds from checking and weighing of raw materials to mixing and then on to filling of bottles, capsules, or tablets and then to packaging and distribution. Quality control is accomplished at various stages of the production process by specialist quality assurance employees. Automation can link different stages of the production process (e.g., mixing ingredients and filling capsules) and substitute for manual labor within any stage (e.g., use of robots for stacking cartons).

Table 9.2 indicates that pharmaceutical production is the sole manufacturing activity at only two of the four sites. The U.K. and Taiwan sites are more complex, especially the former, which also produces chemicals and plastic containers. The latter packages nonpharmaceutical consumer products sold by the company. A second indicator of complexity—exports as a proportion of total sales—shows that the United Kingdom is unique in having to meet special orders (which are usually small-batch) from various parts of Europe and the Middle East.

The worksites and workplaces also vary in size. In 1990, the U.K. site (including the head office) employed more than two thousand employees, slightly more than a third (718) of whom worked in pharmaceuticals. The Australian site/workplace is in the medium-size range, while the sites in Taiwan and Malaysia are smaller in scale; three-quarters of the former site's workers and all of the latter are employed in pharmaceutical production.

Before examining sitewide changes in workforce size since 1985, it is important to note that with the exception of Taiwan, manufacturing workers (as opposed to employees in marketing, sales, finance, and administration) comprise only a minority of the total pharmaceutical employees at each of the four sites: 46.8 percent in the United Kingdom, 54.1 percent in Australia, 43.4 percent in Taiwan, and 46 percent in Malaysia. Women tend to be employed as direct labor—as process and packaging operators—while men work as storepersons and packers (which involve heavier work) and as maintenance personnel.

Table 9.2. Characteristics of PH Work Sites, 1989–1990

Characteristics	United Kingdom	Australia	Taiwan	Malaysia
Nonpharmaceutical production	yes	no	yes	no
Exports as a percentage of sales	50	<10	<10	<10
Pharmaceutical sales in U.S.$: 1990	140	59	9	7.5
Employment sitewide: 1985	3,029	363	220	200
Employment sitewide: 1990	2,079	352	183	126
Pharmaceutical total: 1990	718	352	99	126
Pharmaceutical manufacturing: 1990	336	155	43	58
Percentage female in pharmaceutical manufacturing: 1990	59	54	63	64
Average age of machines (years)	12	14	11	16

Source: Company data.
Sales value data are estimates.

Labor accounts for 15 to 20 percent of the total pharmaceutical production costs, with chemicals comprising the bulk of the costs. Another common feature is that with the exception of two of the managing directors—in Taiwan and Malaysia—and a small number of technical specialists and professionals, managers and employees are recruited locally.

Reductions in employment over the period 1985–90 can be seen from table 9.2: Malaysia reduced its workforce by 37 percent, the United Kingdom by 31.4 percent, Taiwan by 16.8 percent, and Australia by 3 percent. Thus, corporate strictures to "downsize" have had an effect; in two cases—the United Kingdom and Malaysia—this entailed voluntary redundancies. Workers, particularly indirect employees, are aware of continuing pressure to decrease the size of the workforce. It is noteworthy that at all four sites total production in 1990 exceeded that in 1985, indicating substantial increases in labor productivity. Moreover, the average age of the machinery at the various sites, as shown in table 9.2, suggests that this increase was not achieved through dramatic technological change.

Patterns of Workplace Relations

As indicated in the earlier theoretical discussion, workplace relations can be conceptualized in terms of several dimensions. These are included on the left-hand side of table 9.3. I shall proceed by discussing each workplace in turn. Changes under way are discussed in the following section.

British Workplace Relations

Manual employees at PH were employed in jobs that had a narrow task range involving little discretion, and most direct jobs were machine-paced. There were thirty-five different job descriptions[7] and no employee involvement groups in the form of quality circles or similar substructures. Employees were not supervised very intensely, however, as indicated by the relatively low management-employee ratio. But with the comparatively tall management hierarchy, manual workers felt distant from senior plant managers, who were responsible for making the key operating decisions. Being divided along broad product lines, which had quite different technical requirements, middle-level plant managers tended to be parochial. They preferred to retain their autonomy from staff in areas such as human resources, with whom relations were sometimes strained. There were also problems of intraproduct line coordination (e.g., between purchasing, production control, production, and marketing) because of the absence of an advanced computerized materials resource planning system.

Manual employees' jobs were graded according to criteria (complexity, skills, and responsibility) set out in a job evaluation system jointly administered with the unions. Once on the full-ability rate, wage increases were obtained solely through job regrading (which was rare) and through the annual collective agreement. Although there was no provision for

Table 9.3. Workplace Relations among Manual Workers in PH Plants,
1989–1990

	United Kingdom	Australia	Taiwan	Malaysia
Job and work organization				
Job description	narrow	wider	narrow	narrow
Employee involvement	low	medium	low	medium
Management-employee ratio[a]	16.8	10.9	18.8	33.3
Hierarchy index[b]	5	3	2	3–4
Integration[c]	weak	strong	weak	medium
Reward system				
Job grades	17	9	5	6
Ability/skill based	yes, limited	yes	no	yes
Other aspects	—	—	bonus, etc.	bonus, etc.
Equity of system	high	medium-high	medium	high
Employee organization				
Union density (in percent)	100	100	0	+95
Number of unions	3	5	0	1
Steward committee	no	no	no	yes
FTO involvement	very low	medium	no	medium
Rule-setting process				
Union consultation	very high	high	no	high
Collective bargaining	workplace	intermediate	no	workplace
Consultation with employee representatives	uneven	high	medium	high
Other	joint projects	arbitration	—	—
Conflict/cooperation				
Industrial action	none	none	none	none
Absenteeism (in percent)	6.2	3.4 (1988)	8.6	4.5
Turnover (in percent)	13.6 (3.0)[d]	7.0	22.0	2.2
Management-employee rating	fair	good	fair	very good

[a]Refers to the number of line managers, including supervisors, in manufacturing as a percentage of total manual workers.
[b]Refers to the number of reporting levels between manual workers and the manufacturing sector.
[c]Refers to the degree of functional cooperation between units involved in manufacturing.
[d]Figure in brackets refers to voluntary turnover.

recognition of individual merit in the wage system, workers generally deemed their rewards to be reasonably good. Management claimed to pay above the average for similar work, while employees reported that conditions and benefits were better than those offered by most firms in the area.

The U.K. plant is situated in what had previously been a coal mining and iron- and steel-producing area. Unionism is part of the local culture. Accordingly, the plant is technically a closed shop for manual employees, with dues collected by the company on behalf of the unions (the so-called checkoff). Three unions cover manual workers: one has jurisdiction over the semiskilled operators, and the other two are tradespersons' unions. Two separate branches of the union covering operators also cover clerical and technical/managerial employees up to middle management level, and the densities of these branches are about 75 percent. There is no joint shop steward committee at the workplace, but three separate committees exist for stewards of the different unions. During the field work, management consulted extensively with the senior steward of the operators' union, who acted as a full-time convener for all manual workers. Full-time union officials (FTOs) rarely visit the plant, usually only to negotiate the annual collective agreements. Even then, their role has been subsidiary to that of the convener and shop stewards in recent years.

A characteristic of U.K. management is the central role played by the HR department in negotiating change. This has resulted in union cooperation against a background of considerable job insecurity. Some middle line managers complained that this slowed down technological change and the introduction of new work practices, but senior line managers believed that such involvement was ultimately necessary to maintain trust and avoid conflict in order to dispel corporate management's belief that plant performance was unduly constrained by hostile unions.

Relations with the unions, both informally through the convener and formally in the annual workplace negotiations, which involve all the stewards, are the main channels through which management communicates with manual employees. In addition, some line managers have strong bargaining relations with the stewards, mainly on the subject of overtime (which at the time of the fieldwork corporate management claimed to be unduly high[8]). Information is disseminated to stewards on planned changes in technology and work organization, but it varies according to production area. The HR department has involved stewards in major exercises, for example, a project examining ways to reduce absenteeism and, more recently, a task force aimed at developing a new job evaluation system.

According to the indicators in table 9.3, industrial relations have been peaceful. Absenteeism is relatively high, but this was attributed to a small number of offenders rather than viewed as a widespread problem. Few employees have chosen to leave their employer, as signified by the 3 percent voluntary turnover (separation rate) figure. The relatively high turnover of 13.6 percent reflects management efforts to reduce workforce numbers through natural attrition and voluntary redundancies, and an increasing number of workers are employed on nonstandard employment contracts.[9] The consensus among managers and the stewards is that relations are fair but fragile. Employees were apprehensive about their employment prospects given the rumors that changes that were being introduced (discussed later), while management was sensitive to a change in mood among the workforce that could plunge the workplace into conflict.

Australian Workplace Relations

Job descriptions in the Australian plant are similar to those in the United Kingdom, but as part of recent collective agreements, additional maintenance functions have been added to operator jobs. In addition, operators are encouraged to seek ways of resolving quality and wastage problems in accordance with JIT/Total Quality Management (TQM) principles. A variant of quality circles was being used, but they were not in all areas of the plant.

The management hierarchy is relatively flat so that unionized team leaders tend to replace nonunion supervisors as key links between more senior management and employees. Integration is strong, largely as a result of enthusiastic leadership by the manufacturing director and his cohesive team of senior managers in the context of a medium-scale operation whose manufacturing processes are relatively simple compared with those in the United Kingdom.

The extant reward system had only recently been introduced. It has a more limited number of job grades than before. These are divided into three streams (production, maintenance, and stores), which permit up to 30 percent variation in individual earnings within any grade, depending on assessed skill levels. The system also provides for career progression through regrading based on skill acquisition. Increased company support for training is accompanying the new reward system. Pay levels are not significantly higher than those in the local labor market, but with lower-than-average work hours, opportunities for advancement, and good conditions and benefits, employees consider themselves to be relatively well off. This perception is reinforced by a formal management commitment to avoid redundancies except in the most dire of economic circumstances.

A closed-shop and checkoff system exists in Australia involving, until very recently, five occupationally based unions with some jurisdictional overlap. Operators, storepersons, and warehouse employees are covered by separate unions, and two other unions have jurisdiction over tradespersons. There is no steward committee, in part because wages and conditions in the past were set through awards, usually arbitrated beyond the workplace by state or federal tribunals (see Deery and Plowman 1991). In addition, management negotiates separately at the workplace level with the unions representing the four main occupational groups. FTOs do not normally visit the plant, leaving the stewards to conclude their own "over-award" agreements. FTO involvement has increased, however, in response to a trend toward more issues being settled through formalized workplace bargaining and as a result of management efforts to reduce the number of unions at the plant.

Compared with the United Kingdom, there is less consultation with the union in effecting change and more direct communication with employees. This reflects management's policy of limiting union influence while establishing rapport with individual employees. In effecting major changes, however (e.g., in relation to job demarcation, the pay system, training, and hours of work), management consults and negotiates agreements with the unions at the workplace level. This has been encouraged by guidelines set by the federal and state tribunals facilitating lower-level agreements on workplace flexibility and productivity (Curtain 1990).

A new management team was established in the early 1980s following a period of substantial industrial conflict at the plant. Improving employee relations was among the main management objectives. The evidence points to success, as indicated by the data in table 9.3. Management rates employee relations as favorable, a view echoed by the stewards. Senior management, however, believes that employees have been slow to accept change.

Taiwanese Workplace Relations

Job descriptions in Taiwan are narrow, and distinctions between operators, packers, and maintenance workers are similar to those in the United Kingdom and Australia. Management does not systematically involve employees, although there was some experimentation beginning in 1987 with a variant of quality circles, following encouragement from corporate headquarters. Prizes were given to groups that were most successful in improving productivity or quality, but by 1990 the experiment was fading in importance as other issues assumed priority.

A moderately high management-employee ratio reflects management's propensity to monitor employees in order to maintain high levels of in-process product quality. This in turn reduces the need for additional quality assurance personnel and is a key sales attribute, helping to distinguish the company's products from those of local firms. The management hierarchy is relatively flat because of the small number of employees coupled with the almost complete substitution of team leaders (who are responsible for organizing work but not for employee discipline) for supervisors. The lack of supervision means that department managers have to extend their responsibilities to shopfloor details, which limits the time and energy they can devote to dealing with one another about broader issues. Department managers also lacked experience, and the manufacturing director did not provide the necessary leadership to ensure functional integration.

The reward system follows local custom in grading the jobs broadly according to skill, but within the grades there is no differential payment for superior ability or diligence. There is also a year-end bonus, which was equivalent to one and a half months' salary but raised in 1990 to two months, in line with market changes.[10] Other elements of the reward system include a transport and meal allowance and rewards that satisfy local expectations concerning the enterprise's sociability. These include funding for children's scholarships, quarterly birthday parties, May Day and festival gifts, and staff outings. The Employee Welfare Fund Law of 1943 requires employers to establish a welfare fund based on contributions from employer and employees (in prescribed proportions) to support such social activity. The law also requires that responsibility for the fund lies with a welfare committee composed of employee representatives. The line between company rewards and benefits from the fund are subject to negotiation, however, for the company has its own funds—a miscellaneous benefits fund and a community fund—for supporting such activity. As we shall see shortly, the welfare committee and the consultative committee (the latter is required by the Labor Standards Law of 1984)—from which employee representatives can make requests of management—are difficult to disentangle. An estimated 5 percent of workers' earnings is expended annually on these nonwage benefits.

The Trade Union Law of 1929 permits employees in workplaces employing more than thirty employees to join a union; however, management has not encouraged unionism. According to the HR director, no union officials have attempted to organize the plant and employees are ably served by existing mechanisms within the company. He argued that unions tend to promote their own organizational interests and not those of employees while unduly limiting management discretion.

The consultative committee consisted of representatives elected by broad occupational groups, including white-collar workers, and the senior managers. The employee representatives comprised the welfare committee, which dealt with welfare activities supported by the statutorily defined expenditure for this purpose, but since the company contributed more than the minimum, social activities were often included in the deliberations of the consultative committee.

Although this mechanism provided an opportunity for employee participation in decision-making, the employee representatives did not coordinate their claims and had no legitimacy as intermediaries between workers and management; in short, they could articulate worker discontent but not manage it. This, together with the fact that meetings of the consultative committee were held at the company rather than the plant level and were regular but infrequent—once a month—adds up to the assessment that there was medium rather than high consultation, as shown in table 9.3.

Overt collective action had not occurred at the plant, but absenteeism and labor turnover were high relative to the other three plants. These figures need to be seen in the context of the local labor market, whose official statistics for 1989 (Directorate-General of Budget Accounting, 1989 n.d., 21) show labor turnover in manufacturing running at more than 40 percent. Line management claimed to have enjoyed good relations with employees; however, there were indications from a recent company survey that employees were dissatisfied with their earnings and career prospects.

Malaysian Workplace Relations

The nature of work roles is narrowly circumscribed both in content and discretion in Malaysia. There are eleven manual job descriptions, which are used in a job evaluation system that also applies to clerical workers. Manual employees are occasionally rotated between jobs in the same grade. There is no employee involvement scheme, although three work-improvement groups are operating among technical employees. A combination of team prizes and a high management-employee ratio (33.3 percent) nevertheless resulted in the workers being relatively exposed to management ideology and influence. But this did not mean the structure is flat; in fact, quite the contrary, as indicated by the hierarchy score of three to four—the score depending on the presence of an assistant supervisor below supervisor level in some areas. Integration was achieved despite an extended hierarchy, largely because of the manufacturing director's strong and experienced leadership.

The reward system at the Malaysian plant was the most complex, consisting of a collectively bargained pay increase and annual increments up to a maximum amount specified in the contract. In addition, the contract included a cost-of-living allowance and a bonus equivalent to two months' pay. There was also a provision for merit increases of up to 5 percent of pay, which were decided by management on the basis of individual performance appraisals. Furthermore, management had established various prizes, including the General Manager's Excellence Award and the Employee of the Quarter Award, which rewarded outstanding individual creativity and diligence.

Clerical and manual workers were organized by an industrial (chemicals) union. There was no checkoff; responsibility for dues were in the hands of the union secretary, who together with a chairperson and two members, comprised the union committee. Involvement with external union officials occurred only under especially difficult circumstances (e.g., redundancies) and at the time of the triennial negotiations of the collective contract. It is nevertheless noteworthy that the union secretary was also a vice president of the national union.

The company's pay rates and benefits were about average for multinational firms but superior to local companies. This was especially so for medical benefits and pensions. The firm also provided educational subsidies, a scholarship fund for employees' children, festival allowances, and car loans at reduced rates. According to evidence from a company survey, employees were satisfied working at the company, although there was some concern about job security in light of major retrenchment exercises carried out in 1987 and 1988. In addition, the union secretary reported that management gave insufficient information to employees on company developments and that some workers felt their work was monotonous and afforded few career opportunities.

As in the United Kingdom and Australia, the Malaysian collective agreement, which was negotiated at the workplace level, included disputes and disciplinary procedures. Employees tended to process grievances— which were reportedly few in number—through the union secretary. He would then bring the more important problems to the union committee for discussion. The secretary had held the position for eight years and in that time had built up strong bargaining relations with the HR director and manufacturing director. They were appreciative of his role in preventing and resolving problems.

A cooperative industrial relations climate existed at the plant. There had been no industrial action, and absenteeism was low, in fact, lower (3.4 percent) than the 4.5 percent indicated in table 9.3 since this included several people who had been ill for a long period. Labor turnover was low, and both management and the union secretary agreed that relations were very good.

This summary needs to be qualified in two respects: employee commitment to the firm was limited by uncertainty about future corporate intentions regarding the plant, and management was slightly anxious about the upcoming election of union officers and the consequences for renegotiation of the collective agreement.

Preliminary Conclusion regarding Patterns of Workplace Relations

Based on the above, the following observations can be made. First, manual workers' jobs tended to involve low levels of discretion; the Australian plant was different only in degree. The organizational structuring of the work was more varied, however, as evidenced by a comparison of the Taiwanese and Malaysian establishments, which were of similar size yet markedly different in management intensity, hierarchy, and functional integration.

The reward systems represented a variation on the theme of paying employees according to job content and grade, and collective increases in rewards were based mainly on market forces but achieved through bargaining (in unionized establishments) or consultation (Taiwan). Only in the United Kingdom was the job evaluation system formalized and administered jointly. In some plants, notably those in Malaysia and Australia, individual achievement was also rewarded—performance in the former and skill acquisition in the latter.

The reward packages tended to be above average but differed in important respects. In the United Kingdom and Australia, priority was given to pay and working conditions, while in Taiwan especially, but also in Malaysia, welfare benefits and items signifying support for the concept of enterprise community were emphasized. With the exception of the Taiwan plant, where reward increases had tended to lag relative to comparable firms and to the cost of living, employees regarded their rewards as equitable without being particularly favorable.

Union organization varied considerably: the United Kingdom and Taiwan were obvious contrasts. Where unions were present, a cooperative relationship tended to exist based on extensive consultation and workplace collective bargaining, which was constrained in only one country (Australia) by the national industrial relations system. Although there was some variation in the climate of employee relations as perceived by management, such differences—for example, between the United Kingdom and Malaysia—were insubstantial. Taking into account employees' views, however, the picture is less bright: relations in the Australian and Malaysian plants were cooperative, whereas in the United Kingdom and Taiwan, where workers were less satisfied, cooperation was based more on accommodation to the realities of employment than on support for management objectives.

Changes in Workplace Relations

In pursuing policies aimed at attaining workplace output and cost targets, management was introducing changes affecting workplace relations. These changes are summarized in table 9.4 and are discussed more fully below.

Since changes in the various dimensions of workplace relations were part of more complex developments at each establishment, it is important to understand these connections. Hence, I will proceed by examining trends in each plant separately before drawing some general conclusions.

Changes in the United Kingdom

The U.K. plant was in the midst of a substantial program that involved many changes. Four initiatives deserve mention: the automation of the fluids area; the development of a new job evaluation scheme and alteration in union coverage; the introduction of a comprehensive computerized database for materials planning, known as MRP2; and the transfer of sterile products from an overseas affiliate to the U.K. plant. The first two changes are having a more immediate impact on workplace relations and so are discussed briefly below.[11]

The fluids automation project signaled the direction in which work organization was heading. Fluids was the largest business unit, employing 142 persons or 42 percent of the pharmaceutical manufacturing workforce in 1990. Over a two-year period, the plan was to use automation to halve the size of the workforce. Management hoped to achieve this downsizing by attrition and voluntary redundancies. The project involved a change in the shift system (from a morning and afternoon arrangement to a double day shift), permitting machinery to run for longer periods. Major changes were also being made in job descriptions, aimed at increasing job flexibility. These included the reduction of four job categories (packaging opera-

Table 9.4. *Trends in Workplace Relations in PH Plants, 1990*

	United Kingdom	Australia	Taiwan	Malaysia
Job and work organization				
Reduce jobs	yes	yes/limited	yes	no
Broaden jobs	yes	yes	yes/management	no
Emphasis on teamwork	yes	yes	yes/management	yes
Improvement orientation	yes	yes	yes/management	yes/limited
Flatten hierarchy	yes	yes	yes	no
Integrate functions	yes	yes	yes	no
Reward system				
More performance-based	yes	yes	yes	no
Skill development	yes/limited	yes	limited	no
Employee organization				
Reduce union density	no/yes	no	not applicable	no
Reduce number of unions	yes	yes	not applicable	no
Rule-setting process				
Reduce bargaining units	yes	yes	not applicable	no
Increase union consultation	yes	yes	not applicable	no
Increase employee consultation	yes/limited	yes	no	no
Major problems	management morale management and employee skills employee uncertainty union power	low volume management and employee skills union structure	management turnover management disunity and skills employee morale	low volume employee flexibility

tor, line steward or chargehand, inspector, and training operator) into one and the substitution of team leaders for supervisors. Workers would be expected to work together in teams resourced by a team leader. Responsibility for skill formation, performance, and discipline would lie with the line manager.

The new job descriptions provided an opportunity for the HR department to revise the job evaluation system. Unlike the previous system, the new arrangement would apply to semiskilled and skilled manual workers as well as clerical employees. Unionized managerial and technical personnel would be encouraged to leave the union with an attractive pay and benefits offer, thus excluding them from the job evaluation scheme. The result of this plan is shown in table 9.4, which illustrates the attempt to reduce union density among nonmanual employees. These moves laid the foundations for a single bargaining unit instead of the four that existed in 1990. Two further attributes of the scheme are that it is jointly designed and administered with the manual and clerical unions and provides for (not very large) differences in individual pay according to performance, based on regular appraisals.

As indicated in table 9.4, the first major problem in implementing change has been management morale. This is related to the U.K. workplace's position in the region. Essentially, in its drive to rationalize production in Europe, corporate management let it be known that the number of plants was going to be reduced from eleven to about three. With no specific decisions made on plant closure, however, workplace management was anxious about its future. This was fueled by four additional factors. First, headquarters emphasized a "headcount reduction," which diminished local managers' career prospects irrespective of rationalization. Second, it was rumored that the then U.K. chief executive officer was insufficiently active in supporting the U.K. subsidiary's interests at headquarters. This included his failure to counter adequately the prevailing corporate view that the U.K. plant was less orderly than other major European plants on account of union influence. Third, and relatedly, the transfer of the less profitable sterile product line to the United Kingdom suggested limited corporate confidence in the U.K. operation compared with the one in Germany. Fourth, and in the same vein, some managers pointed out that the U.K. plant had not been authorized to produce any of the new products that the corporation had released over the past three years; instead, these had been given to the German and French subsidiaries, which had then enhanced their performance relative to that of the U.K. plant, thereby creating the self-fulfilling prophecy that the United Kingdom plant was less profitable.

Senior plant management countered these arguments by highlighting the major investment made by the company in the fluids automation project and the MRP2 system, as well as improvements leading to higher efficiency in the dry products area. But this message was sometimes lost on account of the new problems managers faced in trying to implement major changes in work systems with limited staff. These problems were compounded by deficiencies in the workforce's qualifications and skills, and by restricted expenditure in this domain.

Uncertainty about the future adversely affected employees, and in some cases their cooperation was tinged with cynicism or was not forthcoming.[12] This withdrawal of cooperation was not reflected in the conduct of industrial relations, but one manager likened the consultation process to "treading treacle": a great deal of activity occurring with little being achieved.

The unions certainly influenced management, making for a complex reality. On the one hand, survey evidence (not presented here) shows the workforce to be strongly labor-oriented and committed to trade unionism. This suggests the possibility of vocal opposition. On the other hand, there is no joint shop steward organization and, as we have seen, no evidence of worker militancy, which may be related to the relatively high proportion of temporary workers at the plant and persistent unemployment in the area.

Changes in Australia

By 1985 a new senior management team had agreed on a strategy to improve manufacturing performance. This was to be a prelude to the introduction of new technology on a larger scale. The four main elements of management's approach, which were widely disseminated among the workforce, included the following: first, a focus on continuous incremental improvements in technology (e.g., a reduction in wastage rates and a linking of previously separate elements related to the production of particular items); second, the adoption of new manufacturing techniques, such as JIT/TQC, which involved new systems, especially regarding materials planning and machinery utilization; and third, the introduction of a more flexible organizational structure, involving greater functional integration of personnel from different parts of the organization by means of project teamwork and flatter hierarchies.

Related to this was the fourth element, which impinged most directly on employees. Greater productivity was fostered by broadening job descriptions, so that operators are expected to perform simple maintenance tasks previously performed by tradespersons. The latter are expected to concentrate on preventive maintenance and to suggest improvements in productivity related to their tasks. Tradespersons are encouraged to cross-skill, with an emphasis on electronics. This is being facilitated by the provision of skills training tied to pay levels, as described earlier in the previous section.[13] In addition, a less directive style of supervision is being introduced, in which unionized team leaders are gradually replacing nonunion supervisors. Teamwork has been institutionalized by the promotion of worker involvement groups whose main objective is to solve productivity and/or quality problems. Although these changes have had the effect of reducing the number of jobs (achieved through attrition), "headcount reduction" is regarded by management as having limited potential for increasing labor productivity.

Union rationalization has been a major goal of senior management. With agreement by the FTOs, HR management encouraged members of one of the skilled workers' unions to join its counterpart, thus consolidating membership of these workers in a single union. Similarly, warehouse employees were persuaded to join the operators' union, leaving management to negotiate in the future with three rather than five unions.

The reduction in unions is part of a broader strategy to negotiate a workplace agreement independent of the main awards, based on a single bargaining unit. This is being assisted by developments at the national level, where there is pressure and there are inducements for unions to amalgamate and rationalize their membership composition (see Frenkel 1993). In addition, it is now possible for companies and unions to opt out of the arbitration system in an orderly and regulated fashion.

Since the changes referred to above affect work and union organization, management has been careful to obtain the consent of the shop stewards. Management favors direct communication with employees, however, and has therefore not introduced representative forms of participation based on union involvement. By contrast, consultation with employees has been stepped up through meetings organized by management and via training programs.

Turning to the impediments to change mentioned in table 9.4, the issue of low volume requires a brief explanation. Essentially, the Australian plant has considerable spare capacity that management is keen to use to boost performance. This increase in turn would help justify larger-scale investment in new technology. The size of the domestic market is limited, however, and there are problems exporting to neighboring countries.[14] This has made it difficult to maintain the momentum for innovation. Further, management and employees have had insufficient background and training in JIT and TQC philosophy and techniques. This limitation is likely to be less significant as workers receive more training, although there is concern that older employees may find it difficult to adapt to work roles that are more flexible, challenging, and often more stressful.

The union structure continues to pose a problem, mainly in impeding job flexibility. Management claims that demarcations between electricians and fitters, operators and tradespersons, and storepersons and warehouse personnel have restricted productivity growth. A further structural problem has been that union officials covering employees in the stores area (the National Union of Workers) have refused to permit their stewards to engage in workplace bargaining, making it impossible for management to establish a single comprehensive workplace agreement.

To conclude on a positive note, the Australian plant has had a superior performance record in recent years. Thus, in 1987, 1988, and 1989, the

:e won manufacturing excellence awards, which are bestowed by
rters on approximately ten of the eighty plants each year.

ᴄᴴᵃⁿᵍᵉs *in Taiwan*

In 1989, the Taiwan subsidiary was in dire straits. Because of declining
financial performance and irregularities, the managing director had re-
signed. This together with a very tight local labor market for managerial
personnel resulted in virtually all the marketing managers and the HR
director leaving the company in the same year. As mentioned earlier, the
managing director from Malaysia was brought in to turn the company
around. His diagnosis was that morale and systems had broken down.
Accordingly, he began selecting and developing a management team that
would set new standards of commitment and efficiency and establish
systems of accountability and control. Monthly meetings of senior management were instituted, and the managing director began taking a keen
interest in manufacturing, which had apparently been neglected by his
predecessor. Building morale among employees through strong, committed
leadership coupled with information sharing was emphasized.

The managing director's longer-term plan for manufacturing was to
eliminate production of less profitable items and concentrate on products
with the most market potential. Some products were therefore being
phased out while reforms were being undertaken to boost profitability.
These included the development of a new market planning and production
scheduling system involving closer cooperation between functional units.
Tighter control over labor costs was exercised, resulting in fewer employees
in manufacturing. This mainly affected production management. Two
supervisors were promoted to management positions without filling their
previous jobs. These managers experienced stress in their broader roles,
since they had no experience and insufficient training for these new
responsibilities. In addition, they received less support than they needed
from the factory manager, whose job was more difficult with fewer staff.
Improved intramanagement relations were developing, however, with the
help of the HR director.

As indicated above, the changes were largely confined to management
and control systems. The new scheduling system was reported to have
decreased idle time among production workers, thereby signaling increased
management efficiency. A revised reward system was also being introduced,
based on the idea of making a third of the bonus payment vary according
to individual performance. Employees would be regularly and systematically appraised by their managers, as in Malaysia. Skill formation had been
suspended while efforts were made to resolve management problems, but
the HR officer intended to introduce a program of training, mainly for
sales and marketing personnel, in 1991.

As indicated above, the high turnover among management personnel in
the recent past and the need to establish new working relations and systems

had preoccupied management. Plant managers were also coming to grips with their new roles and had not yet unified into a team with a common vision of the future. JIT was mentioned, but the knowledge and skills to introduce such a system were lacking. Meanwhile, employee morale, which had been low, was improving as marketing and production became more aligned, with the help of the new scheduling system. More important, the impact of the new managing director was being felt throughout the organization and there was increasing optimism about the future. Indeed, nine months later, the managing director reported that sales were growing at almost double the average rate for the industry. This permitted management to increase wages and allowances by more than in the recent past.

Changes in Malaysia

According to table 9.4, the Malaysian plant is something of an exception to the general trend. Four points can be made, however, that indicate that this is more true of the present than of the past. First, the plant underwent significant change in 1987–88, resulting in a massive decline in the labor force (see table 9.3). This raised labor productivity. There was also a trend toward broader jobs. Given the relatively undereducated workforce, however (only about a third of manual workers can read and write in English, the common language to Malay and Chinese employees) and the low wages by international standards, there was little incentive to use labor more efficiently. Second, in some respects—the reward system, union organization, and bargaining—the Malaysian plant is relatively advanced. Thus, given management's acceptance of unionism in Malaysia, there is no need for substantial change. Third, the managing director in Malaysia—who had been recruited from the U.K. subsidiary—was new and cautious about promoting change before becoming thoroughly acquainted with the local operation. Fourth, and finally, the changes made recently have led to a successful performance record, acknowledged by headquarters in the form of manufacturing excellence awards for 1988 and 1989.

Nevertheless, increasing emphasis was put on teamwork. This was evidenced by new awards, which rewarded group and individual performance. An example was the absenteeism award, introduced in 1990. Management set annual absence targets, and if individuals and teams recorded lower absenteeism than the targets, they received prizes in the form of a dinner and gift vouchers.

Another change, referred to in table 9.4, was in management's orientation. Incremental productivity improvements were pursued mainly through closer relationships with local suppliers of some materials, the upgrading of buildings, and better factory layout. But, low wage costs, and, like the Australian plant, low volume, constrained management's ability to justify corporate investment in new technology. Hence, an emphasis on extending the market for profitable goods and curtailing production of nonprofitable lines, similar to the strategy adopted in Taiwan.

Finally, management regarded manual employees as cooperative yet a constraint on productivity growth. Lack of education and skills coupled with a large proportion of long-serving workers (average length of employment was close to ten years) was said to discourage workers from accepting change. In addition, it is likely that the recent experience of "downsizing" at the plant would have had this effect.

Summary

Based on the foregoing, it appears that comparable workplaces in different countries under common corporate control are tending to converge on what might be called a *cooperative dependent* pattern of workplace relations. The main features of this pattern are a tendency toward greater cooperation with management coupled with enterprise-oriented and rather weak unions; hence, their dependence on, but by no means total subservience to, management. Elements of this pattern are already present in some plants, but three qualifications need to be made. First, there is no certainty that all elements will cohere in the near future at any one plant. There are different impediments of varying magnitudes depending on local circumstance. Second, the emergence of the elements listed below also brings in its wake contradictions, for example, between the development of a more creative and team-oriented workforce and the emergence of more assertive and collectively inclined workers. Third, limited investment in new technology at the four plants has contributed to a relatively slow rate of change. This is likely to change, however, as further rationalization and automation of production continues.

Thus, some workplaces may not have much of a future, in which case they are likely to change along different lines from those indicated below. By contrast, those workplaces favored by corporate management—which appear to include the plants in this study—will upgrade their technology and employ fewer direct workers. Manual workplace relations will come to have characteristics similar to those outlined below.

Jobs will involve more discretion: they will be broader and more flexible, organized on a team basis, and encourage greater use of employees' problem-solving abilities. In this respect, the Taiwanese and Malaysian plants tend to lag. Organic forms of work organization, including flatter hierarchies and stronger functional integration, will be more common, while reward systems will reflect differences in individual performance or skills based on performance appraisals. These will supplement rather than replace collective improvements in rewards achieved through bargaining or consultation (Taiwan). Finally, workplaces will have few or no unions—one, two, or none at all—mainly supporting single or dual bargaining units, featuring more consultation with the union (or employee representatives as in Taiwan) and more direct communication with employees.

Toward an Explanation of Convergence in Workplace Relations

It would be inappropriate in the space available to explain both the similarities and differences in workplace relations and trends in such patterns. I shall therefore concentrate briefly on the latter issue, which has two elements. The first is the general movement toward cooperative dependence; the second is the relative position of plants according to the six dimensions that comprise the concept of workplace relations.

Trend toward Cooperative Dependence

The major sources of the trend toward cooperative dependence lie primarily, though not entirely, with PH's management. To understand this, it is important to begin with the global business environment and corporate strategy. In this regard, the relevant five-year corporate plan notes that "competition has become stronger in all lines of business as a result of the increasing trend towards industry consolidation." As observed earlier, this trend led the company to rationalize production capacity, "downsize," and restructure operations. The corporate plan acknowledges that this "has created strong centralized control." Relations between headquarters and the subsidiaries are changing, however, from ones marked by coordination and control to ones characterized by strategic leadership involving greater decentralization of decision-making for business units within broadly agreed guidelines. Recent corporate strategy has also signaled a shift in geographical market focus, with special emphasis on Europe and Japan, which are seen as crucial markets for longer-term growth. Thus, the U.K. plant is the most important of the four workplaces in corporate strategic calculations. The Australian facility comes second because of its long-term potential as an exporter to Asia. Despite their spare capacity, the Taiwanese and Malaysian plants, as well as other subsidiaries in the region, remain open because of government-imposed import duties and other restrictions that are unlikely to be lifted in the near future.

Headquarters has used several mechanisms for information-gathering and control to ensure improvements in financial and operational performance by the subsidiaries. First, there are the sales and cost plans, which are examined, discussed, and ultimately sanctioned by corporate management. Second, plans for capital investment must be approved by headquarters, and large-scale investment proposals are considered separately. The progress of such investments is monitored by headquarters following implementation. Third, as mentioned earlier, there are the manufacturing excellence awards, which enable corporate management to assess the strengths and weaknesses of plants according to a range of performance criteria. Fourth, there is a special corporate-level productivity measurement unit, which services the regional manufacturing vice presidents. Local manufacturing directors are required to calculate and report productivity levels on an annual basis and are held accountable for lapses in productivity growth. Fifth, there are regular conferences held in various countries or visits to and from headquarters involving senior subsidiary and corporate managers. These are frequently combined with plant inspections, which enable senior managers to exchange ideas and learn from one another in an operating environment. Sixth, and finally, there are temporary international project teams, often involving managers from headquarters and/or a subsidiary, that provide technical assistance, guidance, or training where necessary. All these processes facilitate technical consistency between plants and increase the compatibility between the activities of the subsidiaries and corporate objectives.

Corporate control of manufacturing, however, is not uniform across plants; it also varies in form. Thus, the plants in the United Kingdom and Taiwan were subject to more intense monitoring and feedback requirements than their Australian and Malaysian counterparts. This is explained by variations in recent performance and centrality to corporate strategy (see Hamill 1984). The U.K. and Taiwan plants have performed less satisfactorily, and the former workplace is important vis-à-vis the European market. Interestingly, although the Australian manufacturing director claimed to be relatively independent of headquarters, arguably this was because the subsidiary was comparatively profitable. Moreover, the Australian operation came closest to the corporate ideal in terms of manufacturing systems, so there was less need to exercise corporate control.

What then were the systems corporate management wished to see implemented? The corporate plan speaks of "flexible, state-of-the-art, low cost manufacturing facilities." In 1983, following a series of briefings on JIT and TQC systems by a consultant, corporate management decided to introduce pilot programs in twelve plants located in different countries. The experiences were then analyzed and a program developed involving dissemination of information to the subsidiaries. This was followed up by international training meetings in 1984 where management representatives from various plants in specific regions met with corporate specialists (employed in the productivity services section) to discuss the establishment of a local infrastructure for gradually implementing JIT. In 1987, workshops were arranged on a regional basis by the corporate specialists and attended by subsidiary JIT coordinators (typically moderately senior line managers). These were reinforced by project team visits to plants; the teams consisted of JIT corporate specialists and a knowledgeable senior manager of the subsidiary. Action plans were drawn up to implement what had been agreed to during the visit.

JIT, as applied to pharmaceutical manufacturing, presupposes a form of workplace relations comprising the following characteristics: first, broadened manual employee work roles that include elements of quality control, a culture of employee commitment to continuous innovation based on superior diagnostic skills, and teamwork; second, a formalized method of encouraging worker-based innovations in the form of quality circles; third, work organizations that treat manufacturing as a continuous process involving tight work-flow integration based on strong interfunctional collaboration and a minimum of bureaucracy; fourth, reward systems that encourage cooperative and innovative employee behavior; fifth, union and rule-setting procedures that at best support, and at worst do not prejudice, the development of JIT. Essentially, these elements are identical to those identified under the rubric of cooperative dependence. [15]

The above argument suggests the following question: given the importance assigned to human resources in the JIT system, to what extent and through what means does headquarters attempt to shape plant-level employee relations? To begin with, it is noteworthy that the reward system and core training programs for supervisors and managerial and professional employees are standardized across the corporation. These aim to encourage innovation, teamwork, and leadership styles that are sensitive to differences in task requirements and employee characteristics. In addition, all new middle and senior subsidiary management positions require headquarters' approval. The design of reward systems for manual workers is left to the discretion of subsidiary managers, but the design must be approved by the relevant regional HR vice president. Common norms regarding other aspects of employee relations are encouraged via the triennial human resource audits, including monitoring of subsequent action plans by HR vice presidents. Norms are further reinforced at annual or biennial regional conferences where HR subsidiary directors meet with the regional HR vice president and other corporate HR staff members.

Although subsidiary HR directors saw their overriding objective as supporting manufacturing management in realizing the latter's objectives, this was to be achieved according to principles and guidelines established for the HR function at the corporate level. On the basis of the HR audit manual and interviews with HR managers, it is possible to identify practices that are expected to be implemented by subsidiary HR directors. Some of the more important are as follows[16]: they are expected to provide information to employees on corporate philosophy, goals and performance, and HR procedures; to implement feedback mechanisms for upward communication; to provide clear formal job descriptions for all jobs; to follow disciplinary procedures that are consistent and fair; and to develop quality of working life programs. With regard to nonunion plants, HR management is expected to maintain the status quo by, among other measures, ensuring that employees are aware of their benefits, that a grievance procedure is available and known to employees, and that an employee participation system exists to maintain sound employee relations. Where a union is present, the following guidelines apply: preparations for negotiating the collective contract (which is assumed to be based on the workplace) should be thorough and well researched; grievances and disciplinary cases are to be handled according to formal procedures; and labor-management communications should be shared with all employees. Finally, HR personnel are expected to meet minimum qualifications for their job description and to participate actively in professional organizations.

A positive, cooperative climate of work relations is also fostered by a triennial corporationwide survey administered by headquarters to all employees in supervisory positions and above, although, on request from subsidiary HR directors, the survey can be used for all employee grades. The survey covers a wide range of issues.[17] The results are analyzed and presented by comparison with aggregate national and regional results. The findings are returned to the subsidiaries and then communicated in group meetings to supervisors and management. Action plans for improving employee morale are generated by the subsidiary HR directors and submitted for approval by the relevant regional HR vice president. Responsibility for implementation resides with local HR directors, who report on progress to their regional HR vice presidents.

This summary of human resource guidance mechanisms emphasizes the systematic encouragement of practices consistent with the emergence of the cooperative dependent pattern of workplace relations, in particular, information sharing, participation, effective bargaining procedures, and concern for positive employee relations generally. Beyond a "double-breasted" approach to unionism (working with unions where they exist and attempting to exclude unions where they are absent), however, there are no prescriptions on union structures and bargaining units. So why is there a trend toward single or dual unionism and workplace bargaining based on similar lines?

In brief, this pattern arises because of the interests of the managers of the subsidiaries in improving efficiency. Multiple unionism as practiced in the United Kingdom and Australia has led to four problems that are seen to hamper productivity growth: first, job demarcation, which is inconsistent with the "stretched jobs" presupposed by JIT systems; second, a tendency to institutionalize sectionalism, which makes it difficult to relinquish tight supervision and introduce organic management; and, third, multiple unionism, which tends to encourage more complex bargaining units, which are said to slow down the bargaining process and lead to unstable agreements because more powerful occupational groups tend to receive more favored treatment, leading to perceptions of inequity. A fourth problem, particularly in Australia, is that the larger the number of unions, the greater the probability of external union intervention and hence of difficulties in negotiations.

Management's concern with improving economic performance has been reinforced by external stimuli: publications on best management practice often refer to the Japanese experience, which is being shown to work in the United Kingdom and the United States (Wickens 1987; Womack, Jones, and Roos 1990). More important, governments, employers, and unions are themselves responding to changes in world markets by restructuring wider institutional arrangements into vehicles for management-employee cooperation based on integrative rather than distributive principles. This is certainly evident in Australia (Frenkel 1990b), Taiwan (Frenkel, Hong, and Lee 1993), and Malaysia (Wad 1988; Ponniah and Littler 1993) and is possibly an unintended consequence of Thatcherist policies in the United Kingdom (MacInnes 1987).

Relative Position of Plants Vis-à-Vis Cooperative Dependence

Figure 9.1 summarizes the characteristics of the four workplaces by arranging them relative to one another along the six dimensions of workplace relations.

Figure 9.1. Relative Positions of Four Pharmaceutical Plants along Six Dimensions of Workplace Relations

Dimension	Left end	Positions	Right end
Management Employee relations	Adversarial / Accommodative	T U · M A	Cooperative / Supportive
Rule setting	Multitiered / Multiunion / No consultation	A U · M T	Workplace level / Single/no union / Consultation
Union structure	Multiple	A U · M T	Single/no union
Reward systems	Rate for the job / Nonassessed	T U · A M	Performance related / Assessed
Work organization	Nonorganic	T U · M A	Organic
Job structure	Low discretion/ involvement	T M · U A	High discretion/ involvement

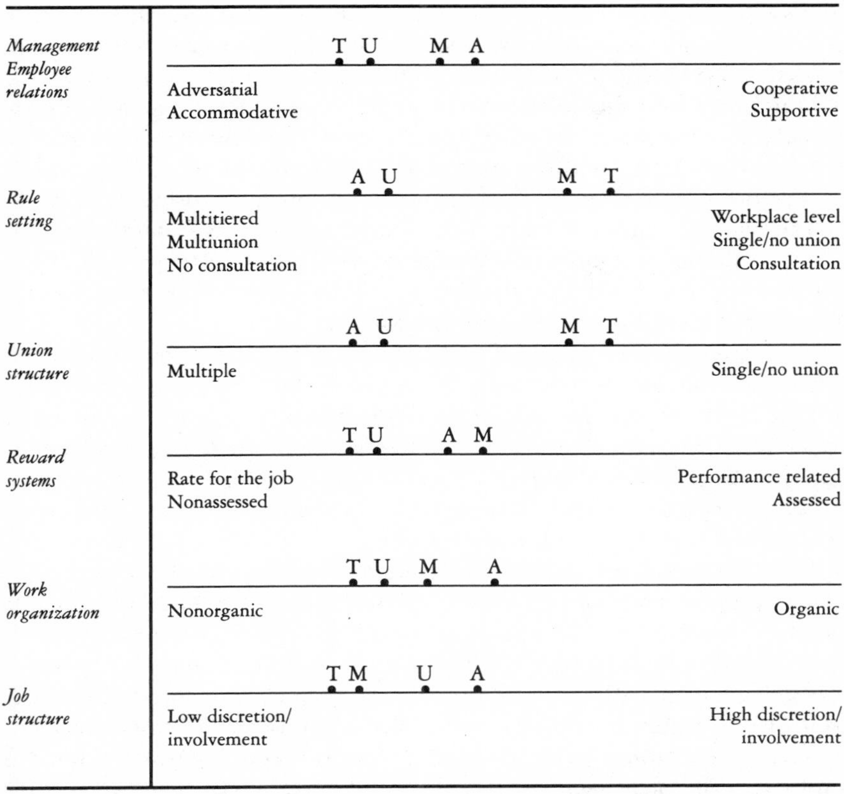

Note: The positions are approximations only.
Abbreviations: U = United Kingdom, A = Australia, T = Taiwan, M = Malaysia.

It is clear that no particular plant is closer to the cooperative dependence model (right-hand side) on all six dimensions shown in figure 9.1, but some patterns are evident. For example, Australia is closer to the ideal in terms of employee relations and, to some extent, reward systems but is least advanced in rule setting and union structure.[18] The United Kingdom is similar in terms of the last two dimensions mentioned above but is least advanced on most of the other dimensions. Taiwan is similar to the United Kingdom in many respects but not regarding unions and rule setting. On these dimensions, Taiwan is like Malaysia, although the latter is more advanced on the other dimensions, except in relation to job structure. It is noteworthy that the plants that most closely approximate the cooperative dependence pattern—Malaysia and Australia—also have the most cooperative employee relations climate and are acknowledged by headquarters as being highly successful performers compared with other workplaces in the corporation.

The various configurations described above can be explained by four major factors: the political power of management of the subsidiary, particularly the influence of senior plant management; the impact of local industrial relations institutions; and, to a lesser extent, the technical complexity and power of employees. Taking Australia first, advancement toward a JIT production and HR model reflects the dynamism of the current manufacturing director and appropriate selection of subordinate managers. Thus, progress has been most clear where management has had the fewest constraints in the areas of job structure and work organization in the broader context of a relatively simple manufacturing system. In areas where the impact of the national industrial relations system is greatest (i.e., on union structure and bargaining units and levels), there is still a way to go. As noted earlier, however, changes in industrial relations arrangements are now assisting in this process.

The recent history of senior management, as noted below, is a major factor in, though not the only explanation for, the limited progress achieved at the U.K. plant. Manufacturing complexity, particularly under conditions of significant change, is also important. At the same time, the external labor market and industrial relations environment have been favorable to management, although, as explained below, past legacies continue to obstruct management's plans.

In 1986, a decision was made by headquarters to close one of two U.K. pharmaceutical manufacturing sites. This had been agreed to in principle some time before, so that the decision was something of a relief when it came. In the meantime, there had been little innovation since management was preoccupied with meeting current requirements to forestall closure. Moreover, a regional manufacturing director was appointed to take responsibility for operations at the case study site. He reportedly took a limited interest in the plant, so, in the words of one senior manager, "The plant became leaderless and various departments went their own way."

Approximately 450 redundancies occurred at the non–case study plant, and some 250 jobs were created at the case study site. Many of the managers moved from the closed site, including a new manufacturing director. This compounded the leadership problem, since the site was highly organized, but the transferred managers had little experience in running a unionized plant. Inefficient labor practices tended to develop, which were magnified by the large-scale transfer of employees and machinery from the closed site. Moreover, all of this was occurring in the broader context of a large complex manufacturing site with a relatively high proportion of customized export products. Inaccurate sales forecasts and a largely manual materials planning system led to fluctuations in workloads that served to institutionalize overtime work and variable worker effort rates. Coping with these problems meant that there was little time to concentrate on JIT.

Although some progress was made by introducing vertically integrated business units in 1987,[19] it was not until 1989, when a new operations director was appointed, that change at the case study plant began to gather momentum to the point that it threatened to overwhelm middle management. In part this was because of lack of preparation and training, but it also reflected management's low morale in view of the impending rationalization of European production capacity. In addition, the union's concerns about protecting workers' interests in the face of job losses has meant that progress has been slower than anticipated. Finally, some of the obstacles to cooperative dependence owe their origins to a broader history. Thus, multiple unionism structured originally according to occupation still exists. More important, there is union power that depends less on labor market strength (since the plant is situated in an area of higher-than-average unemployment) than on workforce traditions of collectivism based on coal mining and the iron and steel industry in the context of a delicately positioned, sensitive management.

As discussed earlier, the factors leading to senior management's instability at the Taiwan subsidiary were quite different from those in the United Kingdom. But the outcome was similar: limited progress in implementing JIT and hence little in the way of associated workplace relations characteristics. In addition, the uncertainty arising from the demise of the previous senior management had reduced employee morale. As noted earlier, however, under the leadership of the new but experienced managing director, a cohesive management team was developing and there were indications of higher performance. Progress toward cooperative dependence was hampered, however, by a reduction in the number of plant managers to a point where inexperienced management threatened future efficiency. This partly reflected the problems of managing a small factory, which although simple compared with the United Kingdom, were complicated by the need to produce many different product lines.

Finally, wider institutional arrangements both constrained and assisted the development of workplace relations. On the one hand, high labor turnover means that strong worker involvement is difficult to achieve outside family enterprises. On the other hand, government labor market policy and the limited role of unions in Taiwan make it easier for management to structure workplace labor relations along cooperative, consultative lines.

In contrast to Taiwan, and with the exception of the managing director, senior management at the Malaysian plant was relatively stable; managers had been with the company for more than five years. This had given the operation continuity. Frequent changes in managing directors, however—as managers progressed from this small subsidiary to a larger one—have meant that there has been no longer-term consistent strategy. The manufacturing director's concern has been with supplying customers without undertaking major changes in production methods other than improving the factory layout. Other conditions—for example, limited pressure from headquarters, insufficient management training in advanced production techniques, difficulties in obtaining small batches of materials quickly from suppliers, and the workforce characteristics mentioned earlier—have militated against the introduction of JIT. The Malaysian plant has a relatively advanced reward system, however, which owes its origins to the work of senior management, especially the HR director, and is similarly placed in terms of union and bargaining structures. These advantages can be explained by external institutions, particularly government labor market policy.

Based on the constraints at the four plants noted above, it is not surprising that corporate management sees manual workers, with few exceptions, as unproblematic constraints. At the same time, the relevant business strategy document notes that one of the company's major weaknesses is lack of management depth: "PH has had a high turnover rate for the past few years; as a result there is a shortage of top level managers who are mobile and have a global perspective. . . . Restoring stability to the management ranks will be a major objective of the strategic plan."

Conclusion

This chapter has explored workplace relations in four pharmaceutical plants producing similar products and owned by the same multinational corporation. Differences were found, particularly regarding work organization, union structure, and rule-setting processes. This is not surprising given the very different institutional characteristics of the societies in which the plants are located. But there were also similarities: in the definitions of work roles, the reward systems, and the climate of employee relations. Moreover, the chapter highlighted a trend toward cooperative dependence, a pattern of workplace relations compatible with the emerging

JIT or "lean" system of production as applied to pharmaceutical manufacturing.

No particular plant was consistently more advanced along the six dimensions comprising workplace relations. The findings in fact challenge stereotypical notions of national patterns. Thus, contrary to the view that Australian plants are backward and dominated by inefficient work practices and that Malaysian workplaces rely solely on cheap labor, these workplaces were shown to be closest to the cooperative dependent pattern. Neither was the Taiwanese plant steeped in paternalism nor was it more efficient. Only in the British case was there some support for the conventional view of comparatively strong trade unionism. But, as argued earlier, this was a less important explanatory factor in shaping workplace relations than corporate and subsidiary management dynamics.

Our analysis suggests several implications for theory and research. Beginning with the source of the framework, the study suggests two observations concerning the efficacy of Fox's analysis of management-employee relations. First, if we take the climate of employee relations as a proxy for trust, the findings show that low trust can be counteracted by benign HR policies. Thus, despite some variation, employee relations in all four plants tended toward cooperation rather than conflict. Second, Fox underplays the role of employment security as a factor influencing management-employee relations. It is this aspect of multinational operations that destabilizes workplace relations, not only at the level of manual workers but also among subsidiary management.

Our research points to national industrial relations institutions as having an important contextual impact on workplace relations but that relations are nevertheless reflected in, and mediated by, product market, firm, and plant characteristics. Because public policy makers are to varying degrees responsive to the need for capital accumulation and growth, some national contexts give management more scope in introducing changes of the kind discussed above. Nevertheless, there has been a general trend in public policy favoring management's search for flexibility and higher productivity growth while limiting union power. This trend has facilitated convergence on the cooperative dependent pattern of workplace relations in the 1980s. Whether this trend will continue throughout the 1990s is a matter that lies beyond the scope of this chapter.

The identification of a broad yet tentative convergence toward cooperative dependence raises questions concerning the similarity of this pattern with tendencies identified by other researchers. Space limitations permit consideration of two alternatives: Burawoy's (1985, 148–52) "hegemonic despotism" and Dore's (1989, 427–30) "organization-oriented" employment system. Burawoy suggests that workers are having to make concessions to employers under the threat of more intense product market competition and higher capital mobility. Alternatively, quality circles and other devices are seen as fads used by management to increase employee commitment to productivity growth. Such developments, according to Burawoy, are not being effectively countered by labor as the balance of power moves further in favor of employers.

Despite some similarities, the notion of cooperative dependence differs from Burawoy's idea of hegemonic despotism in several ways. First, cooperative dependence is a summary term for a more detailed and varied set of arrangements, while hegemonic despotism remains an underdeveloped concept. Second, the research reported in this chapter does not support the contention that concessions by workers (mainly in work-time arrangements and task flexibility) are significant, bearing in mind improvements in wages, conditions, and benefits received. Third, Burawoy's assumption that capital flight in the form of plant relocation is relatively unproblematic, is difficult to sustain. Decisions on this issue are complicated by changing import duties, tax concessions, production restrictions, and so on, which are making relocation decisions more, rather than less, easy for companies in most countries, notwithstanding contrary possibilities in Europe. Fourth, the contention that quality circles and similar schemes are a fad is to misunderstand the growing demand for problem-solving skills associated with new technology and the latent strategic power of team-oriented workers. Management is thus encouraged to institutionalize mechanisms that over the longer term lead to a more highly skilled workforce. Fifth, and finally, as noted earlier, unions have been rationalized but not demobilized by current trends. Certainly, there is no reason to suppose that they are in terminal decline (especially in the industrializing countries) and hence unable to influence state and management policies.

Dore's organization-oriented system is a summary of the major characteristics of large Japanese companies. As such, it contains features that appear to be unique to the Japanese context. These include the following: management being responsible to employees rather than simply to shareholders; lifetime employment; person- rather than position-related reward systems; extensive, continuous training; and enterprise unionism. With respect to other aspects of the organization-oriented system—for example, management commitment to the firm as a community; management responsibility for workers' security and welfare; inculcation of employee involvement and teamwork; and decentralized bargaining—the cooperative dependence pattern resembles Dore's construct. Arguably, under labor market pressure and individualistic consumptionist tendencies, the Japanese employment system is changing (Whittaker 1989). Whether this change is toward a variant of the cooperative dependent pattern is a matter for further research.

In sum, the trend in workplace relations identified in this chapter is neither as inimical to employees' interests as suggested by Burawoy nor as benign as implied by Dore's predictions.

Conclusion
Globalization, National Systems, and the Future of Workplace Industrial Relations

Larry Haiven, P. K. Edwards, and Jacques Bélanger

The purpose of this conclusion is not so much to write an *epilogue* as to present a *prologue*, a challenge to our readers, as it were, to keep alive the spirit of this book by exploring the relevance of comparative workplace studies in the future, examining further the issues raised herein, and pursuing projects and research areas that cry out for the substantive and methodological foci this book has presented. We will discuss two issues. First, what are some of the questions or conundrums raised, and what are some specific projects that scholars attracted by the premise of the book should pursue? Second, what are the implications, for the investigation of national systems of labor regulation, of predictions that a rampant trend to globalization is steamrolling those very differences?

Suggestions for Further Work

The need for comparative ethnographic work is virtually endless. Most of the areas of industrial relations that are interesting to study have seldom been done on a comparative basis, and most of those same areas have seldom been studied at the level of the workplace. Here are some suggestions, albeit brief ones, as to how the program of the book can be developed by scholars attracted by its premise.

We consider below the effect on our project of the trend toward "globalization." We conclude that regardless of the strength of this trend, comparative studies of workplaces will become even more relevant. Indeed, to assess the extent of globalization, it is essential that workplace studies, similar to those of Smith, Shire, and Frenkel in this volume, be done on the introduction by employers in several countries of similar initiatives such as technologies, productivity controls, and teamworking.

This book has been a celebration of the ethnographic tradition, presenting more or less detailed accounts of life on the work floor and justifying their relevance, nay their essentiality, to the learned discourse of industrial relations in any one country or across the world. Methods have ranged from participant observation through open-ended interviews at the workplace, to more generalized information-gathering techniques. Yet none of the researchers purport merely to "tell it like it is." All attempt to locate their inquiries within the national systems and to draw out implications from their studies for those systems. One of the serious problems with such an approach is the lack of authoritative information on what conditions and practices exist across a wide range of workplaces in most countries and of reliable and *directly comparable* data between countries. Ironically, for those doing primarily qualitative research, this calls for the development of better quantitative initiatives. For those doing research on Britain and Australia, the Workplace Industrial Relations Surveys (WIRS and AWIRS) (e.g., Daniel and Millward 1983; Daniel 1987; Millward 1988; Millward and Stevens 1986; Marginson and Whitfield 1989; Callus et al. 1991) conducted in those countries provide absolutely invaluable information. Such surveys do not obviate the need for workplace ethnography; they enhance and complement such study. The continuing nature of WIRS has provided longitudinal data identifying trends in Britain and will do so in Australia. And the replication of the areas of inquiry bodes well for comparative study between the two countries. Prospective researchers in comparative industrial relations from other countries, be they ethnographically or quantitatively oriented, should be demanding that WIRS-like surveys be conducted in their countries.

It is usual for commentators, even Canadians, to lump Canada and the United States together. Often Canada is used as a cleaner and more attractive stand-in for the United States, just as Canadian cities are disguised in countless Hollywood productions to resemble U.S. cities. As mentioned in the introduction, the divergence between the two countries in labor law and in the militancy, politicization, and general strength of the union movement is now significant. Given the continuing strength of the United States and its corporations in the world economy, it is important to address the decline of its labor movement. U.S. scholars and those from other countries are attempting to do this. Yet very little of the work in this area is of a comparative nature. A fair amount compares the United States and Canada, but most of this comparison has been at the legal and institutional level. An important part of unpacking Canada from the United States will be to carry on the work of Herzenberg in comparing *workplace* industrial relations in the two countries.

Shire's look at the introduction of teamworking in highly centralized collective bargaining systems is a step toward tackling another conundrum in comparative industrial relations—how workplace disputes are resolved in centralized systems. Political economy theory on industrial conflict suggests that the process of "political exchange" depoliticizes the workplace. With their major concerns handled at the political forum, workers become less restive. But such a suggestion seems to ignore the realities of the workplace—where the dismissal of a colleague or the denial of a privilege can incite great anger. Of great interest would be comparative studies of discipline in centralized and decentralized collective bargaining systems.

This volume has also concentrated almost exclusively on manufacturing industries. This is primarily because these industries are export-oriented and thus subject to many of the same forces around the world. Yet service industries are also subject to many of the same forces and changes, as Smith demonstrates. More investigation needs to be done on this very important sector. A particularly interesting trend in the service sector is for employers to attempt to gain both numerical flexibility (by offering only nonstandard working hours) and functional flexibility (by demanding employee commitment to show up for work at odd hours and by frequently using highly skilled contractees from the same group of workers).

Dave Robertson and his colleagues (1992) have done a compelling workplace study of the introduction of lean production in the unionized CAMI plant in Ingersoll, Ontario, Canada, and of a strike that followed. It provides much insight into the limits of lean production. It would be good to apply a similar group of research questions to a set of lean production facilities in other countries.

Choosing a matched set of workplaces is an especially useful technique for comparative analysis. It is a good way of eliminating several confounding variables in a qualitative study, as long as the researcher is careful to acknowledge what can easily be controlled and what cannot. The two-by-two (or three-by-three) comparison is especially versatile. The movement beyond a single set allows for a much greater ability to generalize, yet the small number also allows for the intensity of ethnographic investigation.

Finally, more studies (like Frenkel's) should explore the negotiation of order in different national branches of the same multinational corporation. Such studies would be especially useful in discerning just how strong the trend toward globalization is and to what extent national particularities mediate to refract the direction of central initiatives.

Challenge of Globalization for Comparative Workplace Studies

A major issue, raised in the introduction and several chapters, is the challenge of globalization. The word and concept are now common currency, in the dire warnings of the captains of industry, in the business press and in business schools, and in the works of public policy analysts (Reich 1991), diagnosticians of production (Womack, Jones, and Roos 1990), and even neo-Marxist scholars (Ross and Trachte 1990). The message is clear: the nation state as a regulator of production relations is fast becoming ineffective and obsolete as information, capital, raw materials, semifinished goods, and skilled workers become increasingly mobile (in roughly that order of alacrity) on a global scale. There has been a fundamental shift in the structure of capitalism, say Robert Ross and Kent C. Trachte, from monopoly capitalism to global capitalism. As for the workplace, once the repository of diversity and variation both within and across countries, it is now subject to inexorable global production imperatives that will uniformly lower wages, remove legal and contractual protections for workers, eliminate or marginalize trade unions, and assimilate personnel management into the human resources variant. Failing these homogenizing concessions, corporations will simply move their facilities to locations that will provide them.

The nation state can effectively regulate production relations only when productive facilities stay put or have some difficulty moving to another country. Workers and their champions invariably operate in a national arena but can only improve working conditions and transform social relations where at least several stages of production are contained nationally. But, as Ross and Trachte assert,

> The global firm and conglomerate is a design for survival under the competitive conditions of the new era. Its ability to "scan" the globe for investment possibilities makes possible a rational assignment of resources and ruthless pursuit of the exact combination of local policies, labor conditions, transport considerations, and so forth for any commodity or part. (1990, 66)

> Once one ventures beyond the moral critique of corporate behavior, the probability that national regulation of capital allocation in the global context may simply be ineffective in maintaining or enhancing the position of the working class must be confronted. (215)

Considering the above, is a scholarly focus on national systems of labor regulation not doomed to irrelevance or, at the very least, to the pages of history books? Certainly, evidence of a trend toward global production and a new international division of labor cannot be denied, and the challenge is one that cannot be ignored. The possibility and threat of relocation has put new bargaining power at the disposal of the capitalist class. There are indications, however, several of them evident in the chapters of this book, that a focus on international comparative workplace regulation will not only remain important in the future but increase in relevance. The purpose here is not to engage in a protracted discussion but rather, briefly, to touch on some reasons for the increased need for studies on the workplace.

The dominant theme of this book is that *every* workplace must solve the "problem of labor" (turning labor power into labor) through the negotiation of order between workers and management. Whether workers appear grimly oppressed or militant and powerful, bargains are struck, customs are established, and understandings are reached whereby the work of the workplace can proceed. Negotiation does not mean collective bargaining; this is merely a formal and sophisticated variation whereby workers have a collective representative. Precisely because management seeks cooperation, workers will always seek to negotiate compliance on terms more favorable to themselves, using whatever tools are at their disposal. Chung, in this volume, shows ways in which seemingly subjugated women workers in Singapore use irony, humor, flirting, intersupervisor rivalry, and several other techniques informally to negotiate better terms. Armstrong et al. (1981), in their classic study of the negotiation of order in nonunion and weak-union workplaces, show how questions of legitimacy are employed by workers to carve out small areas of autonomy and respite for themselves.

There is no reason to believe that any degree of globalization could ever remove this negotiation of order. Indeed, a belief that the erosion or avoidance of formal collective bargaining means that management has a "free hand" is foolish. A problem encountered in the *maquiladoras* of Mexico illustrates this well. Some naive corporate newcomers from Canada and the United States rush to take advantage of what they think is a compliant, union-free workforce. More savvy employers strike recognition deals with the conservative, ruling party–affiliated Confederacion de Trabajadores de Mexico (see Shaiken, this volume). The former employers often find themselves facing intractable labor troubles and problems of production or militant "unofficial" trade unions. The latter employers have modest collective agreements, but a union that will police, sometimes brutally, any dissension within its ranks.

The relevant point is that the reality of the Mexican national industrial relations system (even in the relatively unregulated free-trade zones) is ignored by employers at their peril. Order must still be negotiated. The order negotiated by the CTM may be only slightly better for Mexican workers than no union at all, but order it is. For employers, that order can be quite a bit better than no union at all. Such situations call out for research, and only a focus on the workplace can fully and accurately capture the deals and "arrangements" that must be negotiated to operationalize production in this and other industrializing countries.

But there is a more important reason the advent of global capitalism presents a false promise of homogenization. If the negotiation of order occurs and cannot be neglected even in workplaces where processes are simple and labor is weak, then this logic will be even more compelling in workplaces where work is complicated, where management relies on workers to add their brain power and initiative, where workers have some real power with which to bargain. Such is the case under lean production. Womack, Jones, and Roos themselves insist that the system, lacking in slack, must rely greatly on the commitment of its workers. To do so, the system must reciprocate:

> Without . . . continual challenges, workers may feel they have reached a
> dead end at an early point in their career. The result: They hold back their
> know-how and commitment, and the main advantage of lean production
> disappears. (1990, 14)

> If management fails to lead and the work force feels that no reciprocal
> obligations are in force, it is quite predictable that lean production will
> revert to mass production. (103)

Thus, workers whose commitment is valued and sought by management must be all the more carefully nurtured and bargained with. "Japanized" enterprises have attempted to counter this problem through careful screening of prospective employees and intense indoctrination. But even this strategy can backfire, as successful applicants are led to believe that they are special and not expendable and as early promises of "a great place to work" meet the reality of close monitoring, excessive regimentation, and the tyranny of the group (Robertson et al. 1992). Thus, the expectation of reciprocity can be heightened rather than lessened by screening and indoctrination.

The just-in-time system for the delivery of parts from suppliers is another feature of lean production that is a double-edged sword for management. While it puts tremendous pressure on workers to deliver quality on time, it also makes work stoppage disastrous—even more disastrous than in conventional Fordist-type production (Turnbull 1986). If disruption is to be avoided at all costs, then the cost of worker happiness rises. Moreover, when stages of production have been disaggregated across national boundaries, disruption at a single plant in one country can halt production in a multitude of plants in several countries. Such is the case for multinational automobile companies in the integrated Canada-U.S. and northern European production system. In light of this fact, Herzenberg's comparison of U.S. and Canadian auto parts plants and any further comparative workplace study of these two countries is especially interesting.

If the globalization imperative is proceeding apace, as some say it is, there is another reason the workplace should become more, not less, important as a focus for study. One of the drives by corporate management in the 1980s that continues is the putative "decentralization" of collective bargaining and personnel management. The rhetoric is to push industrial relations down to the workplace level. Actually, decentralization masks a tightening of central regulation by corporations. It also allows higher managers to distance themselves from responsibility for local problems while still imposing their agenda (see Marginson et al. 1988; Blyton and Turnbull 1992). The corporate strategy has two goals, which often conflict. On the one hand, there is flexibility: the search for local solutions to local problems. On the other, there is uniformity: by weakening the power of trade unions in centralized agreements, local management should have a freer hand in implementing corporate goals at the workplace level, such as the removal of restrictive practices, the realization of multiskilling and multitasking, and the rationalization of payment schemes. It is just this contradiction in moving industrial relations down to the workplace level that makes a focus on the workplace all the more interesting, fruitful, and necessary.

There are also several reasons to question the speed, pervasiveness, and homogenizing effects of the transformation to a global production system. Christian Berggren uncovers some of these reasons in his comparison of teamwork under lean production and in Swedish work organizations. He concludes that an overconcentration on changed product markets and new technology "tends to obscure the significance of labor market conditions and the role of trade unions, government policies, and national institutions in general" (1992, 19). Further, he faults the evangelists of lean production for ignoring the workplace and not separating individual outcomes from composite data:

> This weakness in the flexibility discourse is closely tied to a reductionist perspective in which increased market variation and product flexibility are followed directly by new work forms and more qualified jobs. But which strategies companies use to cope with demands for flexibility and what the consequences for work are cannot be deduced from developments in product markets; rather, these consequences must be traced through empirical study. In the case of the careful empirical investigation of changes in industrial work, . . . the American industrial sociology of the 1950s and the labor process school of the 1970s are superior to the flexibility discourse. (19)

Although the recent closing of some of the Swedish high-participation plants touted by Berggren suggests that the Swedish alternative to lean production may be somewhat less viable than he claims, much of his message is still relevant. The Swedish system of industrial relations is far from collapsing under globalism; indeed, Sweden is not about to become Japan. Britain and the United States, with their short-term market-driven approaches, are even less able to copy the long-term approach of Germany or Japan.

The chapter by Shire demonstrates well the mediating influence of national systems. It makes two points: First, a general move toward teamworking by a major multinational company was introduced differently in Austria and Germany, two countries that, from the outside, appear quite similar in workplace regulation but that are quite dissimilar, a fact not lost on General Motors. Second, knowledge of industrial relations in both these countries reveals that no major initiative such as teamworking could be introduced without operating with and through the unions. Quite a different situation exists in Britain, Canada, and the United States. On the one hand, Wells (1993), using Canadian evidence, argues forcefully that new experiments in human resource management are not compatible with the existence of strong unions. On the other hand, in Germany (and to a lesser extent Austria), the unions have been able to accommodate to the new global imperatives and at the same time insist on a social regime of production that is markedly different from the lean production model.

Why the vast difference between the Anglo-Saxon and the northern European countries in adapting to such global initiatives as lean production? Comparative industrial relations has taught us for some time (Cameron 1984 and Pekkarinen, Pohjola, and Rowthorn 1992, among several others) that corporatism under the German or Swedish model has consistently delivered low inflation and low unemployment. Countries that integrate the workplace with national-level systems are adaptable and perform well and can contain the headlong rush to market solutions that characterizes the Anglo-Saxon countries. What does this tell us about lean production? Its advocates do not consider at all the regime into which it is inserted, or they assume that it must be of the Japanese-type. They do not explore connections between the technical and social organization of work or between the workplace and other levels. Hence, they produce a rather confusing mix of analysis and futurology. We argue, by contrast, that some aspects of lean production are certainly relevant (e.g., quality, JIT) but that the social regulation that accompanies these changes depends on how restructuring is mediated at workplace and national levels. Shire's German case indicates a mediation very different from anywhere else.

The whole idea of a shift in the mode of regulation, although a very useful theoretical construct, often obscures as much as it reveals. A mode of regulation, such as Fordism, is modeled on a *dominant* form of production (and consumption and distribution). In reality, many forms coexist. Indeed, a secondary form may be so powerful and pervasive as to act as a dialectical counterpoint to the primary form. Piore and Sabel (1984) show how craft production, far from disappearing under Fordism, acted as the yin to mass production's yang. As mass production by special-purpose machines increased, craft production of those machines, though always smaller in scale, increased as well. As mentioned in the introduction, "exceptions to the rule" can, by exploring the conditions that bring about the exception, often reveal more about a general tendency than study of the tendency itself. Bélanger in this volume did just that in contemplating the high efficiency of his craftlike subway car production team, despite its apparently inefficient work methods. This enabled him to draw conclusions about the nature of workplace order that no amount of automobile assembly line observation could equal. In much the same way, Berggren's (1992) investigation of the successful Swedish heavy-bus manufacturers was the thin end of the wedge for getting at problems of "lean production."

Another complication in the globalization imperative is that, although there is a definite shift of production from the First to the Third World, the geographic trend is by no means even, simple, universal, or unidirectional. Low wages, weak unions, and lack of workplace regulation are important factors but not the only ones. Individual capitalists may dream of the *perfect* country in which to invest, but no one country or region can meet all criteria. A high percentage of capitalist foreign investment still goes to developed countries, especially those such as Germany, that have highly skilled and highly motivated workforces.

Long-term stability and predictability in production is another prized attribute. Among the NICs, the trend is not simply toward those with the cheapest labor. Chung in this volume points out that factory work has different meanings for women workers in different South Asian countries and thus may affect their level of autonomy and militancy. Singapore, she speculates, has a low level of militancy because factory work is considered more acceptable. This may be connected to the fact that Singapore is "often regarded as the 'labor aristocracy' of Southeast Asia and multinational factories tend to have higher wages and better working conditions." South Korea, by contrast, has a much more militant and independent workforce and a stronger trade union tradition. Yet, despite these complicating factors and the fact that other countries in the region offer lower wages and less militant workers, both countries have received the lion's share of capital investment from First World companies.

With regard to education and the commitment of the workforce, Shaiken's piece sounds a note of caution. It counters the conventional wisdom that only the low-skilled, low-paying jobs from the First World will go to the Third World while the high-skilled, high-paying jobs will remain. Shaiken shows that skilled Mexican workers work for low wages in one of the most efficient automobile assembly plants in the world. Two questions that need exploration, however, are whether "Universal Motors" and the few plants like it have "creamed" a limited "crop" of educated, committed Mexican youth and whether the specific conditions of automobile assembly make it easier to transplant a high-tech turnkey operation to the Third World and simply, as it were, hire appropriate workers and switch the power on.

This brings us to a final point about globalization: the chapters themselves demonstrate the dynamic tension between the enduring autonomy of national systems and the forces of homogenization. Although most highlight the former, those by Frenkel and Shaiken highlight the latter. Without wishing to impose a view on what is evidently controversial, we can identify some possible reasons for the split in opinion. First, the historical pieces stop in the 1970s or early 1980s, and others end by the late 1980s. For this period, national differences were likely to remain salient, whereas Frenkel and Shaiken focus on developments in the present and future. Second, industrial sector may be important. Auto technologies are reasonably standard across the globe, whereas Frenkel's firm also made a range of fairly standard bulk products. Other products may be less readily standardized, in production or marketing. Firms may, accordingly, find it difficult to measure production costs, or feel that it is not worth their while to do so given that they have to be in certain markets in any event. Third, as Frenkel and Shaiken would of course acknowledge, just because there are tendencies toward globalization does not mean that all national differences will be erased. They may well have identified an important new trend toward the coordination of production on a global scale that may become more powerful in the future. Its impact, however, will surely be mediated by a range of other factors, some of them explored above. It is those factors that we encourage other researchers to explore on the floor of the workplace.

Notes

Notes to Chapter 2

1. Clearly, this magazine article was not designed to be a detailed study of empirical work. The analysis was conducted at a very general level, and there were no extensive bibliographic references. In a section on the "peculiarities of American job control," the author goes so far as to suggest that "no other system of union control is comparable to that in the United States. In some countries, in fact, organized labor is not present in the shop at all" (Piore 1982, 9).

2. Indeed, the article mentioned above (Piore 1982) is presented in some detail by Tolliday and Zeitlin as a major piece of evidence in support of the new interpretation (1989, 222–23, and n. 7).

3. It has to be noted, though, that the extent of "fractional bargaining" associated with the application of the collective agreement through the grievance procedure has always been recognized as substantial, and such bargaining was the subject of one of the few classics on workplace industrial relations in North America (Kuhn 1961). It is also worth emphasizing in passing that the volume of shopfloor studies in the United States and Canada is small not only when compared with Britain but with French sociology, which has a very long and rich tradition in this regard.

4. Among the few foreign scholars who made such a contribution, Richard Herding (1972) comes first to mind.

5. In *The Politics of Production*, Burawoy explicitly abandons the concept of internal state (1985, 11) and develops instead the notion of "political apparatuses of production" (chap. 3). But he maintains "a distinction between the labor processes conceived as a particular organization of tasks, and the political apparatuses of production conceived as its mode of regulation. In contrast to Braverman, who ignores the political apparatuses of production, and Edwards, Friedman, Littler and Clawson, who collapse them into the labor process, I treat them as analytically distinct from and causally independent of the labor process" (125).

6. It is worth quoting Kochan, Katz, and McKersie at some length here because what follows represents the classic statement about the interpretation of the North American collective agreement as a source of excessive rigidity:

> Job control unionism entails highly formalized contracts and a quasi-judicial grievance procedure to adjudicate disputes during the term of those contracts. In this system workers' rights and obligations are linked to highly articulated and sharply delineated jobs. For example, what a worker is expected to do on the job is outlined in a job description and a job ladder typically is included in a plant's local collective bargaining agreement. . . . Workers' income is determined by attaching a particular wage rate to each specific job. Unions control career income by seniority rules governing the allocation of internal job vacancies among candidates for promotion. Job security is maintained by a set of rules that specify who gets laid off (after

management decides a layoff is to occur) and how the remaining work is allocated among the workforce.

In this system of job-control unionism, industrial democracy is reduced to a particular form of industrial jurisprudence in which work and disciplinary standards are clearly defined and fairly administered. (1986, 28–29)

7. In his discussion of these matters, Paul Edwards makes a distinction between five sorts of possible generalizations from workplace ethnographic studies (1992, 423–25; also see chap. 1).

8. In the large department that installed equipment, each vehicle would be stable for eight working days, and the work group would move along the line every day. This had the same positive effect on group cohesiveness.

9. To relate this plant located in Quebec to the North American model of labor relations in this way is bound to provoke some criticism. Would the Canadian regime of labor relations not be a more appropriate point of reference? While acknowledging the differences between different *regimes*, between provincial jurisdictions as well as between Canada and the United States, their fundamental principles generally correspond to the same logic, that is, one arising out of the New Deal social compromise, and it seems appropriate to refer to the North American *model* for comparative and analytical purposes (see chap. 1).

10. Under the Thatcher government of the 1980s, several laws were enacted limiting the freedom of unions to strike. While going further than the state had ever gone before, these nevertheless had an arguably negligible impact on the structure of workplace industrial relations.

11. Haiven (1989) paints a somewhat different picture in his comparative study of redundancy in Canadian and British plants. He contends that the potential for conflict is greater in Canada, which uses reverse seniority in large layoffs, whereas the concept of voluntary redundancy in Britain acts effectively to "depoliticize" the issue in that country.

Notes to Chapter 3

1. Hereinafter, the *disciplinary* forums in each respective country will be referred to in capitalized form (i.e., "Arbitration" [Canada] and "Tribunal" [Britain]). To avoid confusion, the generic term for both of these will be "Forum(s)."

2. Canada is a decentralized political entity in which the provinces hold large constitutional jurisdiction. Approximately 90 percent of employers are covered by provincial labor relations law. The federal government regulates labor relations for the remaining 10 percent of employers, which are under its jurisdiction.

3. Henry also postulates a fourth type of discipline called "celebrative-collective," a somewhat utopian system found mostly in cooperative organizations free of the power of a single employer wherein "self-discipline" is taken to its logical conclusion and members of the work community are responsible for adhering to the group's norms. This type of discipline does not apply to this study.

4. Collins also takes much too narrow a view of corporatism, failing to acknowledge that corporatism exists on a number of levels: macro-, meso-, and micro (Rogowski 1985).

5. This percentage has been extrapolated from a survey of the reported decisions of arbitrators in the province of Ontario from 1977 to 1986, compiled from the Ontario Ministry of Labour's *Office of Arbitration Monthly Bulletin* by the Ontario Federation of Labour, assisted by the United Steelworkers of America (District 6); Adams 1978, 40; and Barnacle 1991, 107.

6. Peter J. Barnacle (1991) distinguishes between "express" suspensions (in which Arbitration actively imposes a set suspension in the place of dismissal) and "effective" suspensions (in which Arbitration reinstates the employee with no back pay for the period between dismissal and the arbitral decision). When the latter is considered, the length of suspension increases dramatically.

7. Unlike Canadian Arbitration, in which unions, not employees, are the parties of record, in British Industrial Tribunals, complaints of unfair dismissal are matters between the individual employee and the employer. Only a minority of those parties applying to Tribunals are represented in their complaint by a trade union (Dickens et al. 1985).

8. At the end of the 1960s, the courts briefly ruled that arbitrators had no power to alter disciplinary penalties imposed by employers. So great was the outcry from arbitrators and practitioners (occasioned in no small part by fear of the delegitimizing of arbitration) that suitable legislation was quickly passed in most jurisdictions to allow arbitrators to reinstate grievors and alter penalties (see *Port Arthur Shipbuilding Co. v. Arthurs* [1969] S.C.R. 85, 70 D.L.R. (3d) 693).

9. An employer refusing a recommendation of reemployment can be compelled to pay an "additional award" of compensation (Anderman 1985, 285–86).

10. All of the figures on characteristics and representation of applicants cited here are taken from the Dickens et al. (1985) survey of 1,063 applicants to Tribunals and 596 complainants whose cases were forwarded to a hearing.

11. The Advisory Conciliation and Arbitration Service, a quasi-governmental body, is charged with resolving disputes between collective bargaining parties across the United Kingdom. Use of its services is voluntary. It provides such services as codes of practice, mediators, and (less commonly) arbitrators.

12. Statistics on Tribunal applications are also calculated from reports on Tribunal applications in the *Employment Gazette* (1984, 1986, 1987, appropriate months).

13. To remedy the delay in conventional Arbitration, several Canadian jurisdictions have introduced the option of *expedited Arbitration*, providing for referral either to the labor relations board or to a government-appointed (rather than bilaterally chosen) arbitrator and a quick hearing and decision. If this option is chosen, the parties must accept the intervention of a conciliation officer. In Ontario, settlement officers effect a prehearing settlement in about two-thirds of cases. According to Joseph Rose (1986), however, expedited Arbitration accounted for only 20 percent of all Arbitrations and for 17 percent of all discharge Arbitrations.

14. The nine-year survey of arbitrators cited earlier in this chapter was specifically directed at identifying arbitrators who seemed "more sympathetic" to unions, among an array of arbitral issues. Employers keep similar "box scores." Yet, given the career structure of arbitrators, their "employer" is not any one set of parties but the collective union-management community. And although arbitrators cannot help but be somewhat sensitive to their overall "record" of "pro-union" and "pro-management" awards and to the overall power balance of the parties, this sensitivity does not extend to any *single* set of parties.

15. In Britain, in the rare situations in which Arbitration is chosen voluntarily, it is often done in crisis situations, such as when a strike is in progress and the parties cannot find a face-saving solution themselves.

16. Actually, the initial onus is on the union to prove a few elementary facts: that a collective agreement between the parties exists, that the grievor was an employee, and that discipline took place. The onus then shifts to the employer to prove just cause. The burden of proof shifts back to the union temporarily to show mitigating circumstances, but such circumstances will be considered by the arbitrator only if the employer has fulfilled the burden of proving just cause. If the cause for discharge is akin to a criminal offense, the union may have the burden of proving lack of intent by the grievor (Palmer and Palmer 1991, 258–63).

17. E.g., *British Labor Pump Ltd. v. Byrne*, [1979] IRLR 94, EAT; *Bailey v. BP Oil [Kent Refinery] Ltd.* [1980] IRLR 287, CA; *W & J Wass Ltd. v. Binns* [1982] IRLR 283, CA; *Retarded Children's Aid Society v. Day* [1978] IRLR 128, CA. A more recent case, *Polkey v. A. E. Dayton Services Ltd.* [1987] IRLR 503 HL, claws back some of the damage done to proceduralism in the former cases.

18. Earl Palmer and Bruce Palmer (1991, 231–32) indicate that arbitrators have interpreted these phrases as having the same meaning.

19. *British Home Stores v. Burchell* (1978) IRLR 379, EAT.

20. *Re Levi Strauss*, 29 L.A.C. (2d) 91, at 93 (Arthurs, 1980).

21. *Re Steel Equipment Co. Ltd.* 14 L.A.C. 356 (Reville, 1964), at 356—58.

22. At the present time it is not uncommon for arbitrators' fees to be more than $1,500 per day.

23. Labor relations legislation in all Canadian jurisdictions provides that the decisions of labor relations boards and arbitration boards cannot be challenged in the courts on substantive grounds but only on very narrow procedural grounds.

24. This comparison was calculated as follows: To obtain a number for Canada, the approximate annual number of Ontario dismissal arbitrations, derived from the Ontario Federation of Labour survey, was increased proportionate to the inverse of Ontario's share of the number of employees covered by collective agreements across the country ($\times$ 2.8). This produced a figure of approximately 430 Canadian dismissal arbitrations per year. To correct for the difference in size between Canada and Britain, this figure was further increased by the proportion that Britain exceeds Canada in union membership ($\times$ 3) for a proxy figure of approximately 1,300 arbitrations per year. To obtain a comparison figure for Britain, the survey of British Tribunal applicants in Dickens et al. (1985) was employed. The survey revealed that approximately 12 percent of all applicants appearing at hearings were trade union members represented by their unions (as opposed to nonunionists). This percentage was extrapolated to the total number of hearings held annually to produce a figure of approximately 1,150 Tribunal hearings a year.

25. As mentioned earlier, the number of British arbitrations (as opposed to Industrial Tribunals) on dismissal is negligible. Those that are held are voluntary and tend to be at the larger employers (ACAS 1987, 1986).

26. Complete figures on the rate of discipline over a long enough period to achieve statistical accuracy were not always easy to obtain, especially at BRITBREW and CANMET. Enough information was available, however, to make intelligent estimates.

27. Similar data (rate of dismissal for enterprises across the entire country) are not available for Canada. I suspect, however, that dismissal rates in Canada might be significantly higher than in Britain because of the less paternalistic attitudes among Canadian employers and the illegality of strikes by unions over dismissals, but this cannot be proven at this point.

28. The Donovan Report (Donovan 1968) emerged from a royal commission convened to investigate the disorder and growing unrest in British industrial relations. It found that there were "two systems of industrial relations," of which the informal, shopfloor-based, shop steward—led system predominated.

29. The quotations for this case were taken from documents in the files of the union and management at BRITBREW and from the arbitrator's decision. To preserve the anonymity of the parties, this decision cannot be cited in full. Details can be obtained from the author.

30. Canadian arbitrators have developed two approaches to discipline for incompetence. One is the "nonculpable" or "nondisciplinary" approach, used with employees who are unable to perform duties because of circumstances beyond their control (e.g., illness, injury, and so on). The other is the "culpable" approach, used for employees in control of their actions (e.g., negligence, sabotage, laziness, lack of care, and so on). Although even cases of "nonculpable" incompetence can lead to dismissal (if there is little chance the employee can discharge employment obligations), "culpable" incompetence is dealt with much more harshly by arbitrators (Brown and Beatty 1993, 7:3220).

31. This quotation is from the recorded minutes of the final-step grievance meeting. Note the way the union craftily moves from a "protection of incompetence" argument to a "concern for managerial efficiency" argument, thereby attempting to cast its case in a more legitimate guise (see Armstrong, Goodman, and Hyman 1981).

32. I have mentioned that the Canadian courts are quite restricted by law in the scope of their review of decisions by quasi-judicial tribunals such as Arbitrations. But even within the scope allowed them, the courts have generally taken a hands-off approach to judicial

review of the substance of Arbitration decisions. The general rule is that the courts will interfere only if the decision of the arbitrator is one that the words of the collective agreement cannot reasonably bear (Adams 1985, 202).

33. When divided between disciplinary and nondisciplinary cases, it is evident that Canadian unions have a far higher "win" rate in disciplinary cases and especially in discharge cases (see Haiven 1988, 163–65).

34. One notable exception to the union's refusal to participate in disciplining employees is the CANBREW rule against alcohol on company premises (other than in the canteen). For many years, the company has imposed a one-day suspension for this offense. The company's consistency over such a long period has led the union seldom to challenge these suspensions seriously unless the company has been mistaken. Although there is no explicit participation in the discipline, such passive acquiescence sends a clear message to employees that the union is sympathetic to the employer's policy.

35. At one of CANBREW's sister plants, employees are allowed to "bank" unused sick days and "cash them out" at the end of a period. This is a strong incentive for most employees not to use the sick days but is very costly to the employer and hence very rare among blue-collar workforces.

36. The concept of "nonculpable" or "nonpunitive" absenteeism mirrors that of "nonculpable incompetence" (Brown and Beatty 1993, 7:3210).

37. In Britain, employers can and do impose discipline for a combination of offenses. In Canada, by contrast, as we have seen earlier, the doctrine of "culminating incident" prevails.

38. Barnacle (1991) finds it the fourth most common cause, behind dishonesty, work performance, and attendance.

39. "Job control" is used here not in the sense used by Perlman (1928) and Katz (1985) but rather more as Bélanger uses the term in this volume: to mean the control of the pace and process of the work itself.

40. The BRITBREW industrial relations manager, when presented with evidence of a considerable number of sectional work stoppages in the plant, insisted most were not strikes. "Strikes," he said, "are those stoppages which seriously impair our ability to trade," in other words, that seriously impede the flow of the company's product to market.

41. The dispute revolved around the company's intention to reform a decades' old corrupted incentive earnings plan for draymen. As in many British plants, management had allowed the old system to continue long past the point when it had any meaningful relation to the effort expended. Many workers were making inflated earnings on the old scheme, while others were deprived of incentive pay. The longer management waited to change the system, the more entrenched the workers and the union became in defense of the system. Any attempt to change the system was bound to result in a major industrial dispute.

42. In one case, in which the employer proposed to discipline a union member for drunkenness, the convener made the company aware that the union knew of similar abuse by some managers. In another case, in which the employer wished to discipline an employee for incompetence, the union suspected that a member of management was responsible for an error leading to the loss of product somewhere else. The union stored these bits of information to trade upon at appropriate times. These bits of knowledge have some, though limited, value in mitigating the discipline of union members.

Notes to Chapter 4

1. Bélanger (this volume) takes issue with the way the term "job control unionism" is used in Katz 1985 and in Kochan, Katz, and McKersie 1986.

2. Despite their different perspectives, all those who read the draft perceived it as an

accurate portrayal of shopfloor dynamics at the plant. Although managers and local union officials were given a draft of the Detroit case study, only Erwin Baur provided feedback.

3. Background on the Budd company is a condensation of Herzenberg 1991, chapter 8, with some additional material from chapter 10. More complete references can be found in Herzenberg 1991.

4. See Bélanger (this volume) on the salutary effect of "job-and-finish" on both workers and management in a Canadian plant.

5. The quotations in this and the next paragraph are from interviews with Erwin Baur.

6. In retaining even a limited right to strike during the collective agreement, the UAW was the exception in the United States. In the early 1960s, the U.S. view that arbitration was an alternative to strikes was given legal sanction in a series of Supreme Court cases called the Steelworkers' Trilogy. In its decisions, the Court interpreted a no-strike clause to be implicit on any issue that was arbitrable in a collective agreement, unless a right to strike was explicitly preserved. This contrasts with Canada, where the legal right to strike was removed in 1944 (except in Saskatchewan, which followed the American system until 1983).

7. As a result of the plant's division into units under autonomous superintendents and of workers' race-reinforced sectional loyalties, this provision and seniority-based layoffs operated on a unit basis until the mid-1950s.

8. The information and quotations in this and the next paragraph come from a March 1989 interview with George Merrelli in Washington, D.C.

9. Rather than filing more than proportional numbers of grievances, as they had when shopfloor negotiation often resolved them, wheel workers filed almost none at all in the 1970s.

10. It is impossible to know how drug use after the mid-1960s compares with alcohol abuse before that. Of course, even if the level of abuse was the same, a change in the "drug of choice" could have reinforced generational and racial divisions in the workplace.

11. For a detailed summary of work stoppages at Budd-Detroit from the 1950s to 1980, including the number of people involved, time lost, reason, and settlement terms, see Herzenberg 1991, 695–98.

12. Figures on disciplinary grievances were inflated by union and management agreement that the grievance procedure could be used to give probationary employees a hearing before dismissing them, even though probationary employees had no rights under the collective agreement. The use of the grievance procedure for probationary employees makes it impossible to know how many nonprobationary employees were fired for disciplinary reasons. From 1974 to 1979, 513 Detroit workers in total were "denied reinstatement" after being fired for absenteeism, and another 709 were reinstated; 56 workers were denied reinstatement and 460 were reinstated after firings for being "industrially unemployable" because of an accumulation of absence, poor performance, or other on-the-job infractions.

13. At Chrysler, according to Jefferys (1986, 190), "As recently as 1977 heat walkouts had still been regarded as natural under extreme weather conditions." By 1979, Chrysler "got seven workers sent to prison for a week when they refused to obey injunctions to stop picketing after a [heat strike]."

14. Upon the signing of the Auto Pact, the major auto assembly companies committed themselves to assemble vehicles in Canada with a value roughly equal to the value of their vehicle sales in Canada; and to achieve a Canadian value-added-to-sales ratio of at least 60 percent. These commitments expanded Canada's share of auto employment, especially in assembly, after the Auto Pact.

15. Wide variations in the plant's early years in incentive earnings on different jobs increased supervisory leverage when placing employees (Herzenberg 1991, 417, table 8–9). Variations in earnings still equaled about 25 percent in the mid-1980s. Company data and interviews indicate that the variations were significantly higher earlier, in part because of a wide gap in pay between workers in assembly and in the press shop.

16. The Canadian section of the United Auto Workers union split from its American

parent in 1985. The vast majority of the UAW locals in Canada, including Budd-Kitchener, opted to join the new union.

17. As long as the operation that electrically counted production and measured downtime (the "pay point") was not the slowest in the line, workers could increase their earnings by sabotaging the pay point. During the resulting downtime, workers earned base rate (initially, base rate was paid only after the first two minutes of downtime) and banked parts before the pay point. When the operation started again, workers went at breakneck speed until the bank was used up and the cycle could start again (the learning process followed by Kitchener workers as they tried to maximize earnings under the piece-rate system is reminiscent of that in the plant described by William F. Whyte [1951]). Later in the 1970s, workers did not need to "create" downtime—they openly put the pay point on downtime even if there was nothing wrong and then started the line again when the bank was full.

18. People's memories differed on whether the company ever tried to fire leaders of wildcat strikes. In 1988, Jim Roth, president of Budd-Canada for most of the late 1970s, implied that the company tried to fire strike instigators five or six times. Whatever the details, the company did not manage to fire someone in a way that substantially discouraged collective action.

19. The most common rate issue concerned whether workers should get paid the "Prevailing (i.e., average) Hourly Rate"—PHR—instead of base rate for downtime. PHR was initially reserved for the debugging period on new jobs or for extended periods of downtime beyond workers' control. It became a more important issue because of the mechanical problems associated with high output and as workers demanded it for progressively shorter periods of downtime. Perceptions of inequity also fueled incentive rate disputes on a new part launched in 1979.

20. At Detroit by contrast, the question "Did some workers have more contact with the steward?" almost always elicited no response. Asked if there were nicknames for different kinds of workers, a smile of recognition crossed many workers' faces, but then they would say no. This probably reflected both the workers' general suspicion of management as well as the black workers' mistrust of a white interviewer.

21. At Detroit, blacks, whites, and men all complained that members of the other race or sex got the easiest jobs. In one assembly area, according to workers of both sexes and races, one black steward seen universally as ineffective had gained reelection in part by claiming that a white candidate had said "niggers" would get the worst jobs after he became steward.

22. In Canada, through the 1960s and 1970s, about 25 percent of recorded strikes occurred during the term of the collective agreement and thus were illegal (except in Saskatchewan). This considerably outnumbers midterm strikes in the United States (which are not uniformly illegal) (see Haiven 1988).

23. Katz's entire 1985 book contains two paragraphs on informal pressure tactics and wildcat strikes (see pages 32 and 41).

24. This section relies partly on Herzenberg 1991, chapter 3B.

25. Wells (1986) provides a detailed account of how managers inhibited large-scale wildcats at a Canadian Ford plant and the consequences for worker solidarity.

26. For more on this interplay in assembly situations, see Wells 1986, Zabala 1987, and Watson 1977.

27. Group incentive pay did become less common. In independent parts suppliers, workers on incentive pay of any kind declined from 29 percent of hourly employment in 1950 to 18 percent in 1983 to 13 percent in 1989 (U.S. Department of Labor 1950, 1985, and 1991). Roughly 6 percent of workers were on group piece rates in 1950 and only 3 percent in 1983. Group bonuses applied to roughly 3 percent of workers in 1950 and to 7 percent in 1983.

28. Edwards (1986) developed his typology to encompass all types of manufacturing workers, not just direct production workers. The limited fieldwork on North America makes it harder to support such a broadening of the typology.

29. Casting the net more widely, outside the auto industry, which exemplifies U.S. "job control" unionism, would further increase the proportion of settings in which technology and managerial strategy gave workers leverage beyond that of assembly line workers.

30. Thompson's (1988) comparison of Canada's GM-Oshawa complex and a GM local in Flint, Michigan, finds little difference in the frequency of work stoppages.

Notes to Chapter 5

1. When the change is made in nonnegotiable areas, it usually touches upon some negotiable area, and even when it does not, unions are usually quite adept at trade-offs in negotiable areas for influence in so-called nonnegotiable areas. For the changes examined here, negotiations over a new wage system have ensured local labor influence over work organization.

2. The only similarity in enterprise representation in Austria is the influence Austrian union officials have had on the directorships of the dwindling nationalized sector of industry. By the mid-1980s, the depoliticization of the nationalized sector of Austrian industry had already restricted this exercise of enterprise representation (Gerlach 1989).

3. See Markovits 1986, 53–60, for a discussion of how the 1951 codetermination law covering some heavy industries was diluted in part by later provisions and company practices. See also Streeck 1984a, 402–4, on the constitutional challenge launched by employers after the 1976 codetermination act extended trade union representation on company boards outside the heavy industry sector.

4. The 1970s are an important political context for labor law reform in Austria and Germany because of the strengthening of social democratic rule in both countries. For the first time in the post–World War II period, Austrian social democrats ruled alone and German social democrats, having entered government as part of a Grand Coalition in 1966, took over the leadership of a coalition government with the German Free Democratic party after 1969.

5. Interview with Egon Matzner, Director, Research Area I: "Arbeitsmarkt und Beschäftigungspolitik" Wissenschaftszentrum Berlin für Sozialforschung. December 1987.

6. The Austrian Trade Union Federation openly admits that local bargaining supplements collectively bargained minimums (Österreichischen Gewerkschaftsbundes, n.d.).

7. On the lack of importance of solidarity in Austrian wage policy, see Duda and Tödling 1986, 227–69.

8. Jelle Visser's (1987) study presents the clearest comparison of German trade union capacities with those of other European union movements by delineating between vertical and horizontal integration of worker representation within union organizations.

9. Opel-Germany is the single largest subsidiary of General Motors–Detroit and in the late 1980s held more than a fifth of the German automotive sales market. The Austrian subsidiary, GM-Austria, is a large firm by Austrian standards (the third largest privately owned company in Austria in the mid-1980s) and at the time of its foundation was one of the largest investments by a foreign firm.

10. Those interviewed contributed copies of documents chronicling the development of management strategy and labor demands at the plant and subsidiary level. Permission was requested in March 1991 from management interviewees to identify General Motors in academic publications under the condition that advance copies of these publications would be sent to their public relations offices. To protect the identities of the managers who were interviewed, their departments have not been identified and direct quotes are kept to a minimum.

11. The research focused on plants where management and negotiations were centered: the Rüsselsheim, Germany, office and the GM-Austria Aspern plant. Additional interviews

were conducted with works council representatives at the Bochum, Germany, and Rochester-Products-Austria factories.

12. It is important to emphasize that GM-Austria is one of the largest companies in the Austrian private sector, and although it is much smaller than the German facilities, its position within the Austrian industrial structure is relatively similar.

13. Planning of production for the Austrian engine plant was based in part on sociotechnical studies of motor and transmission production at the German and other European facilities.

14. The most recent development is the introduction of continuous improvement schemes on the model of Japanese *kaizen*. At the time this research was conducted, these schemes were just being introduced, but managers made clear their intention that the goal was to move from local team responsibility for costs and quality toward greater worker identification with the company and management interests.

15. Negotiations over the GM-Austria teamwork design took place more than five years before the first round of interviews, but the managers and labor representatives who were interviewed had no recollection of any conflict over the issue of team leader elections.

16. Interview with Richard Heller, Betriebsrat-Vorsitz, Adam Opel AG, January 1988.

17. The president of the works council at GM-Austria attends joint committee meetings on invitation, as do top managers, and both keep close tabs on consultations through their regularly participating representatives. Joint consultation has had advantages for the local works council. Managers and works council members reported that the works council was given more extensive and earlier information on business decisions than is usually the case in the Austrian private sector.

18. Interview with Peter Haimerl, Gewerkschaft Metall-Bergbau-Energie, September 1988.

19. Interview with Manfred Muster, 1G-Metall, March 1991.

20. This statement was made by a top manager of Adam Opel AG who was guaranteed anonymity as a condition for the interview.

21. Recruitment patterns for GM-Austria were confirmed in interviews with Austrian managers and works council representatives.

22. The quote is from an interview with an Adam Opel AG manager who was granted anonymity.

23. The regulation of local wage increases is improved by making the wage grades congruent with industry-level wage grades, and also insofar as local supplements have been negotiated to increase at the same rate as industry-level agreements, eliminating the possibility of wage drift. (Interview with Armin Herber, Betriebsrat, Adam Opel AG, March 1991.)

24. Interview with Peter Haimerl, Gewerkschaft Metall-Bergbau-Energie, September 1988. According to the same source and the works council president (interview with Werner Lahner, Vorsitzender des Arbeiterbetriebsrates, GM-Austria GmbH, September 1988), this intervention was exceptional within the Austrian context of social democratic bargaining and is explained by the fact that GM management visited the metal workers union to get its approval before the plant was opened with a teamwork organization. Once asked, the union refused to allow the integration of skilled work with unskilled within teams or wage systems. In the Rochester Products Austria case discussed further on, the union was not directly consulted by management.

25. This information is based on management sources and an interview with Hans Jens, Vorsitzender des Arbeiterbetriebsrates, Rochester Products Austria, March 1991. According to these sources, there were a total of 184 blue-collar workers and 22 white-collar workers at Rochester Products in March 1991. Of these, about 40 were certified tradespeople who were hired in 1988 to open and tool the plant.

Notes to Chapter 7

1. The names of the company and the people mentioned in this ethnography have all been changed. The pseudonyms of the women reflect their ethnicity, as their real names

did. Where names such as "Patrick" or "Lilian" have been used, these reflect the adoption of Western names by the people concerned. All the people bearing Western names are Chinese.

2. The majority of the operators were Chinese, and about equal numbers were Malay and Indian. The supervisors and managers were predominantly Chinese. This subject, which is too complex to be interwoven into this text, is treated in depth in my doctoral dissertation (Chung 1989) and in a forthcoming text.

3. The preceding account is not a chronological charting and analysis of the industrial relations system in Singapore nor of the political economy of industrialization in Singapore. I have highlighted only those aspects of the account relevant to an understanding of the ethnography in the wider context. Readers who wish to know more about the industrial relations system in Singapore should refer to Chia 1989, Rodan 1989, Wong, 1992, and to other references cited.

4. Generally, the Chinese women spoke Chinese among themselves (Cantonese, Hokkien, or Mandarin) and with the supervisors. The Malay women spoke Malay among themselves and with the Indian women and a mixture of Malay and English, although a preponderance of English, with the Chinese women and the supervisors. In general meetings, supervisors and/or higher management spoke English. There are varieties of English spoken in Singapore, often referred to locally as Singlish (Singapore English). To be true to the phenomenon, my field notes record the varieties of English spoken. Words that were part of the vocabulary of the workplace such as "drive," "jam," "target," and "OT," were used in their English form.

5. Deepavali is one of the major Indian festivals celebrated by many Indians in Singapore. Devan Nair, an Indian, was president of the Republic of Singapore from October 1981 to March 1985. Tosay is a kind of Indian bread. The tongue-in-cheek humor of Suraya's utterance, which would be quickly "understood" by locals, lies in her "claim" to friendship and familiarity with the president.

6. Note the double use of "sexual" to denote politics between the sexes which is sexual.

Notes to Chapter 8

1. Universal's training manual for an engine plant in a neighboring northern state emphasizes this point. The manual states that "transfers of hourly personnel and their supervisors from [the company's] Mexico operations were not allowed in order to avoid inflated wages/benefits and old work practices" (Shaiken and Herzenberg 1987, 47). The practice of hiring novice workers follows a pattern set by Japanese-owned auto factories in the United States. With the exception of NUMMI—the joint GM-Toyota partnership in Fremont, California—these plants have largely opted to hire workers with no previous auto experience for production jobs, although they have often recruited auto industry veterans for skilled positions.

2. This novel form of work organization takes place primarily in the capital-intensive body shop.

3. In 1991, Universal stopped rotating skilled workers during a major model change. Information on whether the practice has been resumed is unavailable.

4. This represents the compensation cost at the time of the plant's start-up.

5. Prior to the strike, workers earned ninety-six dollars a month and sought a 70 percent increase. They settled for an average of 34.5 percent.

6. Harbour and Associates, a Detroit-area automotive consulting firm, computes an index that reflects the number of production workers required per car. Using this approach, I calculated that the Universal Motors plant utilized 3.12 workers per car in July 1988. (This calculation is based on a line speed of thirty-two cars per hour and on eight hours of daily production, rather than the nine hours actually worked. It also excludes stamping operations.) Based on this result, the Universal plant is the seventh most productive

assembly plant in North America and not far behind the leading plant, which needed 2.72 workers per car. If the stamping area at the plant is included, then it requires 3.53 workers per car, placing it eleventh. This score would still place the Mexican plant ahead of NUMMI, which required 3.73 workers per car. (NUMMI is one of the relatively few U.S. plants to include a stamping area.) Since these numbers do not account for different levels of plant integration—the types of operations performed in an assembly plant can vary— they should be considered as broad benchmarks only. See Harbour and Associates 1990, 138.

7. The export and import data for the automobile industry published by the Banco de Mexico and the National Institute of Statistics, Geography and Information (INEGI) do not include the *maquiladoras*. Based on their data, Mexico had a $942 million trade deficit in the auto industry in 1991, but the figure was actually higher since Ford had closed its highly automated Chihuahua engine plant, a significant source of export dollars, for a major retooling scheduled to last several years. U.S. Department of Commerce figures for Mexico for 1991) show that U.S. imports of passenger cars totaled $2.6 billion, imports of auto parts totaled $5 billion, and exports of automotive parts totaled $5 billion (see *Wall Street Journal*, Sept. 24, 1992, R12).

8. 1980 data from *Comercio Exterior* 1991, 847.

9. It is unclear at this time how many cars from this plant Nissan plans to sell in Mexico.

10. J. Leonard Mertens and Laura Palomares reported similar findings in a 1986 study of sixty electronics plants. See Mertens and Palomares 1988.

11. Although transportation equipment is primarily auto-related, the trade statistics for this sector are grouped with *maquiladoras*, not the automobile industry.

Notes to Chapter 9

1. This is in effect acknowledged by Edwards (1986, chaps. 4 and 5), who analyzes the sources of variation in workplace industrial relations in different societies. There is no integration, however, of the different levels of analysis in relation to the concept of workplace relations.

2. In an article examining studies of workplace relations (Frenkel 1986, 79), I argue that there is a need to define the term "workplace relations" precisely. Four aspects of workplace relations are suggested: the extent and nature of collective employee representation; the level of conflict between management and employees; the dominant mode of rule adjustment at the workplace level; and the reward system. These remained untheorized, but they bear a strong similarity to Fox's ideas.

3. The politics of access is beyond the scope of this chapter, but it is noteworthy that I was denied access to some of the most profitable plants (e.g., in Germany) and some whose performance at the time of the request was reputed to be especially weak (in the Philippines).

4. Research indicates that U.S. multinationals tend to be more centralized than their counterparts (Hamill 1984), whereas product standardization also facilitates centralized decision-making (Marginson et al. 1988, 220). This suggests that the impact of corporate-level management on subsidiaries in matters of production and employee relations may be greater in PH than in non-U.S. (except perhaps Japanese) and more diversified firms. Multinationals are tending to concentrate production in fewer plants, however, and are pursuing global strategies in which the human resource function is assuming increasing strategic importance (Adler and Ghadar 1990, 254). In addition, managers in different countries are being trained in similar best-practice techniques. Hence, the trends found in this study may be typical of workplaces in sectors characterized by relatively simple manufacturing processes. This is clearly a matter for further research, preferably on a longitudinal basis.

5. Different legal processes and restrictions may prevent some products from being sold

in some countries. In addition, new products may be sourced from particular plants, depending on their efficiency, capacity, and product profitability.

6. The voluntary annual submission document requires specific ratios or figures relating to the following items: customer complaints; product recalls; quality failure costs; actual versus planned production; customer service level; equivalent units of product per hour paid; cost of goods relative to sales; cost savings; lost time incidence rate; workdays lost arising from safety problems relative to days worked; energy used per output measure; percentage of employees trained in company core programs; percentage of employees in career development program; absentee rate; labor turnover rate; maintenance hours per output measure; preventive maintenance per total maintenance hours in percent; unscheduled equipment downtime hours per total equipment run hours in percent; total changeover labor hours in percent; total number of changeovers; changeover labor hours per changeover; inventory turns; and inventory amount.

7. The relatively large number of job descriptions at the U.K. plant is explained by the practice of assigning different job descriptions to similar jobs according to the area of the plant in which they are located.

8. Overtime accounted for approximately 20 percent of the total earnings of manual workers.

9. In 1990, nearly 31 percent of manual workers were employed on nonstandard employment contracts. These included workers hired for permanent part-time work and for temporary full-time and part-time employment.

10. The year-end bonus is meant to reflect a sharing of the fruits of the firm's performance over the year, but it has become institutionalized in most Taiwanese firms as part of the total pay package.

11. Nevertheless, the MRP2 project is noteworthy because it has involved line management in the development of a more integrated approach to manufacturing, one that is based on seeking continuous improvement through the use of MRP2 as a diagnostic tool. Frequent interunit meetings have given managers a greater appreciation of one another's problems and how these might be resolved by implementing a common materials planning database. When the system began operating, it became easier to detect inefficiencies, which could then be analyzed and rectified. The system is therefore requiring more skill, job flexibility, and teamwork from employees. The transfer of sterile products—which was confined to the sterile business unit, employing 21 percent of the pharmaceutical production workforce—was part of corporate management's rationalization strategy aimed at concentrating production of the less profitable sterile products in the U.K. plant in order to provide capacity for the allegedly more efficient German facility to specialize in more profitable products. The transfer was accompanied by automation without job loss. With tight control over hiring indirect employees, however, workers have had to work harder and accept greater job flexibility. The relatively rapid transfer placed additional pressure on all those involved, straining relations between the U.K. and German affiliates and between management and employees in the United Kingdom's sterile unit.

12. This was demonstrated in the research process by the fact that very few employees in the fluids area were willing to complete a questionnaire I gave them. Apparently, the prevailing attitude was that, since the questionnaire did not contribute to their job security, it would be a waste of time to cooperate.

13. Because the skill-based reward system has been introduced so recently (late 1990), it is acknowledged as an emerging development in table 9.1. Nothing needs to be added, however, to what has been said in the previous section.

14. These relate to import restrictions and competition with PH's subsidiaries in the region.

15. Since pharmaceutical plants rely on imported chemicals, management has difficulty ensuring rapid and timely delivery of raw materials. This problem severely constrains the implementation of a total JIT system, although it does not negate working with suppliers of bottles, labels, and so on. In addition, other elements, such as zero defects and

continuous productivity improvement, can usefully be introduced. Note that the U.K. plant has an advantage in having chemicals produced on-site.

16. Other norms and practices that relate to the HR function more broadly include guidelines in the following areas: employment and recruitment, orientation of new employees, job evaluation and salary administration, training and development, and succession planning.

17. The 1990 survey comprised nearly 120 forced-choice questions, including a section for comments. The areas covered included job demands, working conditions, pay, employee benefits, friendliness and cooperation of colleagues, supervisor-employee interpersonal relations, confidence in management, technical competence of supervision, effectiveness of administration, adequacy of communication, job security and work relations continuity, status and recognition, identification with the company, opportunity for growth and advancement, and reactions to the survey.

18. Use of the term "advanced" and the general tenor of the discussion should not be interpreted as the author prescribing the cooperative dependent pattern.

19. The idea resulted from a visit by the manufacturing director to a Canadian subsidiary that was operating along these lines. Instead of dividing responsibility on a functional basis, these business units encourage cooperation between functions with respect to particular products, the production of which is ultimately the responsibility of a business unit head.

References

Ackerman, Susan. 1984. "Impact of Industrialisation on the Social Role of Rural Malay Women." In A. Y. Hing, N. S. Karim, and R. Talib, eds., 40–60. *Women in Malaysia.* Kuala Lumpur: Pelanduk Publications.

Adams, George W. 1978. *Grievance Arbitration of Discharge Cases: A Study of the Concepts of Industrial Discipline and Their Results.* Kingston: Industrial Relations Centre, Queen's University.

———. 1985. *Canadian Labour Law.* Aurora: Canada Law Book.

Adams, Roy J., and C. H. Rummel. 1977. "Workers' Participation in Management in West Germany." *Industrial Relations Journal.* 8:4–22.

Adler, Nancy, and Faribarz Ghadar. 1990. "Strategic Human Resource Management: A Global Perspective." In R. Pieper, ed, *Human Resource Management: An International Comparison*, 235–60. New York: Walter de Gruyter.

Advisory Conciliation and Arbitration Service (ACAS). 1986. *Annual Report.* London: ACAS.

———. 1987. *Annual Report.* London: ACAS.

Ahlstrand, Bruce W. 1990. *The Quest for Productivity: A Case Study of Fawley after Flanders.* Cambridge: Cambridge University Press.

Aldcroft, Derek H. 1974. *Studies in Transport History.* Newton Abbot, England: David and Charles.

Altshuler, Alan, Martin Anderson, Daniel Jones, Daniel Roos, and James Womack. 1984. *The Future of the Automobile.* Cambridge: MIT Press.

Amberg, Steve. 1989. "The Triumph of Industrial Orthodoxy." In Nelson Lichtenstein and Stephen Meyer, eds., *On the Line: Essays in the History of Auto Work,* pp. 190–218. Urbana: University of Illinois Press.

Anderman, Steven. 1972. *Voluntary Dismissals Procedures and the Industrial Relations Act.* London: PEP.

———. 1985. *The Law of Unfair Dismissal.* 2d ed. London: Butterworths.

Anders, George. 1992. "Heading South: U.S. Companies Plan Major Moves into Mexico." *Wall Street Journal*, 24 Sept., R1.

Armstrong, Peter J. 1988. "Labour and Monopoly Capital." In Richard Hyman and Wolfgang Streeck, eds., *New Technology and Industrial Relations*, 143–59. Oxford: Blackwell.

Armstrong, Peter J., John F. B. Goodman, and Jeffrey D. Hyman. 1981. *Ideology and Shop-Floor Industrial Relations.* London: Croom Helm.

Arnot, Bob. 1988. *Controlling Soviet Labour.* London: Macmillan.

Ashdown, R. T., and K. H. Baker. 1973. *In Working Order: A Study of Industrial Discipline.* London: HMSO.

Asociación Mexicana de la Industria Automotriz (AMIA). 1988. *La industria automotriz de Mexico en cifras.* Mexico City: AMIA.

Babson, Steve. 1989a. "Pointing the Way: Skilled Workers and Anglo-Gaelic Immigrants in the Rise of the UAW." Ph.D. dissertation, Wayne State University, Detroit.

———. 1989b. "British and Irish Militants in the Detroit UAW in the 1930s." In Robert Asher and Charles Stephenson, eds., *Labor Divided: Race and Ethnicity in United States Labor Struggles, 1835–1960*, 227–45. Albany: SUNY Press.

Baglioni, Guido, and Colin Crouch, eds. 1990. *European Industrial Relations.* London: Sage.

Bagwell, Philip S. 1963. *The Railwaymen.* London: Allen and Unwin.

———. 1968. *The Railway Clearing House in the British Economy, 1842–1922.* London: Allen and Unwin.

Baker, Stephen. 1992. "Detroit South, Mexico's Auto Boom: Who Wins, Who Loses." *Business Week*, March 16:98–103.

Baldamus, William. 1961. *Efficiency and Effort.* London: Tavistock.

Banaji, Jairus, and Rohini Hensman. 1990. *Beyond Multinationalism: Management Policy and Bargaining Relations in International Companies.* New Delhi: Sage.

Banamex (Banco Nacional de Mexico). 1992. "Review of the Economic Situation of Mexico."

Barnacle, Peter J. 1991. *Arbitration of Discharge Grievances in Ontario: Outcomes and Reinstatement Experiences.* Research and Current Issues Series no. 62. Kingston: Industrial Relations Centre, Queen's University.

Batstone, Eric, Ian Boraston, and Stephen Frenkel. 1977. *Shop Stewards in Action: The Organization of Workplace Conflict and Accommodation.* Oxford: Blackwell.

———. 1978. *The Social Organization of Strikes.* Oxford: Blackwell.

Batstone, Eric, and Stephen Gourlay. 1986. *Unions, Unemployment and Innovation.* Oxford: Blackwell.

Batstone, Eric, and Stephen Gourlay, with Hugo Levie and Roy Moore. 1987. *New Technology and the Process of Labour Regulation.* Oxford: Clarendon.

Bélanger, Jacques. 1987. "Job Control after Reform: A Case Study in British Engineering." *Industrial Relations Journal* 18:50–62.

———. 1989. "Job Control and Productivity: New Evidence from Canada." *British Journal of Industrial Relations* 27:347–64.

Bélanger, Jacques, and Stephen Evans. 1988. "Job Controls and Shop Steward Leadership among Semiskilled Engineering Workers." In Michael Terry and P. K. Edwards, eds., *Shopfloor Politics and Job Controls*, 150–84. Oxford: Basil Blackwell.

Bélanger, Jacques, Michèle Bilodeau, and Alain Vinet. 1991. "Contrôle du travail et absences de courte durée: Une étude empirique." *Relations industrielles/Industrial Relations* 46:703–21.

Berggren, Christian. 1992. *Alternatives to Lean Production: Work Organization in the Swedish Auto Industry.* Ithaca: ILR Press.

———. 1993. "Lean Production: The End of History?" *Work, Employment and Society* 7:163–88.

Bernoux, Philippe. 1985. *La sociologie des organisations.* Paris: Éditions du Seuil.

Beynon, Huw. 1984. *Working for Ford.* 2d ed. Harmondsworth, Middlesex: Pelican.

Bijker, Wiebe, Thomas P. Hughes, and Trevor J. Pinch, eds. 1987. *The Social Construction of Technological Systems.* Cambridge, Mass.: Harvard University Press.

Bittner, Egon. 1973. "The Concept of Organisation." In Graeme Salaman and Kenneth Thompson, eds., *People and Organisations.* London: Longman.

Blecker, Robert A. 1991. Testimony before United States Senate Subcommittee on Labor and Human Resources in hearings on the proposed North American Free Trade Agreement with Mexico, April 23, 6.

Blyton, Paul, and Peter Turnbull, eds. 1992. *Reassessing Human Resource Management.* London: Sage.

Bornschier, Volker, and Hanspeter Stamm. 1990. "Transnational Corporations." *Current Sociology* 38:203–29.

Braverman, Harry. 1974. *Labor and Monopoly Capital.* New York: Monthly Review Press.

Brody, David. 1980. *Workers in Industrial America.* New York: Oxford University Press.

———. 1993. "Workplace Contractualism in Comparative Perspective." In Nelson Lichtenstein and Howell J. Harris, eds., *Industrial Democracy in America*, 176–205. New York: Cambridge University Press.

Brooke, Michael Z. 1984. *Centralization and Autonomy.* London: Holt, Rinehart and Winston.

Brown, Donald J. M., and David M. Beatty. 1993. *Canadian Labour Arbitration.* Aurora: Canada Law Book.

Brown, Hedy. 1980. "The Individual in the Organisation." In Graeme Salaman and K. Thompson, eds., *Control and Ideology in Organisations*, 152–66. Milton Keynes: Open University Press.

Brown, R. K., et al. 1973. "Leisure in Work." In M. A. Smith, S. Parker, and C. S. Smith, eds., *Leisure and Society in Britain.* London: Allen Lane.

Brown, William. 1973. *Piecework Bargaining.* London: Heinemann.

Brown, William, ed. 1981. *The Changing Contours of British Industrial Relations.* Oxford: Basil Blackwell.

Brown, William, Robert Ebsworth, and Michael Terry. 1978. "Factors Shaping Shop Steward Organisation in Britain." *British Journal of Industrial Relations* 16:139–59.

Burawoy, Michael. 1979a. "The Anthropology of Industrial Work." *Annual Review of Anthropology* 8:231–66.

———. 1979b. *Manufacturing Consent: Changes in the Labor Process under Monopoly Capitalism.* Chicago: University of Chicago Press.

———. 1983. "Between the Labor Process and the State." *American Sociological Review* 48:587–605.

———. 1985. *The Politics of Production.* London: Verso.

———. 1990. "Marxism as Science." *American Sociological Review* 55:775–93.

Burawoy, Michael, Alice Burton, Ann Arnett Ferguson, Kathryn J. Fox, Joshua Gamson, Nadine Gartrell, Leslie Hurst, Charles Kurzman, Leslie Salzinger, Josepha Schiffman, and Shiori Ui. 1991. *Ethnography Unbound.* Berkeley: University of California Press.

Burawoy, Michael, and Janos Lukacs. 1985. "Mythologies of Work." *American Sociological Review* 50:723–37.

———. 1989. "What Is Socialist about Socialist Production?" In Stephen Wood, ed., *The Transformation of Work?*, 295–316. London: Unwin Hyman.

Business Week. 1983. "The Revolutionary Wage Deal at GM's Packard Electric." August 29.

Callus, Ron, Alison Morehead, Mark Cully and John Buchanan. 1991. *Industrial Relations at Work: The Australian Workplace Industrial Relations Survey.* Canberra: Commonwealth Department of Industrial Relations.

Cameron, David. 1984. "Social Democracy, Corporatism, Labour Quiescence and the Representation of Economic Interest in Advanced Capitalist Society." In John H. Goldthorpe, ed., *Order and Conflict in Contemporary Capitalism*, 143–78. Oxford: Clarendon Press.

Carillo, Jorge V. 1989. "Transformaciones en la industria maquiladora de exportacion." In Bernardo Gonzalez Arechiga and Rocio Barajas Escamilla, eds., *Las maquiladoras: ajuste estructural y desarrollo regional.* Tijuana: El Colegio de la Frontera Norte/Fundàcion Friedrich Ebert.

Chamberlain, Neil. 1948. *The Union Challenge to Management Control.* New York: Harper.

Chandler, Alfred D. 1977. *The Visible Hand.* Cambridge: Harvard University Press.

Chaykowski, Richard, and Anil Verma, eds. 1992. *Industrial Relations in Canadian Industry.* Toronto: Holt, Rinehart and Winston.

Chia, Siow Yue. 1989. "The Character and Progress of Industrialisation." In K. S. Sandhu and P. Wheatley, eds., *Management of Success: The Moulding of Modern Singapore*, 250–79. Singapore: Institute of Southeast Asian Studies.

Child, John. 1972. "Organisation Structure, Environment and Performance: The Role of Strategic Choice." *Sociology* 6:1–22.

Cho, Soon Kyoung. 1985. "The Labor Process and Capital Mobility." *Politics and Society* 14:185–222.

Chung Yuen Kay. 1989. "Gender, Work and Ethnicity: An Ethnography of Female Factory Workers in Singapore." Ph.D. diss., National University of Singapore.

————. Forthcoming. "Elliptical Ethnicity." In N. PuruShotam, ed., *Ethnicity as Discourse in Singapore.*

Clark, Jon, Ian McLoughlin, Howard Rose, and Robin King, eds. 1988. *The Process of Technological Change.* Cambridge: Cambridge University Press.

Clegg, Hugh A. 1976. *Trade Unionism under Collective Bargaining.* Oxford: Blackwell.

Cohen, Robin. 1991. *Contested Domains.* London: Zed.

Coleman, D. C. 1988. Review of Elbaum and Lazonick 1986. *Business History* 30:130–31.

Collins, Hugh. 1982. "Capitalist Discipline and Corporatist Law." *Industrial Law Journal* 11:170.

Concannon, Harcourt. 1980. "Handling Dismissal Disputes by Arbitration." *Industrial Law Journal* 11:12–23.

Copp, Robert. 1977. "Locus of Industrial Relations Decision Making in Multinationals." In Robert F. Banks and Jack Stieber, eds., *Multinationals, Unions, and Labor Relations in Industrialized Countries*, 42–53. Ithaca: New York State School of Industrial and Labor Relations.

Crandall, Robert W. 1986. "Relative Labor Costs, the Newly Industrializing Countries, and Competition in the U.S. Automobile Market." Presentation to the *Automotive News* World Congress, July 28.

Cressey, Peter, and John MacInnes. 1980. "Voting for Ford." *Capital and Class* 11:5–33.

Crouch, Colin. 1993. *Industrial Relations and European State Traditions*. Oxford: Clarendon.

Crozier, Michel. 1963. *Le phénomène bureaucratique*. Paris: Éditions du Seuil.

Curtain, Richard. 1990. "Workplace Change in Australia: Progress, Process and Problems." National Key Centre in Industrial Relations Working Paper no. 8. Monash University, Melbourne.

Daniel, W. W. 1987. *Workplace Industrial Relations and Technical Change*. London: Frances Pinter in association with Policy Studies Institute.

Daniel, W. W., and Neil Millward. 1983. *Workplace Industrial Relations in Britain: The DE/PSI/ESRC Survey*. London: Heinemann.

Daniel, W. W., and Elizabeth Stilgoe. 1978. *The Impact of Employment Protection Laws*. London: Policy Studies Institute.

Deaton, David. 1985. "Management Style and Large Scale Survey Evidence." *Industrial Relations Journal* 162:67–71.

Deery, Stephen, and David Plowman. 1991. *Australian Industrial Relations*. 3rd ed. Sydney: McGraw-Hill.

Deyo, Frederic C. 1989. *Beneath the Miracle*. Berkeley: University of California Press.

Dickens, Linda, and David Cockburn. 1986. "Dispute Settlement Institutions and the Courts." In Roy Lewis, ed., *Labour Law in Britain*, 531–71. Oxford: Basil Blackwell.

Dickens, Linda, Michael Jones, Brian Weekes, and Moira Hart. 1985. *Dismissed: A Study of Unfair Dismissal and the Industrial Tribunal System*. Oxford: Basil Blackwell.

Directorate-General of Budget Accounting and Statistics (DGBAS). Executive Yuan. Republic of China. 1989. "Abstract of Employment and Earnings Statistics in Taiwan Area, Republic of China, 1989."

d'Iribarne, Philippe. 1989. *La logique de l'honneur*. Paris: Éditions du Seuil.

Dohse, Knuth, Ulrich Jürgens, and Thomas Malsch. 1985. "From 'Fordism' to 'Toyotaism'? The Social Organization of the Labor Process in the Japanese Automobile Industry." *Politics and Society* 14:115–46.

Donovan Commission. 1968. *Report of the Royal Commission on Trade Unions and Employers' Associations*. London: HMSO.

Dore, Ronald. 1973. *British Factory—Japanese Factory: The Origins of National Diversity in Industrial Relations*. London: Allen and Unwin.

———. 1989. "Where Are We Now? Musings of an Evolutionist." *Work, Employment and Society* 3:425–46.

Doz, Yves, and C. K. Prahalad. 1986. "Controlled Variety." *Human Resource Management* 25:55–71.

Drucker, Peter. 1988. "Low Wages No Longer Give Competitive Edge." *Wall Street Journal*, March 16.

Duda, Helga, and Franz Tödtling. 1986. "Austrian Trade Unions in the Economic Crisis." In Richard Edwards, Paolo Garonna, and Franz Tödtling, eds., *Unions in Crisis and Beyond: Perspectives from Six Countries*, 227–69. Dover, Mass.: Auburn House.

Edwards, P. K. 1983. "The Political Economy of Industrial Conflict." *Economic and Industrial Democracy* 4:461–500.

———. 1986. *Conflict at Work: A Materialist Analysis of Workplace Relations.* Oxford: Blackwell.

———. 1987. *Managing the Factory.* Oxford: Blackwell.

———. 1988. "Patterns of Conflict and Accommodation." In Duncan Gallie, ed., *Employment in Britain*, 187–217. Oxford: Blackwell.

———. 1989. "The Three Faces of Discipline." In Keith Sisson, ed., *Personnel Management in Britain*, 296–325. Oxford: Blackwell.

———. 1990. "Understanding Conflict in the Labour Process: The Logic and Autonomy of Struggle." In David Knights and Hugh Willmott, eds., *Labour Process Theory*, 125–52. Hampshire: Macmillan.

———. 1991. "Workplace Regulation and Employer Policy in Britain and the United States." Paper presented to International Colloquium on Workplace Industrial Relations and Industrial Conflict in Comparative Perspective, Université Laval, August.

———. 1992a. "Industrial Conflict: Themes and Issues in Recent Research." *British Journal of Industrial Relations* 30:361–404.

———. 1992b. "La recherche comparative en relations industrielles: L'apport de la tradition ethnographique." *Relations industrielles/Industrial Relations* 47:411–37.

Edwards, P. K., Mark Hall, Richard Hyman, Paul Marginson, Keith Sisson, Jeremy Waddington, and David Winchester. 1992. "Great Britain." In Anthony Ferner and Richard Hyman, eds., *Industrial Relations in the New Europe*, 1–68. Oxford: Blackwell.

Edwards, P. K., and Hugh Scullion. 1982. *The Social Organization of Industrial Conflict: Control and Resistance in the Workplace.* Oxford: Blackwell.

Edwards, P. K., and Colin Whitston. 1988. "Factory Discipline, the Control of Attendance and the Subordination of Labour: Towards an Integrated Analysis." Typescript.

———. 1991. "Workers Are Working Harder: Effort and Shop-Floor Relations in the 1980s." *British Journal of Industrial Relations* 29:593–601.

Edwards, Richard. 1979. *Contested Terrain: The Transformation of the Workplace in the Twentieth Century.* London: Heinemann.

Elbaum, Bernard, and William Lazonick, eds. 1986. *The Decline of the British Economy.* Oxford: Clarendon.

Elger, Tony. 1990. "Technical Innovation and Work Reorganisation in British Manufacturing in the 1980s: Continuity, Intensification or Transformation?" *Work, Employment and Society*, May (special issue): 67–101.

Elias, Peter. 1981. "Fairness in Unfair Dismissal: Trends and Tensions." *Industrial Law Journal* 10:201–15.

Emmett, Isabel, and D. H. J. Morgan. 1982. "Max Gluckman and the Manchester Shopfloor Ethnographies." In Ronald Frankenberg, ed., *Custom and Conflict in British Society*, 140–65. Manchester: Manchester University Press.

Enderwick, Peter. 1985. *Multinational Business and Labour.* London: Croom Helm.

Esping-Andersen, Gosta, and Walter Korpi. 1984. "Social Policy as Class Politics in Post-War Capitalism." In John H. Goldthorpe, ed., *Order and Conflict in Contemporary Capitalism*, 179–208. Oxford: Clarendon.

Ferguson, Kathy. 1980. *Self, Society and Womankind: The Dialectic of Liberation.* Westport: Greenwood Press.

Ferner, Antony. 1990. "The Changing Influence of the Personnel Function." *Human Resource Management Journal* 1:12–30.

Fine, Sidney. 1963. *The Automobile under the Blue Eagle*. Ann Arbor: University of Michigan Press.

Flaherty, Sean. 1988. "Mature Collective Bargaining and Rank and File Militancy: Breaking the Peace of the 'Treaty of Detroit.' " *Research in Political Economy* 2:241–80.

Flanders, Allan. 1975. *Management and Unions*. London: Faber.

Florida, Richard, and Martin Kenney. 1991. "Transplanted Organizations: The Transfer of Japanese Industrial Organization to the U.S." *American Sociological Review* 56:381:98.

Fox, Alan. 1974. *Beyond Contract: Work, Power and Trust Relations*. London: Faber.

———. 1985. *History and Heritage*. London: Allen and Unwin.

Franzosi, Roberto. 1989. "Strike Data in Search of a Theory." *Politics and Society* 17:453–87.

Frenkel, Stephen. 1986. "Industrial Sociology and Workplace Relations in Advanced Capitalist Societies." *International Journal of Comparative Sociology* 27:69–86.

———. 1990a. "Containing Dualism through Corporatism: Contemporary Changes in Industrial Relations in Australia." *Bulletin of Comparative Labour Relations* 20:113–45.

———. 1990b. "Industrial Relations in Eight Advanced Societies: A Comparative Overview." *Bulletin of Comparative Labour Relations* 20:191–222.

———. 1991. "State Policies and Workplace Relations: A Comparison between Thatcherism and Accordism." In Harry C. Katz, ed., *The Future of Industrial Relations*, 47–72. Ithaca: ILR Press.

———. 1993. "Australian Trade Unionism and the New Social Structure of Accumulation." In Stephen Frenkel, ed., *Organized Labor in the Asia-Pacific Region: A Comparative Study of Trade Unionism in Nine Countries*, 249–81. Ithaca: ILR Press.

———. 1993. Frenkel, Stephen, Jon-Chao Hong, and Bih-Ling Lee. 1993. "The Resurgence and Fragility of Trade Unions in Taiwan." In Stephen Frenkel, ed., *Organized Labor in the Asia-Pacific Region: A Comparative Study of Trade Unionism in Nine Countries*, 162–86. Ithaca: ILR Press.

Friedman, Andrew L. 1977. *Industry and Labour: Class Struggle at Work and Monopoly Capitalism*. London: Macmillan.

———. 1990. "Managerial Strategies, Activities, Techniques and Technology: Towards a Complex Theory of the Labour Process." In David Knights and Hugh Willmott, eds., *Labour Process Theory*, 177–208. Hampshire: Macmillan.

Fucini, Joseph, and Suzy F. Fucini. 1990. *Working for the Japanese*. New York: Free Press.

Fulcher, James. 1973. "Discontent in a Swedish Shipyard." *British Journal of Industrial Relations* 11:242–58.

———. 1987. "Labour Movement Theory versus Corporatism." *Sociology* 21:231–52.

———. 1988. "On the Explanation of Industrial Relations Diversity." *British Journal of Industrial Relations* 26:246–73.

———. 1991. *Labour Movements, Employers and the State*. Oxford: Clarendon.

Gallie, Duncan. 1978. *In Search of the New Working Class: Automation and Social Integration within the Capitalist Enterprise*. Cambridge: Cambridge University Press.

Gallie, Duncan, ed. 1988. *Employment in Britain*. Oxford: Blackwell.

Gandz, Jeffrey. 1978. "Employee Grievances: Incidence and Patterns of Resolution." Ph.D. diss., York University, Toronto.

Genovese, Eugene D. 1976. *Roll, Jordan, Roll*. New York: Vintage.

Gerlach, Peter. 1989. "Deregulation in Austria." *European Journal of Political Research* 17:209–22.

Gersuny, Carl. 1973. *Punishment and Redress in a Modern Factory*. Lexington, Mass.: Lexington Books.

Giles, Anthony, and Gregor Murray. 1989. "Industrial Relations Theory and Critical Political Economy." Paper presented to the Industrial Relations Research Association Study Group on Industrial Relations Theory, Brussels.

Glasbeek, Harry. 1982. "The Contract of Employment at Common Law." In John C. Anderson and Morley Gunderson, eds., *Union-Management Relations in Canada*, 47–77. Don Mills, Ont.: Addison-Wesley.

———. 1984. "The Utility of Model-Building—Collins' Capitalist Discipline and Corporatist Law." *Industrial Law Journal* 13:133–52.

Glucksmann, Miriam. 1990. *Women Assemble*. London: Routledge.

Goffman, Erving. 1959. *The Presentation of Self in Everyday Life*. Harmondsworth: Penguin.

Gold, Michael, and Mark Hall. 1992. *European-Level Information and Consultation in Multinational Companies: An Evaluation of Practice*. Dublin: European Foundation.

Goldthorpe, John H., ed. 1984a. *Order and Conflict in Contemporary Capitalism*. Oxford: Clarendon.

———. 1984b. "The End of Convergence: Corporatist and Dualist Tendencies in Modern Western Societies." In John Goldthorpe, ed., *Order and Conflict in Contemporary Capitalism*, 315–43. Oxford: Clarendon.

Gordon, David M., Richard Edwards, and Michael Reich. 1982. *Segmented Work, Divided Workers*. Cambridge: Cambridge University Press.

Gospel, Howard F. 1992. *Markets, Firms and the Management of Labour in Modern Britain*. Cambridge: Cambridge University Press.

Gouldner, Alvin. 1954. *Patterns of Industrial Bureaucracy*. New York: Free Press.

Granovetter, Mark. 1985. "Economic Action and Social Structure: The Problem of Embeddedness." *American Journal of Sociology* 91:481–510.

Green, Susan. 1980. "Silicon Valley's Women Workers: A Theoretical Consideration of Sex-Segregation in the Electronics Industry." Impact of Transnational Interactions Project. Culture Learning Institute, East-West Center, Honolulu.

Grossman, Rachael. 1979. "Women's Place in the Integrated Circuit." *Southeast Asia Chronicle* 66:2–17.

Grunberg, Leon. 1986. "Workplace Relations in the Economic Crisis: A Comparison of a British and a French Automobile Plant." *Sociology* 20:503–29.

Guest, David E. 1990a. "Have British Workers Been Working Harder in Thatcher's Britain? A Re-Consideration of the Concept of Effort." *British Journal of Industrial Relations* 28:293–312.

———. 1990b. "Human Resource Management and the American Dream." *Journal of Management Studies* 27:377–97.

Haiven, Larry. 1988. "The Political Apparatuses of Production: Generation and Resolution of Industrial Conflict in Canada and Britain." Ph.D. diss., University of Warwick.

————. 1989. "Industrial Conflict and the Structuring of the Internal Labour Market: The Case of Canada and Great Britain." Paper presented at the annual meeting of the Canadian Industrial Relations Association, May.

————. 1991. "Past Practice and Custom and Practice: 'Adjustment' and Industrial Conflict in North America and the United Kingdom." *Comparative Labour Law Journal* 12:300–34.

Hall, Margie E. 1982. "Class and Stratification in Singapore." Department of Sociology, National University of Singapore. Typescript.

Hall, Peter A. 1986. "The State and Economic Decline." In Bernard Elbaum and William Lazonick, ed., *The Decline of the British Economy*, 266–302. Oxford: Clarendon.

Hamill, James. 1983. "The Labour Relations Practices of Foreign Owned and Indigenous Firms." *Employee Relations* 5:14–16.

————. 1984. "Labour Relations Decision-Making within Multinational Corporations." *Industrial Relations Journal* 15:30–34.

Hancock, Mary A. 1980. "Electronics: The International Industry. An Examination of U.S. Electronic Offshore Production Involving a Female Workforce in Southeast Asia." Impact of Transnational Interactions Project. Culture Learning Institute, East-West Center, Honolulu.

Harbour and Associates, Inc. 1990. *The Harbour Report: A Decade Later: Competitive Assessment of the North American Automotive Industry, 1979–1989*. Rochester, Mich.: Harbour and Associates, Inc.

Harris, Howell J. 1985. "The Snares of Liberalism?" In Stephen Tolliday and Jonathan Zeitlin, ed., *Shop Floor Bargaining and the State*, 148–91. Cambridge: Cambridge University Press.

Haydu, Jeffrey. 1988. "Employers, Unions and American Exceptionalism." *International Review of Social History* 33:25–41.

Henry, Stuart. 1983. *Private Justice: Towards Integrated Theorising in the Sociology of Law*. London: Routledge and Kegan Paul.

————. 1987. "Disciplinary Pluralism: Four Models of Private Justice in the Workplace." *Sociological Review* 35:279–319.

Herding, Richard. 1972. *Job Control and Union Structure*. Rotterdam: Rotterdam University Press.

Heritage, John. 1984. *Garfinkel and Ethnomethodology*. Cambridge: Polity Press.

Herzenberg, Stephen A. 1990. "State Policy, Anglo-Gaelic Immigrants and the Formation of the UAW in the U.S. and Canada." Bureau of International Labor Affairs, U.S. Department of Labor. December. Typescript.

————. 1991. *Towards a Cooperative Commonwealth: Labor and Restructuring in the U.S. and Canadian Auto Industries*. Ph.D. diss., MIT.

————. 1993. "Whither Social Unionism? Labor and Restructuring in the U.S. Auto Industry." In Jane Jenson and Rianne Mahon, eds., *The Challenge of Restructuring: North American Labor Movements Respond*, 314–36. Philadelphia: Temple University Press.

Heyzer, Noeleen. 1981. "From Rural Subsistence to an Industrial Peripheral Workforce: An Examination of Female Malaysian Migrants and Capital Accumulation in Singapore." In Lourdes Beneria, ed., *Woman and Development*, 179–202. New York: Praeger.

————. 1983. "International Production and Social Change: An Analysis of the State, Employment and Trade Unions in Singapore." In Peter Chen, ed.,

Singapore: Development Policies and Trends, 105–28. Singapore: Oxford University Press.

Huxley, Christopher, David Kettler, and James Struthers. 1986. "Is Canada's Experience Especially Instructive?" In Seymour Martin Lipset, ed., *Unions in Transition: Entering the Second Century*, 113–32. San Francisco: Institute for Contemporary Studies.

Hyman, Richard. 1978. "Pluralism, Procedural Consensus and Collective Bargaining." *British Journal of Industrial Relations* 16:16–40.

———. 1987. "Strategy or Structure?: Capital, Labour and Control." *Work, Employment and Society* 1:25–55.

———. 1988. "Flexible Specialization: Miracle or Myth?" In Richard Hyman and Wolfgang Streeck, eds., *New Technology and Industrial Relations*, 48–60. Oxford: Blackwell.

———. 1989a. "Trade Unionism and the State: Some Recent European Developments." In Richard Hyman, ed., *The Political Economy of Industrial Relations: Theory and Practice in a Cold Climate*, 202–23. London: Macmillan.

———. 1989b. *The Political Economy of Industrial Relations: Theory and Practice in a Cold Climate*. London: Macmillan.

Inagami, Takeshi. 1988. *Japanese Workplace Industrial Relations*. Japanese Industrial Relations Series no. 14. Tokyo: Japan Institute of Labor.

Institute of Personnel Management (IPM). 1979. *Disciplinary Procedures and Practice*. IPM Information Report 28. London: IPM.

Jackson, Peter, and Keith Sisson. 1976. "Employers' Confederations in Sweden and the UK and the Significance of Industrial Infrastructure." *British Journal of Industrial Relations* 14:306–23.

Jacobi, Otto, and Walther Müller-Jentsch. 1990. "West Germany: Continuity and Structural Change." In Guido Baglioni and Colin Crouch, eds., *European Industrial Relations*, 127–53. London: Sage.

Jacoby, Sanford M. 1985. *Employing Bureaucracy*. New York: Columbia University Press.

———. 1991. "American Exceptionalism Revisited." In Sanford M. Jacoby, ed., *Masters to Managers*, 173–200. New York: Columbia University Press.

Jain, Hem. 1990. "Human Resource Management in Selected Japanese Firms, Their Foreign Subsidiaries and Locally Owned Counterparts." *International Labour Review* 129:73–89.

Jefferys, Stephen. 1986. *Management and Managed: Fifty Years of Crisis at Chrysler*. London: Cambridge University Press.

Juravich, Tom. 1985. *Chaos on the Shopfloor*. Philadelphia: Temple University Press.

Jürgens, Ulrich, Thomas Malsch, and Kurt Dohse. 1989. *Moderne Zeiten in der Automobilfabrik: Strategien der Produktionsmodernisierung im Länder- und Konzern-envergleich*. Berlin: Springer-Verlag.

Kamata, Satoshi. 1983. *Japan in the Passing Lane*. London: Allen and Unwin.

Katz, Harry C. 1984. "The U.S. Automobile Collective Bargaining System in Transition." *British Journal of Industrial Relations* 22:205–17.

———. 1985. *Shifting Gears: Changing Labor Relations in the U.S. Automobile Industry*. Cambridge: MIT Press.

———. 1988. "Business and Labor Relations Strategies in the U.S. Automobile Industry: The Case of the General Motors Corporation." In Ben Dankbaar, Ulrich Jürgens, and Thomas Malsch, eds., *Die Zunkunft der Arbeit in der Automobilindustrie*, 249–62. Berlin: Edition Sigma.

Keller, Berndt K. 1991. "The Role of the State as Corporate Actor in Industrial Relations Systems." In Roy J. Adams, ed., *Comparative Industrial Relations*, 76–93. London: Harper Collins.

Kelly, John. 1985. "Management's Redesign of Work." In David Knights, Hugh Willmott, and David Collinson, eds., *Job Redesign*, 30–51. Aldershot: Gower.

Kerr, Clark. 1954. "Industrial Conflict and Its Mediation." *American Journal of Sociology* 60:230–45.

Kerr, Clark, John T. Dunlop, Frederick Harbison, and Charles A. Myers. 1960. *Industrialism and Industrial Man*. Cambridge, Mass.: Harvard University Press.

Knight, Thomas R. 1984. "The Impact of Arbitration on the Administration of Disciplinary Procedures." *Arbitration Journal* 39:43–56.

Kochan, Thomas A., Rosemary Batt, and Lee Dyer. 1992. "International Human Resource Studies." In David Lewin, O. S. Mitchell, and P. D. Sherer, eds., *Research Frontiers in Industrial Relations and Human Resources*, 309–37. Madison: Industrial Relations Research Association.

Kochan, Thomas A., and Robert B. McKersie. 1992. "Human Resources, Organizational Governance and Public Policy." In Thomas A. Kochan and Michael Useem, eds., *Transforming Organizations*, 169–86. New York: Oxford University Press.

Kochan, Thomas A., Harry C. Katz, and Robert B. McKersie. 1986. *The Transformation of American Industrial Relations*. New York: Basic Books; Ithaca, N.Y.: ILR Press, 1994.

Kochan, Thomas A., and Michael Piore. 1984. "Will the New Industrial Relations Last? Implications for the American Labor Movement." *The Annals*. AAPSS. 473:177–89.

Kohl, Heribert. 1988. "Teamkonzept im Experimentierstadium: General Motors." In Siegfried Roth and Heribert Kohl, eds., *Perspektive: Gruppenarbeit*. Köln: Bund Verlag.

Koike, Kazuo. 1987. "Human Resource Development and Labor-Management Relations." In Kozo Yamamura and Yasukichi Yasuba, eds., *The Political Economy of Japan*. Vol. 1, *The Domestic Transformation*, 289–330. Stanford: Stanford University Press.

Kondo, Dorinne K. 1990. *Crafting Selves*. Chicago: University of Chicago Press.

Korpi, Walter. 1978. "Workplace Bargaining, the Law and Unofficial Strikes." *British Journal of Industrial Relations* 16:355–68.

———. 1983a. *The Democratic Class Struggle*. London: Routledge & Kegan Paul.

———. 1983b. *The Working Class in Welfare Capitalism*. London: Routledge & Kegan Paul.

Korpi, Walter, and Michael Shalev. 1979. "Strikes, Industrial Relations and Class Conflict in Capitalist Societies." *British Journal of Sociology* 30:164–87.

Kriegler, Roy J. 1980. *Working for the Company*. Melbourne: Oxford University Press.

Kuhn, James W. 1961. *Bargaining in Grievance Settlement: The Power of Industrial Work Groups*. New York: Columbia University Press.

Kung, Lydia. 1983. *Factory Women in Taiwan*. Ann Arbor: UMI Research Press.

Labor Relations Week (no author). 1987. "Electrical Workers Take 8 Percent Pay Cut to Preserve Work at Zenith TV Plant," *Labor Relations Week*, March 25, 268.

Lachs, Thomas. 1976. *Wirtschaftspartnerschaft in Österreich*. Vienna: Verlag des Österrechischen Gewerkschaftsbundes.

Lacroix, Robert. 1986. "Strike Activity in Canada." In Craig Riddell, ed., *Canadian Labour Relations*, 161–210. Toronto: University of Toronto Press.

Lamphere, Louise. 1979. "Fighting the Piece Rate System: New Dimensions of an Old Struggle in the Apparel Industry." In Andrew Zimbalist, ed., *Case Studies on the Labour Process*, 257–76. New York: Monthly Review Press.

Lane, Christel. 1989. *Management and Labour in Europe*. Aldershot, Hampshire: Edward Elgar.

Lazonick, William H. 1981. "Production Relations, Labor Productivity and Choice of Technique." *Journal of Economic History* 41:491–516.

———. 1990. *Competitive Advantage on the Shop Floor*. Cambridge, Mass.: Harvard University Press.

Lehmbruch, Gerhard. 1967. *Proporzdemokratie: Politisches System und politische Kultur in der Schweiz und in Österreich*. Tübingen: J. C. B. Mohr (Paul Siebeck).

Levi, Primo. 1988. *The Wrench*. Translated by William Weaver. London: Abacus.

Levie, Hugo, and Roy Moore. 1984. *Workers and New Technology: Disclosure and Use of Company Information*. Oxford: Ruskin College.

Levie, Hugo, and Ake Sandberg. 1991. "Trade Unions and Workplace Technical Change in Europe." *Economic and Industrial Democracy* 12:231–58.

Levie, Hugo, and Robin Williams. 1983. "User Involvement and Industrial Democracy: Problems and Strategies in Britain." In Ulrich Briefs, C. Ciborra, and L. Schneider, eds., *Systems Design for, with and by the Users*, 265–86. Amsterdam: North-Holland.

Lewchuk, Wayne. 1987. *American Technology and the British Vehicle Industry*. Cambridge: Cambridge University Press.

———. 1989. "Fordism and the Moving Assembly Line in the British System of Mass Production." In Nelson Lichtenstein and Stephen Meyer, eds., *On the Line: Essays in the History of Auto Work*, 17–41. Urbana: University of Illinois Press.

Lewin, David. 1987. "Industrial Relations as a Strategic Variable." In Morris M. Kleiner, Richard Block, Myron Roomkin, and Sidney W. Salsburg, eds., *Human Resources and the Performance of the Firm*, 1–41. Industrial Relations Research Association Series. Madison: Industrial Relations Research Association.

Licht, Walter. 1983. *Working for the Railroad*. Princeton: Princeton University Press.

Lichtenstein, Nelson. 1982. *Labor's War at Home: The CIO in World War Two*. Cambridge: Cambridge University Press.

———. 1986. "Reutherism on the Shop Floor: Union Strategy and Shop-Floor Conflict in the USA, 1946–70." In Steven Tolliday and Jonathan Zeitlin, eds., *The Automobile Industry and Its Workers*, 121–43. Cambridge: Polity Press.

———. 1988. "The Union's Early Days: Shop Stewards and Seniority." In Mike Parker and Jane Slaughter, *Choosing Sides: Unions and the Team Concept*, 65–73. Boston: South End Press.

———. 1989a. " 'The Man in the Middle': A Social History of Automobile Industry Foremen." In Nelson Lichtenstein and Stephen Meyer, eds., *On the Line: Essays in the History of Auto Work*, 153–89. Urbana: University of Illinois Press.

———. 1989b. "Life at the Rouge: A Cycle of Workers' Control." In *Life and Labor: Dimensions of Working-Class History*, 237–59. Albany: SUNY Press.

Lim, Chee Onn. 1982. "Developing Our Most Precious Resource." Secretary-

General's Report to the National Trade Union Congress 4th Triennial Delegates' Conference, April 27–30. Singapore: NTUC.

Lim, Linda Y. C. 1978. "Women Workers in Multinational Corporations: The Case of the Electronics Industry in Malaysia and Singapore." Michigan Occasional Papers no. 9. University of Michigan.

———. 1983. "Multinational Export Factories and Women Workers in the Third World: A Review of Theory and Evidence." In N. El-Sanabury, comp., *Women and Work in the Third World: The Impact of Industrialisation and Global Economic Interdependence*. Center for the Study, Education and Advancement of Women, University of California.

Lincoln, James L., and Arne Kalleberg. 1990. *Culture, Control and Commitment: A Study of Work Organization and Work Attitudes in the United States and Japan*. Cambridge: Cambridge University Press.

Linhart, Robert. 1978. *L'établi*. Paris: Editions de Minuit.

———. 1981. *The Assembly Line*. Translated by M. Crosland. London: John Calder.

Lippert, John. 1983. "Shop-Floor Politics at Fleetwood." In James Green, ed., *Workers' Struggles, Past and Present: A "Radical America" Reader*, 7–37. Philadelphia: Temple University Press.

Littler, Craig. 1990. "The Labour Process Debate: A Theoretical Review, 1974–1988." In David Knights and Hugh Willmott, eds., *Labour Process Theory*, 95–124. Hampshire: Macmillan.

Locke, Richard M. 1992. "The Demise of the National Union in Italy." *Industrial and Labor Relations Review* 45:229–49.

Lukes, Steven. 1974. *Power: A Radical View*. London: Macmillan.

Lupton, Tom. 1963. *On the Shop Floor: Two Studies of Workshop Organisation and Output*. Oxford: Pergamon.

MacInnes, John. 1987. *Thatcherism at Work*. London: Open University Press.

Maitland, Ian. 1983. *The Causes of Industrial Disorder: A Comparison of a British and a German Factory*. London: Routledge & Kegan Paul.

Malsch, Thomas. 1988. "Konzernstrategien und Arbeitsreform in der Automobilindustrie am Beispiel der Arbeitsintegration." Wissenschaftszentrum-Berlin. Typescript.

Manwaring, Tony, and Stephen Wood. 1985. "The Ghost in the Labour Process." In David Knights, Hugh Wilmott, and David Collinson, eds., *Job Redesign: Critical Perspectives on the Labour Process*, 171–96. Aldershot: Gower.

Marginson, Paul, P. K. Edwards, Rod Martin, John Purcell, and Keith Sisson. 1988. *Beyond the Workplace: Managing Industrial Relations in the Multi-Establishment Enterprise*. Oxford: Blackwell.

Marginson, Paul, and Keith Whitfield. 1989. "A Critical Examination of the British Experience with Workplace Industrial Relations Surveys." Working Paper no. 9. Centre for Industrial Relations Research, University of Sydney, and Labour Studies Programme, University of Melbourne.

Marin, Bernd. 1982. *Die Paritätische Kommission: Aufgeklärter Technokorporatismus in Österreich*. Vienna: International Publikationen GmbH.

———. 1985. "Austria—The Paradigm Case of Liberal Corporatism?" In Wyn Grant, ed., *The Political Economy of Corporatism*, 89–125. London: Macmillan.

Markovits, Andrei. 1986. *The Politics of the West German Trade Unions: Strategies of*

Class and Interest Representation in Growth and Crisis. Cambridge: Cambridge University Press.

Mathewson, Stanley B. 1969 [1931]. *Restriction of Output among Unorganized Workers.* Carbondale: University of Southern Illinois Press.

Maurice, Marc, François Sellier, and Jean-Jacques Silvestre. 1986. *The Social Foundations of Industrial Power.* London: MIT Press.

Meier, August, and Elliot Rudwick. 1979. *Black Detroit and the Rise of the UAW.* New York: Oxford University Press.

Mellish, M., and N. Collis-Squires. 1976. "Legal and Social Norms in Discipline and Dismissal." *Industrial Law Journal* 5:164–77.

Mertens, Leonard, and Laura Palomares. 1988. "El surgimiento de un neuvo tipo de trabajador en la industria de alta technologia: El caso de la electronica." In Esthela Gutierrez, ed., *Restructuracion productiva y clase obrera.* Mexico City: Siglo XXI-UNAM.

Milkman, Ruth. 1992. "The Impact of Foreign Investment on U.S. Industrial Relations." *Economic and Industrial Democracy* 13:151–82.

Millward, Neil. 1988. "Descriptive and Analytic Uses of the Workplace Industrial Relations Surveys." Paper presented to the Conference on the Workplace Industrial Relations Surveys, Department of Employment, London.

Millward, Neil, and Mark Stevens. 1986. *British Workplace Industrial Relations: 1980–1984.* Aldershot: Gower.

Misslbeck, Johannes. 1983. *Der Österreichische Gewerkschaftsbund: Analyseiner Korporatistischen Gewerkschaft.* Frankfurt: Wisslit Verlag.

Mitchell, J. Clyde. 1983. "Case and Situation Analysis." *Sociological Review* 31:187–211.

Muster, Manfred. 1988a. "Synopse zur Gruppenarbeit." AbteilungAutomation/Technologie/HdA, IG-Metall, Frankfurt. Typescript.

———. 1988b. "Neue Formen des Arbeitseinsatzes inhochautomatisierten Fertigungsbereichen der Automobilindustrie: An alagen überwachung, Einlegearbeit und Instandhaltung." In Ben Dankbaar, Ulrich Jürgens, and Thomas Malsch, eds., *Die Zukunft der Arbeit in der Automobilindustrie*, 95–113. Berlin: Edition Sigma.

Negrelli, Serafino. 1988. "Management Strategy: Towards New Forms of Regulation?" In Richard Hyman and Wolfgang Streeck, eds., *New Technology and Industrial Relations*, 89–100. Oxford: Blackwell.

Nichols, Theo. 1991. "Labour Intensification, Work Injuries and the Measurement of Percentage Utilization of Labour (PUL)." *British Journal of Industrial Relations* 29:569–92.

Nichols, Theo, and Huw Beynon. 1977. *Living with Capitalism: Class Relations and the Modern Factory.* London: Routledge & Kegan Paul.

Nolan, Peter, and P. K. Edwards. 1984. "Homogenise, Divide, and Rule." *Cambridge Journal of Economics* 8:197–215.

Nomura, Masami. 1991. "Japanese Personnel Management Transferred: Transplants of the Electronic Industry in Asia and Europe." Paper presented at the International Symposium on Production Strategies and Industrial Relations in the Process of Internationalisation, Oct. 14–18, Tohoku University, Sendai, Japan.

Oesterreichischen Gewerkschaftsbundes. 1974. *Arbeitsverfassungsgesetz: Schriftenreihe des OeGB.* No. 116. Vienna: Verlag des OeGB.

Österreichischen Gewerkschaftsbundes. n.d. *Economic and Social Partnership in Austria*. Vienna: Verlag des ÖGB.

Offe, Claus, and Helmut Wiesenthal. 1985. "Two Logics of Collective Action." In Claus Offe, *Disorganized Capitalism*, 170–220. Cambridge: Polity.

Oliver, Nick, and Barry Wilkinson. 1989. "Japanese Manufacturing Techniques and Personnel and Industrial Relations Practices in Britain: Evidence and Implications." *British Journal of Industrial Relations* 27:73–91.

———. 1992. *The Japanization of British Industry*. 2d ed. Oxford: Blackwell.

Ong, Aiwah. 1987. *Spirits of Resistance and Capitalist Discipline*. Albany: SUNY Press.

Ong, Teng Cheong. 1985. "Standing Up for One as Singapore." Secretary-General's Report to the National Trade Union Congress Fifth Triennial Delegates' Conference, April 1–3. Singapore: NTUC.

———. 1988. "Union Leaders' Credibility, Workers' Reputation Enhanced." Secretary-General's Report to the National Trade Union Congress Sixth Triennial Delegates' Conference, April 28–30. Singapore: NTUC.

———. 1991. "Reaching Out for the Best." Secretary-General's Report to the National Trade Union Congress Seventh Triennial Delegates' Conference, April 24–26. Singapore: NTUC.

Opel AG. 1991a. "Betriebsvereinbarung Nr. 180: Opel—Prämienlohn." Typescript.

Opel AG. 1991b. "Betriebsvereinbarung Nr. 179: Gruppenarbeit." Typescript.

Osterman, Paul. 1987. "Choice of Employment Systems in Internal Labor Markets." *Industrial Relations* 26:46–67.

Palmer, Earl E., and Bruce M. Palmer. 1991. *Collective Agreement Arbitration in Canada*. 3rd ed. Toronto: Butterworths.

Panitch, Leo. 1981. "Trade Unions and the Capitalist State." *New Left Review* 125:21–44.

Parker, Mike, and Jane Slaughter. 1988. *Choosing Sides: Unions and the Team Concept*. Boston: South End Press.

Pekkarinen, Jukka, Matti Pohjola, and Bob Rowthorn, eds. 1992. *Social Corporatism: A Superior Economic System?* Oxford: Clarendon.

Pelinka, Anton. 1980. *Gewerkschaften im Parteienstaat: Ein Vergleich zwischen dem Deutschen und dem Österreichischen Gewerkschaftsbund*. Berlin: Duncker & Humbolt.

Perlman, Selig. 1928. *A Theory of the Labor Movement*. New York: Macmillan.

Pfeffer, Richard M. 1979. *Working for Capitalism*. New York: Columbia University Press.

Phelps-Brown, Henry. 1986. *The Origins of Trade Union Power*. Oxford: Oxford University Press.

Piore, Michael J. 1982. "American Labor and the Industrial Crisis." *Challenge* 25:5–11.

Piore, Michael J., and Charles F. Sabel. 1984. *The Second Industrial Divide: Possibilities for Prosperity*. New York: Basic Books.

Pizzorno, Alessandro. 1978. "Political Exchange and Collective Identity in Industrial Conflict." In Colin Crouch and Alessandro Pizzorno, eds., *The Resurgence of Class Conflict in Western Europe since 1968* 2:277–89. London: Macmillan.

Pollert, Anna. 1983. "Women, Gender Relations and Wage Labour." In Eve Garmarnikow, David Morgan, June Purvis, and Daphne Taylorson, eds., *Gender, Class and Work*, 69–114. Aldershot: Gower.

Ponniah, Arudsothy, and Craig Littler. 1993. "State Regulation and Union Fragmentation in Malaysia." In Stephen Frenkel, ed., *Organized Labor in the Asia-Pacific Region: A Comparative Study of Trade Unionism in Nine Countries*, 107–30. Ithaca: ILR Press.

Poole, Michael. 1986. *Towards a New Industrial Democracy*. London: Routledge & Kegan Paul.

Porter, Michael E. 1990. *The Competitive Advantage of Nations*. London: Macmillan.

Poulantzas, Nicos. 1973. *Political Power and Social Classes*. London: New Left Books.

Purcell, John. 1981. *Good Industrial Relations: Theory and Practice*. London: Macmillan.

———. 1987. "Mapping Management Styles in Employee Relations." *Journal of Management Studies* 24:533–48.

Purcell, John, Paul Marginson, P. K. Edwards, and Keith Sisson. 1987. "The Industrial Relations Practices of Multi-plant Foreign-Owned Firms." *Industrial Relations Journal* 18:130–37.

Rada, Juan F. N.d. "Development, Telecommunications and the Emerging Service Economy." International Management Institute, Geneva. Typescript.

Ram, Monder. 1991. "Control and Autonomy in Small Firms." *Work, Employment and Society* 5:601–20.

———. 1994. *Managing to Survive: Working Lives in Small Firms*. Oxford: Blackwell.

Reich, Robert B. 1991. *The Work of Nations*. London: Simon and Schuster.

Richardson, Reed C. 1963. *The Locomotive Engineer, 1863–1963*. Ann Arbor: Graduate School of Business Administration, University of Michigan.

Roberts, Wayne. 1983. "Workplace Justice: Grievance Arbitration Has Become Too Costly." *Facts*, July-Aug., 20–21.

Robertson, Dave, James Rinehart, Chris Huxley, and the CAW Research Group on CAMI. 1992. "Team Concept and 'Kaizen': Japanese Production Management in a Unionized Canadian Auto Plant." *Studies in Political Economy* 39:77–108.

Robinson, Ian. 1990. "Organizing Labour: Explaining Canada-U.S. Density Divergence in the Post-War Period." Ph.D. diss., Yale University.

Rodan, Garry. 1989. *The Political Economy of Singapore's Industrialisation: National State and International Capital*. London: Macmillan.

Rodger, N.A.M. 1986. *The Wooden World*. London: Collins.

Rogowski, Ralf. 1985. "Meso-Corporatism and Labour Conflict Resolution: The Theory and Its Application to the Analysis of Labour Judiciaries in France, the Federal Republic of Germany, Great Britain and the United States." *International Journal of Comparative Law and Industrial Relations* 12:143–

Rose, Joseph. 1986. "Statutory Expedited Grievance Arbitration: The Case of Ontario." Working Paper no. 257. Hamilton: McMaster University Faculty of Business.

Rosen, Michael. 1991. "Coming to Terms with the Field." *Journal of Management Studies* 28:1–24.

Ross, Arthur M., and Paul T. Hartman. 1960. *Changing Patterns of Industrial Conflict*. New York: Wiley.

Ross, Robert J. S., and Kent C. Trachte. 1990. *Global Capitalism: The New Leviathan*. Albany: SUNY Press.

Roy, Donald. 1952. "Quota Restriction and Goldbricking in a Machine Shop." *American Journal of Sociology* 57:427–42.

———. 1954. "Efficiency and 'the Fix.' " *American Journal of Sociology* 60:255–66.

———. 1973. "Banana Time: Job Satisfaction and Informal Interaction." In Graeme Salaman and Kenneth Thompson, eds., *People and Organisations*, 205–22. London: Longman.

Sabel, Charles F. 1981. "The Internal Politics of Trade Unions." In Suzanne Berger, ed., *Organizing Interests in Western Europe*, 209–44. Cambridge: Cambridge University Press.

———. 1982. *Work and Politics: The Division of Labor in Industry*. Cambridge: Cambridge University Press.

Sabel, Charles F., and David Stark. 1982. "Planning, Politics and Shop-Floor Power." *Politics and Society* 11:439–75.

Salaman, Graeme. 1985. "Factory Work." In Rosemary Deem and Graeme Salaman, eds., *Work, Culture and Society*, 1–21. Milton Keynes: Open University Press.

Sandberg, Ake. 1986. "Socio-Technical Design." In E. Mumford, ed., *Research Methods in Information Processing*. Amsterdam: North-Holland.

Schatz, Ronald W. 1983. *The Electrical Workers: A History of Labor at General Electric and Westinghouse*. Urbana: University of Illinois Press.

Schmitter, Philippe. 1979. "Still the Century of Corporatism?" In Philippe Schmitter and Gerhardt Lehmbruch, eds., *Trends towards Corporatist Intermediation*, 1–35. Beverly Hills: Sage.

Schutz, Alfred. 1970. *Reflections on the Problem of Relevance*. New Haven: Yale University Press.

Schutz, Alfred, and Thomas Luckmann. 1974. *Structures of the Life-World*. London: Heinemann Education.

Scott, James C. 1985. *Weapons of the Weak*. New Haven: Yale University Press.

Screpanti, Ernesto. 1987. "Long Cycles of Strike Activity." *British Journal of Industrial Relations* 25:99–124.

Sengenberger, Werner, G. Loveman, and Michael J. Piore, eds. 1990. *The Re-Emergence of Small Enterprises: Industrial Restructuring in Industrialised Countries*. Geneva: International Institute for Labour Studies.

Sewell, Graham, and Barry Wilkinson. 1992. " 'Someone to Watch over Me.' " *Sociology* 26:271–90.

Shaiken, Harley, with Sarah Kuhn and Stephen Herzenberg. 1984. "Case Studies on the Introduction of Programmable Automation in Manufacturing." Washington, D.C.: Office of Technology Assessment.

Shaiken, Harley, and Stephen Herzenberg. 1987. *Automation and Global Production: Automobile Engine Production in Mexico, the United States, and Canada*. Monograph Series no. 26. San Diego: Center for U.S.-Mexican Studies, University of California.

Shapiro-Perl, Nina. 1979. "The Piece-Rate: Class Struggle on the Shop Floor. Evidence from the Costume Jewelry Industry in Providence, Rhode Island." In Andrew Zimbalist, ed., *Case Studies on the Labour Process*, 277–298. New York: Monthly Review Press.

Sharrock, Bob, and Wes Anderson. 1986. *The Ethnomethodologists*. Chichester: Ellis Horwood.

Shire, Karen. 1993. "Nouvelles formes d'organization et de systèmes de rémunération: le cas de General Motors en Allemagne et en Autriche." *Cahiers de recherche sociologique* 18–19: 217–38.

Shorter, Edward, and Charles Tilly. 1974. *Strikes in France, 1830–1968.* Cambridge: Cambridge University Press.

Silver, Beverley. 1991. "World-Scale Patterns of Labour-capital Conflict." In Inga Brandell, ed., *Workers in Third World Industrialization*, 145–72. London: Macmillan.

Simmons, Jack. 1978. *The Railways in England and Wales, 1830–1914.* Vol. 1. *The System and Its Working.* Leicester: Leicester University Press.

Sisson, Keith. 1987. *The Management of Collective Bargaining.* Oxford: Blackwell.

———. 1989. "Personnel Management in Perspective." In Keith Sisson, ed., *Personnel Management in Britain*, 3–21. Oxford: Blackwell.

Skocpol, Theda. 1980. "Political Response to Capitalist Crisis." *Politics and Society* 10:155–201.

Slichter, Sumner, James Healy, and E. Robert Livernash. 1960. *The Impact of Collective Bargaining on Management.* Washington, D.C.: Brookings Institution.

Smith, Anthony E. 1991. "New Technology and the Non-Manual Labour Process in Britain." *Relations Industrielles/Industrial Relations* 46:306–28.

Smith, Chris, John Child, and Michael Rowlinson. 1990. *Reshaping Work.* Cambridge: Cambridge University Press.

Snyder, David. 1975. "Institutional Setting and Industrial Conflict." *American Sociological Review* 40:259–78.

Sorge, Arndt, G. Hartmann, Malcolm Warner, and I. Nicholas. 1983. *Microelectronics and Manpower in Manufacturing.* Aldershot: Gower.

Sorge, Arndt, and Malcolm Warner. 1986. *Comparative Factory Organization: An Anglo-German Comparison of Management and Manpower in Manufacturing.* Gower: WZB Publications.

Stanley, L. 1987. *Essays on Women's Work and Leisure and Hidden Work Studies in Sexual Politics* No. 18, Department of Sociology, University of Manchester.

Stephens, John D. 1979. *The Transition from Capitalism to Socialism.* London: Macmillan.

Storey, John. 1985. "The Means of Management Control." *Sociology* 19:193–211.

Strauss, Anselm, et al. 1973. "The Hospital and Its Negotiated Order." In K. Thompson and G. Salaman, eds., *People and Organisations*, 303–20. London: Longman.

Strauss, George. 1990. "Toward the Study of Human Resource Policy" in James Chelius and Hames Dworkin, eds. *Reflections on the Transformation of Industrial Relations*, 73–95. Metuchen: IMLR Press/Rutgers University and the Scarecrow Press.

Streeck, Wolfgang. 1984a. "Co-Determination: The Fourth Decade." In B. Wilpert and Arndt Sorge, eds., *International Perspectives on Organizational Democracy.* Sussex: John Wiley and Sons.

———. 1984b. *Industrial Relations in West Germany.* London: Heinemann.

———. 1987. "The Uncertainties of Management in the Management of Uncertainty: Employers, Labour Relations and Industrial Adjustment in the 1980s." *Work, Employment and Society* 1:98–106.

———. 1992. *Social Institutions and Economic Performance.* London: Sage.

Swenson, Peter. 1989. *Fair Shares: Unions, Pay, and Politics in Sweden and West Germany*. Ithaca: Cornell University Press.

Tallard, Michèle. 1988. "Bargaining over New Technology: A Comparison of France and West Germany." In Richard Hyman and Wolfgang Streeck, eds., *New Technology and Industrial Relations*, 284–96. Oxford: Blackwell.

Taylor, Cecil. 1977. "The Bias of Arbitration." *Ontario Report* 2:9.

Terry, Michael, and P. K. Edwards, eds. 1988. *Shopfloor Politics and Job Controls: The Post-War Engineering Industry*. Oxford: Basil Blackwell.

Thomas, Robert J. 1986. "Participation and Control: New Trends in Labor Relations in the Auto Industry." Paper prepared under the auspices of the Joint U.S.-Japan Automotive Industry Study administered through the Center for Japanese Studies, University of Michigan, Ann Arbor.

Thompson, Heather Ann. 1985. "Detroit: Wildcat 1973." Honors Thesis, University of Michigan.

———. 1988. "Labor, the State, and Militancy: Canadian/American Exceptionalism, 1950–1973." Department of History, Princeton University. Typescript.

Thompson, Paul. 1990. "Crawling from the Wreckage: The Labour Process and the Politics of Production." In David Knights and Hugh Willmott, eds., *Labour Process Theory*, 95–124. London: Macmillan.

Thomson, Andrew. 1981. "A View from Abroad." In Jack Stieber, Robert B. McKersie, and D. Quinn Mills, eds., *U.S. Industrial Relations, 1950–80*, 297–342. Madison: Industrial Relations Research Association.

Tolliday, Steven, and Jonathan Zeitlin. 1986. "Shop Floor Bargaining, Contract Unionism, and Job Control: An Anglo-American Comparison." In Steven Tolliday and Jonathan Zeitlin, eds., *The Automobile Industry and Its Workers*, 99–120. Cambridge: Polity Press.

———. 1989. "Shop Floor Bargaining, Contract Unionism, and Job Control: An Anglo-American Comparison." In Nelson Lichtenstein and Steven Meyer, eds., *On The Line*, 219–44. Urbana: University of Illinois Press.

———. 1991a. "Employers and Industrial Relations between Theory and History." In Steven Tolliday, and Jonathan Zeitlin, eds., *The Power to Manage?* 1–43. London: Routledge.

———. 1991b. "Conclusion: National Models and International Variations in Labour Management and Employer Organization." In Steven Tolliday and Jonathan Zeitlin, eds., *The Power to Manage?* 273–343. London: Routledge.

———, eds. 1991c. *The Power to Manage?* London: Routledge.

Tomlins, Christopher L. 1985. *The State and the Unions*. Cambridge: Cambridge University Press.

Traxler, Franz. 1982. *Evolution gewerkschaftlicher Interessenvertretung: Entwicklungslogik und Organisationsdynamik gewerkschaftlichen Handelns am Beispiel Österreich*. Frankfurt: Campus Verlag.

Treu, Tiziano. 1981. "Italy." In Roger Blanpain, ed., *International Encyclopaedia for Labour Law and Industrial Relations*. Kluwer: Deventer.

Turnbull, Peter. 1986. "The Limits to Japanization." *New Technology, Work and Employment* 3:7–20.

Turner, H. A., Geoffrey Roberts, and David Roberts. 1977. *Management Characteristics and Labour Conflict: A Study of Managerial Organisation Attitudes and Industrial Relations*. Cambridge: Cambridge University Press.

U.S. Department of Labor. 1951. *Wage Structure: Motor Vehicles and Parts, 1950.* BLS Bulletin 1015. Washington, D.C.: Bureau of Labor Statistics.

———. 1985. *Industry Wage Survey: Motor Vehicles and Parts, May 1983.* BLS Bulletin 2223. Washington, D.C.: Bureau of Labor Statistics.

———. *Industry Wage Survey: Motor Vehicles and Parts. Part I: Motor Vehicles, June 1989. Part II: Motor Vehicle Parts, August 1989.* Washington, D.C.: Bureau of Labor Statistics. Forthcoming.

U.S. International Trade Commission. 1992. "The U.S. Automobile Industry Monthly Report on Selected Economic Indicators."

Useem, Michael. 1990. "Business Restructuring, Management Control, and Corporate Organization." *Theory and Society* 19:681–707.

Visser, Jelle. 1987. "In Search of Inclusive Unionism: A Comparative Analysis." Ph.D. diss., Amsterdam University.

Wad, Peter. 1988. "The Japanization of the Malaysian Trade Union Movement." In Roger Southall, ed., *Trade Unions and the New Industrialisation of the Third World*, 210–29. London: Zed.

Walton, Richard E. 1985. "From Control to Commitment in the Workplace." *Harvard Business Review* 52:77–84.

Waters, Malcolm. 1982. *Strikes in Australia.* Sydney: Allen and Unwin.

Watson, Bill. 1977. "Counter-Planning on the Shop Floor." *Radical America*

Watson, Tony J. 1980. *Sociology, Work and Industry.* London: Routledge & Kegan Paul.

Weir, Margaret, and Theda Skocpol. 1985. "State Structures and the Possibilities for 'Keynesian' Response to the Great Depression in Sweden, Britain and the U.S." In Peter B. Evans, Dietrich Rueschemeyer, and Theda Skocpol, eds., *Bringing the State Back In*, 107–68. Cambridge: Cambridge University Press.

Wells, Donald M. 1986. "Autoworkers on the Firing Line." In Craig Heron and Robert Storey, eds., *On the Job: Confronting the Labour Process in Canada*, 327–52. Kingston and Montreal: McGill-Queens University Press.

———. 1993. "Are Strong Unions Compatible with the New Model of Human Resource Management?" *Relations industrielles/Industrial Relations* 48:56–85.

Whittaker, D. H. 1989. "The End of Japanese-Style Employment?" *Work, Employment and Society* 4:321–47.

Whyte, William F. 1951. *Patterns for Industrial Peace.* New York: Harper.

Wickens, Peter. 1987. *The Road to Nissan: Flexibility, Quality, Teamwork.* London: Macmillan.

Wilkinson, Barry. 1983. *The Shop Floor Politics of New Technology.* London: Heinemann.

Williams, Karel, John Williams, and Dennis Thomas. 1983. *Why Are the British Bad at Manufacturing?* London: Routledge & Kegan Paul.

Womack, James P. 1989. "Seeking Mutual Gain: North American Responses to Mexican Liberalization of Its Motor Vehicle Industry." Paper prepared for the forty-fourth annual plenary meeting, Mexico-U.S. Business Committee, Orlando, Fla., Nov. 9.

Womack, James P., Daniel T. Jones, and Daniel Roos. 1990. *The Machine That Changed the World.* New York: Harper Perennial.

Wong, Evelyn, 1992. "Labour Policies and Industrial Relations," in Linda Low and Toh Mun Heng, eds., *Public Policies in Singapore: Changes in the 1980s and Future Signposts*, 144–69. Singapore: Times Academic Press.

Woodward, Joan. 1980. *Industrial Organisation: Theory and Practice*. Oxford: Oxford University Press.

Yates, Charlotte A. B. "From Plant to Politics: The Canadian UAW, 1936–84." Ph.D. diss., Carleton University, Ottawa.

Zabala, Craig A. 1983. "Collective Bargaining at UAW Local 645, General Motors Assembly Division, Van Nuys, California, 1976–1982." Ph.D. diss., University of California, Los Angeles.

———. 1989. "Sabotage at General Motors' Van Nuys Assembly Plant, 1975–83." *Industrial Relations Journal* 20:16–32.

Zeitlin, Jonathan. 1985. "Shop Floor Bargaining and the State: A Contradictory Relationship." In Steven Tolliday and Jonathan Zeitlin, eds., *Shop Floor Bargaining and the State*, 1–45. Cambridge: Cambridge University Press.

———. 1990. "The Triumph of Adversarial Bargaining." *Politics and Society* 18:405–26.

Zimmerman, Don. 1973. "The Practicalities of Rule Use." In Graeme Salaman and K. Thompson, eds., *People and Organisations*, 250–63. London: Longman.

About the Contributors

Jacques Bélanger is a professor in the Department of Industrial Relations, Laval University, Québec. He received his Ph.D. from the University of Warwick. The results of field research he conducted in British and Canadian factories have appeared in various industrial relations and sociological journals, and he has also contributed chapters to several books. Current research, based on direct observation and interviewing, focuses on the evolution of work organization and labor relations in comparative perspective.

Chung Yuen Kay is a sociologist who lives and works in Singapore. She obtained her M.A., with distinction, from the University of Manchester, England, and her Ph.D. from the National University of Singapore. The chapter in this book is based on her Ph.D. dissertation, "Gender, Work and Ethnicity: An Ethnography of Female Factory Workers in Singapore." Her publications include "At the Palace: Researching Gender and Ethnicity in a Chinese Restaurant," in Liz Stanley, ed. *Feminist Praxis* (Routledge 1990); "A Factory Life, A Woman's Life," in *Commentary: Journal of the National University of Singapore Society*; and conference papers on women wage earners and female migrant workers.

P. K. Edwards is a professor of industrial relations and the deputy director of the Industrial Relations Research Unit, University of Warwick. His research interests include the comparative development of shopfloor industrial relations in Britain and the United States and the pattern of conflict and consent within the workplace. His publications include *Strikes in the United States, 1881–1974* (1981); *Conflict at Work* (1986); and, with Colin Whitston, *Attending to Work* (1993).

Stephen Frenkel is a professor at the Centre for Corporate Change in the Australian Graduate School of Management at the University of New South Wales. He has a Ph.D. in economics and politics from Cambridge University. His major publications include *Shop Stewards in Action* (1977, coauthored with Eric Batstone and Ian Boraston); *Unions Against Capitalism?* (1984, coauthored with A. Coolican); and *Organized Labor in the Asia-Pacific*

Region (1993, editor). He is currently completing a book on workplace relations in the global corporation.

Larry Haiven is an associate professor of Industrial Relations in the College of Commerce at the University of Saskatchewan. He received his Ph.D. from the University of Warwick. He conducts research on international comparative industrial relations, the state and labor regulation, public sector labor relations, and women and technology. Among his publications are *Regulating Labor: The State, Neo-Conservatism, and Industrial Relations* (co-edited with Stephen McBride and John Shields); "Past Practice and Custom and Practice: 'Adjustment' and Industrial Conflict in North America and the United Kingdom" in *Comparative Labour Law Journal*; and *On Bringing Back the Right to Strike and Lockout in Mid-Term* (York University Centre for the Study of Work and Society 1992).

Stephen Herzenberg received his Ph.D. in Economics from the Massachusetts Institute of Technology in 1991. He works at the Office of Technology Assessment of the U.S. Congress. From 1987 to 1993 he worked at the Bureau of International Labor Affairs of the U.S. Department of Labor, where he helped negotiate the labor supplemental agreement to the North American Free Trade Agreement. His recent writings on labor and the auto industry include essays in *The Challenge of Restructuring* (Temple University Press 1993), and *Driving Continentally* (Carleton University Press 1993). He was a major contributor to *U.S.-Mexico Trade: Pulling Together or Pulling Apart?*, prepared for the U.S. Congress in 1992. Dr. Herzenberg and Harley Shaiken coauthored *Automation and Global Production* (University of California, San Diego 1987), and "The Work Process under More Flexible Production," *Industrial Relations* (Spring 1986).

Harley Shaiken is a professor in social and cultural studies at the Graduate School of Education, University of California, Berkeley, where he specializes in issues of work, technology, and global production. He is also affiliated with the Institute of Industrial Relations and the Center for Latin American Studies at Berkeley. He is a research associate of the Center for U.S.-Mexican Studies, University of California, San Diego. He is author of three books: *Work Transformed: Automation and Labor in the Computer Age*; *Automation and Global Production*; and *Mexico in the Global Economy*, as well as numerous articles and reports in both scholarly and popular journals. He is a frequent guest on the "MacNeil-Lehrer News Hour" (PBS), National Public Radio, and other news programs.

Karen Shire received her Ph.D. in sociology from the University of Wisconsin–Madison. She is an assistant professor of political and industrial sociology in the Division of Social Science of the International Christian University in Tokyo. She has published articles about the social implications of the pay-for-knowledge wage system at General Motors Europe and the division of domestic labor in Sweden and the United States. At present she is finishing a book on the ideology of economic democracy and industrial relations institutions in Germany and Austria. She is also engaged in research about knowledge and power in Japanese industry.

Anthony E. Smith is an associate professor of industrial relations at the University of New Brunswick. He holds a diploma in labor studies from the University of Oxford and an M.A. and Ph.D. in industrial relations from the University of Warwick. He has contributed to books and published journal articles on white-collar unionism, workplace industrial relations, and technological change. His current research interests include the role of management in industrial relations, and cross-national perspectives on new technology and industrial relations.

Index